FAMILY CHILD CARE

2020 Tax Workbook & Organizer

Being a Family Child Care Professional

Family child care is a special profession for those who love young children. As a professional family child care provider, you must balance the skills required to care for children with those required to operate your business. Here are some tips that will keep your family child care business as healthy and successful as possible:

- Learn the child care regulations for your area, and follow them.
- Join your local family child care association.
- Sign up with your local child care resource and referral agency.
- Join the Child and Adult Care Food Program (CACFP).
- Find good professional advisers (such as a tax professional, insurance agent, and lawyer).
- Participate in training to acquire and improve your professional skills.

Additional Resources

Redleaf Press (www.redleafpress.org; 800-423-8309) publishes resources for family child care professionals. Redleaf Press offers the following publications to support your business:

- Starting a family child care business:
  Family Child Care Business Planning Guide
- Promoting your business:
  Family Child Care Marketing Guide, 2nd edition
- Creating contracts and policies:
  Family Child Care Contracts and Policies, 4th edition
  Sharing in the Caring: Agreement Packet for Parents and Providers
  The Redleaf Complete Forms Kit for Both Family Child Care and Center-Based Programs, Revised edition
- Keeping accurate records and filing your taxes:
  Family Child Care Record-Keeping Guide, 9th edition
  The Redleaf Calendar-Keeper: A Record-Keeping System for Family Child Care Professionals
  Family Child Care Tax Workbook and Organizer
  Family Child Care Tax Companion
  The Business of Family Child Care: Record-Keeping DVD
- Reducing business risks:
  Family Child Care Legal and Insurance Guide
- Managing your money and planning for retirement:
  Family Child Care Money Management and Retirement Guide

FAMILY CHILD CARE

2020 Tax Workbook & Organizer

TOM COPELAND, JD

Redleaf Press®
www.redleafpress.org
800-423-8309

Tom Copeland is a licensed attorney and has conducted tax workshops for family child care providers since 1982. In 2017 his website (www.tomcopelandblog.com) was chosen as one of the Top 75 Childcare Blogs and Websites for Childcare Providers and Parents by Feedspot (ranked second in the United States). In 2014 his blog was chosen as one of the top 50 money management blogs in the country by Direct Capital, a national financing company. In 1998 he won the Child Care Advocate of the Year award from the Minnesota Licensed Family Child Care Association. In 2003 he received the Friend of the National Association for Family Child Care (NAFCC) award from NAFCC. In 2004 Tom received the Advocate of the Year award from NAFCC. Tom is the author of *Family Child Care Business Planning Guide*, *Family Child Care Contracts and Policies*, *Family Child Care Legal and Insurance Guide* (with Mari Millard), *Family Child Care Marketing Guide*, *Family Child Care Money Management and Retirement Guide*, *Family Child Care Record-Keeping Guide*, and *Family Child Care Tax Companion.* Tom Copeland can be reached by email at tomcopeland@live.com, by phone at 651-280-5991, or through his website at www.tomcopelandblog.com.

Published by Redleaf Press
10 Yorkton Court
St. Paul, MN 55117
www.redleafpress.org

Cover design by Jim Handrigan
Cover photograph © iStockphoto.com/DNY59
Typeset in Times
Printed in the United States of America
ISBN 978-1-60554-734-3

Contents

Part I The Tax Organizer

Part II The Tax Workbook

Acknowledgments

Thanks to the many tax preparers who helped answer my questions for this edition and for previous editions. Any errors in this book are my responsibility.

Thanks to Douglas Schmitz for his editorial and production help.

Readers may contact Tom Copeland directly by email at tomcopeland@live.com, by phone at 651-280-5991, or through his website at www.tomcopelandblog.com.

Highlights of the New Tax Laws

- The COVID-19 crisis has created many tax and record-keeping problems and questions. See page xi for a comprehensive description of how to handle them.
- The standard meal allowance rates for 2020 are $1.33 for breakfast, $2.49 for lunch and supper, and $0.74 for snacks. The rates are higher for Alaska and Hawaii. See page 96.
- The standard mileage rate for 2020 is $0.575 per business mile. See page 116.
- The income eligibility limits for the Earned Income Credit have increased to $47,646 (for married couples filing jointly with one child) and $41,756 (if single with one child). See page 125.
- The income limits to qualify for the IRS Saver's Credit has increased to $65,000 (adjusted gross income for couples filing jointly) and $32,500 for individuals or married people filing separately. See page 127.

The Tax Implications of COVID-19 for 2020

What a year! Most family child care providers have suffered financially because of the massive economic disruptions caused by COVID-19. Many providers have had to close for a number of months. Others have experienced reduced enrollment because of parent fears about bringing their children to child care. The year 2020 may be the last in business for some providers. Other providers have not been significantly impacted by the economic downturn.

All of this has made preparing your taxes for 2020 extremely complicated. In this chapter we will cover the following:

- how to report Stimulus checks
- how to report unemployment benefits
- how to treat SBA loan programs: Paycheck Protection Program and Economic Injury Disaster Loan
- how to handle state and local grants
- how to report parent and subsidy payments made to you when you were closed
- how to calculate your Time-Space Percentage if you were closed for a month or more
- what's deductible because of COVID-19

This chapter will answer questions related to all of the above topics and their impact on your 2020 tax return.

How to report Stimulus checks

The federal government sent out Stimulus checks in early 2020. Eligible individuals received $1,200 and married couples received $2,400. If you had a child age sixteen or under, you received an additional $500 per child.

This money is not taxable income and should not be reported on your 2020 federal or state tax return. This money will not reduce your tax refund or increase your IRS taxes in 2020. It will not affect any back taxes you may owe the IRS. You can use the money for anything you want, business or personal. If you buy something that is used for your business, you can deduct the business portion on your Schedule C.

How to report unemployment benefits

Many providers were entitled to receive unemployment benefits during the COVID-19 pandemic. You may have received state unemployment benefits only, or you may have received the weekly $600 federal benefit. In either case, these amounts are taxable income. They should be reported on IRS **Form 1040** Schedule 1, line 7. You may have received a **Form 1099-G** showing these benefits. If you had some taxes withheld from your unemployment payment, show these taxes on IRS **Form 1040**, line 25b. You will only owe federal income taxes on unemployment benefits, not Social Security/Medicare taxes.

How to treat SBA loan programs: Paycheck Protection Program and Economic Injury Disaster Loan

Many family child care providers received money from two Small Business Administration (SBA) loan programs. These are the Paycheck Protection Program (PPP) and the Economic Injury Disaster Loan (EIDL).

PPP

If you received money from the PPP, this amount is not taxable income and should not be reported anywhere on your tax return. This is true even if all the money was not forgiven by the SBA and you kept some of the money as a 1% loan. Any interest you paid on this loan is tax deductible.

The IRS has said the PPP money you used for utilities, mortgage loan interest, or rent is not deductible on your tax return. For example: Let's say your total utility bill was $2,000 during the weeks you spent your PPP money. Let's assume your Time-Space Percentage was 30% and you used $600 of the PPP money for your utilities. Under an IRS ruling, you would not be able to deduct this $600 as a business expense on your taxes. Let's also say that your total utility bill for the year was $6,000 x 30% = $1,800, which would be the normal amount you could deduct as a utility expense for the year. However, under this IRS ruling you would only be able to deduct $1,200 ($1,800–$600 = $1,200). We don't know yet if the IRS will reverse this position and allow you to deduct the full $1,800.

If you spent some or all of the PPP money on payroll for yourself, this is not a business deduction. However, if you paid yourself $2,000 on payroll for yourself, and turned around and spent the $2,000 on an item used 100% for your business, you can deduct 100% of this expense. If you spent money on payroll for your employee(s), this is also a business expense.

If you don't spend all of the PPP money on your payroll, utilities, mortgage loan interest, and rent, you could keep any remaining money, which will turn into a 1% interest loan. If you did pay any interest on this loan, it is a business deduction that you would report on Schedule C, line 16a.

EIDL

There are two loan programs called EIDL: the EIDL "advance" and the EIDL "loan." Providers who received $1,000 for themselves or an additional $1,000 for their employees got the EIDL "advance." It does not have to be paid back. When you used this money to pay for business expenses, you can deduct them on either **Schedule C** or **Form 8829** depending on what you spent the money on. Congress has not determined whether this money is taxable income or not.

The EIDL "loan" is not taxable income and should not be reported on your tax return. You can deduct the business items you purchase with this money on either **Schedule C** or **Form 8829**. If you spent the money on payroll for yourself, you cannot deduct this as a business expense.

How to handle state and local grants

Many states distributed grants to family child care providers in the form of one-time payments or reoccurring payments. State grants are taxable income and should be reported on **Schedule C**. If your state issued you a **Form 1099**, report the grant on line 6, so the IRS will see that you did report it. Grants are taxable income whether or not your state issues **Form 1099**. If your state issued you a training voucher or equipment, this is still considered taxable income.

Some states may limit how you can spend your grant money. When you spend the grant money on items for your business, you can deduct them as business expenses. Items used 100% for your business can be fully deducted in one year. You can deduct the business portion of items that are used for both business and personal purposes. Use your Time-Space Percentage on such shared items.

How to report parent and subsidy payments made to you when you were closed

Many providers closed for part of 2020 and had parents pay them while they were closed. Any money you received from parents, whether you were closed temporarily or not, still must be reported as taxable income. The answer is the same if you received payments from your state's subsidy program for low-income families and were paid by them for weeks that you were closed. If you charged families a holding fee during 2020 to hold their spot until you reopened, that is also taxable income in 2020.

Some providers charged parents less while they were closed. Some providers accepted less money from parents during COVID-19. Some providers gave discounts. In all cases, you should report as income the money you received. You cannot deduct as a business expense any money you did not receive. In other words, if your normal rate was $180 per week and you allowed a parent to pay you $90 for 10 weeks, you received $900 which is taxable. The other $900 you did not receive is not a business expense.

How to calculate your Time-Space Percentage if you were closed for a month or more

With the advent of COVID-19, many family child care providers have shut down for a number of months or reduced their hours in 2020. Doing so means that your Time-Space Percentage will be lower.

A lower Time-Space Percentage means a reduction in the amount of house expenses you can deduct. Such expenses include property tax, mortgage interest, utilities, repairs, homeowners insurance, and house depreciation. It will also lower your deductions for shared business and personal expenses such as supplies, toys, office expenses, computer, household items, and more. This loss of deductions means you will pay higher taxes this year.

How can you calculate your Time-Space Percentage under these unusual circumstances in 2020? You will need to focus on how to keep records to mitigate some of these higher taxes by tracking all the extra hours you work in your home because of COVID-19.

First, let's look at the Space percentage. You can count the square footage of a room in your home as business space if it is "regularly" used for your business. "Regular use" means you are using it two to three times per week for some business purpose. For a more detailed explanation, see chapter 1.

How does being shut down for weeks or months affect your Space percentage in 2020?

It shouldn't. You can still consider a room as regularly used for your business even if you were closed for several months in 2020. Child care providers who closed for summers before 2020 did not have to reduce their Space percentage, so closing for several months in 2020 because of COVID-19 should not be treated differently.

What about exclusive use rooms? Some providers use rooms in their home exclusively for their business and are able to significantly increase their Time-Space Percentage. Again, shutting down for several months should not prevent you from continuing to claim a room as being used exclusively. If you do use such a room for personal purposes while you are shut down, you will not be able to claim it as exclusively business use. For more about exclusive-use rooms, see chapter 1.

Calculating your Time Percentage

This calculation becomes much more difficult in 2020 if you are closed for a period of time. The Time percentage is based on the total number of hours you use your home for business. This includes the number of hours children are present as well as the number of hours children are not present and you are doing business activities such as cleaning, activity preparation, meal preparation, talking to parents on the phone, record keeping, time on the internet, and so on.

When you are not caring for children for several weeks or months, this will significantly reduce your Time percentage. What can you do to help offset the reduction of some of these hours?

First, you want to make sure you keep careful records of the hours when children were present. Ideally, this means keeping a daily record of the time the first child arrives to when the last child leaves. It doesn't matter what it says in your contract about when you are open, and it doesn't matter when the parent signs out at pickup time. You want to know when the last child walks off your property.

If your pickup time is 6:00 p.m. and the last parent walks out at 6:30 after talking with you for a half hour, you want to track that half hour. Why? Because a half hour every day is equal to 1% of the year. A 1% increase in your Time percentage, multiplied by thousands of dollars of house-related expenses, adds up and is worth tracking.

If you didn't keep a careful record of these hours in 2020, it's not too late to reconstruct them by entering these hours on a 2020 calendar or some other place. Then include these hours on **Form 8829**, line 4.

Tracking hours when children are not present

Tracking these hours will make the biggest difference in helping to offset the loss of hours caring for children.

Before 2020, I advised providers to keep careful records for two months of the hours they worked in their home when children were not present. Then, I recommended using the average of these two months for the rest of the year. So, if you kept records showing you worked 40 hours in January and 44 hours in June, your average would be 42 hours a month x 12 months = 504 extra hours for the year. That is equal to 5.7% of the year, a significant increase in your Time percentage. For detailed information on how to track these hours, see my book *Family Child Care Record-Keeping Guide*.

But, with the disruption in 2020, here's how to calculate your Time percentage for 2020. First, determine the average number of hours you spent on these activities for the months you were open. Ideally, you want to carefully track this for two months and use the average for those two months for all the months you were open.

Next, you want to track the hours you are doing work in your home when you were closed for any part of the year. Such hours can include extra cleaning, distance learning with children, talking to parents/children on the phone, talking to licensors/unemployment offices, activity preparation, record keeping, Zoom meetings, time on the internet/Facebook, reading books, taking CDA classes, fixing up children's rooms, or filling out SBA loan applications.

Look back to the time when you first closed and start adding up all the hours you spent on these activities up until the day you reopened. Make notes on a calendar about when you did these activities and how long they lasted. So, your records could say, "Monday, April 6: home deep cleaning, 3 hours; Wednesday, April 8: Zoom learning session with Selena Gomez, 30 minutes."

You probably did not track these hours, so do this as soon as possible so you won't forget what you did and when. Estimate the days and hours to the best of your ability. If you were closed for multiple months, tracking this carefully for one month may only be necessary if you can say that the hours in that month were typical of the hours you spent in the other months. Now look at how many hours you spent on these activities once you did reopen. Do your best to reconstruct them for at least a month or two so you can establish an average number of hours for the months you were open.

Example #1

Let's say you were open January through March and closed April through August. Then you reopened from September through December. You cared for children 11 hours a day during the months you were open and worked 40 hours in January and 46 hours in October conducting business activities in your home when children were not present. You worked 20 hours in April and 26 hours in August doing business activities when children were not present.

Your home is 2,000 square feet and you used 1,800 square feet on a regular basis during the year.

- Hours children present: January, February, March, September, October, November, December = 153 days x 11 hours a day = 1,683 hours.
- Hours children not present during months open: 40 January hours + 46 October hours = 86 hours ÷ two = 43 hours a month average x 7 months open = 301 hours
- Hours children not present during months closed: 20 April hours + 26 August hours = 46 hours ÷ two = 23 hours x 5 months closed = 115 hours
- Total hours worked: 1,683 + 301 + 115 = 2,099
- 2,099 business hours ÷ 8,760 hours in 2020 = 24% Time percentage
- Space percentage: 1,800 ÷ 2,000 square feet = 90%
- 24% Time percentage x 90% Space percentage = 21.6% Time-Space percentage

You will enter your hours and space on IRS **Form 8829 Expenses for Business Use of Your Home**. You can also use my Time-Space Calculator which will do the math for you. See http://tomcopelandblog.com/calculate-your-own-time-space-percentage.

Note: If you had not tracked all the hours you worked in your home when children were not present, your Time percentage would have been 1,683 hours ÷ 8,760 hours = 19.2%. Your Time-Space Percentage would have been 19.2% x 90% Space = 17.3%. That 5% reduction is significant when multiplied by thousands of dollars of your house-related expenses.

When calculating your Time-Space Percentage for 2020, you will still apply your percentage to 12 months of house expenses, even if you were closed for several months.

Example #2

There is another way to calculate your Time-Space Percentage when you are closed for a month or more. To use this method, calculate your Time-Space Percentage based on the months you were open, and then apply this percentage to your house expenses for the months you were open.

For example, if you were closed from April through August, you would add up all the hours you worked for the other seven months and divide this number by the number of hours in those seven months. Then you would multiply your Time-Space Percentage by your house expenses for those seven months.

Let's use the numbers from Example #1 to see how this would work.

We would use the same number of hours caring for children when you were open: 1,683.

We would use the same number of hours you worked in your home when children were not present during the months you were open: 301

We would not count the number of hours you worked in your home when children were not present during the months you were closed.

Total number of hours worked in the year: 1,984 (1,683 + 301)

1,984 business hours divided by the number of hours in the seven months you were open or 5,160 hours = 38.4%

38.4% x 90% Space percentage = 34.6% Time-Space percentage

Let's assume your house expenses for the year were $12,000.

In Example #1, you would be able to deduct 21.6% of $12,000, or $2,592.

In Example #2, you would be able to deduct seven months of $12,000, or $7,000 x 34.6%, or $2,422.

Conclusion: Using the method in Example #1 is more work and gives you a slightly higher deduction. The higher your house expenses and other shared business and personal expenses, the better the first method will be for you. If you were closed for less than a month, use Example #1. If you were not closed for full months, this method is easier to calculate. If before COVID-19 you normally close for three months in the summer, you can calculate your Time-Space percentage using either of the above methods.

Note: I've created a Time-Space percentage online calculator that you can use here: http://tomcopelandblog.com/calculate-your-own-time-space-percentage.

What's deductible because of COVID-19

You probably spent more money on business items because of COVID-19. Here are some examples of such expenses: cleaning supplies, masks, gloves, paper towels, thermometers, soap, hand sanitizers, bleach, room dividers, disinfectant spray, computers for distance learning, Zoom subscription, deep cleaning or private sanitation services, food deliveries and other delivery expenses, curriculum expenses, expenses associated with reopening (painting, construction, remodeling, and so on), taking CDA classes or getting the National Association for Family Child Care Accreditation, and so on.

If you are spending money to respond to COVID-19 because of your business, you can deduct 100% of the cost. Should you list these COVID-19 expenses in a separate expense category on your tax return or lump them with other business expenses? The answer is that it doesn't matter. If you want to list them separately, label them as "COVID-19 expenses" using one of the blank lines on the back of **Schedule C**.

In light of all these extra expenses, some of which you may still be paying for, you may want to consider raising your rates. Call it "A COVID-19 surcharge."

Introduction

The purpose of the *Family Child Care Tax Workbook and Organizer* is to guide you as you prepare your federal tax forms for your family child care business. Since this book covers only the federal income tax rules and forms, you may also need to complete additional forms for your state and local tax returns. Because the tax laws can change every year, the *Tax Workbook and Organizer* is updated each year to reflect the latest changes in the tax rules and forms. For this reason, it's important to use only the current year's edition of this book.

Note: If Congress makes any changes in the tax rules after this book goes to print, I will post changes that affect family child care providers on my website: http://tomcopelandblog.com/2020-family-child-care-tax-workbook-organizer.

Note: Family child care providers who operate as a partnership or corporation should not use this book to file their taxes, because they must use different tax forms. Providers who are set up as a single-person limited liability company (LLC) will use all the forms as described in this book.

Getting Help

The *Family Child Care Tax Workbook and Organizer* is designed to enable you to fill out important tax forms for your business. The following resources are available if you need further help:

Getting Help from the IRS

- Call the IRS Business and Specialty Tax Line at 800-829-4933 with your questions. This number is for business-related questions. Tax help is also available at IRS offices nationwide.
- Visit the IRS website (www.irs.gov) to download tax forms, publications, and instructions or to search for answers to your questions.
- You can call 800-829-3676 to order a free copy of any IRS publication or form. Many post offices and libraries also carry the more common IRS forms and instructions.
- If you are running out of time, you can get a six-month extension (to October 15) to file your taxes. You must still pay the taxes you owe by April 15 or pay interest on the amount you owe.

- For a list of IRS resources, revenue rulings, court cases, and publications relevant to family child care providers, see appendix C.

Getting Help from a Tax Professional

- If you need help finding a tax professional, visit my website (www.tomcopelandblog.com) for a tax preparer directory.

Finding IRS Publications and Other Resources

- For copies of all the relevant IRS publications, tax forms, revenue rulings, court cases, and other materials, visit my website at www.tomcopelandblog.com.

Notes on This Edition

New Record-Keeping and Tax Tips is a regular feature that includes IRS updates and new information to help you keep your records, file your tax return, and deal with the IRS. This year's tips cover the following topics:

- Should You Take a Distribution from Your IRA?
- Should You Claim Social Security Benefits Early?
- Time to Invest in Your 2021 IRA!
- 2021 Webinars with Tom Copeland
- Retirement Plan Limits for 2020

IRS Child Care Provider Audit Technique Guide

The IRS **Child Care Provider Audit Technique Guide** is one of a series of audit guides that the IRS produced to help auditors better understand specific businesses. I refer to this guide several times in this book. I have posted a copy of the guide on my website, www.tomcopelandblog.com, along with a more detailed commentary about the guide.

How to Find a Tax Professional

Many family child care providers use tax professionals to help prepare their tax returns; however, many tax preparers aren't familiar with how the IRS Tax Code affects family child care businesses. You need to find out if the tax preparer you are considering is aware of the unique tax rules for your business. (The *Record-Keeping Guide* contains more information about hiring and working with a tax preparer.) Here are some ways that you can find a qualified tax preparer:

- Ask other family child care providers or the members of your family child care association for the names of their tax preparers.

- Find out if there are any community resources you can use. For example, some communities have taxpayer assistance services for low-income people. Contact your local United Way for more information about these programs.
- Three national tax preparer organizations offer state listings of their members: the National Association of Enrolled Agents (www.naea.org or 202-822-6232), the National Association of Tax Professionals (www.natptax.com or 800-558-3402), and the National Society of Accountants (www.nsacct.org or 800-966-6679). You can also look online to find the local chapter of any of these organizations.

Using Tax Preparation Software

An increasing number of family child care providers are using tax preparation software to do their own taxes. The three leading tax preparation software programs are TurboTax, H&R Block at Home, and TaxAct. The IRS has a program by which you can use these tax preparation software programs for free if you are income eligible: https://apps.irs.gov/app/freeFile/jsp/index.jsp?ck. These programs can be helpful in doing math calculations (such as depreciation) and completing your tax forms; they may also help catch some of your mistakes. They do, however, have drawbacks—specifically, tax software *will not* do the following:

- Identify the items you can deduct for your business. The software will merely list the category (for example, Supplies); it will be up to you to figure out what you can claim on that line.
- Explain how to deduct items that are used both for business and personal purposes. You will need to figure out how to claim not only the supplies you use exclusively for your business but also the supplies you use for both business and personal purposes. Here's an example: Let's say that you spent $120 on arts and crafts supplies that were used only by the children in your care and $600 on household cleaning supplies that were used by both your business and your family. In this case, you can deduct the full amount of the arts and crafts supplies but not of the cleaning supplies. You must multiply that $600 by your Time-Space percentage and add that amount to the $120 for arts and crafts supplies. The total is the number that you enter on **Schedule C**, line 22. If you don't know that you can't claim either $720 or the Time-Space percentage of $720 for your supplies, then you shouldn't be using a tax software program.
- Alert you to all the special rules that apply to your business. For example, it won't remind you that the reimbursements you received from the Food Program for your own children are not taxable income.
- Ask you detailed questions to make sure you are reporting the highest Time-Space percentage and business deductions you are allowed to claim.

Using Tax Software

- Enter your business expenses (advertising, supplies) *after* applying your Time-Space percentage or actual business-use percentage.
- Be sure to keep records of how you calculated your business-use percentage (if you will not be using your Time-Space percentage).

- Read chapter 3 for a clear explanation of depreciation rules and how to use them. Unless you know a lot about depreciation, it is easy to make a mistake claiming depreciation expenses.
- Before filing your return, compare **Form 8829**, **Form 4562**, and **Schedule C** with the numbers you entered into the Tax Workbook and the Tax Organizer to see if all your deductions are properly reported. Sometimes it's easy to lose track of a deduction you enter into a software program.

Every year I write detailed reviews of each software program in early January on my website: www.tomcopelandblog.com.

How to Use This Book

Although filling out tax forms isn't a pleasant task, it's an essential part of operating a family child care business. Many family child care providers don't claim all the business deductions they're entitled to because they're unaware of the tax rules and don't think the deductions are worth the time it takes to learn the tax rules. As a result, providers end up paying more taxes than they need to. Taking advantage of all the legal business deductions that you're entitled to, however, ends up lowering your tax bill.

Because a family child care business requires you to use your home for business purposes, the tax rules for your business are unlike those that apply to most other small businesses. A professional tax adviser might not be familiar with all the details of the tax laws as they apply to your business, which is why you need to take an active role in learning the tax rules and what they mean for your business.

This book is designed to guide you through all aspects of preparing your taxes and filling out your federal tax forms for the current year. (In most states, you will also have to pay state income taxes, but there are no special state tax forms to file if you are a family child care provider.) The *Family Child Care Record-Keeping Guide* provides additional tax preparation information about how to keep good records and how to determine which expenses are deductible.

Careful, accurate business records are an essential part of preparing your taxes; when family child care providers get into trouble with the IRS, it's usually because they can't separate their deductible business expenses from their nondeductible personal expenses. These personal and business expenses are usually closely intertwined, and the IRS requires you to have written evidence for all your business deductions.

This book provides you with two different approaches to preparing your taxes—the Tax Organizer and the Tax Workbook—as well as copies of the common tax forms that most providers need to file for their business.

The Tax Organizer

The Tax Organizer is a set of worksheets on which you can gather, calculate, and organize all the information you need to fill out your tax forms. The Tax Organizer doesn't include a lot of explanation of the tax laws, but if you don't have any unusual tax issues, it can be a great way to gather all your data, thus making it much easier to complete your tax forms. There are many ways you might use this section of the book. You might complete the Tax Organizer (referring to the Tax Workbook if you need more information about a particular topic) and then transfer the information directly to your tax forms. You might complete the Tax Organizer and then give the information to a professional tax preparer. Or if you just need information on a particular tax form or topic (such as depreciation or the Food Program), you might skip the Tax Organizer completely and just use the Tax Workbook.

The Tax Organizer worksheets help you record and organize all your business income and expenses. Once you fill in the information, the Tax Organizer provides specific directions about where to enter each line on your tax forms. After you complete the Tax Organizer, tear it out of this book and save it with your other tax records. Since the tax laws and forms are always changing, this Tax Organizer applies only to the year 2020; don't use it for any other year.

The Tax Workbook

The second section of this book is the Tax Workbook, which is designed to guide you line by line through the key tax forms you need to file for your business. For each form, it's important to read the instructions carefully and take the time to understand the rules. Most of the tax issues covered in this book are discussed in more detail in the *Family Child Care Record-Keeping Guide.* If any of your tax-preparation questions aren't addressed in this book, you can refer to the *Record-Keeping Guide* or my website (www.tomcopelandblog.com), or you can contact the IRS (www.irs.gov) for more information (also see appendix C).

Tax Forms

The final section of this book (Part V) includes copies of forms **W-10**, **1040**, **1040 Schedule C**, **1040 Schedule SE**, **4562**, and **8829**. It's best to tear out these forms, copy them, and then do your rough work on the copies so you can make adjustments as you go along. Once you have your final numbers, write them on a clean copy before submitting your forms to the IRS.

You may also need forms for special situations. For example, if you're making estimated tax payments, you'll need to file **Form 1040-ES Estimated Tax for Individuals**. If you want to change your tax return for an earlier year, you'll need to file **Form 1040X Amended U.S. Individual Income Tax Return**. In addition, if you hire employees, you must file a series of tax forms throughout the year. Copies of those tax forms are available at www.irs.gov.

Complete Your Tax Forms in the Correct Order

Since some tax forms must be filled out before others can be completed, it's important to fill out your tax forms in the proper order. For example, **Form 8829**, **Form 4562**, and **Schedule C** are closely linked; you can't complete **Schedule C** before you've completed **Form 4562**. You need to fill out Part I of **Form 8829** before you can complete most of **Form 4562** and **Schedule C**. And you need to complete most of **Schedule C** before you can finish **Form 8829**. Here's the best way to proceed:

1. Start by filling out Part I of **Form 8829** (lines 1–7) and determining your Time-Space percentage (see chapters 2 and 1, respectively).
2. Complete **Form 4562** (see chapter 3); enter the amount on line 22 of **Form 4562** on line 13 of **Schedule C**.
3. Complete lines 1–29 of **Schedule C** (see chapter 5), and enter the amount on line 29 of **Schedule C** on line 8 of **Form 8829**.
4. Finish filling out **Form 8829**; enter the amount on line 35 of **Form 8829** on line 30 of **Schedule C**.
5. Finish filling out **Schedule C** and any other tax forms you need to complete, such as your **Form 1040** and your state tax forms.

Here's a flowchart that shows the proper order for filling out your tax forms:

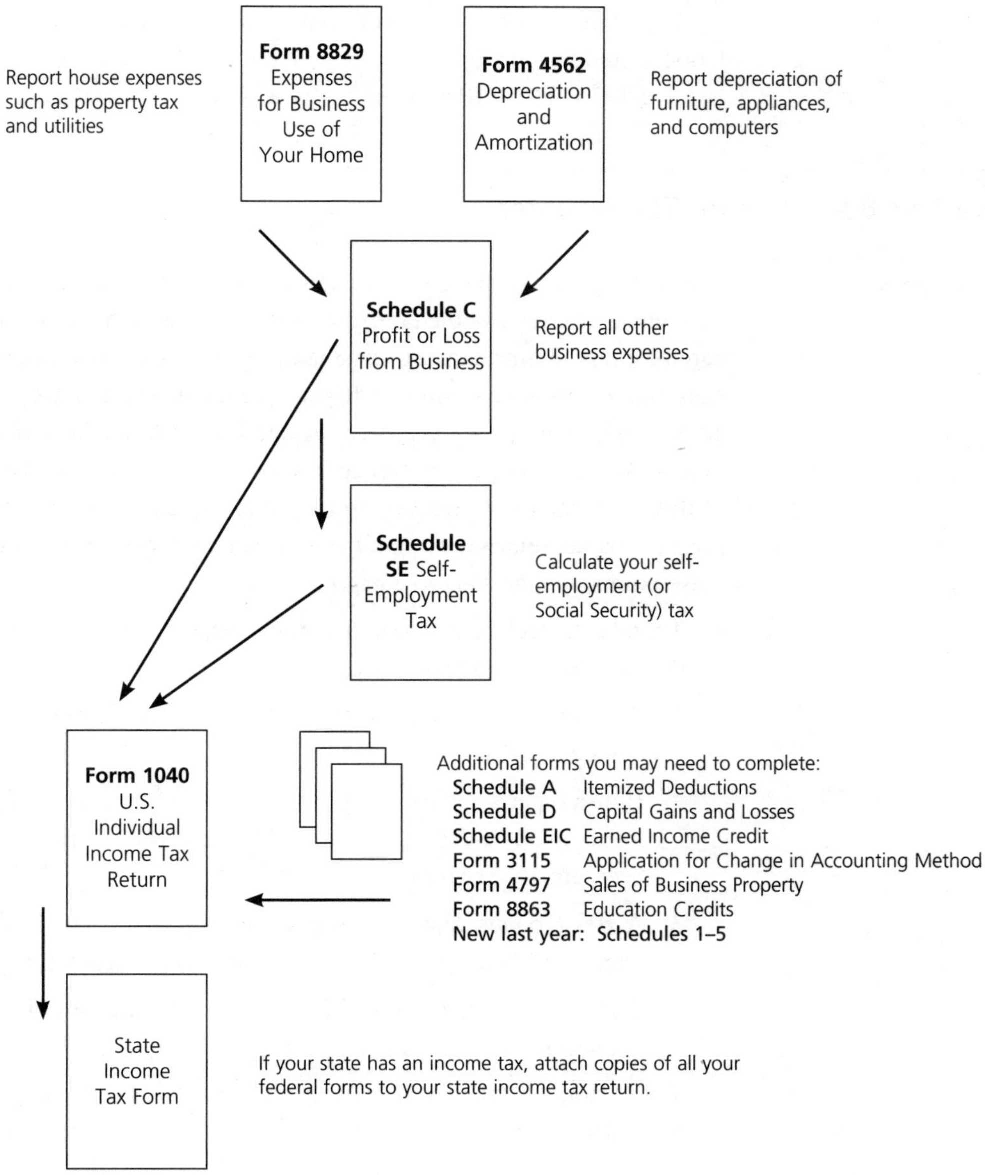

About the Math in This Book

The calculations in this book use exact amounts so you can track how to do the calculations; however, the IRS allows you to round numbers to the nearest dollar, and we recommend that you do so on your tax forms. Here's a reminder of how to round numbers correctly: If the cents portion of an amount is $0.49 or less, round down to the nearest dollar (for example, round $3.39 down to $3.00). If the cents portion of an amount is $0.50 or more, round up to the nearest dollar (for example, round $3.68 up to $4.00).

In this book we also do a lot of multiplying by percentages. Here's a reminder of how to do this: Let's say that you want to multiply $500 by 30%. To multiply by a percentage, you need to move the decimal point two places to the left before you multiply—in this case 30% becomes 0.30. Here's the calculation:

$500 × 0.30 = $150

To multiply $500 by 3%, you first need to convert 3% to 0.03. In this case, the calculation would be

$500 × 0.03 = $15

Give This Book to Your Tax Preparer

If you decide to complete the Tax Organizer and then hire a professional tax preparer to do your return, remind the preparer about tax rules that are unique to the family child care business. Unfortunately, some tax preparers don't understand the nature of this business and therefore can't do an adequate job of interpreting the tax law in your favor. (For advice on selecting a tax preparer, see the *Family Child Care Record-Keeping Guide*.) It may make an important difference in your tax return if you give your tax preparer a copy of this book and draw attention to the following eleven points that are the foundation of preparing a tax return for a family child care business. (For more information on any of these points, see the *Record-Keeping Guide*.)

- There have been four major changes in depreciation rules in the past several years that will benefit all providers:
    1. Providers can deduct any expense of less than $2,500 in one year, rather than depreciating it.
    2. House repairs can be deducted in one year, regardless of the cost. Home improvements must be depreciated over 39 years. The definition of what is a repair has been greatly expanded.
    3. A 100% bonus depreciation rule allows providers to deduct all items costing more than $2,500 except for the home, home improvement, and home addition.
    4. The Safe Harbor for Small Taxpayers rule allows eligible providers to deduct home improvements in one year.
- The standard "ordinary and necessary" test for business expenses casts a wide net in the family child care business. Child care is the only home-based business that is

allowed to use hundreds of common household items for both personal and business purposes. Such items include toothpaste, lightbulbs, toilet paper, garbage bags, a lawn mower, sheets, and towels. (See the *Record-Keeping Guide* for a list of more than a 1,000 allowable deductions.)

- The standard for claiming a room in the home as business use is regular use, not exclusive use. The children in a provider's care need not be present in a room for it to be used regularly for the business (storage, laundry, and so on). (See chapter 1.)
- A garage (either attached to the home or detached) and basement should be included in the total square footage of the home when calculating the business use of the home. Most family child care providers use their garage and basement on a regular basis for their business because they have a laundry room, storage room, or furnace area there. They may store a car, bicycles, tools, lawn maintenance items, firewood, or other items used for business in these spaces. (See chapter 1.)
- Providers can claim a higher business-use percentage of their home if they have one or more rooms that are used exclusively in their business. The tax preparer should add the Space percentage of this exclusive-use area to the Time-Space percentage of the rest of the home to determine the total business-use percentage of the home. (See chapter 1.)
- When counting the number of hours the home is used for business, include the number of hours the children in the provider's care are present as well as the number of hours the provider spends on business activities when the children are not present. These hours include the time the provider spends cleaning, preparing activities, interviewing parents, keeping records, and preparing meals. (See chapter 1.)
- Reimbursements from the Child and Adult Care Food Program (CACFP) are taxable income to the provider. Reimbursements for the provider's own child (if the provider is income eligible) are not taxable income. Providers are entitled to deduct all the food they serve to the children in their care, even if their food expenses are greater than their Food Program reimbursements. (See chapter 4.)
- Providers who are not licensed or registered under their state law are still entitled to claim their home expenses as business use if they have applied for a license or are exempt from local regulations. (See page 6.)
- All providers are better off financially if they claim depreciation on their home as a business expense. When a provider sells her home, she will have to pay a tax on any depreciation she claims (or was entitled to claim) after May 6, 1997. She will owe this tax even if she hasn't claimed any home depreciation as a business deduction. (See chapter 12.)
- Providers who use their home for business can avoid paying taxes on the profit on the sale of the home if they have owned the home and lived in it for at least two of the last five years before the sale. (See chapter 12 and the *Record-Keeping Guide*.)
- Providers are entitled to use the Start-Up Rule and deduct any items they owned before their business began and are used in their business, including a computer, TV, VCR, DVD player, washer, dryer, refrigerator, sofa or bed, and many other types of property. In addition, providers who have not deducted these items or not depreciated

items they were entitled to in previous years can use IRS Form 3115 to recapture all previously unclaimed depreciation on the current year tax return. This can mean hundreds of dollars in deductions for providers who have been in business for a number of years. (See chapter 10.)

If You File Electronically

If you will be filing your tax return electronically (or if your tax preparer will be doing so), be sure to keep paper copies of all your backup documentation, such as your depreciation schedules, the calculations for your Time-Space percentage, and your mileage records. The electronic documents can get lost, and you will need paper copies to provide evidence that your numbers are accurate if you are ever audited.

A Few Other Issues before We Get Started

What If You Aren't Licensed or Certified?

For tax purposes, you don't need to have a business name, be registered with your state or Chamber of Commerce, or even meet the requirements of your local regulations in order to be considered a business. Your child care business begins when you are ready to care for children and are advertising that you are ready to accept children. At this point, you can begin claiming all "ordinary and necessary" expenses for your business. You don't have to be licensed or actually caring for children to be considered a business and start claiming your expenses.

Suppose you're paid to care for children but don't meet the requirements of your local regulations. You may still deduct many expenses as business deductions, as long as you report your income. You can deduct all direct expenses, such as car expenses, depreciation on personal property (such as furniture and appliances), office expenses, equipment rental, repairs, supplies, education, food, and other miscellaneous home expenses. You may deduct these expenses even if you are caring for more children than your local regulations allow. Although we don't recommend operating outside of your local regulations, you should be aware of the tax advantages of deducting these expenses from your business income on **Schedule C**.

The only expenses you aren't entitled to deduct if you don't meet your local requirements are your home utilities, mortgage interest, home repairs, homeowners insurance, home depreciation, and real estate taxes. (These expenses appear on **Form 8829**. If you aren't entitled to claim expenses on **Form 8829**, you can still deduct all your mortgage interest and real estate taxes by itemizing on **Schedule A**.)

If your local regulations are voluntary, or if you are exempt from them, you may claim all the same business deductions as a licensed or certified provider. For example, your state rules may require that child care providers be licensed only if they care for more than four children. If you care for three children, you are exempt from the licensing rules and thus are able to deduct the same business expenses as a licensed provider.

Do You Need an Employer Identification Number?

If parents want to claim the child care tax credit, they will ask you for your Social Security or employer identification number (EIN). Because of privacy concerns, I strongly recommend that you get an EIN for your business. Using an EIN can reduce the chances that your Social Security number will get into the wrong hands and cause you problems with identity theft. If you hire an employee, you are required to have an EIN. You can get an EIN by filing **Form SS-4** (go to www.tomcopelandblog.com and click on "2020 IRS Tax Forms" to download the form) or by calling the IRS Business and Specialty Tax Line at 800-829-4933.

Another easy way to get your EIN is by going online. The application process is quicker, with fewer questions, and a simpler format to follow. Go to www.irs.gov and enter "EIN" in the search box. Once you fill out the application online, you will instantly get your EIN. You'll be asked, "Why is the sole proprietor requesting an EIN?" This question includes the following choices for answers: started a new business, hired employee(s), banking purposes, changed type of organization, or purchased active business. Always answer "started a new business" to this question, unless you are hiring employees. This may seem like a strange answer if you've been in business for a long time, but the instructions say to choose an answer that is closest to your situation.

If you have an EIN, you should use it instead of your Social Security number on forms **Schedule C** and **Schedule SE**. On all other forms, including **Form 1040** and **Form 1040-ES**, you should use your Social Security number.

About Parent Payments and Form W-10

If the parents of children in your care want to claim the child care tax credit, they will ask you to fill out **Form W-10**. **Form W-10** is easy to complete: simply enter your name, address, and Social Security or employer identification number, and sign the form. If you have an employer identification number, you must use it, rather than your Social Security number, on this form.

If you don't fill out **Form W-10** when a parent asks you to do so, you face a penalty of $50, even if you don't file tax returns or meet state regulations. Since the parents are responsible for giving you this form, you don't have to track them down and give it to them if they don't ask for it. Don't, however, refuse to sign **Form W-10** in the hope of hiding some of your income from the IRS. Not signing this form is one of the things that can trigger an IRS audit of your tax return.

Parents don't file **Form W-10** with their tax return. Instead, they keep it for their records. When they file **Form 2441**, they take the information from **Form W-10** and record each provider's name, address, and employer identification number, and the amount paid to each provider. The IRS uses this information to check whether the providers listed filed tax returns and reported all their income.

In the past, some parents overstated the number of their dependent children, and some providers understated the amount of their income. The IRS is trying to reduce such false reporting by requiring parents to list the Social Security or employer identification number of each provider. Still, some parents may report child care expenses on their **Form 2441** that are higher than what they paid you. This can happen, for example, when parents use two providers but report all of their child care expenses under one provider because they don't have the other provider's Social Security or employer identification number.

To protect yourself, you need to keep careful records of how much each parent paid you during the year. You should also get a signed receipt from each parent that indicates how much they paid you that year and keep the receipt with your tax records.

Providing Receipts for Parent Payments

There are three types of receipts that you can use, as shown in the examples below.

1. One type of receipt is **Form W-10**, which shows the amount paid and the parent's signature. Keep a copy of all the **Form W-10**s that you fill out. You can also fill out copies of **Form W-10** and give them to parents in January each year. (See the example below.) Parents find this helpful, and it's a professional touch that many will appreciate. There's a blank copy of **Form W-10** in the back of this book that you can use.

Form **W-10** (Rev. October 2020) Department of the Treasury Internal Revenue Service

Dependent Care Provider's Identification and Certification

▶ Do NOT file Form W-10 with your tax return. Instead, keep it for your records.
▶ Go to *www.irs.gov/FormW10* for the latest information.

Part I **Dependent Care Provider's Identification** (see instructions)

Please Print or Type	Name of dependent care provider Lori Uphus	Provider's taxpayer identification number 123-45-6789
	Address (number, street, and apt. no.) 1423 Claire Street	If the above number is a social security number, check here ▶ ☐
	City, state, and ZIP code New York, NY 10109	

Certification and Signature of Dependent Care Provider. Under penalties of perjury, I, as the dependent care provider, certify that my name, address, and taxpayer identification number shown above are correct.

Please Sign Here	Dependent care provider's signature *Lori Uphus*	Date 1/1/2021

Part II **Name and Address of Person Requesting Part I Information** (see instructions)

Name, street address, apt. no., city, state, and ZIP code of person requesting information

For child care of Manny Gordon in 2020, Phyllis Gordon paid $4,000.

2. Another option is to use a standard book of sales receipts that you can buy in a stationery or office supply store. (See the example below.)

Date 01/05/2021

M.

Address

Reg. No.	Clerk	Account Forward		
1	2020 child care for			
2	Manny Gordon			
3				
4				
5	Paid $4,000			
6				
7	Phyllis Gordon			
8				
9	123-45-6789			
10				
11				
12				
13				
14				
15	1785-42			

Your Account Stated to Date - If Error is Found, Return at Once

3. You can also use the receipts in the *Family Child Care Business Receipt Book,* which are designed especially for family child care providers. (See the example below.)

Business Receipt for Child Care Services ©2002 Redleaf Press, St. Paul, MN

No. 10 Month/Day 01/05 Year 2021

Received from Phyllis Gordon (parent/guardian name) $ 4,000

Four thousand and 00/100 Dollars

Name of child(ren) Manny Gordon

☐ Cash ☐ Check #

For Child Care Services from 01/01/2020 (M D Y) to 12/31/2020 (M D Y)

123-45-6789
Provider's SS# or Taxpayer ID#

Provider's Signature *Lori Uphus*

Parent/Guardian Signature *Phyllis Gordon*

New Record-Keeping and Tax Tips

These tips are exclusive to this edition of the *Tax Workbook and Organizer*. They highlight the tax changes and issues that have been identified over the past year.

New Tom Copeland Record-Keeping DVD

Redleaf Press has released my first DVD, *The Business of Family Child Care: Record-Keeping* featuring Tom Copeland. In this DVD, I share everything that new and experienced family child care providers need to know about record keeping.

The DVD is designed to be used by both trainers and family child care providers. The three-hour DVD covers the following topics:

- the three-step process for claiming business expenses
- which business deductions you can claim
- how to calculate your Time-Space percentage
- deducting your house and home improvements
- why the Food Program is so important and how to claim food expenses
- and much more!

Organizations that support providers can choose some or all of the sections of the DVD to cover in live workshops. Individual providers can watch all or parts of the DVD at their convenience.

Should You Take a Distribution from Your IRA?

These are very difficult times financially for family child care providers. Many are looking for ways to pay their bills and stay in business. One option some may want to consider is to take an early distribution from their Individual Retirement Account (IRA). Is this a good idea?

Normally, it is not advisable to take money out of your IRA early. The rules have always been that if you do so before you are age 59 ½ you will owe a 10% penalty on the amount you take out. In addition, you will have to pay income taxes on the amount distributed. This represents a big tax bill.

However, under a new law you can now take out up to $100,000 without this 10% penalty. You will still owe income taxes on the money you take out, but you are allowed three years to pay these taxes. You can also redeposit the money back into your IRA, rather than treating it as a loan.

To be eligible for this new rule,

- you must have been closed or reduced your hours of business because of COVID-19;
- you must have had your income reduced due to COVID-19;
- you or a family member must have been diagnosed with COVID-19; or
- other reasons

IRS rules have always allowed you to borrow money from your IRA, but because of the high monthly loan payments, it usually makes more sense to take a distribution, which does not require monthly payments. In addition, you must pay back the loan within five years. Your IRA administrator sets the interest rate on the loan. If you default on the loan, the 10% penalty comes back. With the distribution, you have three years to pay the income tax only and the 10% penalty is always waived.

A general warning about taking an IRA distribution or IRA loan: The decision to take a distribution or loan can have significant financial implications. Either one should only be taken as a last resort if you cannot avoid a major financial catastrophe otherwise.

Contact your IRA administrator for more details.

Should You Claim Social Security Benefits Early?

The financial crisis has caused some providers to consider taking their Social Security benefits earlier than they had originally planned. Is this a good idea?

You are eligible to start claiming your Social Security benefits as early as age 62. The amount you will receive goes up each year that you wait to claim your benefits. The last year you must start claiming benefits is age 70. Your full retirement age is either age 66 (if you were born before 1960) or 67 (if you were born in 1960 or later).

To find out how much you can expect to get in Social Security benefits, go to www.socialsecurity.gov and create your own account. You will see your annual Social Security statement, which will tell you how much you can expect to get if you start claiming benefits at age 62, your full retirement age, and age 70. These numbers are based on the assumption that you will be earning the same amount of money as you earned in 2019 until you reach these ages. If you earn more in the coming years, your benefit will rise and if you earn less, your benefit will decline.

If you start claiming Social Security benefits before your full retirement age and earn more than $18,960 in 2021, your benefit will be reduced. Once you reach your full retirement age, you can earn as much money as you want, and it will have no impact on your Social Security benefits.

Ideally, you should wait for as long as you can before claiming Social Security benefits. For every year you wait after your full retirement age, your benefit will rise by about 8% a year, which is significant. I strongly recommend that you look at the online calculator at www.opensocialsecurity.com to see the month and year you should start collecting your benefits that will give you the most income over the lifetimes of you and your spouse.

Before making the decision to start claiming Social Security benefits earlier because of COVID-19, consider the reduction in benefits over your lifetime if you take this step. It could mean a loss of tens of thousands to hundreds of thousands of dollars. I would try your hardest to meet the financial crisis you may be facing by doing everything else possible before taking this step.

Social Security is complicated, so I would not make any decision until you talk with a financial planner.

How Much Money Do You Want to Make?

You may want to know the answer to this question because you are considering raising your rates and need help justifying higher rates. Or, you are just curious. Whatever the reason, here's the simplest way to figure this out:

First, take the number from IRS **Schedule C**, line 31. This represents your profit from last year. It takes into account all your business income minus all your business expenses. It's your profit.

Second, take the number from last year's IRS **Form 8829 Expenses for Business Use of Your Home**, line 4. This represents how many hours you worked last year.

Third, divide your profit (line 31 of **Schedule C**) by the number of hours you worked (line 4 of **Form 8829**). The result is the amount you earned per hour for your work last year.

For example, if your profit was $25,000 and you worked 3,000 hours, you earned $8.33 per hour ($25,000 ÷ 3,000).

Many providers underestimate how many hours they work by not carefully counting all the hours they spent on business activities in their home when children were not present. If this is the case for you, your hourly wage will be lower if you include all of these hours.

Some providers underreport their business expenses by not claiming all the expenses they are entitled to. My book *Family Child Care Record-Keeping Guide* lists over 1,000 allowable deductions.

How can you use this information?

If you want to raise your hourly wage, multiply the hourly wage you want by line 4 on **Form 8829** to see what your profit must be. So, in the above example, if you want to earn $10 an hour, multiply $10 by 3,000 hours = $30,000 profit.

To reach this goal you would need to earn an additional $5,000 per year. If you care for four children, you could raise your rates by $1,250 per year or $24 per week. Or, you could cut your business expenses by $5,000 per year.

Sometimes parents look at how much they pay you, see how many other children are in your care, and assume you are earning a lot more money than you really are. The next time parents question your rates, tell them how much you make per hour.

Who Needs an Emergency Fund?

The obvious answer is that we all do.

Life is full of unexpected events. Are you ready for them?

- Your car breaks down and requires a major repair.
- You fall and break your arm and are unable to provide child care for four to six weeks.
- Your roof springs a leak and your homeowners insurance has a $1,000 deductible.
- Your mother becomes ill, and you leave town to stay with her until she recovers.
- The largest employer in your town shuts down, and three families tell you they are leaving.

If you think about it, unexpected events are such a fact of life that we really should call them expected events.

Since you are almost guaranteed to encounter a major financial disruption at some time in the next few years, you should plan ahead by setting aside at least three months of living expenses in an emergency fund.

Deposit this money in a money market fund or bank account where it can be easily accessed and has little or no risk of losing its value.

Here's what three family child care providers said about emergency funds:

> "After five years of struggling, the best thing I did was to put six months' worth of living expenses into a savings account. This completely changed the way I did business, because I didn't have to worry about the money factor when making business decisions about terminating or enrolling new children."

> "I think it's important for child care providers to have a plan B—a backup plan. Plan for bad weather, power outages, becoming ill and not being able to work, and car breakdowns and repairs. Think of everything you can that could affect your income, and develop a backup plan that will help offset the loss of income in those situations."

> "Make sure you have a three-month emergency fund before you spend any money on more supplies—and I actually feel you need more than three months. My goal is to have a six-to-eight-month backup fund. Because we have those reserves, if a family doesn't work out, I can feel okay letting them go."

Saving money for an emergency fund may not sound like an exciting project, but it's an important financial goal you should take seriously.

Don't let the prospect of setting aside three months of living expenses intimidate you. The first step is to set a specific goal ($5,000, $10,000, whatever three months of living expenses are for your family). Don't worry if this number seems impossibly high.

Second, establish a place where you are going to put the money and commit yourself to not spending this on anything except an emergency. It can be a separate savings account or a money market fund. Don't put it into a Certificate of Deposit (CD), because there is usually a penalty for taking it out early.

Third, make regular (monthly) contributions to your emergency fund. Start small: $25 a month is fine. Maintain the discipline of a monthly contribution. To start with, establishing the habit of a consistent contribution is more important than the amount of the contribution. Review your progress at the end of each year and make plans for how much you will save each month next year.

Don't be discouraged if your progress is slow. Slow but steady wins the race. As your emergency fund grows, so will your financial confidence. You will start to feel a sense of freedom and relief that will make all your hard work worthwhile!

Time to Invest in Your 2021 IRA!

Many family child care providers wait until they file their 2020 tax return before making a contribution to their 2020 IRA. Here's a simple way to boost your retirement savings. Contribute to your IRA at the beginning of the year. This will generate substantially higher returns than if you wait until after the year is over.

The reason is that money invested in January will take full advantage of the power of compound interest. Money you invest at the beginning of 2021 will earn interest throughout the year. Over the long run, money invested early in the year will make a big difference in your retirement. Let's look at some examples.

Providers Kim and Teresa are the same age. They invest $5,000 each year in their IRA and earn the same rate of interest (5%) each year. Kim invests her $5,000 each January, while Teresa waits until April of the following year to invest her $5,000. This means that Kim's contribution is earning interest for 15 extra months (January 2020–April 2021) each year.

After 30 years Kim will have $16,000 more in her IRA, and after 40 years she will have $34,000 more.

If they both earned 9% (the historic long-term return of the stock market), Kim would have $75,000 more than Teresa after 30 years and $193,000 more over 40 years.

What if Kim invested her money on January 1, 2020, for her 2019 IRA and Teresa invested on April 15? Even the 3.5 month difference would add up to $30,000 more in Kim's pocket after 30 years and $45,000 over 40 years (at 9% a year).

In all these scenarios, that's a lot of money!

It's Not Too Late

If you are in your 50s, it's not to late to boost your retirement savings. If you are age 55 and you contribute $2,400 on January 1 each year for 10 years (earning 7% a year), you will have $273,000 at age 65. Not bad.

So when is the best time to start saving money for your retirement? Answer: Today! When is the next best time? Answer: Tomorrow! Now is the time to contribute toward your 2020 IRA.

Retirement Plan Limits for 2020

Here are the contribution limits for various individual retirement account (IRA) plans for 2020:

- Traditional IRA and Roth IRA: $6,000, plus an additional $1,000 if you are age 50 or over

- SIMPLE IRA: $13,500 of your net profit, plus an additional $3,000 if you are age 50 or over (Note: you must have established a SIMPLE IRA by October 1, 2020, to make a 2020 contribution.)
- SEP IRA: 18.58% of your net profit

The deadline for your contribution to your IRA is April 15, 2021.

PART I

The Tax Organizer

The Tax Organizer

The Tax Organizer is a series of worksheets that help you organize all the income and expenses for your family child care business and show you where to enter the information on your tax forms. After you complete the Tax Organizer, cut it out and save it with your other tax records for the current tax season. Because the tax laws change constantly, do not use this Tax Organizer for any year other than 2020.

If you plan to give this Tax Organizer to your tax preparer, show it to the preparer before you start recording information. Some tax preparers have their own tax organizer that they will ask you to use, but ask your tax preparer if you can use this one instead. This Tax Organizer can help your tax preparer better understand the deductions that you're entitled to claim for your child care business and can save her a lot of time as she completes your tax return. Before you give your completed Tax Organizer to your tax preparer, be sure to make a copy for your records.

Once your tax return is complete, review the deductions in your Tax Organizer and make sure they've all been entered on your tax forms. If it appears that any of the deductions you listed aren't included, ask the tax preparer why.

There are several record-keeping books that can help you record and organize your tax records, including the following:

Redleaf Calendar-Keeper
Inventory-Keeper
Mileage-Keeper

If you use these products to track your income and expenses throughout the year, you will be able to complete this Tax Organizer much more quickly (and your tax return will be more accurate). Each part of the Tax Organizer explains how to get the information from these other tools and enter it in the Tax Organizer.

Let's start with some identifying information:

Name ______________________________

Address ______________________________

____

Social Security or employer ID number ______________________________

Your Income

In the chart below, list all the child care income you received from both parent fees and county or state subsidy programs for parents. If necessary, continue on another sheet of paper.

Name of Parent	Income from Parents Jan 1–Dec 31	Income from Subsidy Programs Jan 1–Dec 31
____________	____________	____________
____________	____________	____________
____________	____________	____________
____________	____________	____________
____________	____________	____________
____________	____________	____________
____________	____________	____________
____________	____________	____________
____________	____________	____________
____________	____________	____________
Totals	**(A)** ____________	**(B)** ____________

Total parent fees **(A + B)**		____________
Plus government grants	+	____________
Enter on **Schedule C**, line 1	=	____________
Food Program reimbursements received Jan 1–Dec 31		____________
Less Food Program reimbursements for your own children (total **[C]** from page 31 of this Tax Organizer)	–	____________
Other income	=	____________

Enter the total “other income” on **Schedule C**, line 6.

Your Time Percentage

Your Time percentage is the ratio of hours spent on business activities in your home during this tax year to the total hours in a year. There are two ways to calculate this ratio, depending on whether the care you provide for children is on a regular or irregular schedule throughout the year. In either case, you need to have written records of the hours you worked.

A. If You Cared for Children on a Regular Schedule throughout the Year

Complete this section if the hours you cared for children were fairly consistent from week to week during this tax year. If the hours weren't consistent, go to section B on page 21.

HOURS CARING FOR CHILDREN ON A REGULAR BASIS

	________	Time the first child regularly arrived at your home
	________	Time the last child regularly left your home
	________	**(A)** Number of hours in a day the children were present, from the time the first child regularly arrived until the last child regularly left
x	________	Number of days you worked per week
=	________	Hours you worked in a week
x	________	52 weeks
=	________	**(B)** Tentative hours caring for children

You cannot count time spent on vacations, holidays, illnesses, or other days your business was closed. Below, record these days for the entire year and subtract this total from the tentative hours caring for children:

	________	Vacations
+	________	Holidays
+	________	Illnesses
+	________	Other (describe: ______________________________________)
=	________	Total days closed
x	________	**(A)** Hours worked in a typical day
=	________	**(C)** Total hours closed
	________	**(B)** Tentative hours caring for children
–	________	**(C)** Total hours closed
=	________	**(D)** Total hours caring for children on a regular basis

ADDITIONAL HOURS CARING FOR CHILDREN

	Average # Hours		# Times per Year		
Children arriving early or staying late	_____	x	_____	=	_______
Children staying overnight	_____	x	_____	=	+ _______
Occasional care on weekends	_____	x	_____	=	+ _______
Other (describe: __________________)	_____	x	_____	=	+ _______
Total additional hours caring for children				**(E)** =	_______

Business Hours in the Home When Children Were Not Present

Activity Worked	Average # Hours		# Weeks in Business		Hours
Business phone calls	______	x	______	=	______
Cleaning	______	x	______	=	+ ______
Email/internet activity	______	x	______	=	+ ______
Family child care association activities	______	x	______	=	+ ______
Food Program paperwork	______	x	______	=	+ ______
Meal preparation	______	x	______	=	+ ______
Parent interviews	______	x	______	=	+ ______
Planning/preparing activities	______	x	______	=	+ ______
Record keeping	______	x	______	=	+ ______
Other (identify: ________________)	______	x	______	=	+ ______
Other (identify: ________________)	______	x	______	=	+ ______
Total business hours when children were not present				**(F)** =	______

Summary of Business Hours

Total hours caring for children on a regular basis	**(D)** =	______
Total additional hours caring for children	**(E)** +	______
Total business hours when children were not present	**(F)** +	______
Total business hours	**(G)** =	______

Enter the Total business hours **(G)** amount on **Form 8829**, line 4.

If you were not in business as of January 1 of last year, cross out the amount on **Form 8829**, line 5 (8,760 hours), and enter the number of hours in the year from the day you started your business until December 31 of last year.

If You Use the *Redleaf Calendar-Keeper*

The total number of hours you worked should be recorded on the year-to-date total line in the box in the upper-right corner of the December calendar page. Enter this amount in **(G)** above or directly on **Form 8829**, line 4.

B. If You Cared for Children on an Irregular Schedule

If your hours of business were not on a regular schedule throughout the year, you will have to carefully track your hours worked for each month. Calculate the number of hours you cared for children each day, from the moment the first child arrived until the last child left. Don't count any days that your business was closed because of vacations, holidays, or illnesses. Next, calculate your business hours when children were not present by filling out the table Business Hours in the Home When Children Were Not Present on page 20.

	# Hours Caring for Children
January	______
February	+ ______
March	+ ______
April	+ ______
May	+ ______
June	+ ______
July	+ ______
August	+ ______
September	+ ______
October	+ ______
November	+ ______
December	+ ______

Total hours caring for children: **(H)** = ______

Summary of Business Hours

Total hours caring for children	**(H)**	______
Total business hours when children were not present	**(F)** +	______
Total business hours	**(I)** =	______

Enter the Total business hours **(I)** amount on **Form 8829**, line 4.

If You Use the *Redleaf Calendar-Keeper*

Follow the same directions as listed above to report your total number of business hours.

Your Space Percentage

List all the rooms in your home (including the basement and garage). Enter the square footage of each room in the column that best applies to how that space is used.

Room	Used 100% for Business	Used Regularly for Business	Not Used Regularly for Business
__________	________	________	________
__________	________	________	________
__________	________	________	________
__________	________	________	________
__________	________	________	________
__________	________	________	________
__________	________	________	________
__________	________	________	________
__________	________	________	________
__________	________	________	________
__________	________	________	________
__________	________	________	________
__________	________	________	________
Total square feet	________ **(J)**	________ **(K)**	________ **(L)**

Total square footage of your home: (J + K + L = M) **(M)** = ________

Your Time-Space Percentage

1) If you have no entries in column **(J)**:
Enter the amount from line **(K)** on **Form 8829**, line 1.
Enter the amount from line **(M)** on **Form 8829**, line 2.

2) If you have any entries in column **(J)**, you have one or more rooms that are used *exclusively* for your business. Calculate your Time-Space percentage for these rooms as follows:

Enter the amount on line **(J)** __________
Enter the amount on line **(M)** __________
Divide **(J)** by **(M)** = __________% **(N)** Space percentage for exclusive-use rooms

Enter the amount on line **(K)** __________
Enter the amount on line **(M)** __________
Divide **(K)** by **(M)** = __________% **(O)** Space percentage for regularly used rooms

Enter the amount from line **(G)** or **(I)** = __________ **(P)**
Enter the total number of hours in the year from **Form 8829**, line 5* ______ **(Q)**
Divide **(P)** by **(Q)** = __________ **(R)** Time percentage for regularly used rooms

Multiply:

(O) __________
x **(R)** __________
= __________ **(S)** Time-Space percentage for regularly used rooms

Add:

(N) __________
\+ **(S)** __________
= __________ **(T)** Final Time-Space percentage

Enter the Final Time-Space percentage **(T)** amount on **Form 8829**, line 7.
Do not fill in lines 1–6. Attach a copy of these calculations to **Form 8829**.

*If you weren't in business as of January 1 of last year, enter the number of hours in the year from the day you started your business until December 31 of last year.

Your Business Expenses

Start by entering your business expenses in the categories below, then transfer the amounts to the indicated lines on **Schedule C**. (See the *Record-Keeping Guide* for a list of more than one thousand deductions.)

Advertising	________	Enter on **Schedule C**, line 8
Liability insurance	________	Enter on **Schedule C**, line 15
Legal and professional services (for your business)	________	Enter on **Schedule C**, line 17
Business taxes and licenses (payroll taxes and child care licenses)	________	Enter on **Schedule C**, line 23
Business travel expenses (vehicle expenses go on line 9)	________	Enter on **Schedule C**, line 24a
Business meals and entertainment	________	Enter on **Schedule C**, line 24b
Wages (paid to both family and nonfamily employees)	________	Enter on **Schedule C**, line 26

Your expenses may be 100% deductible or partly deductible, based on either the Time-Space percentage or the actual business-use percentage:

- **100% business use**: Items that are never used for personal purposes after business hours. Do not claim something as 100% business use unless it meets this qualification.
- **Time-Space percentage**: Items that are used for both business and personal purposes. To calculate your Time-Space percentage, see pages 41–46.
- **Actual business-use percentage**: Items that are used extensively but not exclusively for business purposes. Calculate the percentage of time the item is actually used in your business (each item will usually have a different business-use percentage). You must have written records to show how you arrived at each business-use percentage. Most providers reserve this method for more expensive items they use considerably more than items in their Time-Space percentage.

For each business category that follows, enter your expenses:

Credit Card Interest

100% business use				$ ________
Time-Space percentage	$_________	x ______% =		+ $ ________
Actual business-use percentage	$_________	x ______% =		+ $ ________
Enter the total on **Schedule C**, line 16b				= $ ________

Office Expenses

100% business use			$ ________
Time-Space percentage	$__________	x ______% =	+ $ ________
Actual business-use percentage	$__________	x ______% =	+ $ ________
Enter the total on **Schedule C**, line 18			= $ ________

Rent of Items

100% business use			$ ________
Time-Space percentage	$__________	x ______% =	+ $ ________
Actual business-use percentage	$__________	x ______% =	+ $ ________
Enter the total on **Schedule C**, line 20b			= $ ________

Repairs and Maintenance on Business Property

(doesn't include home repairs)

100% business use			$ ________
Time-Space percentage	$__________	x ______% =	+ $ ________
Actual business-use percentage	$__________	x ______% =	+ $ ________
Enter the total on **Schedule C**, line 21			= $ ________

Supplies

(includes children's supplies and kitchen supplies)

100% business use			$ ________
Time-Space percentage	$__________	x ______% =	+ $ ________
Actual business-use percentage	$__________	x ______% =	+ $ ________
Enter the total on **Schedule C**, line 22			= $ ________

Toys

100% business use			$ ________
Time-Space percentage	$__________	x ______% =	+ $ ________
Actual business-use percentage	$__________	x ______% =	+ $ ________
Enter the total on one of the blank lines on **Schedule C**, Part V			= $ ________

Household Items

(includes yard expenses, safety items, tools)

100% business use			$ ________
Time-Space percentage	$__________	x ______% =	+ $ ________
Actual business-use percentage	$__________	x ______% =	+ $ ________
Enter the total on one of the blank lines on **Schedule C**, Part V			= $ ________

Cleaning Supplies

100% business use			$ ________
Time-Space percentage	$__________	x ______% =	+ $ ________
Actual business-use percentage	$__________	x ______% =	+ $ ________
Enter the total on one of the blank lines on **Schedule C**, Part V			= $ ________

Activity Expenses

(includes field trips, birthday parties, special activities)

100% business use		$ _______
Time-Space percentage	$_________ x ______% =	+ $ _______
Actual business-use percentage	$_________ x ______% =	+ $ _______
Enter the total on one of the blank lines on **Schedule C**, Part V		= $ _______

Other Expenses

(items not included in any of the above expense categories)

100% business use		$ _______
Time-Space percentage	$_________ x ______% =	+ $ _______
Actual business-use percentage	$_________ x ______% =	+ $ _______
Enter the total on one of the blank lines on **Schedule C**, Part V		= $ _______

IF YOU USE THE *REDLEAF CALENDAR-KEEPER*

There are two places where you can find the totals of your **Schedule C** deductions. One is the year-to-date total at the bottom of the monthly expense report for December. The second is the list of direct business expenses on the income tax worksheet. Take the totals that best represent your deductions, and enter them in the appropriate expense category in the Tax Organizer.

Your Vehicle Expenses

To calculate the miles that you drove on trips for which the primary purpose was business, enter information from your written records, such as the *Redleaf Calendar-Keeper*, the *Mileage-Keeper*, receipts, and canceled checks on the lines below. If you used more than one vehicle for your business last year, photocopy this part of the Tax Organizer and fill out one worksheet for each vehicle you used.

Odometer Readings

Make and model of vehicle	_________________
Year first used in your business	_________
Purchase price of vehicle	_________
Odometer reading December 31 of last year	_________
Odometer reading January 1 of last year	– _________
Total miles vehicle was driven last year	**(A)** _________

Business Mileage

Add up your business mileage and then multiply it by the standard mileage rate.

Business miles January 1–December 31 ____	x	0.575	= ________	
Total mileage deduction			= ________	(C)

Business-Use Percentage of Vehicle

Total business miles last year		________	(B)
Divided by total miles vehicle was driven last year	÷	________	(A)
Business-use percentage of vehicle	=	________	(D)

Other Vehicle Expenses

Parking/tolls/ferry		________	
Vehicle loan interest	+	________	
Vehicle property tax (if applicable)	+	________	
Total other vehicle expenses	=	________	
Multiplied by business-use percentage of vehicle	x	________	(D)
Business-use percentage of other vehicle expenses	=	________	(E)

Standard Mileage Rate Method

Mileage deduction		________	(C)
Total business-use percentage of other vehicle expenses	+	________	(E)
Total business deduction (standard mileage rate method)	=	________	

Enter the Total business deduction on **Schedule C**, line 9

Actual Vehicle Expenses Method

To use this method, you must have recorded all your vehicle expenses so that you can add them up at the end of the year.

Gas		________	
Oil/lube/filter	+	________	
Tune-up/repairs/tires	+	________	
Lease payment	+	________	
Wash/wax	+	________	
Supplies	+	________	
Vehicle insurance	+	________	
Other	+	________	
Total actual vehicle expenses	=	________	
Multiplied by business-use percentage of vehicle	x	________	(D)
Business deduction for actual vehicle expenses	=	________	(F)

Vehicle Depreciation

Fair market value of vehicle when first used for business ________

Business-use percentage of vehicle x ________ **(D)**

= ________

Depreciation percentage (from tables on page 94) x ________ %*

Depreciation deduction ________ **(G)**

Actual Business-Use Deduction

Business deduction for actual vehicle expenses ________ **(F)**

Extra business endorsement on vehicle insurance (if any) + ________

Depreciation deduction + ________ **(G)**

Business-use percentage of other vehicle expenses + ________ **(E)**

Total business deduction (actual vehicle expenses method) = ________

Enter the Total business deduction on **Schedule C**, line 9

Compare your total business deduction under the standard mileage rate method and the actual vehicle expenses method. If you began your business last year or used the standard mileage rate method for this vehicle in earlier years, you may choose to use the total from either method. If you used the actual vehicle expenses method for this vehicle in earlier years, you must continue using this method. (For more information, see chapter 5.)

If You Use the *Redleaf Calendar-Keeper*

Refer to the year-to-date total mileage at the bottom of the December expense report. If you tracked your actual vehicle expense in one of the monthly expense columns, enter the year total from December on the appropriate lines above.

If You Use the *Mileage-Keeper*

Enter the amounts recorded for mileage and actual vehicle expenses from pages 34–35 (if you use the standard mileage rate method) or pages 44–45 (if you use the actual vehicle expenses method) on the appropriate lines above.

*See chapter 3 for limitations on the depreciation deduction each year. Also, if you purchased a vehicle last year, see the Section 179 rules in chapter 3.

Your Food Expenses

You have two choices when calculating your food expenses. You can use the standard meal allowance rate or the actual cost of food. The standard meal allowance rate was established by the IRS so that providers could claim their food expenses without having to keep food receipts. (For a complete discussion of how to report Food Program reimbursements and food expenses on **Schedule C**, see chapter 4. For a detailed discussion of how to track food costs, see the *Record-Keeping Guide*.) Here's a summary of these two methods:

Using the Standard Meal Allowance Rate

You must keep the following records throughout the year: each child's name, dates and hours of attendance, and number of meals served. If you were on the Food Program during the year, save your monthly claim forms, which contain this information. Track nonreimbursed meals on your copy of the claim form or someplace else. Use the meal form to track nonreimbursed meals for last year (or all meals if you weren't on the Food Program). Use the year-end meal tally to total your reimbursed and nonreimbursed meals for last year.

Using the Actual Cost of Food

There are many ways to calculate your actual food costs. One way to do this is to buy and store your business food separately from buying and storing food for your personal use. Probably the simplest and most accurate method is to estimate the average cost per child per meal and multiply that number by the number of meals and snacks served. To calculate the average cost, track the ingredients you served for four typical menus for breakfast, lunch, supper, and snacks. Estimate the cost of the food for each menu, and divide that number by the number of children served. (For more information about how to calculate the actual cost of food, see the *Record-Keeping Guide*.)

If You Use the *Redleaf Calendar-Keeper*

If you tracked your food expenses each month, your yearly total will be on page 83 of your December expense report. You may also have entered your food expenses on the income tax worksheet as direct business expenses on page 85. If you haven't estimated your business food expenses, you may want to fill out the meal form and year-end meal tally in this book to get a more accurate deduction rather than using the totals on your *Redleaf Calendar-Keeper*.

Calculating Food Program Reimbursements for Your Own Children

If you received Food Program reimbursements for your own children this year, subtract this amount before reporting your reimbursements as taxable income on **Schedule C**. To calculate the reimbursements for your own children, you'll need to calculate the first and the second half of the year separately, because the reimbursement rates go up on July 1 every year.

Begin by filling out the two worksheets below, taking the information requested from the meal counts on your monthly claim forms.

Worksheet 1:
Food Program Reimbursements
for Your Own Children, January–June 2020

Number of Meals	Breakfasts	Lunches	Snacks	Dinners
January	______	______	______	______
February	______	______	______	______
March	______	______	______	______
April	______	______	______	______
May	______	______	______	______
June	______	______	______	______
Total meals	______	______	______	______
Total meals times CACFP Tier 1 reimbursement rate	x $ 1.33 (Alaska: $2.12) (Hawaii: $1.54)	x $2.49 (Alaska: $4.04) (Hawaii: $2.92)	x $0.74 (Alaska: $1.20) (Hawaii: $0.87)	x $2.49 (Alaska: $4.04) (Hawaii: $2.92)
CACFP reimbursements for your own children =	______ (1)	______ (2)	______ (3)	______ (4)

Add reimbursement totals 1–4 to get the total reimbursements for your own children, Jan–June = ________ **(A)**

Worksheet 2:
Food Program Reimbursements
for Your Own Children, July–December 2020

Number of Meals	Breakfasts	Lunches	Snacks	Dinners
July	______	______	______	______
August	______	______	______	______
September	______	______	______	______
October	______	______	______	______
November	______	______	______	______
December	______	______	______	______
Total meals	______	______	______	______
Total meals times CACFP Tier 1 reimbursement rate	x $1.39 (Alaska: $2.22) (Hawaii: $1.62)	x $2.61 (Alaska: $4.24) (Hawaii: $3.06)	x $0.78 (Alaska: $1.26) (Hawaii: $0.91)	x $2.61 (Alaska: $4.24) (Hawaii: $3.06)
CACFP reimbursements for your own children =	______ (1)	______ (2)	______ (3)	______ (4)

Add reimbursement totals 1–4 to get the total reimbursements for your own children, July–Dec = __________ **(B)**

Once you have calculated amounts (**A**) and (**B**), add them together to get the total (**C**):

Reimbursements for your own children, Jan–June		__________**(A)**
Reimbursements for your own children, Jul–Dec	+	__________**(B)**
Total reimbursements for your own children	=	__________**(C)**

Enter the total reimbursements for your own children **(C)** amount on page 18 of this Tax Organizer.

MEAL FORM Week of ________________ 2020

Child	Mon	Tue	Wed	Thu	Fri	Sat	Sun	Totals	Child	Mon	Tue	Wed	Thu	Fri	Sat	Sun	Totals
	Bkst ___ Lun ___ Din ___ Sn1 ___ Sn2 ___ Sn3 ___	Bkst ___ Lun ___ Din ___ Sn1 ___ Sn2 ___ Sn3 ___	Bkst ___ Lun ___ Din ___ Sn1 ___ Sn2 ___ Sn3 ___	Bkst ___ Lun ___ Din ___ Sn1 ___ Sn2 ___ Sn3 ___	Bkst ___ Lun ___ Din ___ Sn1 ___ Sn2 ___ Sn3 ___	Bkst ___ Lun ___ Din ___ Sn1 ___ Sn2 ___ Sn3 ___	Bkst ___ Lun ___ Din ___ Sn1 ___ Sn2 ___ Sn3 ___	B ___ L ___ D ___ S ___		Bkst ___ Lun ___ Din ___ Sn1 ___ Sn2 ___ Sn3 ___	Bkst ___ Lun ___ Din ___ Sn1 ___ Sn2 ___ Sn3 ___	Bkst ___ Lun ___ Din ___ Sn1 ___ Sn2 ___ Sn3 ___	Bkst ___ Lun ___ Din ___ Sn1 ___ Sn2 ___ Sn3 ___	Bkst ___ Lun ___ Din ___ Sn1 ___ Sn2 ___ Sn3 ___	Bkst ___ Lun ___ Din ___ Sn1 ___ Sn2 ___ Sn3 ___	Bkst ___ Lun ___ Din ___ Sn1 ___ Sn2 ___ Sn3 ___	B ___ L ___ D ___ S ___
	Bkst ___ Lun ___ Din ___ Sn1 ___ Sn2 ___ Sn3 ___	Bkst ___ Lun ___ Din ___ Sn1 ___ Sn2 ___ Sn3 ___	Bkst ___ Lun ___ Din ___ Sn1 ___ Sn2 ___ Sn3 ___	Bkst ___ Lun ___ Din ___ Sn1 ___ Sn2 ___ Sn3 ___	Bkst ___ Lun ___ Din ___ Sn1 ___ Sn2 ___ Sn3 ___	Bkst ___ Lun ___ Din ___ Sn1 ___ Sn2 ___ Sn3 ___	Bkst ___ Lun ___ Din ___ Sn1 ___ Sn2 ___ Sn3 ___	B ___ L ___ D ___ S ___		Bkst ___ Lun ___ Din ___ Sn1 ___ Sn2 ___ Sn3 ___	Bkst ___ Lun ___ Din ___ Sn1 ___ Sn2 ___ Sn3 ___	Bkst ___ Lun ___ Din ___ Sn1 ___ Sn2 ___ Sn3 ___	Bkst ___ Lun ___ Din ___ Sn1 ___ Sn2 ___ Sn3 ___	Bkst ___ Lun ___ Din ___ Sn1 ___ Sn2 ___ Sn3 ___	Bkst ___ Lun ___ Din ___ Sn1 ___ Sn2 ___ Sn3 ___	Bkst ___ Lun ___ Din ___ Sn1 ___ Sn2 ___ Sn3 ___	B ___ L ___ D ___ S ___
	Bkst ___ Lun ___ Din ___ Sn1 ___ Sn2 ___ Sn3 ___	Bkst ___ Lun ___ Din ___ Sn1 ___ Sn2 ___ Sn3 ___	Bkst ___ Lun ___ Din ___ Sn1 ___ Sn2 ___ Sn3 ___	Bkst ___ Lun ___ Din ___ Sn1 ___ Sn2 ___ Sn3 ___	Bkst ___ Lun ___ Din ___ Sn1 ___ Sn2 ___ Sn3 ___	Bkst ___ Lun ___ Din ___ Sn1 ___ Sn2 ___ Sn3 ___	Bkst ___ Lun ___ Din ___ Sn1 ___ Sn2 ___ Sn3 ___	B ___ L ___ D ___ S ___		Bkst ___ Lun ___ Din ___ Sn1 ___ Sn2 ___ Sn3 ___	Bkst ___ Lun ___ Din ___ Sn1 ___ Sn2 ___ Sn3 ___	Bkst ___ Lun ___ Din ___ Sn1 ___ Sn2 ___ Sn3 ___	Bkst ___ Lun ___ Din ___ Sn1 ___ Sn2 ___ Sn3 ___	Bkst ___ Lun ___ Din ___ Sn1 ___ Sn2 ___ Sn3 ___	Bkst ___ Lun ___ Din ___ Sn1 ___ Sn2 ___ Sn3 ___	Bkst ___ Lun ___ Din ___ Sn1 ___ Sn2 ___ Sn3 ___	B ___ L ___ D ___ S ___
	Bkst ___ Lun ___ Din ___ Sn1 ___ Sn2 ___ Sn3 ___	Bkst ___ Lun ___ Din ___ Sn1 ___ Sn2 ___ Sn3 ___	Bkst ___ Lun ___ Din ___ Sn1 ___ Sn2 ___ Sn3 ___	Bkst ___ Lun ___ Din ___ Sn1 ___ Sn2 ___ Sn3 ___	Bkst ___ Lun ___ Din ___ Sn1 ___ Sn2 ___ Sn3 ___	Bkst ___ Lun ___ Din ___ Sn1 ___ Sn2 ___ Sn3 ___	Bkst ___ Lun ___ Din ___ Sn1 ___ Sn2 ___ Sn3 ___	B ___ L ___ D ___ S ___		Bkst ___ Lun ___ Din ___ Sn1 ___ Sn2 ___ Sn3 ___	Bkst ___ Lun ___ Din ___ Sn1 ___ Sn2 ___ Sn3 ___	Bkst ___ Lun ___ Din ___ Sn1 ___ Sn2 ___ Sn3 ___	Bkst ___ Lun ___ Din ___ Sn1 ___ Sn2 ___ Sn3 ___	Bkst ___ Lun ___ Din ___ Sn1 ___ Sn2 ___ Sn3 ___	Bkst ___ Lun ___ Din ___ Sn1 ___ Sn2 ___ Sn3 ___	Bkst ___ Lun ___ Din ___ Sn1 ___ Sn2 ___ Sn3 ___	B ___ L ___ D ___ S ___
	Bkst ___ Lun ___ Din ___ Sn1 ___ Sn2 ___ Sn3 ___	Bkst ___ Lun ___ Din ___ Sn1 ___ Sn2 ___ Sn3 ___	Bkst ___ Lun ___ Din ___ Sn1 ___ Sn2 ___ Sn3 ___	Bkst ___ Lun ___ Din ___ Sn1 ___ Sn2 ___ Sn3 ___	Bkst ___ Lun ___ Din ___ Sn1 ___ Sn2 ___ Sn3 ___	Bkst ___ Lun ___ Din ___ Sn1 ___ Sn2 ___ Sn3 ___	Bkst ___ Lun ___ Din ___ Sn1 ___ Sn2 ___ Sn3 ___	B ___ L ___ D ___ S ___		Bkst ___ Lun ___ Din ___ Sn1 ___ Sn2 ___ Sn3 ___	Bkst ___ Lun ___ Din ___ Sn1 ___ Sn2 ___ Sn3 ___	Bkst ___ Lun ___ Din ___ Sn1 ___ Sn2 ___ Sn3 ___	Bkst ___ Lun ___ Din ___ Sn1 ___ Sn2 ___ Sn3 ___	Bkst ___ Lun ___ Din ___ Sn1 ___ Sn2 ___ Sn3 ___	Bkst ___ Lun ___ Din ___ Sn1 ___ Sn2 ___ Sn3 ___	Bkst ___ Lun ___ Din ___ Sn1 ___ Sn2 ___ Sn3 ___	B ___ L ___ D ___ S ___
	Bkst ___ Lun ___ Din ___ Sn1 ___ Sn2 ___ Sn3 ___	Bkst ___ Lun ___ Din ___ Sn1 ___ Sn2 ___ Sn3 ___	Bkst ___ Lun ___ Din ___ Sn1 ___ Sn2 ___ Sn3 ___	Bkst ___ Lun ___ Din ___ Sn1 ___ Sn2 ___ Sn3 ___	Bkst ___ Lun ___ Din ___ Sn1 ___ Sn2 ___ Sn3 ___	Bkst ___ Lun ___ Din ___ Sn1 ___ Sn2 ___ Sn3 ___	Bkst ___ Lun ___ Din ___ Sn1 ___ Sn2 ___ Sn3 ___	B ___ L ___ D ___ S ___		Bkst ___ Lun ___ Din ___ Sn1 ___ Sn2 ___ Sn3 ___	Bkst ___ Lun ___ Din ___ Sn1 ___ Sn2 ___ Sn3 ___	Bkst ___ Lun ___ Din ___ Sn1 ___ Sn2 ___ Sn3 ___	Bkst ___ Lun ___ Din ___ Sn1 ___ Sn2 ___ Sn3 ___	Bkst ___ Lun ___ Din ___ Sn1 ___ Sn2 ___ Sn3 ___	Bkst ___ Lun ___ Din ___ Sn1 ___ Sn2 ___ Sn3 ___	Bkst ___ Lun ___ Din ___ Sn1 ___ Sn2 ___ Sn3 ___	B ___ L ___ D ___ S ___

Place a check mark (✓) next to each meal or snack you serve. Do not count meals served to your own children. If you are on the Food Program, use this form to track your nonreimbursed meals only. Add the reimbursed meals from your monthly claim forms and the nonreimbursed meals from this form together, and put the totals on the year-end meal tally on page 33. If you are not on the Food Program, use this form to track all your meals, and put the totals on the year-end meal tally on page 33.

Make copies of this form for each week of the year. If you have six or fewer children in your program, you can use one form for two weeks. You can download this form at the Redleaf Press website. Go to www.redleafpress.org, and find the page for the *Redleaf Calendar-Keeper 2020*. There will be a link to this form.

Weekly Totals

Breakfasts ________ Dinners ________

Lunches ________ Snacks ________

YEAR-END MEAL TALLY

If you are not on the Food Program, enter all meals and snacks in the column labeled "Number Not Reimbursed by Food Program."

	Breakfasts		Lunches		Dinners		Snacks	
	Number Reimbursed by Food Program	Number Not Reimbursed by Food Program	Number Reimbursed by Food Program	Number Not Reimbursed by Food Program	Number Reimbursed by Food Program	Number Not Reimbursed by Food Program	Number Reimbursed by Food Program	Number Not Reimbursed by Food Program
January								
February								
March								
April								
May								
June								
July								
August								
September								
October								
November								
December								
TOTAL								

2020 Standard Meal Allowance Rate*

Number of Breakfasts	______ X	$1.33	=	$__________
Number of Lunches	______ X	$2.49	=	$__________
Number of Dinners	______ X	$2.49	=	$__________
Number of Snacks	______ X	$0.74	=	$__________
	Total Food Deductions			$__________†

Do not report any meals served to your own children (even if they are reimbursed by the Food Program).

* The IRS standard meal allowance rate for 2020 used in these calculations is based on the Tier I rate as of January 1, 2020. This rate is used for all meals and snacks served throughout 2020, even though the Tier I rate goes up every July. All providers, whether on Tier I or Tier II (and all providers not on the Food Program), will use the rates listed.

† Enter this amount on Form 1040 Schedule C, Part V. Be sure to enter any reimbursements from the Food Program (with the exception of reimbursements for your own children) as income on Form 1040 Schedule C, line 6.

Your Home Expenses

Casualty losses	________	Enter on **Form 8829**, line 9, col. b
Mortgage interest paid last year	________	Enter on **Form 8829**, line 10, col. b
Real estate taxes paid last year	________	Enter on **Form 8829**, line 11, col. b
Homeowners/renters insurance	________	Enter on **Form 8829**, line 17, col. b
Home repairs and maintenance	________	Enter on **Form 8829**, line 19, col. b
Other assessments	________	Enter on **Form 8829**, line 21, col. b

Utilities

Gas	________	
Oil	________	
Electricity	________	
Water	________	
Sewer	________	
Garbage	________	
Cable TV	________	
Total utilities	________	Enter on **Form 8829**, line 20, col. b
Apartment or home rent	________	Enter on **Form 8829**, line 18, col. b

You can never claim monthly costs associated with the first phone line in your home. If you have a second phone line in your home, you may claim part of its monthly costs based on your business-use percentage. Calculate your business-use percentage by tracking your business and personal use for at least two months. Divide your business hours by the total (business and personal) hours of use.

Cost of second phone line	________	
Actual business-use percentage	x ________	%
	= ________	Enter on **Form 8829**, line 20, col. a

IF YOU USE THE *REDLEAF CALENDAR-KEEPER*

Enter the amounts in the Total column (not the FCC Business Expense column) from the house expenses worksheet.

Your Depreciation

Enter all the depreciable items you bought last year on the worksheet. (Use the depreciation tables in chapter 3 to fill in the Table % column in the depreciation worksheet.) Enter your depreciation deductions on **Form 4562**. For depreciable items you bought before last year and after you went into business, fill out copies of this page. Enter depreciation for each year on **Form 4562**. Enter the first year of depreciation as described in chapter 3. After the first year, enter depreciation (except home and home/land improvements) on **Form 4562**, line 17.

Your Home Depreciation (including home and land improvements)

Purchase price of your home	________	
Value of land (at time of purchase)	– ________	
Value of any improvements to your home or land that you completed *before* your business began (see below)	+ ________	**(A)**
Your home's adjusted value	= ________	

Enter your home's adjusted value on **Form 8829**, line 36

Improvements Completed before Your Business Began

Description of Project	Month/Year Completed	Cost of Project
________	________	________
________	________	+ ________
________	________	+ ________
________	________	+ ________
________	________	+ ________
________	________	+ ________
Total cost of all projects		= ________ **(A)**

IF YOU USE THE *INVENTORY-KEEPER*

Use the numbers from page 53.

Depreciation Worksheet

Depreciation Category[1]	Date Put into Service	Cost or Other Basis[2]	Method/ Convention	Business-Use %[3]	Business Basis[4]	Table %	Depreciation Deduction	Section 179 Deduction
Computers/printers								
Furniture/appliances								
Home improvements								
Land improvements								

[1] See chapter 3 for a definition of what items belong in each depreciation category.

[2] Enter the original cost or the fair market value of the item when it was first used for business last year, whichever is lower.

[3] Enter one of the following percentages: 100% business use, Time-Space percentage, or actual business-use percentage. See chapter 5 for a definition of each option.

[4] Multiply the amount in the Cost or Other Basis column by the percentage in the Business-Use % column.

Your Employee Payroll Tax Record

Your Employee Payroll Tax Record

Employee Name	Date Paid	Gross Amt. Pd.	Social Sec./ Medicare Withheld[1]	Fed. Inc. Tax Withheld	State Inc. Tax Withheld	Total Deductions[2]
Totals						
Enter on:		Schedule C, line 26	Schedule C, line 23	Schedule C, line 23	Schedule C, line 23	

[1] 6.2% Social Security + 1.45% Medicare = 7.65%

[2] Social Security/Medicare Amount Withheld + Federal Income Tax Withheld + State Income Tax Withheld

PART II

The Tax Workbook

CHAPTER 1

Calculating Your Time-Space Percentage

Note: See page xiv for how to calculate your Time-Space percentage if you were closed for a month or more in 2020.

Before you start filling out your tax forms, calculate your Time-Space percentage for this tax year. This percentage is one of the most important numbers you will use for your taxes because it determines how much of your key expenses you will be able to deduct as business expenses. For example, the Time-Space percentage is used in calculating home expenses on **Form 8829**, personal property depreciation expenses on **Form 4562**, and shared household supplies and other expenses on **Schedule C**. The specific deductions that are based on the Time-Space percentage include these:

- casualty losses
- mortgage interest
- real estate taxes
- homeowners insurance
- home repairs and maintenance
- utilities
- rent of a house or apartment
- home depreciation
- personal property depreciation
- home improvements
- land improvements
- household supplies and toys

Since the total of these costs is usually a significant amount, it's important to calculate your Time-Space percentage correctly. The Tax Organizer includes worksheets you can use to calculate your Time-Space percentage quickly; this chapter provides a more detailed description of that process.

Computing your Time-Space percentage is a three-step process. First you calculate your Time percentage, then you calculate your Space percentage, and then you multiply the two together. The formula you will use looks like this:

$$\frac{\text{\# hours your home is used for business}}{\text{Total \# hours in a year}} \times \frac{\text{\# square feet of your home used regularly for business}}{\text{Total \# square feet in your home}} = \text{Time-Space percentage}$$

Step One: Calculate Your Time Percentage

The Time percentage is how much time your home is used for your business. You calculate it by using the following formula:

$$\frac{\text{\# hours your home is used for business}}{\text{Total \# hours in a year}} = \text{Time percentage}$$

You can include the following activities in calculating how many hours your home is used for your business:

- caring for children
- cleaning the home for your business
- cooking for the children in your care
- planning and preparing activities for your business
- keeping business records, including paperwork for the Child and Adult Care Food Program (CACFP)
- conducting interviews with parents
- talking to parents on the telephone about your business
- locating resources and information on the internet
- any other business-related activities you do in your home

In calculating your Time percentage, you may not count time you spend outside your home on activities such as shopping or transporting children to school. For those activities, you are not using your home for business purposes.

Maximize Your Claim

Many family child care providers don't include all their working hours in calculating their Time percentage and therefore do not take full advantage of the law. Although there is no maximum Time percentage, it is important to track your working hours so that you have evidence to back up your claim. Also, you must recalculate your Time percentage each year because the number of hours you work usually isn't exactly the same from year to year. Here are some tips for recording your business hours:

Hours Spent Caring for Children

Throughout the year, keep records that show how much time you spend caring for the children in your business. Keep attendance records, or save a copy of a document that describes your normal working day, such as a parent contract or a flyer advertising your business.

> Example
>
> This year you cared for children from 7:00 a.m. to 5:00 p.m. five days a week and took one week of vacation. In this case, you spent 2,550 hours caring for children (10 hours a day x 5 days a week x 51 weeks = 2,550 hours).

To come up with this number, count all the hours when children are in your care from the time the first child arrives to the time the last child leaves. If you usually work from 7:00 a.m. to 5:00 p.m. but a child regularly arrives early or stays late, note this on a calendar or in your record book and count the additional time. If a child stays overnight occasionally, count all the hours the child is in your house. If you regularly care for children overnight, your Time percentage could be very high. In this case, it is extremely important to keep exact records of when children are present.

If you take a vacation, don't count this time as business hours. You probably should not count the hours for paid holidays, either, although there are no IRS guidelines on this point.

Hours Working When Children Are Not Present

In addition to counting all the hours you spend caring for children, you should also include all the hours your home is used for business purposes when the children in your care are not present. This includes time spent cleaning, cooking, planning activities, keeping records, interviewing, making phone calls, and doing other activities related to your business. Don't count hours spent on general home repairs or maintenance activities, such as cutting the lawn, repairing fixtures, or putting up storm windows.

You may not count the same hours twice. For example, if you clean the house during the day while the children sleep, you cannot count the cleaning hours because you are already counting this time as caring for children. You may only count these hours if the children you care for are not present. For example, if between 7:00 a.m. and 8:00 a.m. you are preparing breakfast for the children in your care and your spouse is cleaning your home, you can only count one hour toward your Time percentage. If your spouse did the cleaning the night before while you were not conducting business activities, then you can count the time spent doing both tasks.

Keep records showing that you spent these hours on business activities and not on personal activities. If you spend one hour cleaning after the children leave, count this hour as business time. If you are cleaning your house in general, count only the time that is associated with the mess created by your business. Mark on a calendar when you do these business activities, or make up a weekly schedule that you regularly follow.

> Example
>
> In addition to the 2,550 hours you spent actually caring for children, you spent 60 hours a month (720 hours a year) on business activities such as cleaning, preparing meals, planning activities, record keeping, meeting parents, and making business phone calls. You add this to your total business hours for the year and get 3,270 hours, which gives you a Time percentage of 37% (3,270 ÷ 8,760 hours [24 hours a day x 365 days = 8,760 hours]).

Step Two: Calculate Your Space Percentage

The Space percentage is how much space you use in your home on a regular basis for your business. You calculate it by using the following formula:

$$\frac{\text{\# square feet of your home used regularly for business}}{\text{Total \# square feet in your home}} = \text{Space percentage}$$

For a room to be counted as child care space, it must be used on a *regular* basis for your business. Regular means consistent, customary use. Using a room only occasionally for business is not regular use. A room doesn't have to be used every day to be considered regularly used, but using it once every two weeks probably isn't regular use. If the children in your care sleep in your bedroom for an hour a day, count the bedroom as being regularly used for the business. However, using the bedroom for sick children once a month would not be regular use.

If there are any rooms in your home that you use exclusively for your business, refer to the section titled Exclusive-Use Rooms (in this chapter) before you calculate your Space percentage.

In the total square footage of your home, include every area of your home, including your basement, porch, deck, carport, detached garage, basement, and other structures on your land, such as a barn. Do not include the following spaces: lawn, garden area, driveway, sidewalk, sandbox, or outdoor play space.

IRS Child Care Provider Audit Technique Guide on the Space Percentage

The guide explicitly states that providers should count both their basements and garages as part of the total square footage of their home. A Tax Court case (see the *Uphus and Walker v. Commissioner* case in appendix C) has also ruled that providers can claim their laundry room, storage room, and garage as regularly used in the business, even if the children in care never use the rooms.

This means that when you count your basement in the total square footage of your home, you may be able to count areas such as the following as regularly used by your business: the furnace and water heater area (if used regularly to heat the home and water used by the business), the laundry room (if used regularly to wash children's clothes, bedding, and blankets), and the storage areas (if used regularly to store toys, holiday decorations, or home maintenance equipment used in the business).

The inclusion of basements and garages into the Space percentage calculation can have different consequences for providers. For providers who use these areas on a regular basis for their business and have other rooms that are not regularly used in their business, this is good news because it will increase their Space percentage. For providers who have exclusive-use rooms and did not previously count these areas, this is bad news because it will decrease their Space percentage. For providers who use all their rooms on a regular basis for their business as well as their basement and garage, this will not make any difference. In my experience working with thousands of child care providers, I have found that it is very common for providers to use all the rooms of their home on a regular basis for their business. If this applies to you, don't hesitate to claim 100% Space percentage.

Let's look at an example of a Space percentage calculation:

	Used regularly for business?	Count as business space	Don't count as business space
Living room	Yes	300 sq ft	
Dining room	Yes	200 sq ft	
Kitchen	Yes	150 sq ft	
Entryway or stairs	Yes	150 sq ft	
Second-floor hallway	Yes	75 sq ft	
Master bedroom	Yes	200 sq ft	
Child's bedroom	Yes	150 sq ft	
Child's bedroom	No		250 sq ft
Bathroom	Yes	100 sq ft	
Basement playroom	Yes	275 sq ft	
Basement furnace/ laundry area	Yes	50 sq ft	
Basement storage area	Yes/No	150 sq ft	250 sq ft
Garage/carport	Yes	200 sq ft	
Total		2,000 sq ft	500 sq ft

$$\frac{\text{\# square feet of your home used regularly for business}}{\text{Total \# square feet in your home}} = \frac{2{,}000}{2{,}500} = 80\% \text{ Space percentage}$$

Step Three: Calculate Your Time-Space Percentage

To find your Time-Space percentage, multiply your Time percentage by your Space percentage. In our example:

37% Time x 80% Space = 30% Time-Space percentage

Here's the Time-Space percentage formula again:

$$\frac{\text{\# hours your home is used for business}}{\text{Total \# hours in a year}} \times \frac{\text{\# square feet of your home used regularly for business}}{\text{Total \# square feet in your home}} = \text{Time-Space percentage}$$

Use your 2020 Time-Space percentage only for the expenses you are claiming in 2019. *Remember that you will have to recalculate your Time-Space percentage each year and apply the new percentage to your expenses.*

If you discover that in previous years you have not been counting all the business space in your home or all your business hours, you may want to file **Form 1040X** (see chapter 9) to amend your previous tax returns and collect refunds from the IRS.

Exclusive-Use Rooms

If you use one or more of the rooms in your home exclusively for your business, you will need to calculate your Space percentage a bit differently. For example, an exclusive-use room might be a separate playroom that is used only by the children in your care. Exclusive use means 100% business use—it means that you don't use the room for any personal purposes at all, at any time. You can walk through the area during your personal time to get to another room or to go outside, but if you use the room for personal use at all, it is no longer used exclusively for business.

Let's say that in the example on the previous page the basement playroom is an exclusive-use room that is used 100% for the child care business. This room will serve as an example of how to calculate the Space percentage if you have an exclusive-use room:

1. Divide the square feet of the exclusive-use room by the total square feet of the home: 275 ÷ 2,500 = 11%
2. Divide the square feet of the rooms used regularly for business by the total square feet of the home: 1,725 ÷ 2,500 = 69%
3. Multiply the Space percentage of the shared rooms by the Time percentage: 69% x 37% = 26%
4. Add the percentages that resulted from Step 1 and Step 3: 11% + 26% = 37% Time-Space percentage

Notice that this Time-Space percentage is significantly greater than the 30% that we calculated previously for this example. If you use any rooms exclusively for your business, you should use this formula and claim the higher Time-Space percentage.

If you use some rooms exclusively for business, try not to set aside any other rooms exclusively for personal use, if you can avoid it. If you use one room exclusively for business and all your other rooms regularly for business, you will have a higher Time-Space percentage than if you use one room exclusively for business and all your other rooms exclusively for personal use.

You don't need to have a physical barrier around an area that is used exclusively for business. If a room has an area used exclusively for business but is otherwise a personal area, measure the two parts of the room and claim the exclusive-use rule for the exclusive area.

Because of the significant impact that an exclusive-use room can have on your Time-Space percentage, an IRS auditor is likely to look closely at the measurements of these rooms. If you claim any exclusive-use rooms, draw a simple diagram of your home showing which areas you used exclusively for your business, and keep this diagram with your records. This is important because your use of the rooms or the square footage of the rooms may change (if you remodel, for example). Save any copies of your house plans, blueprints, or other documents that can verify the square footage of your home.

Actual Business-Use Percentage

An actual business-use percentage is an alternative to the Time-Space percentage for items that you regularly use for business. It results in a much higher rate than your Time-Space percentage. You determine an item's actual business-use percentage by dividing the number of hours you use it for business by the total number of hours you use it for all purposes. If you use this method, you must document your business use in writing and be prepared to back up your number if the IRS challenges it.

Here's an example: You bought a swing set this year for $1,000; your Time-Space percentage is 25%. Using your Time-Space percentage, you could only depreciate $250 ($1,000 x 25%) of this expense this year. (See chapter 3 for an explanation of depreciation.) You determine that the children in your care use the swing set 10 hours a week (2 hours/day x 5 days), while your own children only use it 7 hours a week (1 hour/day x 7 days). In this case, your business-use percentage would be 59% (10 hours of business use ÷ 17 hours of total use), and you would be able to depreciate $590 ($1,000 x 59%). Since this item represents a large expense, and 59% is significantly greater than 25%, you should definitely use your business-use percentage in this case.

If you use a business-use percentage, you must keep records to support your calculation. If the IRS challenges it, it will be up to you to prove that your figure is accurate. This doesn't mean that you have to keep a log every day to show the business use, but you may need several weeks or months of logs to show a pattern. The higher your business-use percentage, the more evidence the IRS may request to justify your number.

You may use a business-use percentage for a few items and your Time-Space percentage for everything else. You can use either method for any items you are depreciating.

For more information about the tax issues discussed in this chapter, refer to the related topics in the other chapters of this book and the Redleaf Press *Family Child Care Record-Keeping Guide.*

CHAPTER 2

Claiming Your Home Expenses: Form 8829

This chapter explains how to fill out **Form 8829 Expenses for Business Use of Your Home**. The following expenses are listed on this form:

- casualty losses
- mortgage interest
- real estate taxes
- homeowners insurance
- home repairs and maintenance
- utilities
- rent
- home depreciation

The goal of **Form 8829** is to determine how much of your home expenses you can claim as a business deduction. There are limits on this amount; for example, you cannot claim a loss from your business because of home expenses (other than real estate taxes and mortgage interest). You can carry forward any home expenses that aren't allowable this year and claim them in a later year. (If you live on a military base and pay no home-related expenses, you don't need to fill out **Form 8829**.)

To finish **Form 8829**, you will have to complete **Schedule C** through line 29 (see chapter 5). It's a good idea to read this chapter first so you'll know what to do when you reach that point on **Form 8829**. You may want to begin **Form 8829** while the Time-Space percentage calculation is fresh in your mind, then switch to other forms needed to complete **Schedule C** and return to **Form 8829** when you're done with **Schedule C**.

New Simplified Method

You may use a new IRS Simplified Method to claim up to $1,500 of your house expenses without receipts on **Schedule C**, line 30. If you choose to use this new rule, you will not fill out IRS **Form 8829** and you will not be able to deduct house depreciation, utilities, property tax, mortgage interest, homeowners insurance, or house repairs. You will be able to claim 100% of your property tax and mortgage interest on **Schedule A Itemized Deductions**. The vast majority of providers should not use this Simplified Method. See chapter 5 for an explanation.

How to Fill Out Form 8829

This section explains how to fill out **Form 8829** for your business by taking you through the form line by line and referring to the filled-out example at the end of this chapter. Before you start filling out **Form 8829**, you should also skim the section titled Special Cases for **Form 8829** on page 57 to see if any of the situations described there apply to your business in this tax year.

Part I: Part of Your Home Used for Business

Line 1: Enter the number of square feet of your home that you use regularly for your business. Ignore the phrase "area used exclusively for business" on this line. Every other kind of business is only allowed to count the space that is used exclusively for business, but family child care providers are exempt from this regulation (see IRS **Publication 587 Business Use of Your Home**).

Line 2: Enter the total square footage of your home. Some providers use the number of rooms in their home on lines 1 and 2 instead of the square footage of those rooms. This might lower your business use of your home by a greater margin than if you were counting square feet.

Line 3: Divide line 1 by line 2 to get your Space percentage. If you used 2,200 square feet of your 2,200-square-foot home regularly for your business, you would enter 100% on this line (2,200 ÷ 2,200 = 100%).

Line 4: Enter the number of hours you used your home for business purposes in this tax year. Be sure to include both the hours that children were present and the hours you spent on business activities when they weren't present.

Line 5: This line shows the total number of hours in a year (365 days x 24 hours = 8,760 hours). If you didn't operate your business every day of the year, cross this number out and enter the total number of hours your home was available for business use. To find this number, multiply the number of days you were in business by 24 hours. Include Saturdays, Sundays, and holidays between working days. Here's an example: You began your business on April 1 of last year and were still in business at the end of the year. Since there are 275 days between April 1 and December 31, on line 5 you would enter 6,600 hours (275 days x 24 hours).

Line 6: Divide line 4 by line 5. If you worked 3,514 hours last year and you were in business the entire year, your Time percentage would be 40% (3,514 ÷ 8,760).

Line 7: Multiply line 6 by line 3. If your Space percentage was 100% and your Time percentage was 40%, your Time-Space percentage would be 40% (100% x 40%). This percentage will affect your other tax forms, so be sure to double-check your math. An error will mean mistakes on all your tax forms. Be sure to save the records that show how you calculated your numbers for Part I. The Time-Space percentage is a favorite area for IRS audits, so it's important to have good, clear documentation.

If You Weren't in Business the Entire Year

Recall that the total number of hours your home was available for business use was calculated on line 5 of Part I. When you enter your home expenses in Part II, you may list only the expenses that you incurred when your home was available for business use; the dates of your expenses must match the dates you used for that calculation.

If you based that calculation on the 275 days between April 1 and December 31 of last year, you may enter only expenses you incurred between April and December. You may not include the March utility bill that you paid in April, but you may include the January bill for December's utilities.

You will also need to enter a prorated amount of your home expenses for the year, such as property tax and homeowners insurance. In our example, you would enter 75% of these yearly expenses (275 days ÷ 365 days = 75%).

Let's look at an example to see how being in business for less than the full year will affect **Form 8829** and **Schedule A**. Last year you began your business on April 1, and your Time-Space percentage between April 1 and December 31 was 40%. Your mortgage interest for the year was $5,000, and your property tax was $2,000. Since you were in business for only 75% of the year, multiply these expenses by this percentage:

Mortgage interest	$5,000 x 75% = $3,750
Property tax	$2,000 x 75% = $1,500

Next, multiply the results by your Time-Space percentage (40%):

Mortgage interest	$3,750 x 40% = $1,500
Property tax	$1,500 x 40% = $600

These numbers represent the amount you can deduct on **Form 8829**. If you itemize your tax return, enter the remaining amounts on **Schedule A**:

Mortgage interest	$5,000 – $1,500 = $3,500
Property tax	$2,000 – $600 = $1,400

Remember, the amount you claim for mortgage interest and property tax on **Form 8829** and **Schedule A** should equal (and never exceed) 100%.

Part II: Figure Your Allowable Deduction

Before you fill out this part of **Form 8829**, go to **Schedule C** and complete lines 1–29 (see chapter 5). Then return to this point and continue.

Line 8: Enter the amount from **Schedule C**, line 29. If you sold any items you used in your business during the last year (see chapter 11), add the net gain or loss from these items on this line. If you sold your home last year, don't include the net gain or loss from the sale on this line.

If there is a negative number on line 8, your mortgage interest and real estate taxes (lines 10 and 11) will be the only home expenses you can claim this year. Complete the rest of this form anyway, because you may be able to carry over any excess expenses to next year.

The next several lines of **Form 8829** include two columns. The following numbers are an example of how you might fill out lines 9–36. For this example, assume that the provider was in business for the entire year.

Time-Space percentage	40%
Net income from line 29 of **Schedule C**	$3,500
Casualty losses	$0
Mortgage interest	$2,000
Real estate taxes	$1,500

Home insurance	$900
Child care homeowners insurance endorsement	$400
Repairs and maintenance	$800
Utilities	$1,000

Col. (a): Under column (a) you will enter only your *direct* expenses—expenses that were incurred 100% for your business or for which you are using an actual business-use percentage instead of a Time-Space percentage. Continue reading for a description of each line in this column.

Col. (b): Under column (b) you will enter your *indirect* expenses—expenses that were incurred partly for your business and partly for your personal use. Continue reading for a description of each line in this column.

Line 9: Hurricanes and fires have certainly made people aware of the terrible damage that can be caused by a natural disaster. A casualty loss is defined as the damage, destruction, or loss of property resulting from an identifiable event that is sudden, unexpected, or unusual, such as an earthquake, tornado, flood, storm, fire, vandalism, theft, or car accident.

You must file an insurance claim in a timely manner in order to deduct a sudden or unexpected loss. If your insurance fully covers your losses, then you can't claim them as losses for tax purposes. If your insurance doesn't fully cover them (for example, if you have to pay a deductible or are underinsured), then you may be able to claim some business deductions that will reduce your taxes at the end of the year.

You are entitled to deduct any casualty losses of items used in your business (not covered by insurance), including your home, furniture, appliances, and business equipment. Expenses that result from a casualty loss or theft may also be deductible. These expenses include medical treatment, cleanup, minor repairs, temporary housing, a rental car, replacing spoiled food, and boarding up your home or sandbagging your property in anticipation of a flood.

If a natural disaster forces you to shut down your business temporarily, you cannot deduct your loss of income as a business expense. You will simply report less income on your tax return and therefore pay less in taxes.

If an item is completely destroyed, the business loss is the purchase price of the item minus the depreciation you have claimed on it or were entitled to claim on it. For example, let's say that you have a Time-Space percentage of 40% and are uninsured. You buy a swing set for $1,000 and depreciate it for two years, and then it is destroyed in a fire. In this case, your business loss would be $245 ($1,000 x 40% = $400 – $155 [two years of depreciation deductions] = $245).

If you received an insurance payment of $200 for this loss, the business portion of that payment would be $80 ($200 x 40% Time-Space), and your business loss would be $165 ($245 – $80). If you received a payment of $1,000 for this loss, you would have a business gain of $155 ($245 – $400 [$1,000 x 40% Time-Space = $400] = – $155), which you would report on **Form 4797**.

If an item you use in your business is damaged but not destroyed, use the lower of the adjusted value of the property (the original cost minus the depreciation claimed) or the difference between the fair market value of the item immediately before and immediately after the casualty. In other words, in the above example the adjusted value of the swing set was $245. If the business portion of the swing set's value before damage was $300 and its value after the damage was $100, the difference would be $200 ($300 – $100 = $200). You would compare the $200 to the adjusted value ($245) and use the lower number ($200) as your business loss.

Calculate your business loss (or gain) on a separate piece of paper and enter the total on line 9, column (a). Notice that the expenses entered on this line are taken out on line 34 and transferred to **Form 4684**. From that form, the business losses (or gains) are transferred to **Form 4797** and then to **Form 1040**, where they are deducted. This means that you will not actually claim your business losses as an expense on **Form 8829**. (Personal losses are calculated on **Form 4684** and then transferred from there to **Schedule A**.)

Although casualty losses can't create a loss on **Form 8829** (see the IRS instructions for **Form 8829**), you can carry the excess amount forward to next year. If you suffer a loss in an event that leads to your community being declared a federal disaster area, see the instructions to **Form 4684**. If you buy new property to replace the damaged or destroyed property, begin depreciating the new property under the rules described in chapter 3.

An Insurance Note

Many homeowners insurance policies only cover up to $2,000 worth of property used in a family child care business. Examine your policy to find out if your business property is properly covered. If it's not, you should purchase additional business property insurance. Business liability insurance usually will not cover the loss of business property. See the *Family Child Care Legal and Insurance Guide* for detailed information about how to protect your home and business through insurance.

To help prepare for a natural disaster, you should conduct an inventory of all the property in your home. Use the *Family Child Care Inventory-Keeper* to help you identify and track all your property and estimate its fair market value. Take photographs of all the rooms in your home, and store the photographs and your inventory records in a safe-deposit box.

Line 10: If you itemized your deductible mortgage interest using **Schedule A**, enter you total deductible mortgage interest in column (b), including any interest paid on a contract-for-deed mortgage. If you used the standard deduction on **Form 1040**, enter your total deductible mortgage interest on line 16, column (b). Don't include interest on a mortgage loan that didn't benefit your home (such as a second mortgage used to pay off your credit cards or buy a car).

Refinancing Points

The points, or mortgage closing fees, paid on a home loan are treated as prepaid interest. You can deduct on line 10, column (b), the business portion of points paid on a loan to buy, build, remodel, or improve a home in the same year. (Deduct the personal portion of the points on **Schedule A** as personal interest.) You must deduct any points paid to refinance a loan over the term of the loan.

If you refinance with the same lender, add the remaining points of the old loan to the points of the new loan and spread the total over the life of the new loan. For example, let's say that you're paying $200 a year in points for a twenty-year loan. Six years into the loan, you refinance with the same lender and get a new twenty-year loan, and the points for the new loan amount to $3,000. Add the remaining points of the old loan ($4,000 – $1,200 = $2,800) to the new points ($3,000) and spread the total ($5,800) over twenty years, at $290 a year. Put $290 on line 10, column (b) each year for the next twenty years (where it will be multiplied by your Time-Space percentage to calculate business use).

If you refinance with another lender, you can deduct all the remaining points from the old loan on line 10, column (b) in the year you refinance.

Line 11: If you itemized your real estate taxes using **Schedule A**, enter this total amount in column (b). Enter your total real estate taxes in column (b). You will be able to deduct only part of this amount on **Form 8829**, but you will be able to claim the remaining amount of your real estate taxes on **Schedule A**, line 6. If you used the standard deduction on **Form 1040**, enter your total real estate taxes on line 17, column (b).

You are always entitled to claim the business portion of property tax and mortgage interest on **Form 8829** whether or not you itemize your personal taxes using **Schedule A**.

Line 12: Enter the total of lines 9, 10, and 11. (In the example at the end of this chapter, $0 + $2,000 + $1,500 = $3,500.)

Line 13: Enter the total of line 12, column (b), multiplied by line 7. (In the example, $3,500 x 40% = $1,400.)

Line 14: Enter the total of line 12, column (a), and line 13. (In the example, $0 + $1,400 = $1,400.)

Line 15: Enter the total of line 8 minus line 14. (In the example, $3,500 – $1,400 = $2,100.)

The amount on line 15 ($2,100) is the most that you can claim on **Form 8829** for the remaining home expenses. You *must* claim the business amount of your mortgage interest and real estate taxes on this form; you can claim the rest of these expenses as itemized deductions on **Schedule A**. Use your Time-Space percentage to determine your business deduction. Here's the calculation, building on the previous example, using a 40% Time-Space percentage:

	Total Expense	**Form 8829 Expense 40%**	**Schedule A Expense 60%**
Mortgage interest	$2,000	$800	$1,200
Property tax	$1,500	$600	$900

You may wish to claim all of your mortgage interest and real estate taxes on **Schedule A** rather than dividing them between **Schedule A** and **Form 8829**; however, this is both against the law and not in your best interests. Unlike your personal income, your business income is subject to Social Security and Medicare taxes as well as income tax. For this reason, a business deduction will reduce your taxes more than a personal deduction will.

Don't make the error of claiming your Time-Space percentage of these expenses on **Form 8829** and then claiming 100% of the same expenses on **Schedule A**. You are never allowed to claim more than 100% of any deduction. In addition, if your state offers a property tax rebate, you must calculate the amount of your rebate based on your personal-use percentage of the property tax, not the business- and personal-use percentage of the property tax. For example, if a family child care provider has a Time-Space percentage of 40%, then her personal use of the home is 60%, and she is entitled to use only 60% of her property tax to calculate her rebate.

Remember that only mortgage interest and real estate taxes can create a loss on **Form 8829**. What happens if they do? Building on the previous example, if the business share of the mortgage interest and real estate taxes was greater than $3,500, that amount could be claimed as a loss for the business. If the mortgage interest was $6,000 and real estate taxes were $4,000, the amount on line 12 would be $10,000. Multiply this by 40% (line 7), and line 13 would be $4,000 ($10,000 x 40%). Line 14 would also be $4,000. Since $4,000 is more than $3,500 (line 8), 0 would be entered on line 15.

No other expenses could be claimed on **Form 8829**. Line 34 would be $4,000, and this amount would transfer to **Schedule C**, line 30, where it would create a $500 loss on that form. The other expenses on this form would be put on Part IV and carried over to **Form 8829** in the next year.

Line 16: If you used the standard deduction to claim your deductible mortgage interest, enter it here on column (b). Note: As of 2018 you may deduct mortgage interest only if the loan is used to improve your home. So, a home equity loan that you use to buy a car or boat or anything else besides improving your home is no longer deductible. If you used the standard deduction to claim your real estate taxes, enter it here on column (b).

Line 18: Enter your homeowners insurance in column (b). If you purchased a special policy just for your business or bought a business endorsement for your homeowners insurance policy, enter this amount in column (a). You can deduct the Time-Space percentage of your home mortgage insurance premiums. If your adjusted gross income (**Form 1040**, line 37) is more than $109,000 (married filing jointly), the amount you can deduct is reduced. You cannot deduct home mortgage insurance premiums paid on cash-out refinances or home equity loans.

Line 19: If you rent your home, enter your total rent payments in column (b). As a renter, you may claim the Time-Space percentage of your monthly rent and any utilities you pay, plus a portion of any home improvements you make and any losses due to the theft of personal property used in your business.

Line 20: Enter your home repair and maintenance expenses in column (b). (See chapter 3 for a discussion of the difference between a repair and a home improvement.) Repairs (painting, wallpapering, fixing a broken window, or mending a leak) keep your home in good working order. Repairs to an exclusive-use room are 100% deductible; enter these expenses in column (a).

Line 21: Enter your total utility expenses (gas, electricity, water, sewage, garbage, and cable TV) in column (b), even if you rent your home. Monthly fees for telephone service are not deductible. If your phone service includes charges on a cost-per-minute basis, however, you can deduct the cost of your local business calls. Enter the cost of local business calls on line 20, column (a).

Actual Business-Use Percentage of Utilities Costs

Because of the significant cost of heating oil, gas, and electricity, you may benefit from using your actual business-use percentage of utility expenses. The actual business-use percentage of utilities costs for heating a home during the day for ten or more hours, Monday through Friday, is probably significantly more than the cost calculated by using a typical 30%–40% Time-Space percentage, especially since you can turn down the heat in the evening.

How can you determine the actual business-use percentage of your utility expenses? If you have been in business only for a short time, look at your energy usage before and after your business began. You might also call your local utility company to see if it can determine your energy usage during daytime hours.

If you decide to use a method other than your Time-Space percentage to calculate your utility expenses, be sure to keep careful records of your calculations and save them. Enter the actual business-use amount of your utilities on line 20, column (a).

Line 22: If you have other house expenses not claimed elsewhere, claim them here.

Line 23: Enter the total of lines 16–22. (In the example, $0 + $900 + $0 + $800 + $1,000 + $0 = $2,700.)

Line 24: Enter the total of line 23, column (b), multiplied by line 7. (In the example, $2,700 x 40% = $1,080.)

Line 25: If you had any home operating expenses in 2018 that you were unable to deduct that year because of the home expense limitation, enter that amount here.

Line 26: Enter the total of line 23, column (a), and lines 24–25. (In the example, $400 + $1,080 + $0 = $1,480.)

Line 27: Compare the amounts on line 15 and line 26, and enter whichever is the least. (In the example, $2,100 is the larger of the two, so $1,480 is entered.)

Line 28: Enter the amount of line 15 minus line 27. (In the example, $2,100 – $1,480 = $620.) In the example, this is the upper limit of the home depreciation expenses that can be claimed.

Line 29: Enter any excess casualty losses.

Line 30: Enter your home depreciation total from line 42. (The same example will be used in the next section to illustrate how to depreciate a home.) In the example, $963 is entered ($11 will be added later for a home improvement; see the instructions for line 42 on page 56).

Line 31: Enter any excess casualty losses and depreciation you carried over from 2019.

Line 32: Enter the total of your home depreciation, excess casualty losses, and carryover of excess casualty losses and home depreciation from 2019. In the example, $963 is entered.

Line 33: Compare the amounts on line 28 and line 32, and enter whichever is the least. (In the example, $620 is entered because it is less than $963.)

Line 34: Enter the total of lines 14, 27, and 33. (In the example, $1,400 + $1,480 + $620 = $3,500.)

Line 35: If you had any casualty loss from line 14 or 33, enter that amount here. The example does not have anything to record.

Line 36: Subtract line 33 from line 34. (In our example, $3,500 – $0 = $3,500.)

Line 36 has the allowable expenses for the business use of your home that you can claim on **Schedule C**. Enter this amount on **Schedule C**, line 30.

Using an Actual Business-Use Percentage

Although in most cases you will apply the Time-Space percentage from line 7 to all your indirect home expenses on **Form 8829**, in some cases you can use an actual business-use percentage instead. (See the section titled Actual Business-Use Percentage at the end of chapter 1 for a discussion.)

If a home expense is partly for your business and partly for personal use, you would normally enter it in column (b) and use the Time-Space percentage from line 7 to calculate the allowable business portion of the expense.

You aren't required to use the Time-Space percentage if you can show that one or more of your home expenses should be allocated in a different way. This is most common in the case of repairs to a room that is used heavily, but not exclusively, for your business. (If the room was used exclusively for business, you would enter 100% of the cost of the repair in column [a].)

Let's say that your Time-Space percentage is 37%, and you incurred a $200 repair to fix the radiator in a room that you use 80% of the time for your business. In this case you can claim 80% of the cost of this repair, or $160. To do this, simply enter the amount you calculate according to the business-use percentage in column (a), and enter nothing in column (b). In this example, you would list $160 in column (a). All the amounts you list in column (a) are deducted 100% as business expenses.

Part III: Depreciation of Your Home

If you first began using your home for your business last year, you must fill out **Form 4562**, line 19i (see chapter 3). Next, fill out lines 36–41 of **Form 8829**. If you used your home for your business before last year, don't enter any information about home depreciation on **Form 4562**; just fill out lines 36–41 of **Form 8829**, as described below.

Line 37: Enter your home's adjusted basis or its fair market value, whichever is the least. In the example, this amount is $103,800. Your home's adjusted basis is the sum of the purchase price of your home plus the value of any home improvements before you began using your home for your business (for more information, see chapter 3).

Line 38: Enter the value of the land at the time you purchased your home ($10,000 in the example). This amount should be included in the purchase price of your home on line 36; however, land can't be claimed as a business expense.

Line 39: Subtract line 38 from line 37. This is the basis of your home ($93,800 in the example). This number doesn't change from year to year. You'll enter the same numbers on lines 37–38 of **Form 8829** each year that you own this home.

Line 40: Enter the amount of line 39 multiplied by line 7 ($37,520 in the example). This is the business basis of your home.

Line 41: If you first began using your home for business before 1987, consult IRS **Publication 534 Depreciating Property Placed in Service Before 1987** to determine what rules were in effect when you began using your home for business. If you first used your home for business after 1986 but before May 13, 1993, enter 3.175% on this line. If you first used your home for business after May 12, 1993, but before last year, enter 2.564% on this line.

If you first began using your home for business last year, enter the percentage from the chart below, based on the first month you used your home for business:

January	2.461%	July	1.177%
February	2.247%	August	0.963%
March	2.033%	September	0.749%
April	1.819%	October	0.535%
May	1.605%	November	0.321%
June	1.391%	December	0.107%

In the example, the business began in January, so 2.461% is entered on this line. For years 2 through 39, 2.564% will be used for our depreciation calculations (for information about home depreciation, see chapter 3).

Line 42: Enter the amount of line 40 multiplied by line 41. This is the amount of home depreciation you can claim. In the example, this amount is $922. After $41 is added for a home improvement, the total ($963) is entered on line 30. (See the example form at the end of this chapter.)

Part IV: Carryover of Unallowed Expenses

Line 43: Subtract line 27 from line 26. A positive number here represents excess operating expenses that can't be deducted this tax season but can be carried forward and deducted next tax season. If you have a carryover here, put a copy of your **Form 8829** in your files for next tax season so you won't forget to claim it.

Line 44: Subtract line 33 from line 32 ($963 – $620 = $343). A positive number here represents excess casualty losses and home depreciation that can't be deducted this tax season but can be carried forward and deducted next tax season. If you have a carryover here, put a copy of your **Form 8829** in your files for next tax season so you won't forget to claim it.

If you go out of business in a tax year and don't operate your business the following year, you won't be able to claim any carryover expenses. If you go back into business in a later year, however, you will be able to claim your carryover expenses at that time.

What You Can't Claim on Form 8829

You can't claim the following kinds of expenses on **Form 8829**:

- **Property assessments**
  Property assessments (sidewalks, sewer, other improvements to your land made by your local government) are usually included with your property tax bill. Subtract them from your property tax before you enter your property tax on line 11. The cost of a property assessment can be deducted as a land improvement. For an explanation of how to deduct these expenses, see pages 85–86.

- **Monthly mortgage payments**
  Don't put your monthly mortgage payments on **Form 8829**. These payments consist of interest and payments toward the principal of your loan. Your monthly principal payments have nothing to do with how much you can deduct as a business expense. Your mortgage interest is claimed on line 10, column (b), of **Form 8829**. The principal is accounted for when you depreciate your home. Your home depreciation is based on the purchase price of your home, which you claim on line 29 of **Form 8829**.

- **Home expenses if you aren't a sole proprietor**
  If you have formed a partnership or a corporation and are working out of your home, you can't claim your home expenses on **Form 8829** because a partnership or a

corporation can't file **Form 8829**; it is for individuals only. If you have established a single-person limited liability company (LLC), however, you are entitled to claim all home expenses on **Form 8829**.

Special Cases for Form 8829

If You Have Any Exclusive-Use Rooms

You can claim a higher Time-Space percentage on **Form 8829** if you use one or more rooms in your home exclusively for business. The following example shows you how to calculate the Time-Space percentage in this situation:

- Polly Jones's home totals 2,000 square feet.
- She has one 300-square-foot room that she uses exclusively for her business.
- She uses the other 1,700 square feet regularly for her business.
- Polly works 2,628 hours during the year in the 1,700-square-foot area.

Because Polly has a room she uses exclusively for her business, she can't complete Part I of **Form 8829**. Instead, she will have to write "see attached" across Part I of the form and attach a separate sheet of paper that shows her Time-Space calculation.

Here's what her attachment would say:

Supporting Statement for Form 8829, Part I

Name: Polly Jones
Social Security #146-28-3333
Total square footage of home: 2,000
Square footage of room used exclusively for business: 300
Remaining 1,700 square feet are used regularly for child care
Hours 1,700-square-foot area is used for child care: 2,628

300 ÷ 2,000	= 15% actual business-use percentage of exclusive-use area
1,700 ÷ 2,000	= 85% Space percentage for business use of remainder of home
2,628 ÷ 8,760	= 30% Time percentage for business use of remainder of home
85% x 30%	= 25.5% Time-Space percentage for business use of remainder of home
15% + 25.5%	= 40.5% Time-Space percentage for business use of entire home

If You Provide Child Care Outside Your Home

Child care providers operating at locations other than their own homes is a growing trend. If you only provide child care in a building that's separate from your home, you can claim 100% of the expenses associated with that space, such as rent, utilities, furniture, and supplies. But if you operate out of another building, or two separate locations, you won't be eligible to file **Form 8829**. Instead, you will show your expenses for the other building on **Form 4562** and **Schedule C**, as follows:

ENTER ON **FORM 4562**

- depreciation (line 19i)

ENTER ON **SCHEDULE C**

- insurance (line 15)
- mortgage interest (line 16a)
- rent (line 20b)
- repairs and maintenance (line 21)
- property taxes (line 23)
- utilities (line 25)

Since you can only claim one location for your business, you won't be able to claim a Time-Space percentage for your home expenses if you're using both your home and a building separate from your home for your business. This is true even if you're still using your home for business activities such as keeping records and planning lessons. You can claim part of the cost of the business equipment that you use in your home, such as your computer, printer, file cabinet, and desk. Follow the depreciation rules described in chapter 3, and use your actual business-use percentage.

You won't be eligible to claim travel to and from your home and your place of business as business trips; this travel will be considered commuting to work. You can still count a trip for business purposes as business mileage if you are departing from and returning to your place of business.

If you provide child care at a location other than your home, you won't be eligible to use the IRS standard meal allowance rate in calculating your food expenses (see chapter 4). In addition, you may not be eligible to participate in the Food Program (check with your sponsor). Also, check your state regulations, which may prohibit you from providing child care in a home that you do not live in.

If You Receive a Military Housing Allowance

The IRS **Child Care Provider Audit Technique Guide** clarifies how to treat housing allowances if you are a family child care provider living in military housing.

If you live in on-base housing, you can't claim any home expenses except for those you pay out of your own pocket. Since you have no property tax or mortgage interest expenses, you can't deduct these expenses. If you spend your own money on a home repair, fence, or improvement, you can deduct the business portion of this expense on **Form 8829** or **Form 4562**.

If you live in off-base housing, you're entitled to claim the Time-Space percentage of your property tax and mortgage interest on **Form 8829** and the personal portion of these expenses on **Schedule A**. (You can do this even if your housing allowance covers these expenses.)

The **Child Care Provider Audit Technique Guide** offers a detailed formula to determine how much of your other home expenses not covered by your housing allowance (such as utilities, home depreciation, homeowners insurance, and home repairs) you can deduct as a business expense. Enter the allowable portion of these expenses on **Form 8829**, line 21, column (a). (For more information about how to claim these expenses, see the *Record-Keeping Guide*.)

If You Went Out of Business

If you went out of business last year, you can't claim a full year's worth of home depreciation. Instead, you can claim a prorated percentage of the full year's depreciation based on how many months you used your home for your business. Count the month that you stop using your home for business as a half month (this is according to the Mid-Month Convention rule; see chapter 3).

For example, let's say that you went out of business in November of last year. The business basis of your home is $17,550 and you have been in business for three years. Normally, your depreciation deduction would be $449.98 ($17,550 x 2.564% [the percentage of depreciation for a 39-year-old property]); however, in this case your deduction would be $449.98 x (10.5 months ÷ 12 months), or $393.73.

If Your Spouse Also Claims a Home Office Deduction

If your spouse is self-employed and also claims a deduction for home office expenses, you must file **Form 8829** and **Schedule C** for your business, and your spouse must file his own **Form 8829** and **Schedule C** for his business. Since the space that he claims for his business cannot also be claimed as space for your child care business, your Space percentage will be less than 100%.

If your spouse uses 10% of the home exclusively for his business, then he can claim 10% of the home expenses (such as utilities, real estate taxes, and mortgage interest). If you regularly use the rest of the home for your child care business, your Space percentage will be 90%. If your Time percentage is 35%, your Time-Space percentage will be 31.5% (90% x 35%), and you will claim 31.5% of the home expenses on your **Form 8829**.

If your spouse doesn't use any rooms exclusively for his business, then he won't file **Form 8829** because he won't be entitled to claim any home expenses (although he can still claim other business expenses on his **Schedule C**).

If you both use the same office for your business, he is using it nonexclusively, and you are using it regularly, you can claim the office space in your Time-Space calculation. Under these circumstances, you might have a Space percentage of 100% even if your husband runs his business in the home.

If You Made Home Improvements

If you made a home improvement before your business began, include the cost of the improvement in the cost of your home when you depreciate it in Part III of **Form 8829**.

If you made a home improvement after your business began but before 2017, calculate the depreciation deduction (see chapter 3), and include that amount on **Form 8829**, line 40. Write "see attached" next to this line, and attach a supporting statement showing how you calculated your home improvement deduction.

Here's an example:

Supporting Statement for Form 8829, Part III

Name: Polly Jones
Social Security #146-28-3333
Total square footage of home: 2,000
$4,000 new deck installed in 2015
x 40% Time-Space percentage
$1,600
x 2.564% depreciation amount for 39-year-old property
$41.02 enter on line 42

If you made a home improvement in 2020, first fill out **Form 4562**, line 19i (see chapter 3). Transfer the depreciation deduction from **Form 4562**, column (g), line 19i, to **Form 8829**, line 42. Don't include this amount in the depreciation deduction carried forward from **Form 4562**, line 22, to **Schedule C**, line 13. You can't claim an expense twice.

If You Moved

If you moved during the last year and continued to provide child care in your new home, you must file two copies of **Form 8829**, one for each home. You will need to calculate a separate Time-Space percentage for each home. On both forms, cross out the number printed on line 5 (8,760), and enter the number of hours you occupied the home during the last year. For example, if you moved on May 1, enter 2,880 hours (January–April = 120 days x 24 hours) on line 5 for the first house and 5,880 hours (May–December = 245 days x 24 hours) on line 5 for the second house. List your expenses for each home on the appropriate form. Add together lines 35 on both forms, and enter the total on **Schedule C**, line 30.

To determine what Time-Space percentage to use on shared items you are claiming on **Schedule C** (toys, household items, activity expenses, cleaning supplies, and so on), use the average of the two Time-Space percentages for each home. To account for the different number of months that each house was used for your business, use the following formula: multiply your Time-Space percentage for each house by the number of months the business was in each home. Add the two totals together and divide by 12. This is the Time-Space percentage to use for all shared expenses on **Schedule C**. For example, your Time-Space percentage was 35% for your first home (used January–April), and it was 25% for the second home (May–December): 35% x 4 months = 140%; 25% x 8 months = 200%; 140% + 200% = 340%, divided by 12 months = 28%.

For more information about the tax issues discussed in this chapter, refer to the related topics in the other chapters of this book and the Redleaf Press *Family Child Care Record-Keeping Guide.*

Form **8829**

Department of the Treasury
Internal Revenue Service (99)

Expenses for Business Use of Your Home

▶ File only with Schedule C (Form 1040). Use a separate Form 8829 for each home you used for business during the year.

▶ Go to *www.irs.gov/Form8829* for instructions and the latest information.

OMB No. 1545-0074

2020

Attachment Sequence No. **176**

Name(s) of proprietor(s)	Your social security number
POLLY JONES	123-45-6789

Part I Part of Your Home Used for Business

1	Area used regularly and exclusively for business, regularly for daycare, or for storage of inventory or product samples (see instructions)			1	2,200
2	Total area of home			2	2,200
3	Divide line 1 by line 2. Enter the result as a percentage			3	100 %
	For daycare facilities not used exclusively for business, go to line 4. All others, go to line 7.				
4	Multiply days used for daycare during year by hours used per day	4	3,514 hr.		
5	If you started or stopped using your home for daycare during the year, see instructions; otherwise, enter 8,784	5	8,760 hr.		
6	Divide line 4 by line 5. Enter the result as a decimal amount	6	.40		
7	Business percentage. For daycare facilities not used exclusively for business, multiply line 6 by line 3 (enter the result as a percentage). All others, enter the amount from line 3 ▶			7	40 %

Part II Figure Your Allowable Deduction

			(a) Direct expenses	(b) Indirect expenses		
8	Enter the amount from Schedule C, line 29, **plus** any gain derived from the business use of your home, **minus** any loss from the trade or business not derived from the business use of your home. See instructions.				8	$3,500
	See instructions for columns (a) and (b) before completing lines 9–22.					
9	Casualty losses (see instructions)	9				
10	Deductible mortgage interest (see instructions)	10				
11	Real estate taxes (see instructions)	11				
12	Add lines 9, 10, and 11	12				
13	Multiply line 12, column (b), by line 7	13				
14	Add line 12, column (a), and line 13				14	0
15	Subtract line 14 from line 8. If zero or less, enter -0-				15	$3,500
16	Excess mortgage interest (see instructions)	16		$2,000		
17	Excess real estate taxes (see instructions)	17	$400	$1,500		
18	Insurance	18		$900		
19	Rent	19				
20	Repairs and maintenance	20		$800		
21	Utilities	21		$1,000		
22	Other expenses (see instructions)	22				
23	Add lines 16 through 22	23	$400	$6,200		
24	Multiply line 23, column (b), by line 7	24		$2,480		
25	Carryover of prior year operating expenses (see instructions)	25				
26	Add line 23, column (a), line 24, and line 25				26	$2,880
27	Allowable operating expenses. Enter the **smaller** of line 15 or line 26				27	$2,880
28	Limit on excess casualty losses and depreciation. Subtract line 27 from line 15				28	$620
29	Excess casualty losses (see instructions)	29				
30	Depreciation of your home from line 42 below	30		$963		
31	Carryover of prior year excess casualty losses and depreciation (see instructions)	31				
32	Add lines 29 through 31				32	$963
33	Allowable excess casualty losses and depreciation. Enter the **smaller** of line 28 or line 32				33	$620
34	Add lines 14, 27, and 33				34	$3,500
35	Casualty loss portion, if any, from lines 14 and 33. Carry amount to **Form 4684.** See instructions				35	
36	**Allowable expenses for business use of your home.** Subtract line 35 from line 34. Enter here and on Schedule C, line 30. If your home was used for more than one business, see instructions. ▶				36	$3,500

Part III Depreciation of Your Home

37	Enter the **smaller** of your home's adjusted basis or its fair market value. See instructions	37	$103,800
38	Value of land included on line 37	38	$10,000
39	Basis of building. Subtract line 38 from line 37	39	$93,800
40	Business basis of building. Multiply line 39 by line 7	40	$37,520
41	Depreciation percentage (see instructions)	41	2.431 %
42	Depreciation allowable (see instructions). Multiply line 40 by line 41. Enter here and on line 30 above	42	$963

Part IV Carryover of Unallowed Expenses to 2021

43	Operating expenses. Subtract line 27 from line 26. If less than zero, enter -0-	43	
44	Excess casualty losses and depreciation. Subtract line 33 from line 32. If less than zero, enter -0-	44	$343

For Paperwork Reduction Act Notice, see your tax return instructions. Cat. No. 13232M Form **8829** (2020)

CHAPTER 3

Calculating Your Depreciation: Form 4562

Major Change in Depreciation Rules

As a result of a significant change in depreciation rules, as of 2018 providers no longer have to depreciate any expense except for their home, a home improvement, and a home addition! This means most providers will not have to depreciate items. This is great news because it allows providers to deduct in one year expenses that would normally have to be deducted over a number of years.

In some situations, you may want to spread your deductions over the years rather than claiming them all in 2020. This may happen if you want to show more profit in 2020 because you are applying for a loan, or your tax bracket is going up in later years, or other personal circumstances. If any of these apply to you, then this chapter can explain how to depreciate larger expenses.

But in general, you probably want to take advantage of the new tax laws and not depreciate expenses for your business, except for a home, a home improvement, and a home addition. A deck, new garage, or large shed would be considered a home addition. Here is a summary of these changes:

- Any item you purchase that costs $200 or less may be deducted in one year.
- Any item you purchase that costs between $201 and $2,500 may be deducted in one year, as long as you attach a special statement to your tax return.
- House-related repairs can be deducted in one year as always. However, there is a new, expanded definition of what can be treated as a repair, rather than a home improvement, that includes roof shingles, windows, wood and tile floors, and more.
- **Any item you purchase that costs more than $2,500 may also be deducted in one year, with the exception of a home, a home improvement, or home addition. This is called the 100% bonus depreciation rule and is the major change that will be in effect through 2022!**

$2,500 Rule

For decades, the IRS rules said that you must depreciate items costing more than $100 (with certain exceptions). As of 2015, according to Treasury Regulation Section 1.263(a), providers may deduct in one year any item costing $200 or less. You may also deduct items costing between $201 and $2,500 in one year as long as you attach a special statement to your tax return.

This rule applies to any individual purchase, and there is no limit as to how many items you can deduct. Therefore, you could buy twelve items costing less than $2,500 each and apply this rule to all of them. If you use an item 100% for your business, you can deduct 100% of its cost in 2020. If you also use this item for personal purposes, multiply the cost by your Time-Space percentage (see chapter 1) and deduct the business portion in 2020.

To use this $2,500 rule, you must elect it by filing the following statement with your tax return:

"Section 1.263(a)-1(f) De Minimis Safe Harbor Election

[Your name, address, and EIN or Social Security number]

For the year ending December 31, 2020, I am electing the de minimis safe harbor under Treas. Reg. Section 1.263(a)-1(f) for my business expenses of less than $2,500."

You must file such a statement for each year you wish to use this $2,500 rule. Put this deduction on **Schedule C**, Part V, line 27a, and call it "De minimis Equipment." Doing so will make it clear that you elected this rule. See page 247 for a copy of this statement.

When you choose to use the $2,500 rule, you must apply it to all items purchased that year costing between $201 and $2,500. You may still use the Section 179 rule for selected items. Using this $2,500 rule is a choice, so you can decide whether to depreciate items under the rules described in this chapter or deduct them in one year.

What About 2017, 2018, or 2019? What can you do if you were eligible to use this rule in 2017, 2018, or 2019 but you instead depreciated an item instead of deducting it in one year? You cannot amend your return back to these years, elect to use this new Treasury Regulation, and deduct the cost in one year. This is because you did not attach the statement of election to your tax return. Once you elect to use this rule, you cannot later amend your tax return to undo it.

The Old 50% Bonus Depreciation Rule

In 2017 a 50% bonus depreciation rule allowed providers to deduct 50% of the normal depreciation of most items in one year. Exceptions to this rule were home improvements, the home itself, and home additions. For example, if you bought a $4,000 swing set in 2017 and used it 100% for your business, you could have deducted $2,000 (50% of the cost) in one year and depreciated the other $2,000 over seven years.

With the new 100% bonus depreciation rule (see below), it no longer makes sense to use the 50% bonus depreciation rule for items purchased in 2020 because it fell to zero in 2020 and after.

New 100% Bonus Depreciation Rule

The Tax Cuts and Jobs Act (www.congress.gov/115/plaws/publ97/PLAW-115publ97.pdf) passed in December 2017. As of 2018, the act allows providers to deduct in one year the business portion of all expenses except for a home, a home improvement, and home addition. Computers and other office equipment must be used more than 50% of the time to qualify for this rule. Effectively, this amends the old 50% bonus depreciation rule to a 100% bonus depreciation rule.

In other words, if you purchased a $10,000 fence and your Time-Space percentage is 40%, you can deduct $4,000 on your 2020 tax return, with no depreciation necessary. Enter $4,000 on **Form 4562**, line 14.

The 100% bonus rule applies to the purchase of both new and used items. It is available for the tax years 2018–2022. In 2023 it will be reduced to 80%, then 60% in 2024, 40% in 2025, and 20% in 2026.

This is one of the most important tax changes for family child care providers in decades! No longer will you have to depreciate your furniture, appliances, fences, playground equipment, patio, or driveway. If you go out of business in the next few years, there is no recapture of these deductions. In other words, you won't ever have to pay back these deductions. You do not have to attach a statement to your tax return electing this rule as you must do for items that cost less than $2,500. You are considered to have automatically elected this rule unless you specifically elect out by doing so on your tax return. Claiming expenses under the 100% bonus depreciation rule can create a loss for your business on **Schedule C**. If you realized you should have used the 100% bonus depreciation rule in 2018, you can amend your tax return and claim this deduction and get a refund.

Note: The 100% bonus depreciation rule applies to your federal taxes, not your state taxes. Your state may not adopt this rule when calculating your state income taxes. If it does, your business profit will be higher for state tax purposes. Contact your state department of revenue to see if they have adopted this rule or not.

Home Improvements

Home improvements are a complicated topic, one that has seen many changes recently. In general, home improvements made in 2020 must be depreciated over 39 years. There are three possible situations where you may be able to deduct them in one year:

1. A home improvement may meet the definition of a repair.
2. You use the home improvement for more than 50% of the time in your business.
3. You qualify for the Safe Harbor for Small Taxpayers rule.

Home Improvements vs. Repairs

Treasury Regulation Section 1.263(a) expands what can be treated as a repair and offers the clearest explanation yet of the difference between a repair and a home improvement. A repair may be deducted in one year, regardless of the cost, while a home improvement must be depreciated over 39 years. This is a big difference!

Repairs deal with normal wear and tear and routine maintenance. They are expenses that do not materially add to the value of a home or prolong its life: they simply keep it in good operating condition. Examples of repairs include painting, wallpapering, fixing a broken window, and mending leaks. Repairs also include replacing the shingles on a home or garage. If you replaced the shingles and the roofing boards underneath the shingles, the work should be treated as a home improvement.

A home improvement is something that results in the betterment of the property, restores the property, or adapts the property to a new or different use. If you replace a significant or substantial portion of a major component of your home (walls, windows, floors, plumbing, electrical, or heating), you must depreciate these items over 39 years. Examples of home improvements include building a new addition, installing a furnace, remodeling your kitchen or bathroom, and adding a deck or garage.

It's not exactly clear what replacing a "substantial portion" of a major component of your home means. I talked to the author of the Treasury Regulation, who said that replacing 20% of the windows or floors would not be a "substantial portion" and could be treated as a repair. When asked if replacing fewer than 50% of windows or floors would be considered a repair, she said, "Maybe" and wouldn't be more precise.

This creates a problem for providers trying to determine when they can treat an expense as a repair or home improvement. In the examples provided with the new regulations described in Section 1.263(a), the replacement of 8 of 20 sinks (40%) was treated as a repair, as was the replacement of 100 of 300 windows (33%). Replacing 200 of 300 windows (67%) was treated as an improvement. In my opinion, you can argue that the replacement of less than half of a major component of the home could be treated as a repair. I think this is a reasonable interpretation of the rule, but I can't guarantee that's what an IRS auditor would conclude.

Under my interpretation, if you replace 8 out of 20 windows, treat the cost as a repair and deduct the Time-Space percentage of the cost in one year (regardless of the cost). If you replace 12 of 20 windows, depreciate the cost as a home improvement over 39 years. If you add a new wood or tile floor that represents less than half the square footage of your home, treat it as a repair. Note: carpeting should always be considered eligible for the 100% bonus depreciation rule and thus can be deducted in one year, regardless of the cost. If you have two bathrooms and remodel one of them, treat it as a home improvement. If you have three bathrooms and remodel one of them, I believe you could treat it as a repair. If you remodel your kitchen, it's a home improvement.

Remember, if something is a home improvement but costs less than $2,500, you can still deduct the business portion of the cost in one year.

Because this rule is relatively new, we can expect future clarifications about what is a repair versus a home improvement. Talk to your tax professional for further guidance. As I receive more information on this issue, I will write about it on my website: www.tomcopelandblog.com.

The Section 179 Rule Exception

If you used your home improvement (but not a home addition) more than 50% of the time for your business, you can now use the Section 179 rule and deduct the business portion in one year for 2020. To take advantage of this rule, your Time-Space percentage should be more than 50%. If it's not, you should keep records to show that you did use the home improvement more than 50% of the time for your business. The best way to show that is to track the hours of business and personal use on a calendar for several months.

For example, if you spent $6,000 to build a deck that is filled with child care toys and equipment and you have no children of your own, you could probably claim that you use the deck more than 50% for your business. After tracking your actual use of the deck for two months, you determine that it's used 60% for your business. You can then deduct $3,600 ($6,000 x 60%) on **Form 4562**, Part I. See pages 74–76 for an expanded discussion of the Section 179 rule.

Should you use the Section 179 exception? The drawback to using this exception is that if you go out of business or use the item 50% or less in later years, you will have to pay back some of the deduction you claimed. For example, if you go out of business five years after deducting the $3,600 for the deck, you will have to report the $3,600 as income, minus the amount of depreciation you would have taken over five years instead. Five years of depreciation on a deck amounts to $461 ($3,600 ÷ 39 years x 5 years = $461). Assuming you are in the same tax bracket (30%) in five years, you will owe $942 in taxes when you go out of business ($3,600 – $461 x 30% = $942). However, by deducting $3,600 in the first year, you saved $1,080 in taxes ($3,600 x 30% = $1,080). The longer you use the deck before you go out of business, the greater the tax advantage of using this exception. So financially you are always better off using the Section 179 exception. However, you must fill out **Form 4797 Sale of Business Property** when you do go out of business. See chapter 11 for more details on how to recapture depreciation when using the Section 179 rule.

Note: Using the Section 179 rule can't create a business loss on your tax return. See page 74.

Safe Harbor for Small Taxpayers Rule Exception

This rule also allows some providers to deduct in one year the cost of home improvements but not home additions.

Here's how this works. If the amount of home improvements you make in one year plus the amount of any home repairs made in that year is the lesser amount of $10,000 or 2% of the unadjusted basis of your home, you may deduct the business portion of the home/land improvements in one year.

Let's sort this out.

The unadjusted basis of your home is the purchase price of your home minus the value of the land at the time you bought it, plus the value of any home improvements you made before the year you are using this rule. For example, if you purchased your home for $300,000, and the value of land when you bought it was $30,000, and you made $50,000 in home improvements before 2020, the unadjusted basis of your home would be $320,000 ($300,000 – $30,000 + $50,000 = $320,000). Therefore, the lesser of $10,000 or 2% of the unadjusted basis of your home is $6,400 ($320,000 x 2% = $6,400, which is less than $10,000).

Let's look at two examples.

EXAMPLE #1

Bernice installed a new deck for $4,500 and made no home repairs in 2020. Her Time-Space percentage is 40%. Her home's unadjusted basis is $250,000. Because $4,500 is less than $5,000 ($250,000 x 2% = $5,000), she can use this rule. She could deduct $1,800 for the deck in one year ($4,500 x 40% = $1,800). Enter on **Form 4562**, line 14. To use this rule you must elect it by filing a statement with your tax return.

EXAMPLE #2

Bernice installed the same deck but also spent $2,000 on house repairs. She can't use this rule because the $6,500 of repairs and improvements ($4,500 + $2,000) is higher than $5,000. She can deduct $800 of the repairs ($2,000 x 40% = $800) in one year, but she must depreciate the deck over 39 years.

Note: Repairs to your personal property (items not attached to your home or land) are not counted as a home repair. For example, Keri had the following expenses in 2020: $4,000 kitchen remodel, $500 to recover a sofa, $600 for deck stain, $250 furnace and duct cleaning, and $250 computer repair. Her Time-Space percentage is 35%. The unadjusted basis of her home is $260,000. Her deduction limitation is $5,200 ($260,000 x 2% = $5,200). She can deduct separately the business portion of her sofa and computer expenses because these are considered repairs to her personal property, not to her home. Therefore, she can deduct $500 + $250 = $750 x 35% = $262.50 in 2020. The remaining expenses total $4,850 ($4,000 + $600 + $250). Since this is less than $5,200, she can deduct $1,698 ($4,850 x 35% = $1,698) in 2020.

To use this rule you must elect it by filing a statement with your tax return. Here's the statement you should use:

"Section 1.263(a)-3(h) Safe Harbor Election for Small Taxpayers

[Your name, address, and EIN or Social Security number]

For the year ending December 31, 2020, I am electing the safe harbor election for small taxpayers under Treas. Reg. Section 1.263(a)-3(g) for the following: [list your improvements]."

You must file such a statement each year you use this small taxpayer safe harbor rule. See page 247 for a copy of this statement.

Notes on the safe harbor election for small taxpayers: What can you do if you were eligible to use this rule before 2020 but you instead depreciated a home improvement? You cannot amend your return and elect to use this new Treasury Regulation and deduct the cost in one year. This is because you must have attached the statement of election to your tax return in the year you purchased it. Once you elect to use this rule, you cannot later amend your tax return to change it. You can use the safe harbor election if you rent your home and spend money on a home improvement.

Summary

These new tax rules are fantastic news for many family child care providers! They allow providers to deduct in one year many items that in previous years had to be depreciated. In fact, any purchase other than a home, a home improvement, and home addition can be deducted in one year, regardless of the cost. This eliminates practically all depreciation, and thus providers can skip over much of the rest of this chapter!

Here's a summary of depreciation rules. If an item costs $200 or less, you can deduct it in one year. Later in this chapter I explain how to depreciate each type of expense in detail.

OFFICE EQUIPMENT

Costing less than $2,500: deduct in one year and attach statement to your tax return

Costing more than $2,500:

If you use less than 50% for your business, depreciate over five years

If you use 50% or more for your business:

- Use the Section 179 rule, or
- Use the 100% bonus depreciation rule and deduct in one year, or
- Depreciate over five years

PERSONAL PROPERTY

Costing less than $2,500: deduct in one year and attach statement to your tax return

Costing more than $2,500:

Use the 100% bonus depreciation rule and deduct in one year, or

Depreciate over seven years

If you use 50% or more for your business:

- Can use the Section 179 rule

LAND IMPROVEMENT

Costing less than $2,500: deduct in one year and attach statement to your tax return

Costing more than $2,500:

Use the 100% bonus depreciation rule and deduct in one year

- Can depreciate over 15 years

HOME IMPROVEMENT

Costing less than $2,500: deduct in one year and attach statement to your tax return

Costing more than $2,500:

Depreciate over 39 years

If used more than 50% for business, can use the Section 179 rule

Does the Safe Harbor for Small Taxpayers rule apply (effective for 2014 and after)?

- If yes, deduct in one year

HOME

Depreciate over 39 years

See appendix B for a chart summarizing these rules.

General Rules about Depreciation

The following is a discussion about how to apply the rules for items you are depreciating. Since the vast majority of providers will take advantage of either the $2,500 rule or the 100% bonus depreciation rule, much of what follows in this chapter is irrelevant. If you are using the 100% bonus depreciation rule, enter your deductions on **Form 4562**, line 14. The exceptions to this are depreciations of the home, home improvement, home additions, and vehicles. See pages 86–91 for details on these items.

This chapter explains how to fill out **Form 4562 Depreciation and Amortization**. Many child care providers feel that depreciation is the most complex tax concept that they have to deal with, so I will try to keep it as simple as possible. Basically, depreciation is a way to spread the deductible cost of an item over several years by deducting a certain percentage of the total amount each year. (When dealing with depreciation, remember that the deductible portion of any expense depends on how the item is used; for more information, see chapter 5.)

If you buy an item before your business begins and later start using it in your business, the following rules apply (see the section titled Start-Up Costs on page 91).

If you began depreciating an item last year, you must continue depreciating this item according to the depreciation rules for that year, even if the rules change in later years.

The IRS divides depreciable items into categories and sets a depreciation period for the items in each category—in other words, it tells you over how many years you must spread the cost for items in each category. The depreciation method and the length of the depreciation period determine the percentage of the total amount you can deduct each year. The depreciation tables at the end of this chapter show the percentages that will be used this year.

Here are the categories of items and the number of years the IRS says you must depreciate them. Every item you depreciate must fall into one of these categories:

Category	Number of Years of Depreciation
Personal computers/office equipment	5
Other personal property	7
Home improvements	39
Land improvements	15
Home	39
Vehicle	5

The years of depreciation rules for 2020 (as shown above) are the same as those for 2019. This chapter describes how to apply those depreciation rules and fill out **Form 4562**. In many cases, home depreciation will be shown on **Form 8829**. Bear in mind that before you fill out **Form 4562**, you should complete Part I of **Form 8829**, since you will need your Time-Space percentage calculation from **Form 8829** to determine your depreciation deductions on **Form 4562**.

IRS Child Care Provider Audit Technique Guide on Depreciation

The guide lists a number of items that are commonly depreciated in the family child care business, including computers, office equipment, kitchen equipment, playground equipment, furniture, appliances, DVD players, televisions, and pianos. The guide clearly states that providers may depreciate items that were purchased before their business began that were originally exclusively personal use and then later put into business use. The guide states, "The fact that the asset was only used for personal purposes prior to being placed in service does not disqualify it from being converted to use in the business."

The Benefits of Depreciation

If you began your business before 2020 and haven't been depreciating your home, home or land improvements, and household items, you may be entitled to recapture this previously unclaimed depreciation on **Form 3115**, which could result in hundreds or even thousands of dollars of deductions this year (see chapter 10 for more information).

Taking a Household Inventory

Are you claiming *all* of your allowable depreciation deductions? To find out, conduct an inventory of the items in your home that are used regularly in your business. All new providers should take an inventory their first year in business, and experienced providers should review their inventory each year.

To conduct an inventory, record all the items you are using in your business, room by room. Include any home improvements that were made before and after your business began. Estimate the fair market value of each item at the time you began using it in your business. Next, determine the depreciation of each item as a business expense.

Gather and keep records that support your business deductions for these items. You can do this with receipts or photographs of the property. To claim depreciation, you must have written evidence. When filling out **Form 4562**, always answer yes to the questions on lines 24a and 24b that ask whether you have evidence to support your claim and whether the evidence is written. *Failure to answer these questions could trigger an audit.* See page 91 for a discussion of how to deduct items you owned before you went into business.

Need Inventory Help?

The *Family Child Care Inventory-Keeper* includes a series of forms that make it easy to inventory your property and claim depreciation. The *Inventory-Keeper* includes detailed room-by-room listings of household items and charts for your home and for home and land improvements, as well as instructions on how to estimate the fair market value of depreciable items.

Determining Your Depreciation

The following section of this chapter goes into detail about how to depreciate an item rather than using the 100% bonus depreciation rule for everything except a home, a home improvement, and a home addition. The depreciation rules can be difficult to understand because there are so many of them. To simplify things, the depreciation process is broken down here into four steps. You must go through these four steps for each item you are depreciating.

Step One: What Is the Business Amount of the Item?

The first step is to determine the business amount of the property you are depreciating. Start with the lower of (a) the cost of the property or (b) its fair market value at the time you first used it for business. If you bought the item (new or used) last year, use its actual cost. Multiply the value of the item by your Time-Space percentage or an actual business-use percentage (as described in chapter 1). The result is the business amount (or business basis) of the item you are depreciating.

EXAMPLE

You bought playground equipment in 2020 for $3,000. If your 2020 Time-Space percentage is 35%, the business amount of this item would be $3,000 x 35% = $1,050.

You could then deduct $1,050 in 2020. If you decided to depreciate the playground equipment over seven years, your Time-Space percentage could change over that time. If so, it will affect the amount of business deduction that you can claim. In the following example, $3,000 worth of playground equipment is depreciated using seven-year straight-line depreciation. Watch what happens as the Time-Space percentage (T/S%) changes:

2020	$3,000 x	35%	(T/S%)	= 1,050	x 7.14%	= $74.97
2021	$3,000 x	30%	(T/S%)	= 900	x 14.29%	= $128.61
2022	$3,000 x	31%	(T/S%)	= 930	x 14.29%	= $132.90
2023	$3,000 x	32%	(T/S%)	= 960	x 14.28%	= $137.09

Step Two: How Long Must You Depreciate the Item?

The next step is to determine the number of years over which the property must be depreciated. You must put all your depreciable items into one of the categories listed on page 69. The category that an item falls into determines the number of years over which it must be depreciated. Once you begin depreciating an item, you must stick to the number of years on this chart, even if the rules change in later years.

Step Three: What Depreciation Method Can You Use?

The third step is to determine which depreciation method to use. In some cases, you will have a choice between the straight-line method and the accelerated method, which is also called the 150% or 200% declining balance method. (For a summary of these methods, see the depreciation tables at the end of this chapter.)

- Under the straight-line method, you claim an equal amount of depreciation each year. Generally, you can't use this method unless you choose it the first year you use the property for business.
- Under the accelerated depreciation method, you claim more depreciation in the first few years and less in later years. Although the accelerated method is usually more beneficial, you may not want to use it if doing so would cause a loss for your business this year or large fluctuations in your deductions from year to year.

EXAMPLE

You decide to use the 200% declining balance depreciation method for your playground equipment, which entitles you to deduct 28.58% of the $1,050 business amount in the first year. Using this method, the amount of depreciation you could claim in the first year would be $1,050 x 28.58% = $300. (See below to determine if you must use the Half-Year Convention rule.)

Once you choose a depreciation method for an item, you must continue using that method for the life of that item; you can't change methods. Also, you must use the same method for all the items in each category that you start depreciating in the same year. For example, if you use straight-line depreciation for a freezer you bought last year, you must use that method for all other personal property you bought or first used for business last year. You can use another method for a land improvement (such as a fence) that you purchased in that year. (This rule doesn't apply to the Section 179 rule; you can use Section 179 for one furniture item and still use accelerated or straight-line depreciation for other furniture items you bought that year.)

Each year you can choose again for the items you buy and start depreciating that year. So for last year's purchases, you could use accelerated depreciation for other personal property and straight-line depreciation for land improvements, but this year you can make a different choice for your new purchases in those categories.

Step Four: Do Any Special Rules Apply?

The final step is to determine if there are any special depreciation rules that apply to the item. There are five special depreciation rules—three conventions, the 100% bonus depreciation rule, and Section 179. Section 179 allows you to deduct the entire cost of some depreciable items in the first year, and the three convention rules are applied to items in the first year they are used for business. These rules—the Half-Year Convention, the Mid-Month Convention, and the Mid-Quarter Convention—may affect the first-year depreciation you can take in certain circumstances.

The 100% Bonus Depreciation Rule

As described on pages 62–63, this new rule as of 2018 allows you to deduct the business portion of all expenses in one year without having to depreciate them. The exceptions to this rule are the home, a home improvement, and a home addition.

The Half-Year Convention

Since the items you're depreciating were bought at various times during the year, the IRS won't allow you to claim a full year's worth of depreciation the first year you use an item in your business. Instead, for all items except home improvements and home depreciation, you must apply the Half-Year Convention rule in the first year of depreciation.

This rule says that no matter when you purchased the item or put it into business use, it will be treated as if it were put into business use in the middle of the year. This means that you only get one-half of the normal depreciation deduction in the first year. The other half of that year's deduction is picked up at the end of the depreciation period. In other words, if you are using seven-year straight-line depreciation rules, you will claim half of the normal depreciation in the first year, then six years of full depreciation, and then another half year. This means that you must actually depreciate the item over eight calendar years. In the depreciation tables at the end of this chapter, the Half-Year Convention rules are already built into the percentages listed.

The Mid-Month Convention

To depreciate your home and home improvements, you must apply the Mid-Month Convention rule instead of the Half-Year Convention rule. Under this rule, the deduction for the first year is based on the month that you first used the home or home improvement in the business, and it doesn't matter when during the month. The rule treats every item as if it was first put into business use in the middle of the first month that it was used for business. The percentages for each month are listed in the depreciation table for home and home improvements.

The Mid-Quarter Convention

This rule applies if you purchased over 40% of items costing more than $2,500 during the last quarter of last year, which might happen, for example, if you started your business during that quarter. If you didn't purchase over 40% of such items during the last quarter of the year, this rule doesn't apply to you. There are some expenses that you don't have to include in your capital expenditures in determining if you must apply the Mid-Quarter Convention rule:

- property that you purchase and sell in the same tax year
- the purchase of a home

- home improvements (you still have to include land improvements)
- deductions for personal property that you claim under Section 179 rules

When you apply the Mid-Quarter Convention in computing your depreciation, it imposes limits on the amount of depreciation you can claim this year for the items you purchased in each quarter of the year. The depreciation limits for the items you purchased in each quarter are as follows:

First quarter	(January, February, March)	87.5%
Second quarter	(April, May, June)	62.5%
Third quarter	(July, August, September)	37.5%
Fourth quarter	(October, November, December)	12.5%

If this convention applies to you, you will only be able to deduct 87.5% of what you would otherwise be entitled to for the items you purchased in the first quarter of the year. And you will only be able to deduct 12.5% of the depreciation you would otherwise be entitled to for the items you purchased in the last quarter of the year.

Example

You purchased a $2,800 swing set in November last year and a $3,000 jungle gym in February last year, and these are your only capital expenditures in this tax year. Your Time-Space percentage is 25%. If you choose to apply seven-year straight-line depreciation to these items, you would get the following results:

$2,800 swing set	x 25%	=	$700	x 7.14%	= $49.98
$3,000 jungle gym	x 25%	=	$750	x 7.14%	= $53.55

Since you purchased more than 40% of your capital expenditures during the last quarter of last year, however, you must apply the Mid-Quarter Convention. Under the straight-line depreciation rules, 7.14% represents only one-half of the first year of depreciation. This means that you must multiply by two before applying the limitations:

$2,800 swing set purchased in fourth quarter:	$49.95 x 2 x 12.5% = $12.50
$3,000 jungle gym purchased in first quarter:	$53.55 x 2 x 87.5% = $93.71
Total	$106.21

In the second year of depreciation for these items (and beyond), you will be able to claim the full amount of your normal depreciation:

$2,800 swing set	x 25%	=	$700	x 14.29%	= $100.03
$3,000 sofa	x 25%	=	$750	x 14.29%	= $121.47
Total					$221.50

Is all this work worth it? In our example, the first year doesn't look like much. However, in subsequent years, the numbers will add up. If the Mid-Quarter Convention drives you crazy, you might consider forfeiting the depreciation on your capital expenditures for the first year and begin by claiming the second year of depreciation. In this example, you would lose $106.21 this tax season, but you would be able to claim $221.50 next tax season.

These calculations get far more complicated if you use accelerated depreciation instead of straight-line depreciation, because in every subsequent depreciation year you have to readjust the amount of the item being depreciated by the depreciation you claimed in the first year. Because of this, you may want to always choose straight-line depreciation whenever you use the Mid-Quarter Convention rule.

Section 179

Section 179 is a special rule that allows you to claim up to $1,020,000 (2019 rule) of your new or used items purchased in the year they are incurred. This rule does not apply to land improvements or home depreciation. **Note: As discussed earlier, home improvements may be eligible for the Section 179 rule as of 2018.**

To be eligible to apply it to an item, you must meet all four of these conditions:

1. You must use the rule that applies to the year you first used the item in your business. This means you can't use Section 179 on your tax return for any item you used in your business before last year. But you can claim Section 179 if you amend your taxes for earlier years (see Changing Your Election of Section 179 on page 75).
2. The expenses you claim under Section 179 can't result in a loss on your tax return for this year. (But you can carry forward any unused Section 179 deductions to the next tax year.) If you file jointly, Section 179 expenses can't create a loss on the combined taxable income of both spouses. In other words, any wage income your spouse reports on your joint **Form 1040** can offset Section 179 losses from your business. If your **Schedule C** shows $5,000 in losses and your spouse reports more than $5,000 in wages on **Form 1040**, you can claim those losses. However, if your spouse has self-employment income, this cannot offset your Section 179 losses. If you file separately, your spouse's tax return doesn't play any role in these limits.
3. You must be using the item more than 50% of the time for your business. Most child care providers use their Time-Space percentage to calculate their personal property depreciation. It's unusual to have a Time-Space percentage greater than 50%, so few providers can use Section 179 for these items.
4. You may not use Section 179 for an item you purchased from a related party, such as a spouse, child, parent, grandparent, or grandchild (siblings—that is, brothers and sisters—are not covered by this restriction). You can't use Section 179 if you acquired the property as a gift or inheritance.

Note: Your state may or may not recognize the Section 179 rule. If not, you may be required to add back to your income (for state income tax purposes) the amount of extra depreciation you claimed because of this rule.

Put Your Section 179 Expenses on the Right Form

To take advantage of the Section 179 rule, you must claim the expense on **Form 4562**, Part I, not on **Schedule C**. So if you purchased an item that cost over $2,500 this year, used it mostly for business, and want to claim the entire deduction this year, be sure to put it on **Form 4562**.

The Consequences of Using Section 179

There are some potentially negative consequences of using Section 179 that you should take into consideration before you decide to use this method:

1. If you go out of business before the end of the normal depreciation period for the item, you will have to pay back (recapture) some of the depreciation you claimed and file **Form 4797** (see chapter 11) to report it as income. The sooner you go out of business, the more income you will have to report. Before using Section 179, consider whether you plan to be in business at the end of the normal depreciation period

for that item (five years for a personal computer or a car; seven years for other personal property). If you shut down your business for several months and then start up again, your Section 179 deductions will not be affected.

2. Recapturing some of the depreciation you claimed also comes into play if you sell an item before the end of its normal depreciation period. If this is the case, you must also fill out **Form 4797** (see chapter 11). If you sell the item for a gain, you have to report the gain as income. If you sell it for a loss while you are still in business, you can deduct that loss on your **Form 1040**.
3. You will also have to recapture some of the depreciation you claimed if your business-use percentage of a Section 179 item falls to 50% or less in a later year. To avoid this, only apply Section 179 to items you will be using more than 50% of the time for business over their entire lives.

When Should You Use the Section 179 Rule?

Now that I've explained all the restrictions and potential negative consequences of using the Section 179 rule, you might wonder: are there any circumstances when you should consider using it? In most situations, the items you purchased are eligible for either the $2,500 rule or the 100% bonus depreciation rule, allowing you to deduct the business portion in one year without regard to having to be used more than 50% in your business.

As we discussed on pages 64–65, using the Section 179 rule on a home improvement does make sense rather than depreciating it over 39 years.

Section 179 after the First Year

Once you use Section 179 to claim the business deduction for an item, you can't claim any further deductions for that item in future years. In other words, you won't record anything on **Form 4562** for this item in any future years. However, if your business use falls below 50%, you will need to recapture some of the depreciation you claimed. See chapter 11 for details.

Changing Your Election of Section 179

The IRS allows you to choose or revoke your choice of the Section 179 rule by amending your tax return for the tax years 2017 through 2019. Once you amend your return to elect or revoke the Section 179 rule, this change cannot be reversed without the consent of the IRS. If you did not take advantage of the Section 179 rule between 2017 and 2019, you may want to consider amending your tax return to get a refund. Here's an example of how this rule might benefit you. Let's say that you bought a computer in 2017 for $2,600 and used it 80% of the time in your business. You depreciated the computer over five years and claimed $320 in depreciation deductions ($2,600 x 80% business use x 20% first-year accelerated depreciation = $416).

If you amend your tax return and elect to use the Section 179 rule, you can claim $1,664 as a deduction on your 2017 amended tax return ($2,600 x 80% = $1,600 – $416 = $1,664). This will mean a tax refund of about $499 (30% tax bracket) or $655 (40% tax bracket). If you use this rule, it will eliminate any depreciation deduction for this item on your 2020 tax return.

Depreciation Tip
Don't subtract the first year's depreciation deduction from the cost of the property before calculating the depreciation for the second year. Use the original cost to calculate your depreciation each year.

Calculating Depreciation by Category

The rest of this chapter will review each of the categories of depreciable items in more detail, explaining the specific rules and options that apply to each one. The examples will show the straight-line method, an accelerated method, and Section 179 (where applicable) but will always show the straight-line method first. Straight-line depreciation is the easiest to use, and there are many pitfalls and restrictions involved in using Section 179.

You may prefer to use accelerated rules rather than the straight-line rules. If you depreciate an item under the accelerated rules and go out of business before the end of the recovery period, you won't have to recapture (pay back) any of the depreciation you've claimed. If you sell an item you've used for your business, however, there may be some tax consequences, and if you were using accelerated rules, you'd be more likely to owe tax at this point than if you'd been using straight-line rules (see chapter 11).

Check the Tables for More Information

As you read the following examples, refer to the tables at the end of this chapter. These tables list the percentages that you can deduct each year under each of the depreciation methods described on the following pages.

Keep Written Records of All Your Business Deductions
Remember that you need to keep written records to support all the business deductions you claim, in the form of receipts, canceled checks, or other records.

Personal Computer/Office Equipment

Under a new IRS regulation, you can deduct in one year office equipment that individually costs less than $2,500! If it cost more than $2,500, it may be eligible for the Section 179 rule or 100% bonus depreciation rule and therefore not be subject to depreciation. This category of depreciation includes personal computers and office equipment, including printers, fax machines, copiers, scanners, and electric typewriters. If you do use the 100% bonus depreciation rule, enter the deduction on **Form 4562**, line 14. We'll use a computer as an example. You can use your Time-Space percentage or an actual business-use percentage to depreciate the items in this category. If you use an actual business-use percentage, track how much time you use each item for your business (children's games, business record keeping, and so on) and how much time you use it for personal purposes. Divide the number of hours of business use by the total number of hours you use the item. For example, if you use your computer three hours a week for business and nine hours a week for personal purposes, your business-use percentage would be 25% (3 ÷ [3 + 9]).

In this category, your options for depreciation methods are based on your business-use percentage. If it is 50% or less, you must depreciate the item over five years. If it is higher, you can choose from three depreciation periods as described below, after an explanation about a change in recommendations for depreciating listed property.

100% Bonus Depreciation Rule

In the first example below, we will not use the 100% bonus depreciation rule because the computer was not used more than 50% for business. In the second example, we will use the new rule because the computer was used 70% for business.

What Is Listed Property?

Clearly, a cell phone and a vehicle weighing less than 6,000 pounds would both be listed property and should be depreciated on **Form 4562**, Part V. See pages 78–79 for an example of how to fill out Part V. The IRS Regulation Section 1.280F-6 says, "Exception for computers. The term 'listed property' shall not include any computer (including peripheral equipment) used exclusively at a regular business establishment. For purposes of the preceding sentence, a portion of a dwelling unit shall be treated as a regular business establishment if (and only if) the requirements of Section 280A(c)(1) are met with respect to that portion."

Family child care providers don't meet the requirements under Tax Code Section 280A(c)(1) because it allows taxpayers to claim expenses for their home only if they use part of the home exclusively in their business. Family child care providers have their own rule under Section 280A(c)(4), which allows them to claim expenses for their home if they're using rooms on a regular basis. But technically that doesn't meet the requirements under Section 280A(c)(1), so a provider's computer should be listed property.

The one exception is that a provider who has an exclusive-use room and uses a computer in that room would be able to claim that the computer was not listed property because it meets the above exception. However, providers who use their computer in a regularly used room in their home do not meet this exception and must claim their computer as listed property.

Claiming a computer as listed property means providers must keep track of business use based on the hours the computer is used for business purposes. The IRS **Child Care Provider Audit Technique Guide** indicates that auditors may be stricter about demanding logs showing the business use of computers. Most providers, as a practical matter, do not keep such logs and instead use their Time percentage. This could be challenged in an audit. You must keep careful records to show this computer use. Such a record might be a log that tracks business and personal use for several months.

Business Use Equal to or Less Than 50%

If your business-use percentage is 50% or less, use the five-year straight-line depreciation rule. See the tables at the end of this chapter for the percentages that you can deduct each year. If you bought a $3,000 computer last year and your business-use percentage was 25%, the amount you can claim as a business expense would be $75:

Five-Year Straight-Line

$3,000 computer x 25% business use	=	$750 business basis
$750 x 10% (1st-year depreciation)	=	$75

Enter this amount on **Form 4562**, Part V, line 27. column (h).

Form 4562 (2020) Page **2**

Part V **Listed Property** (Include automobiles, certain other vehicles, certain aircraft, and property used for entertainment, recreation, or amusement.)

Note: For any vehicle for which you are using the standard mileage rate or deducting lease expense, complete **only** 24a, 24b, columns (a) through (c) of Section A, all of Section B, and Section C if applicable.

Section A—Depreciation and Other Information (Caution: See the instructions for limits for passenger automobiles.)

24a Do you have evidence to support the business/investment use claimed? ☐ **Yes** ☐ **No** | **24b** If "Yes," is the evidence written? ☐ **Yes** ☐ **No**

(a) Type of property (list vehicles first)	(b) Date placed in service	(c) Business/ investment use percentage	(d) Cost or other basis	(e) Basis for depreciation (business/investment use only)	(f) Recovery period	(g) Method/ Convention	(h) Depreciation deduction	(i) Elected section 179 cost
25 Special depreciation allowance for qualified listed property placed in service during the tax year and used more than 50% in a qualified business use. See instructions . **25**								
26 Property used more than 50% in a qualified business use:								
		%						
		%						
		%						
27 Property used 50% or less in a qualified business use:								
COMPUTER	1/1/2020	25 %	$3,000	$750	5 YEAR	S/L – HY	$75	
		%				S/L –		
		%				S/L –		
28 Add amounts in column (h), lines 25 through 27. Enter here and on line 21, page 1 . **28**							$75	
29 Add amounts in column (i), line 26. Enter here and on line 7, page 1 . . . . **29**								

Business Use Greater Than 50%

If your business-use percentage is more than 50%, you have four choices—you can use the five-year straight-line method, the five-year 200% declining balance method, the 100% bonus depreciation rule, or Section 179. (To use the Section 179 rule, you must have bought the computer in 2019.) If your business-use percentage is 70%, this is what these three calculations would look like (refer to the tables at the end of this chapter for more information).

Five-Year Straight-Line

$3,000 computer x 70% business use	=	$2,100
$2,100 x 10%	=	$210

Enter this amount on **Form 4562**, Part V, line 26, column (h).

Five-Year 200% Declining Balance

$3,000 computer x 70% business use	=	$2,100
$2,100 x 20%	=	$420

Enter this amount on **Form 4562**, Part V, line 26, column (h).

100% Bonus Depreciation

$3,000 computer x 70% business use	=	$2,100
$2,100 x 100%	=	$2,100

Enter this amount on **Form 4562**, Part V, line 14

Form 4562 (2020) Page **2**

Part V **Listed Property** (Include automobiles, certain other vehicles, certain aircraft, and property used for entertainment, recreation, or amusement.)

Note: For any vehicle for which you are using the standard mileage rate or deducting lease expense, complete **only** 24a, 24b, columns (a) through (c) of Section A, all of Section B, and Section C if applicable.

Section A—Depreciation and Other Information (Caution: See the instructions for limits for passenger automobiles.**)**

24a Do you have evidence to support the business/investment use claimed? ☐ **Yes** ☐ **No** **24b** If "Yes," is the evidence written? ☐ **Yes** ☐ **No**

(a) Type of property (list vehicles first)	(b) Date placed in service	(c) Business/ investment use percentage	(d) Cost or other basis	(e) Basis for depreciation (business/investment use only)	(f) Recovery period	(g) Method/ Convention	(h) Depreciation deduction	(i) Elected section 179 cost
25 Special depreciation allowance for qualified listed property placed in service during the tax year and used more than 50% in a qualified business use. See instructions . **25**							$2,100	
26 Property used more than 50% in a qualified business use:								
COMPUTER	1/1/2020	70 %	$2,100	$1,550	5 YEAR	DB	$210	
		%						
		%						
27 Property used 50% or less in a qualified business use:								
		%				S/L –		
		%				S/L –		
		%				S/L –		
28 Add amounts in column (h), lines 25 through 27. Enter here and on line 21, page 1 . **28**								
29 Add amounts in column (i), line 26. Enter here and on line 7, page 1 . . . . **29**								

Section 179

$3,000 computer x 70% business use = $2,100

Using this method, you can claim the entire business-use percentage of the expense. If you go out of business within five years, however, you will have to pay back some of it. Enter $2,100 on **Form 4562**, Part I, line 2.

After filling out Part I, line 2, notice that there is a limitation amount for line 1 ($1,000,000) and a business income limitation on line 11 (see the IRS instructions for **Form 4562**). Your business income is your earned income—your net profit from line 31 of **Schedule C**, plus the wages you (or your spouse) report on line 7 of **Form 1040**. Because of these limitations, you can't take more than the lesser of $1,000,000 or your earned income as a Section 179 deduction.

If your business income is $25,000, you will enter $25,000 on line 11, since this is the lesser of the two amounts (see example). If this is the case, you will have no problem claiming the full $2,100 for your computer this year, since it is far less than the lower of the two limitations.

Form **4562**

Department of the Treasury Internal Revenue Service (99)

Depreciation and Amortization
(Including Information on Listed Property)
▶ **Attach to your tax return.**
▶ **Go to *www.irs.gov/Form4562* for instructions and the latest information.**

OMB No. 1545-0172
2020
Attachment Sequence No. **179**

Name(s) shown on return | Business or activity to which this form relates | **Identifying number**

Part I **Election To Expense Certain Property Under Section 179**
Note: If you have any listed property, complete Part V before you complete Part I.

1	Maximum amount (see instructions)	**1**	
2	Total cost of section 179 property placed in service (see instructions)	**2**	$2,100
3	Threshold cost of section 179 property before reduction in limitation (see instructions) . . .	**3**	
4	Reduction in limitation. Subtract line 3 from line 2. If zero or less, enter -0-	**4**	
5	Dollar limitation for tax year. Subtract line 4 from line 1. If zero or less, enter -0-. If married filing separately, see instructions	**5**	

6 (a) Description of property	(b) Cost (business use only)	(c) Elected cost
COMPUTER	$2,100	$2,100

7	Listed property. Enter the amount from line 29 . . . . **7**		
8	Total elected cost of section 179 property. Add amounts in column (c), lines 6 and 7	**8**	$2,100
9	Tentative deduction. Enter the **smaller** of line 5 or line 8	**9**	$2,100
10	Carryover of disallowed deduction from line 13 of your 2019 Form 4562	**10**	
11	Business income limitation. Enter the smaller of business income (not less than zero) or line 5. See instructions	**11**	$25,000
12	Section 179 expense deduction. Add lines 9 and 10, but don't enter more than line 11	**12**	$2,100
13	Carryover of disallowed deduction to 2021. Add lines 9 and 10, less line 12 ▶ **13**		

Computer Software

Because any computer software you purchase will cost less than $2,500, you can deduct the cost in one year. Apply your Time-Space percentage if you use it for business and personal use.

Other Personal Property

Under a new IRS regulation, you can deduct in one year personal property that individually costs less than $2,500! If it cost more than $2,500, you can use the 100% bonus depreciation rule and deduct it in one year. If you do use the 100% bonus depreciation rule, enter the deduction on **Form 4562**, line 14. Therefore, it's unlikely you will chose to depreciate this category of expenses unless you want to show a higher profit this year. For example, if you bought a $4,000 swing set used 40% in your business, you can enter $1,600 ($4,000 x 40%) on **Form 4562**, line 14.

If you do wish to depreciate these expenses, you should depreciate them over seven years using either the seven-year straight-line method or the 200% declining balance method. To demonstrate, we'll use the example of a purchase of a $4,000 swing set used 40% in your business.

This category of depreciation includes all personal property other than computers and computer software. It includes large play equipment, furniture, appliances, TVs, VCRs, DVD players, lawn and garden equipment, household tools, and other household expenditures.

SEVEN-YEAR STRAIGHT-LINE

To use this method, you would prepare a supporting schedule such as the following.

2020 Tax Return
Supporting Schedule for Form 4562, Part III, line 19c
Polly Jones
Social Security #474-66-1234

Item	Date Put in Service	Method	Cost	Business-Use %	Business Basis	Table % Year 1	Deduction 2020
Swing set	1/20	7 YR/SL	$4,000	40%	$1,600.00	7.14%	$114.24
Total			$4,000		$1,600.00		$114.24

Using this method, the amount you can claim as a depreciation expense this year is $114.24. Enter this amount on **Form 4562**, Part III, line 19c, column (g). In column (e), enter "HY" for the Half-Year Convention (see pages 72–73). If you're depreciating more than three items, include your supporting schedule with your tax return.

Part III MACRS Depreciation (Don't include listed property. See instructions.)

Section A

17 MACRS deductions for assets placed in service in tax years beginning before 2020 17

18 If you are electing to group any assets placed in service during the tax year into one or more general asset accounts, check here . . . . ▶ ☐

Section B—Assets Placed in Service During 2020 Tax Year Using the General Depreciation System

(a) Classification of property	(b) Month and year placed in service	(c) Basis for depreciation (business/investment use only—see instructions)	(d) Recovery period	(e) Convention	(f) Method	(g) Depreciation deduction
19a 3-year property						
b 5-year property						
c 7-year property		$1,600	7 YEAR	HY	S/L	$114
d 10-year property						
e 15-year property						
f 20-year property						
g 25-year property			25 yrs.		S/L	
h Residential rental			27.5 yrs.	MM	S/L	
property			27.5 yrs.	MM	S/L	
i Nonresidential real			39 yrs.	MM	S/L	
property				MM	S/L	

SEVEN-YEAR 200% DECLINING BALANCE

To use this method, you would prepare a supporting schedule, such as the following.

2020 Tax Return
Supporting Schedule for Form 4562, Part III, line 19c
Polly Jones
Social Security #474-66-1234

Item	Date Put in Service	Method	Cost	Business-Use %	Business Basis	Table % Year 1	Deduction 2020
Swing set	1/20	7YR/200% DB	$4,000	40%	$1,600.00	14.29%	$228.64
Total			$4,000		$1,600.00		$228.64

Using this method, the amount you can claim as a depreciation expense this year is $228.64. Enter this amount on **Form 4562**, Part III, line 19c, column (g). Enter "HY" in column (e). If you're depreciating more than three items, include a supporting schedule.

Part III MACRS Depreciation (Don't include listed property. See instructions.)

Section A

17 MACRS deductions for assets placed in service in tax years beginning before 2020 17

18 If you are electing to group any assets placed in service during the tax year into one or more general asset accounts, check here . . . . ▶ ☐

Section B—Assets Placed in Service During 2020 Tax Year Using the General Depreciation System

(a) Classification of property	(b) Month and year placed in service	(c) Basis for depreciation (business/investment use only—see instructions)	(d) Recovery period	(e) Convention	(f) Method	(g) Depreciation deduction
19a 3-year property						
b 5-year property						
c 7-year property		$1,600	7 YEAR	HY	200%	$229
d 10-year property						
e 15-year property						
f 20-year property						
g 25-year property			25 yrs.		S/L	
h Residential rental			27.5 yrs.	MM	S/L	
property			27.5 yrs.	MM	S/L	
i Nonresidential real			39 yrs.	MM	S/L	
property				MM	S/L	

If you used the swing set more than 50% of the time for your business, you can use the Section 179 rule:

SECTION 179

2020 Tax Return
Supporting Schedule for Form 4562, Part I
Polly Jones
Social Security #474-66-1234

Item	Method	Cost		Business Use %		Business Basis	Deduction 2020
Swing set	Section 179	$4,000	x	75%	=	$3,000	$3,000
Total		$4,000				$3,000	$3,000

Using this method, the amount you can claim as a depreciation expense this year is $3,000. Enter this amount on **Form 4562**, Part I.

Personal Property Expenses before Last Year

If you were in business before last year, enter your depreciation deductions for the items first used in your business before last year on **Form 4562** as follows:

- Enter computer depreciation on **Form 4562**, line 17.
- Enter other personal property depreciation on **Form 4562**, line 17.

You do not have to attach a supporting schedule to your tax return after the first year you begin depreciating an item. Just enter the proper amount of depreciation for the items from earlier years onto the lines noted above.

Warning: Choose Wisely!
Remember that once you begin depreciating an item using one of the methods described in this chapter, you must continue using that method for the entire life of the item, even if the depreciation rules change in later years.

Home Improvements

A home improvement is something that is attached to your home and adds to its value or substantially prolongs its useful life. Home improvements include room additions, a new garage, or an outdoor deck. If you made home improvements since you began using your home for business, you must depreciate these improvements separately from your home depreciation. Remember, you may be able to deduct a home improvement in one year if it meets the definition of a repair, you use it more than 50% of the time in your business, or you meet the requirements for the safe harbor election for small taxpayers. See pages 62–65.

You may depreciate a home improvement expense even if you are renting your home or apartment. The only requirement is that you must be the person who paid for the improvement. If you have paid for the home improvement in lieu of rent payments, you should claim the cost of the home improvement as rent and deduct it all in the current year. Enter this amount on **Form 8829**, line 18. Remember, you can elect out of using the 100% bonus depreciation rule if you want to show lower expenses this year.

Home improvements are depreciated with the same method used for the home itself, the 39-year straight-line method. To calculate the depreciation deduction for a home improvement, first multiply the cost of the improvement by your Time-Space percentage to get the business basis of the improvement. (When your Time-Space percentage changes, the total you can depreciate will also change.) Multiply the business basis by the percentage for the month you completed the improvement (as listed in the depreciation tables at the end of this chapter).

If you completed a $3,000 garage remodeling project in April of last year, your depreciation calculation might look something like this:

$3,000	Total cost of garage remodeling
x 25%	Time-Space percentage
$ 750	
x 1.819%	Depreciation percentage for April
$13.64	Amount you can deduct

The amount you can claim as a depreciation expense this year for your garage remodeling project is $13.64. Enter this amount on **Form 4562**, Part III, line 19i, column (g). After the first year of depreciation, you will use 2.564% each year to calculate your deduction.

You can use your actual business-use percentage instead of your Time-Space percentage in calculating your home improvement depreciation. It may make sense to do this if your business-use percentage is much higher than your Time-Space percentage. If you do use your business-use percentage, you'll need written evidence to support it. It probably isn't possible to claim a higher business-use percentage for home improvements that are an integral part of the structure of your home, such as a new roof or new windows.

Depreciating Unfinished Home Improvement Projects

If you started a home improvement project last year but won't finish it until this year, you can depreciate part of the project this tax season if you were able to start using the improvement by the end of last year. Here are your options:

- Wait to take any depreciation on the project until it is finished. If you started a project in 2020 and didn't use the improvement at all that year, start depreciating the project in 2021 in the month the project is finished.
- Treat the unfinished home improvement as two projects. If you began using part of the improvement in December of last year, you can depreciate your expenses for the project starting that month. Depreciate your expenses for this year starting the month the project is finished.

Section A						
17 MACRS deductions for assets placed in service in tax years beginning before 2020					17	
18 If you are electing to group any assets placed in service during the tax year into one or more general asset accounts, check here . . . . ▶ ☐						
Section B—Assets Placed in Service During 2020 Tax Year Using the General Depreciation System						
(a) Classification of property	(b) Month and year placed in service	(c) Basis for depreciation (business/investment use only—see instructions)	(d) Recovery period	(e) Convention	(f) Method	(g) Depreciation deduction
19a 3-year property						
b 5-year property						
c 7-year property		$1,600	7 YEAR	HY	200%	$229
d 10-year property						
e 15-year property						
f 20-year property						
g 25-year property			25 yrs.		S/L	
h Residential rental			27.5 yrs.	MM	S/L	
property			27.5 yrs.	MM	S/L	
i Nonresidential real			39 yrs.	MM	S/L	
property				MM	S/L	

Home Improvement Savings Are Small

Since home improvements must be depreciated over 39 years, the amount you will be able to claim in any one year will be relatively small. Some providers spend thousands of dollars fixing up their homes for their businesses under the mistaken belief that they will be able to write off much of the cost in the first year. As they soon discover, spending money on home improvements is not a good way to create deductions for your business.

In the previous example, a $3,000 remodeling expense resulted in a $13.64 deduction in the first year. If you are in the 15% income tax bracket, this would be a federal tax savings of only $3.68 (15% income tax plus 12% net Social Security tax rate). Your state income taxes will also produce a small tax savings. If you make a home improvement, it's always good to take the depreciation deduction, no matter how small, because it will run for many years. But remember that large home improvement expenses for your business will not translate into significant tax savings.

The Mid-Quarter Convention rule (see pages 72–73) doesn't apply to home improvements. You can now take Section 179 for home improvements. If you make home improvements that are necessary to become licensed or regulated or to maintain your license, you may be able to depreciate 100% of the cost.

Home Improvements before Last Year

Use Part III of **Form 4562** only for improvements that you paid for last year. If you made a home improvement before last year and before you began using your home for business, determine whether the cost of the improvement or its fair market value at the time your home was first used for your business is the lesser amount. (Since most home improvements increase in value along with the home, the lower number will usually be the original cost.) Add this amount to the cost of your home, and depreciate it as part of your home depreciation.

If you made a home improvement before last year but after you began using your home for your business, enter the depreciation for that improvement on **Form 8829**, following the instructions given in chapter 2. Calculate the depreciation deduction separately from your home and add that amount to **Form 8829**, line 41. The home improvements you make after you begin using your home for business aren't depreciated with your home because the depreciation periods end on different dates. If you are using tax preparation software and it won't allow you to enter your home improvement on line 41, enter it on line 21 (other expenses), column (b).

Land Improvements

Land improvements are eligible for either the $2,500 rule or the 100% bonus depreciation rule and therefore do not have to be depreciated. If you do use the 100% bonus depreciation rule, enter the deduction on **Form 4562**, line 14. Land improvements are not eligible for the Section 179 rule. Land improvements include installing a fence around your property or a patio, paving your driveway, adding a cement walkway, or installing a well.

To calculate the depreciation deduction for a land improvement, first multiply its cost by your Time-Space percentage to get the business basis of the improvement. (When your Time-Space percentage changes, the total you can depreciate will also change.) If you purchased a fence in 2020 for $11,000, your depreciation calculation might look something like this:

Cost of fence $11,000 x 30% Time-Space percentage = $3,300
$3,300 x 5% (first year using 15-year 150% declining balance method) = $165.00
Enter this on **Form 4562**, Part III, line 19c, column (e).

Part II **Special Depreciation Allowance and Other Depreciation (Don't** include listed property. See instructions.**)**

14 Special depreciation allowance for qualified property (other than listed property) placed in service during the tax year. See instructions	14	$1,650
15 Property subject to section 168(f)(1) election	15	
16 Other depreciation (including ACRS)	16	

Part III **MACRS Depreciation (Don't** include listed property. See instructions.**)**

Section A

17 MACRS deductions for assets placed in service in tax years beginning before 2020	17	
18 If you are electing to group any assets placed in service during the tax year into one or more general asset accounts, check here ▶ ☐		

Section B—Assets Placed in Service During 2020 Tax Year Using the General Depreciation System

(a) Classification of property	(b) Month and year placed in service	(c) Basis for depreciation (business/investment use only—see instructions)	(d) Recovery period	(e) Convention	(f) Method	(g) Depreciation deduction
19a 3-year property						
b 5-year property						
c 7-year property						
d 10-year property						
e 15-year property		$3,300	15 YEARS	HY	150% DB	$165
f 20-year property						
g 25-year property			25 yrs.		S/L	
h Residential rental			27.5 yrs.	MM	S/L	
property			27.5 yrs.	MM	S/L	
i Nonresidential real			39 yrs.	MM	S/L	
property				MM	S/L	

Again, you may want to use your actual business-use percentage instead of your Time-Space percentage in calculating the depreciation for land improvements. This may make sense for a fence that you install for your business if you have no young children of your own or if you can show that it is mostly for your business. As noted above, you must be able to support this business-use claim.

Landscaping Is Not a Land Improvement

Landscaping includes trees, shrubbery, sod, plantings, grading, and landscape architect's fees. Deduct it in one year as a repair on **Form 4562**, line 19 (see page 81). If your landscaping is located immediately adjacent to your home and would be destroyed if your home was moved or replaced, then it should be treated as a home improvement and depreciated over 39 years. Landscaping that costs more than $2,500, is installed away from your home and would not be harmed if your home was moved or replaced is considered part of the land and cannot be depreciated at all.

Land Improvements before Last Year

Use Part II of **Form 4562** only for the land improvements you paid for last year. If you made a land improvement before you began your business, determine whether the cost of the improvement or its fair market value at the time it was first used in your business is the lesser amount. (Since many land improvements increase in value along with the home, the original cost will often be the lower number.) Add this amount to the cost of your home when determining the depreciation deduction for your home.

If you made a land improvement before last year but after you began using your home for your business, enter the depreciation for that land improvement on **Form 8829**. (Follow the instructions under Home Improvements.) Calculate your depreciation deduction and add that amount to **Form 8829**, line 41.

Home Depreciation

The purchase of a home is not eligible for the 100% bonus depreciation rule or the Safe Harbor for Small Taxpayers rule (see pages 62–67). It's always financially beneficial to depreciate your home. There are two important reasons to depreciate your home. First, it will reduce your taxable income while you're in business. Second, any higher taxes that you may have to pay later because you used your home in your business will be the same whether or not you claimed the depreciation you were entitled to. (The rules about the tax consequences when you sell your home don't change the fact that you are still better off claiming all the home depreciation you're entitled to; see chapter 12.)

If you own a mobile home that is fastened to the land and connected to local utilities, use the home depreciation rules described in this section. If your mobile home wears out within 39 years, you can deduct all the unused depreciation in the final year.

Most taxpayers must show that they use part of their home regularly and exclusively for business purposes to qualify to deduct depreciation for their home. Family child care providers are exempt from this requirement. You only need to show that you use part of your home regularly for your business. If that is the case, you can claim part of the value of your home as a depreciation expense each year you are in business.

If you're married and your name isn't on the deed of the home, you can still claim home depreciation for your business. If you aren't married and your companion owns the home, you can't claim home depreciation (see the *Record-Keeping Guide*). You can't take a business deduction for your mortgage payments; instead, depreciate your home using the rules described below.

If You Rent Your Home

If you rent your home instead of own it, deduct your Time-Space percentage of your rent instead of depreciation. To do this, enter your total rent payments on **Form 8829**, line 18, column (b) (see chapter 2).

If You Started Claiming Home Depreciation before Last Year

If you claimed depreciation on your home before last year, enter your depreciation by filling out **Form 8829**, lines 36–42. Don't claim this deduction on **Form 4562**.

If you or your spouse claimed home depreciation in earlier years for another business, continue depreciating your home under the rules for that business. Once your child care business begins, start a separate depreciation calculation for your home for this business. In other words, use two different depreciation schedules to depreciate your home for the two different businesses.

If You Started Claiming Home Depreciation Last Year

If you first began using your home for your business last year, you must enter information on **Form 4562**, Part III, line 19i. Enter the month you started using your home for business in column (b). Enter the business basis of your home in column (c). To calculate the business basis of your home, follow these steps:

Step One

Record the purchase price of your home. If you hired a contractor or built part of the home yourself, record only the amount of money you actually spent to build your home; don't include the value of your labor.

The basis for depreciating your home is either its purchase price or its fair market value at the time you first started to use it for your business, whichever is lower. Therefore, if you bought your home in 2011 for $150,000 and its fair market value when you started using it for your business in 2020 was $180,000, use $150,000 as the basis of your home.

Note: If the fair market value of your home declines after you begin using it for business, don't reduce its value in calculating your home depreciation in later years.

Step Two

Add to the above amount the value of any home improvements you made before you first used your home for business. These improvements might include remodeling expenses, a new roof, room additions, siding, or a new deck. Don't include repairs or maintenance expenses, such as painting, wallpapering, or fixing a broken window.

Step Three

Subtract from the above the value of the land (land is not depreciable) to get the adjusted basis of your home. If you don't know the value of the land when you bought the house, use the relationship between the value of your land and home today to calculate the value of your land when you bought your house. Check your property tax statement, or call your county assessor's office for an estimate of the value of your land today.

> Example
>
> You bought your home in 2014 for $100,000. According to your property tax statement, it's worth $120,000 now. Your county assessor says the land is worth $12,000 today, and $12,000 ÷ $120,000 = 10%. Therefore the value of your land in 2014 was roughly 10% of the purchase price of your home, or $10,000 ($100,000 x 10% = $10,000). Keep a copy of your tax assessment report for your records.

If you buy more land or are given land and pay for surveying, you can't claim these expenses as business deductions. (For more information, see the *Record-Keeping Guide*.)

Step Four

Multiply the adjusted basis of your home by your Time-Space percentage to get the business basis of your home—the amount you can depreciate. Enter this number in column (c) of **Form 4562**, Part III, line 19i. Here are the calculations:

Step One:	$100,000	purchase price of home in 2014
Step Two:	+ $3,800	new roof in 2015
	$103,800	
Step Three:	–$10,000	value of land in 2014
	$93,800	adjusted basis of home
Step Four:	x 30%	Time-Space percentage
	$28,140	business basis of home

The next step is to determine the percentage of the business basis of your home that you can deduct in the first year of business. This depends on the month you began your business last year; see the depreciation tables at the end of this chapter.

Let's use our example to calculate your first year's home depreciation deduction. If you went into business in January 2020, you would use 2.461%:

$28,140	business basis of home
x 2.461%	began business in January
$692.53	home depreciation deduction

Enter the amount you calculate here in line 19i, column (g). After the first year of depreciation, you will use 2.564% each year to calculate your deduction.

Part III MACRS Depreciation (Don't include listed property. See instructions.)

Section A

17 MACRS deductions for assets placed in service in tax years beginning before 2020 17

18 If you are electing to group any assets placed in service during the tax year into one or more general asset accounts, check here . . . . . ▶ ☐

Section B—Assets Placed in Service During 2020 Tax Year Using the General Depreciation System

(a) Classification of property	(b) Month and year placed in service	(c) Basis for depreciation (business/investment use only—see instructions)	(d) Recovery period	(e) Convention	(f) Method	(g) Depreciation deduction
19a 3-year property						
b 5-year property						
c 7-year property						
d 10-year property						
e 15-year property						
f 20-year property						
g 25-year property			25 yrs.		S/L	
h Residential rental			27.5 yrs.	MM	S/L	
property			27.5 yrs.	MM	S/L	
i Nonresidential real		$28,140	39 yrs.	MM	S/L	$693
property				MM	S/L	

If you first began using your home for your business last year, fill out Part III of **Form 4562**, as described above. Enter the depreciation deduction ($692.53 in our example) on **Form 4562**, line 22. Don't carry this deduction forward to **Schedule C**, line 13. You will claim your home depreciation on **Form 8829**.

Vehicle Depreciation

You can use either the standard mileage rate method or the actual vehicle expenses method to deduct the vehicle expenses for your business (see chapter 5 and the *Record-Keeping Guide* for information on claiming other expenses for your vehicle). No matter which method you use to claim vehicle expenses, if you used more than one vehicle in your business during the year, report your business miles on **Form 4562** (lines 30–36), not on **Schedule C** (see Vehicle Expenses in chapter 5). If you choose the actual vehicle expenses method, you may take a depreciation deduction on your vehicle. Vehicles are subject to the Mid-Quarter Convention rule (see pages 72–73).

To calculate the depreciation on your vehicle, fill out **Form 4562**, Part V, Section A. (If you began depreciating your vehicle in an earlier year, you must continue depreciating it under the rules that were in effect when you began to depreciate it.)

Caution

If you decide to use the actual vehicle expenses method in the first year you use a vehicle in your business, you'll be locked into this method for the life of that vehicle; you can't switch back to the standard mileage rate method in later years. This means that you'll have to keep detailed records of all your vehicle expenses for every year you use the vehicle in your business.

To depreciate your vehicle, you must first determine if it weighs more or less than 6,000 pounds gross vehicle weight. Look for this information on the inside front door panel of your vehicle. (Vehicles that weigh more than 6,000 pounds include the Dodge Durango SUV, the Ford Econoline Van E150, the GMC Savana Van 1500, and the Chevrolet Express Van 1500.) Next, figure out if the vehicle was used more or less than 50% for your business. Once you have these two facts, follow the instructions below that apply to your situation.

The depreciation you claim for your vehicle cannot create a loss for your business. This may be an issue if your vehicle weighs more than 6,000 pounds and you are using it more than 50% in your business.

If the Vehicle Weighs Less Than 6,000 Pounds

Vehicles are normally depreciated over five years. Your depreciation deduction is subject to limitations each year, based on the first year the vehicle is used for your business and when you purchased the vehicle. If you purchased your vehicle after September 27, 2017, and first started using it in your business in 2020, the first-year depreciation limit is $10,100 for 2020, $16,100 for 2021, $9,700 for 2022, and $5,760 each year thereafter until the vehicle is fully depreciated. If you use the 100% bonus depreciation rule, the limit is $18,100 for 2020, and the same limits as described above for the subsequent years. If you purchased the vehicle before September 28, 2017, and first started using it for your business in 2020, the extra 100% bonus depreciation is $4,800, not $8,000. The regular depreciation limits are the same as described above.

You must reduce these limitations by your business-use percentage of the vehicle. In other words, if you use a car 35% of the time for your business, your depreciation limit in 2020 would be $3,535 ($10,100 x 35%) or $6,335 ($18,100 x 35%) if you used the 100% bonus rule.

For example, if you bought a $30,000 vehicle (new or used) and your business use was 40%, your depreciation deduction would be $12,000. If you did not use the 100% bonus rule, your deduction would be subject to the $10,100 limitation, but if you used the 100% bonus rule, you could deduct the full $12,000 (since it's less than the $18,100 limit). Enter either $10,100 or $12,000 on **Form 4562**, Part V, line 27.

If the Vehicle Weighs 6,000 Pounds or More

If the business use of the vehicle was under 50%, the depreciation deduction limitations are the same each year as above ($10,100 or $18,000) and you would depreciate the vehicle over five years. If the business use was 50% or more, there is no limitation and you can deduct the entire business portion in the first year, using the 100% bonus rule.

For example, if you bought a vehicle for $40,000 and your business use was 60%, you could deduct the entire $24,000 in 2020, using the 100% bonus rule. Enter on **Form 4562**, Part V, line 26.

Note: If you are able to claim all the vehicle depreciation in the first year, you are not entitled to any further depreciation in later years. If you weren't able to claim all the depreciation in the first year, the calculation to determine how much you can depreciate in later years is very complicated. For example, if you use the vehicle less than 50% of the time for your business and claim the 100% bonus rule, and your deduction is more than the limitation, you won't be able to claim the remaining depreciation for another six years. Use an online tax preparation software or a tax preparer to help you calculate depreciation in later years.

Part V **Listed Property** (Include automobiles, certain other vehicles, certain aircraft, and property used for entertainment, recreation, or amusement.)

Note: For any vehicle for which you are using the standard mileage rate or deducting lease expense, complete **only** 24a, 24b, columns (a) through (c) of Section A, all of Section B, and Section C if applicable.

Section A—Depreciation and Other Information (Caution: See the instructions for limits for passenger automobiles.)

24a Do you have evidence to support the business/investment use claimed? ☐ **Yes** ☐ **No** | **24b** If "Yes," is the evidence written? ☐ **Yes** ☐ **No**

(a) Type of property (list vehicles first)	(b) Date placed in service	(c) Business/ investment use percentage	(d) Cost or other basis	(e) Basis for depreciation (business/investment use only)	(f) Recovery period	(g) Method/ Convention	(h) Depreciation deduction	(i) Elected section 179 cost
25 Special depreciation allowance for qualified listed property placed in service during the tax year and used more than 50% in a qualified business use. See instructions .						**25**		
26 Property used more than 50% in a qualified business use:								
		%						
		%						
		%						
27 Property used 50% or less in a qualified business use:								
VAN	1/1/2019	40 %	$30,000	$12,000	5 YEAR	S/L – HY	$12,000	
		%				S/L –		
		%				S/L –		
28 Add amounts in column (h), lines 25 through 27. Enter here and on line 21, page 1 .						**28**	$12,000	
29 Add amounts in column (i), line 26. Enter here and on line 7, page 1							**29**	

Depreciation and Vehicle Expenses

In addition to depreciation, you can claim actual vehicle expenses on **Schedule C**, line 13 (see Vehicle Expenses in chapter 5). If you depreciate a vehicle you first started using in business last year, you can't use the standard mileage rate to claim expenses for it in later years. If you use Section 179 and go out of business, or use the vehicle 50% or less within five years, you'll have to file **Form 4797** to recapture some of the depreciation you claimed (see chapter 11).

If You Sold Your Vehicle Last Year

If you've been depreciating your vehicle before last year and you sold it last year, use the following to determine how much depreciation to claim.

If you placed your vehicle in business use between January 1 and September 30 of the first year you used it in your business, you can deduct one half of the regular depreciation amount. If you placed your vehicle in business use between October 1 and December 31 of the first year you used it in your business, multiply the full-year depreciation amount by the following percentages, based on the month you sold the vehicle:

January–March	12.5%
April–June	37.5%
July–September	62.5%
October–December	87.5%

(For a description of the tax consequences of selling a vehicle, see chapter 11.)

Congratulations!

You have entered your depreciation expenses on either **Form 4562** or **Form 8829**. Now enter the total of all your depreciation deductions on **Schedule C**, line 13.

Next, take a deep breath. The most difficult part of doing your taxes is done! Nothing else you'll do on your tax forms will be as complicated as what you have just completed. Your next step will be completing **Schedule C**.

Start-Up Costs: A Special Rule

To the IRS, your business begins when you're ready to enroll children and are advertising that fact to the public. Whether you are licensed or have any children in your care at that point is not important. Here's an example: In February you are ready to care for your first child and put up a sign at your church announcing your business. In March you apply for your license, in April you get your license, and in May you enroll your first child. In this case, the IRS would say that your business began in February. On the other hand, if you get your license in June and aren't ready to care for your first child until August, then the IRS would say that your business began in August.

You are entitled to deduct items you owned before your business began. Conduct an inventory of all these items and estimate their value at the time your business began. See my *Family Child Care Record-Keeping Guide* for an explanation of how to do this.

If you went into business in 2020 or 2019, you can use the Start-Up Rule to deduct in one year up to $5,000 worth of items that cost $200 or less. Amounts over $5,000 can be amortized over 180 months using **Form 4562**, Part VI. Items that cost more than $200 can be deducted in one year using the 100% bonus depreciation rule. Remember, there is an exception to this rule for the home, home improvements, and home additions. If you didn't claim these expenses in 2019, you can amend your tax return.

For example, let's say you owned 150 items before you went into business in 2020 (washer, dryer, refrigerator, tables, couch, bed, pots and pans, lawn mower, patio furniture, rugs, and so on). The total amount of items valued at $200 or less was $6,000 and the total value of items costing more than $200 was $4,000. Let's assume these values are determined after applying your Time-Space percentage. You can deduct $5,000 of the $6,000 as start-up expenses and amortize the other $1,000 over 180 months. You can also deduct the $4,000 in 2020 under the 100% bonus depreciation rule.

If you went into business before 2017 and didn't claim the items you owned before you went into business, you can use IRS **Form 3115** to recapture previously unclaimed depreciation. See chapter 10 for how to do this.

Special Cases for Depreciation

If You've Gone In and Out of Business

What if you started depreciating an item, went out of business, and then started up your business again? When you start up again, determine whether the fair market value of the item at that time or the adjusted basis of the item is the lesser amount. The adjusted basis is the cost of the item minus the amount of depreciation you claimed (or were entitled to claim) while you were in business. Then begin depreciating the item as Year 1 for this new amount.

> EXAMPLE
>
> In Year 1 you bought a $4,000 fence. You started using the fence in your business in Year 2; its fair market value at that time was $3,000. From Year 2 through Year 4, you claimed $369 in depreciation (fifteen-year straight-line depreciation with a 40% Time-Space percentatge). You stopped doing child care in Year 5 and Year 6.
>
> In Year 7 you started up your business again. At that time, the fair market value of the fence was $1,000. The adjusted basis is the original cost ($4,000) less the depreciation you have claimed ($369), or $3,631. Since the fair market value is lower than the adjusted basis of the item, use $1,000 to begin depreciating all over again using the fifteen-year depreciation rules. The depreciation you can now claim in the new Year 1 is $20 ($1,000 x 5% first year depreciation = $20).

If You Haven't Been Taking All Your Depreciation

What if you discover that you didn't take all the depreciation you were entitled to in a previous year? What if you haven't been taking any depreciation at all on your home or some other item? In these cases, you have three options:

1. You can file amended tax returns for 2017, 2018, and 2019 and claim the depreciation you were entitled to for those years. You will get a refund plus interest. (You can only amend your return three years back.)
2. If you didn't deduct the full amount of depreciation you were entitled to and the error goes back more than three years, you should file **Form 3115** to recapture all the unclaimed depreciation you are entitled to. (For instructions on filing **Form 3115**, see chapter 10.) To use **Form 3115**, you must have failed to claim the full amount of your depreciation for at least two consecutive years.
3. You can decide not to take advantage of **Form 3115** and just claim the depreciation you would be entitled to this year if you had depreciated the previous years correctly. To do this, calculate the amount of depreciation you are entitled to under the rules that were in effect when the depreciation period began. If you bought the item for

your business in 2015, for example, you would claim depreciation based on the fourth year of the seven-year depreciation tables. If you choose this option, you would forget about your unclaimed depreciation from earlier years.

If You Incurred Expenses to Meet Local Regulations

In some parts of the country, the local regulations require you to purchase safety equipment (such as smoke detectors or fire extinguishers) or make home improvements (such as enlarging a basement window or installing a fence) in order to operate a family child care business. These expenses aren't automatically 100% deductible. What matters is how you use the item, not why you bought it.

- In the case of smoke detectors and fire extinguishers, you can deduct only your Time-Space or business-use percentage of the cost. If these items are in an exclusive-use room, however, you can deduct 100% of the cost.
- If you enlarge a basement window in order to become licensed and you use that area of the basement 100% for your business, you can deduct the total cost as a repair. If you use that area of the basement for both business and personal purposes, you must apply your Time-Space or business-use percentage to the cost before deducting it.

If an Item Wears Out during the Depreciation Period

If an item wears out before its depreciation period ends, you're normally entitled to claim all the remaining depreciation as a business deduction in the year it wears out (start-up costs are an exception to this rule). For instructions on how to claim this amount, see chapter 11. If you buy a new item to replace the old one, you will start a new depreciation period for the new item.

Obtain a Copy of Your Depreciation Schedule

When your tax preparer depreciates items for your business, he or she will prepare a depreciation schedule showing each item, cost, depreciation method, and convention. It's important to ask your tax preparer for a copy of this schedule each year. This can be extremely useful for you in preparing future tax returns whether you do them yourself or use a new tax preparer.

For more information about the tax issues discussed in this chapter, refer to the related topics in the other chapters of this book and the Redleaf Press *Family Child Care Record-Keeping Guide*.

2020 Depreciation Tables

	3-Year Straight-Line (computer software)	**5-Year Straight-Line** (computers, office equipment, and vehicles)	**5-Year 200% Declining Balance** (computers, office equipment, and vehicles)
Year 1	16.67%	10%	20%
Year 2	33.33%	20%	32%
Year 3	33.33%	20%	19.20%
Year 4	16.67%	20%	11.52%
Year 5		20%	11.52%
Year 6		10%	5.76%
Section 179?	Maybe	No	Yes

	7-Year Straight-Line (furniture and appliances)	**7-Year 200% Declining Balance** (furniture and appliances)
Year 1	7.14%	14.29%
Year 2	14.29%	24.49%
Year 3	14.29%	17.49%
Year 4	14.28%	12.49%
Year 5	14.29%	8.93%
Year 6	14.28%	8.92%
Year 7	14.29%	8.93%
Year 8	7.14%	4.46%
Section 179?	Maybe	Yes

	15-Year Straight-Line (land improvements)	**15-Year 150% Declining Balance** (land improvements)
Year 1	3.33%	5.00%
Year 2	6.67%	9.50%
Year 3	6.67%	8.55%
Year 4	6.67%	7.70%
Year 5	6.67%	6.93%
Year 6	6.67%	6.23%
Year 7	6.67%	5.90%
Year 8	6.66%	5.90%
Year 9	6.67%	5.91%
Year 10	6.66%	5.90%
Year 11	6.67%	5.91%
Year 12	6.66%	5.90%
Year 13	6.67%	5.91%
Year 14	6.66%	5.90%
Year 15	6.67%	5.91%
Year 16	3.33%	2.95%
Section 179?	Maybe	Maybe

39-Year Straight-Line (home and home improvements)

	For the first year of depreciation, use this table:	*After the first year of depreciation, use:*
January	2.461%	2.564%
February	2.247%	
March	2.033%	
April	1.819%	
May	1.605%	
June	1.391%	
July	1.177%	
August	0.963%	
September	0.749%	
October	0.535%	
November	0.321%	
December	0.107%	
Section 179?	No	No

CHAPTER 4

Reporting Your Food Program Income and Food Expenses

The first part of this chapter explains how to report your income from the Child and Adult Care Food Program (CACFP). The Food Program is a federal program that reimburses family child care providers for serving nutritious food. The second part of this chapter explains how to claim your food expenses. It's important to claim these expenses properly because food is the single biggest business deduction most family child care providers have. The standard meal allowance rates for 2020 are $1.33 for breakfast, $2.49 for lunch or supper, and $0.74 for snack. The rates are higher for Alaska and Hawaii. See page 96.

Reporting Your Income from the Food Program

All family child care providers who meet their state regulation standards are eligible to participate in the CACFP. All family child care providers should participate in the Food Program because it offers a major source of income. (For a full discussion of the benefits of the Food Program, see the *Record-Keeping Guide.*)

Reimbursement Rates

The Food Program's reimbursement rates are raised on July 1 every year. If you have a low income, live in a low-income area, or serve low-income children, you will be eligible for the Tier I reimbursement rates. If you don't have at least one of these qualifications, you will get the Tier II reimbursement rates.

For your family to be considered low income in 2020, you must meet the following income eligibility guidelines (July 1, 2020–June 30, 2021):

Annual Income	Family of one	Family of two	Each additional person
All states except Alaska and Hawaii	$23,606	$31,894	$8,288
Alaska	$29,508	$39,868	$10,360
Hawaii	$27,158	$36,686	$9,528

FOOD PROGRAM REIMBURSEMENT RATES (PER SERVING)

	Tier I Regular Rate		Tier II Reduced Rate	
	Jan–June	July–Dec	Jan–June	July–Dec
Breakfast	$1.33	$1.39	$0.48	$0.50
Lunch/Supper	$2.49	$2.61	$1.50	$1.58
Snack	$0.74	$0.78	$0.20	$0.21
Total	$4.56	$4.78	$2.18	$2.29

If you live in Alaska and Hawaii, the reimbursement rates are higher:

Alaska				
Breakfast	$2.12	$2.22	$0.75	$0.78
Lunch/Supper	$4.04	$4.24	$2.44	$2.55
Snack	$1.20	$1.26	$0.33	$0.35
Total	$7.36	$7.72	$3.52	$3.68

Hawaii				
Breakfast	$1.54	$1.62	$0.56	$0.58
Lunch/Supper	$2.92	$3.06	$1.76	$1.84
Snack	$0.87	$0.91	$0.24	$0.25
Total	$5.33	$5.59	$2.56	$2.67

As of July 1, 2020, the Tier I reimbursement per child equaled $1,242 per year for serving a daily breakfast, lunch, and snack. The Tier II reimbursement equaled $595 per year.

These rates are based on a consumer price index that tracks the cost of food served in a home on a national basis. After stagnating for several years, the increase as of July 2020 is welcome. Despite the fact that the Food Program reimbursement rate has not increased as fast as providers would like, you are still always better off financially by joining and remaining on the Food Program.

Reporting CACFP Reimbursements

I recommend that you enter your Food Program reimbursements on **Schedule C**, line 6, and write "CACFP Income" next to this number. This will clearly show the IRS that you are reporting this income. Some providers prefer to include these reimbursements in the parent fees they report on line 1; however, the IRS is always on the alert for unreported income in the child care field. If you combine your Food Program reimbursements with your parent fees, they won't be as identifiable. The IRS may wonder if you have reported all this income properly and might audit your return to find out.

F	Accounting method: (1) ☑ Cash (2) ☐ Accrual (3) ☐ Other (specify) ▶		
G	Did you "materially participate" in the operation of this business during 2020? If "No," see instructions for limit on losses	☑ Yes ☐ No	
H	If you started or acquired this business during 2020, check here ▶	☐	
I	Did you make any payments in 2020 that would require you to file Form(s) 1099? See instructions	☐ Yes ☐ No	
J	If "Yes," did you or will you file required Form(s) 1099?	☐ Yes ☐ No	
Part I	**Income**		
1	Gross receipts or sales. See instructions for line 1 and check the box if this income was reported to you on Form W-2 and the "Statutory employee" box on that form was checked ▶ ☐	1	
2	Returns and allowances	2	
3	Subtract line 2 from line 1	3	
4	Cost of goods sold (from line 42)	4	
5	**Gross profit.** Subtract line 4 from line 3	5	
6	Other income, including federal and state gasoline or fuel tax credit or refund (see instructions)	6	CACFP $4,250
7	**Gross income.** Add lines 5 and 6 ▶	7	

Form 1099

If you have received **Form 1099 Miscellaneous Income** from your Food Program sponsor, be sure to put the amount listed on it on line 6 and identify it as "1099 Income" instead of "CACFP Income." The IRS computers can check whether all **Form 1099** income was properly reported by those who received this form. You want to make sure that anyone who looks at your **Schedule C** can see that you have reported all of your **Form 1099** income.

Reimbursements for Your Own Children

If you received reimbursements from the Food Program for your own children last year, this income is not taxable; however, most Food Program sponsors don't tell you how much of your monthly reimbursement is for your own children. To calculate how much you were reimbursed for your own children, you can use the worksheets in the Tax Organizer (see pages 30–31). Once you've calculated the total reimbursement for your own children, subtract it from your total reimbursements for the year and enter the result on line 6 of **Schedule C**. Show how you got this total in the space next to line 6 ("$5,000 CACFP, $750 own child").

The IRS can find out the total amount you received from the Food Program and is likely to look for this number on your **Schedule C**. By showing how you got the amount entered there, you'll explain why line 6 doesn't match your total reimbursement amount.

If in a previous year you reported the reimbursements for your own child as income and claimed the same amount as a food expense, then the two amounts almost canceled each other out, and no damage was done. If you reported the reimbursements for your own child as income but didn't claim your food expenses for that child, you should file an amended tax return to get a refund, plus interest (see chapter 9).

Reimbursements for a Foster Child

If you have a foster child and you receive Food Program reimbursements for that child, treat these reimbursements the same way you would for your own children. You're receiving them because your family is income eligible. Therefore, these reimbursements are not taxable income, and the food you serve to a foster child is not a deductible business expense.

Food Stamps

If you receive food stamps, don't report them as income on **Schedule C**, because they are not taxable income. This means that the food you purchase with food stamps can't be deducted as a business expense either. If you receive food stamps, be sure to save records that show how much you received in food stamps.

If One of Your Employees Receives a Check from the Food Program

Some family child care providers operate their business from more than one location and hire employees to care for the children in one or both locations. In this situation, the Food Program will probably issue some of the reimbursement checks to your employee, and your employee should turn over the checks to you. Here's how to handle this transaction on your tax forms:

If your Food Program sponsor sends a **Form 1099** to the employee, the employee should send a **Form 1099** back to you. If the sponsor doesn't use this form, the employee shouldn't do so either. In either case, the employee should show the reimbursement as income on her own **Schedule C** and report the same amount as an expense under line 27 (other expenses). If she does this, she won't owe any tax on this income. You should show the reimbursements as income on your **Schedule C**, line 6 (other income).

Don't Assume That Food Expenses Equal Food Program Reimbursements
Instead of keeping careful food records, some providers just assume that their food expenses equal their Food Program reimbursements, so they report neither of these amounts on their tax return on the assumption that they will "wash out." For example, a provider who received $3,000 from the Food Program would assume that she spent $3,000 on food and not report either number on her **Schedule C**. This is a bad practice.

If you are a Tier I provider, you can justify your deduction by using the standard meal allowance rule and show the IRS your monthly Food Program claim forms to defend your position. If you served extra meals and snacks that weren't reimbursed by the Food Program, then your food deduction will be too low. You can easily claim a higher food deduction by tracking the nonreimbursed meals you serve.

If you are a Tier II provider who evens out her food income and expenses, you are probably cheating yourself out of hundreds of dollars. If you use the standard meal allowance rule, you will always be able to claim food deductions that are at least twice as much as your Food Program income, because you will be claiming food expenses based on the Tier I rate, while reporting income based on the lower Tier II rate. It makes no sense not to claim this extra deduction.

Why Should You Report Your Food Reimbursements This Way?

The instructions in **Publication 587** tell you to report only your net income or expense for food reimbursements. This means that if you received $3,000 in reimbursements and spent $3,500 on business food, you would report no income and a $500 food expense. I recommend that you always show your taxable reimbursement on line 6 and all deductible food expenses on line 27 of **Schedule C**. The tax result is the same with both methods, but showing only the net income or expense is likely to increase your chance of being audited. Many providers spend far more on food than they receive from the Food Program, and showing a large food expense on **Schedule C** without any reimbursement income will draw attention from the IRS, especially for a Tier II provider.

For example, let's say that you are a Tier II provider who has received $2,000 in reimbursements and spent $5,000 on food. If you follow the IRS instructions, you would report $0 income and $3,000 in food expenses. In this case the IRS may assume that you didn't report your Food Program reimbursements and will audit you to find out if you did. All the IRS agents I have consulted recommend that you show your taxable Food Program reimbursements and all your business food deductions on **Schedule C**.

IRS Child Care Provider Audit Technique Guide on Food Expenses
The guide clearly rejects the netting method described in **Publication 587** saying, "The netting method is not a preferred method since an Examiner will always be looking for the food reimbursement amounts." The guide says that the recommended method is to report Food Program reimbursements as income and report all food expenses as expenses on **Schedule C**.

Determining the Cost of Your Food

You now have two choices for how to claim your food expenses: use the IRS standard meal allowance rule or estimate your actual cost of business food. See the *Record-Keeping Guide* for a complete discussion of these two choices.

Using the Standard Meal Allowance Rule

The IRS meal allowance rule allows you to calculate your food expenses by multiplying the meals and snacks you serve to the children in your care by the Tier I Food Program reimbursement rates in effect at the beginning of the calendar year. The rates for calendar year 2020 are $1.33 for breakfast, $2.49 for lunch or supper, and $0.74 for snacks. (The rates are higher in Alaska and Hawaii; see page 96.) **If you use these rates, you won't have to save any of your business or personal food receipts.**

You can use the meal allowance for up to one breakfast, one lunch, one supper, and three snacks per child per day. (The Food Program rules haven't changed; they still only reimburse up to three servings a day.) You must actually serve a meal in order to count it.

All family child care providers are eligible to use this rule, including those who aren't licensed or registered, those who receive the lower Tier II reimbursement rate, those who aren't on the Food Program, and those who are operating illegally. You can use the meal allowance one year and estimate your actual cost of food the next year. If you spend less on food than the standard meal allowance, you can still use it.

You can't use the meal allowance rate if you provide care in a building that isn't your home, and you may not count a meal if the child's parent has supplied the food. You also can't count any meals you serve to your own child. (Food Program reimbursements for your own children aren't taxable income.)

You can count meals you serve to employees as an actual food cost separate from the meal allowance rate (you must save the receipts). Or you could use the standard meal allowance. You may deduct only 50% of the cost of food served to employees while they are working. So either deduct 50% of the actual food cost or 50% of the standard meal allowance rate. If you hire your child to work for you, you can deduct the actual cost of the food served to your child if that child is eating in the middle of his workday. You may deduct any food you serve as part of an activity (rather than a meal or snack) as a separate activity expense rather than a food expense. For example, you can deduct the cost of a cake that you serve at a birthday party or the ingredients for a gingerbread house. Nonfood meal preparation supplies, such as containers, paper products, and utensils, continue to be deductible.

To use the standard meal allowance rule, you must maintain the following records: the name of each child, the dates and hours each child was in your care, and the number of breakfasts, lunches, suppers, and snacks served. The IRS provides a meal and snack log you can use to track this information. In addition, the *Redleaf Calendar-Keeper* has two pages of charts that meet IRS requirements, and those are included in Part I of this book.

Estimating Your Actual Cost of Food

If you are trying to decide whether to use the standard meal allowance rule or your actual cost of food, you may want to estimate the actual cost of the food you serve based on several weeks of menus and compare it with the standard meal allowance rate. It's important to keep in mind that if you choose to estimate your actual cost of food rather than using the standard meal allowance, you will have to keep receipts for all the business and personal food you purchase.

There are many ways to estimate your actual food expenses (the *Record-Keeping Guide* describes several). Usually the simplest and most accurate method is to estimate your average cost per meal per child, and then multiply this by the total number of meals you served.

Reporting Your Food Expenses

It's best to claim your deduction for food expenses on one of the blank lines in **Schedule C**, Part V, Other Expenses, although you can also put it elsewhere on this form. Wherever you choose to put it, be sure to identify it clearly as "Food" rather than including it under a general heading, such as "Other," because the IRS will be looking for it. If you're a Tier II provider who spends thousands of dollars more for food than you're reimbursed by the Food Program, you should identify yourself as such by writing "Food (Tier II Provider)" next to your food deduction, rather than simply "Food."

Since large individual expense amounts on **Schedule C** can trigger an audit, don't include any nonfood items in your food expenses. Remove items such as paper products and kitchen supplies from your food receipts and claim them on a different line, such as line 22 (supplies). The food expenses you list on Part V are carried over to line 27 (other expenses) on the front page of **Schedule C**.

If you serve meals to your employees, you can deduct 50% of the cost of the food, and your employees don't have to report these meals as income. You can either include this cost with your other food expenses or list it separately as "Employee meals" on one of the blank lines in Part V. You could enter employee meals on line 24b. (If you are reporting "Employee meals," make sure you have filed all the proper payroll forms for these employees [see chapter 8].)

Part V **Other Expenses.** List below business expenses not included on lines 8–26 or line 30.	
FOOD	$5,540
or NOT ON FOOD PROGRAM	$5,540
or FOOD (TIER II PROVIDER)	$5,540
EMPLOYEE MEALS	$600

Summary of Food Income and Expenses

Here's a summary of the rules about which food expenses you can deduct as a business expense and how to treat your income from the Food Program and food stamps:

	Report as Taxable Income?	**Deduct as a Food Expense?**
FOOD INCOME		
Food Program reimbursements for children in your care	Yes	
Food Program reimbursements for your own child	No	
Food Program reimbursements for your foster child	No	
Food stamps for your own family	No	
FOOD EXPENSES		
Food eaten by the children in your care		Yes
Food eaten by you during business hours at home		No
Food eaten by your own child during business hours		No
Lunch leftovers eaten by your family		No
Nonreimbursed meals eaten by the children in your care		Yes
Noncreditable food (ice cream, potato chips, and so on) eaten by the children in your care		Yes
Food eaten by a paid employee during business hours		Yes (but only 50% of the cost)
Food eaten by foster children		No

For more information about the tax issues discussed in this chapter, refer to the related topics in the other chapters of this book and the Redleaf Press *Family Child Care Record-Keeping Guide*.

CHAPTER 5

Reporting Your Business Income and Expenses: Schedule C

This chapter explains how to fill out **Schedule C** Profit or Loss from Business. On this form you'll report both your business income and your business expenses. You'll find more information about how to calculate and report specific kinds of business income and expenses, such as depreciation, in other chapters of this book. This chapter will take you step-by-step through **Schedule C**. (A copy of **Schedule C** is included in the tax forms at the back of this book.)

If you and your husband work side by side caring for children, you may want to consider filing two **Schedule C**s (see pages 120–121). You can then split the income and expenses between the two of you. This may be an option if you want your husband to show more income to increase his Social Security benefits. Before taking this step, consult with a Social Security expert to see the long-term impact on Social Security benefits for both of you. Before reading about how to fill out each line of **Schedule C**, some general issues about how to enter your income and expenses on this form will be addressed.

Reporting Income (Part I of Schedule C)

Part I of **Schedule C** is where you will enter all your income. In addition to parent fees, you must report as income any payments you received from county social service agencies for care you provide to low-income parents. Report all of this income on **Schedule C**, line 1b. If you received reimbursements from the Food Program, see chapter 4 for instructions on how to report this income.

IRS Child Care Provider Audit Technique Guide on Reporting Income
The guide makes it clear that the IRS will look very closely to make sure a provider is reporting all her income. They may examine a provider's contract and policies to see if she got paid additional amounts for late pickup, overnight care, transportation, diaper fees, holding fees, and so on. Providers should keep careful records showing the source of all deposits into checking and savings accounts (both business and personal). If you did not receive the full amount from a parent, as stated in your contract, make a note of the reason. For example, if your contract says that your fee is $150 a week, the IRS would assume you received $7,800 a year from the parent ($150 x 52 weeks). Reasons why you may not have received this full amount could include unpaid vacation or

sick time, part-time care, forgiving payments for a laid-off parent, or debt from a parent who left child care. Without records showing deposits of parent payments, you may have trouble showing why you earned less than the full amount.

Cash Payments

If you receive any cash payments, you should record them in a cash journal. Enter the dates you provided child care, the child's and parent's names, the amount, and the date of payment. The IRS is always looking for signs of unreported income, and a cash journal will help your case if you need to show that you didn't earn any more money than you reported. Here's a sample entry from a cash journal:

CASH JOURNAL

Dates of Care	Child/Parent	Amount Pd.	Date Pd.
Jan 3–Jan 7	Jenny/Carol Martinez	$100	Jan 3
Jan 10–Jan 14	Jenny/Carol Martinez	$100	Jan 10

Here's how to report some of the other kinds of business income you may have received last year.

Grants

If you received grants from a government agency (usually for start-up expenses or home renovations), this money is most likely taxable income. If the granting agency has sent you **Form 1099G** Certain Government Payments, the IRS will be sure to check to see that you have reported this income. Even if you didn't receive **Form 1099G**, you should report the grant as income. Enter your income from grants on **Schedule C**, not on **Form 1040**.

Since you are reporting the grant as income, you will deduct the items you buy with the grant money according to the usual rules for claiming deductions. For example, if you use the grant money to buy a home improvement (such as a deck), you will have to depreciate that expense over several years (see chapter 3). This will reduce your deductions and increase your taxes in the current year.

The only situation in which you don't have to report a grant as income is if you qualify for it because your family has a low income. If a grant is offered only to low-income families, it may be considered a welfare payment (like food stamps) rather than taxable income. (If you don't know if your grant qualifies, contact the granting agency.) You can't deduct the items you buy with nontaxable grant money as a business deduction.

Loans

Some loans given to family child care providers for purchasing business equipment are structured so that the loan is forgiven (you don't have to pay it back) if you stay in business for two years. Normally you don't have to report a loan as income; however, when a business loan is forgiven, you need to report the amount of the loan as income on **Schedule C**, line 6. In the year you receive the loan, don't report any of the money as income; simply deduct the items that you purchased with the loan money as business expenses.

Gifts from Parents

In general you must report as business income any cash, gift certificates, or items you receive from the parents of the children in your care. Report these gifts on **Schedule C**, line 1. However, if a parent gives you a gift that is not directly related to your business, you do not have to report these gifts as income. Examples would include birthday gifts or holiday gifts. If you use any of these gifts in your business, don't treat them as an expense.

If a parent gives you a noncash gift as a partial or total payment for child care services, then the item isn't really a gift, and you do have to report it as income. For example, if the parent gives you a $20 scarf as partial payment for child care, you have to report it as income.

Refunds to Parents

Some providers offer a discount to parents who pay for blocks of time in advance. If one of your parents moves away before the end of the paid-up period and you refund some of her money, then subtract the refund from the original payment and report only the net income. If you reported the original payment as income in one year and gave the refund in the next year, the refund becomes a business expense, and you will report it on **Schedule C**, Part V.

Military Housing Allowances

Some family child care providers receive military housing allowances that are called BAQ (Basic Allowance for Quarters) or VHA (Variable Housing Allowance). These housing allowances are not taxable income, so don't report them on **Schedule C**. If you receive a housing allowance but live off-base, see page 58. See the *Record-Keeping Guide* for a full discussion of military housing allowances.

Foster Care Allowances

Some family child care providers receive payments for child or foster care under an arrangement with a charitable organization or governmental agency. These payments don't have to be reported on **Schedule C** if they are received from a foster care placement agency that is licensed or certified by a state or local government or from an agency that is designated by a state or local government to make such payments, because those payments are exempt from federal taxes. Since the payments aren't taxable, you can't deduct any expenses you incur for these children. See the *Record-Keeping Guide* for a full discussion of foster care allowances.

Respite Care Payments

If you receive payments from a government agency for offering respite care for a family, this money is taxable income. (Respite care is usually provided for families that need to be separated from their children on a short-term basis.) Report these payments as income on **Schedule C**, line 1. You can deduct the expenses you incur in caring for a child in respite care in the same way you do your expenses for regular child care children.

Interest

If you have earned any interest on a business checking or savings account, don't enter it on **Schedule C**. You must report that type of interest income on **Schedule B**.

Claiming Expenses (Part II of Schedule C)

Part II of **Schedule C** is where you will show all the deductions for your business expenses (sometimes after transferring the information from another tax form). The major expense lines that are listed on **Schedule C** are as follows:

- Line 8: Advertising
- Line 9: Car and truck expenses
- Line 13: Depreciation
- Line 14: Employee benefit programs
- Line 15: Insurance (other than health)
- Line 16: Interest
- Line 17: Legal and professional services
- Line 18: Office expenses
- Line 20: Rent or lease
- Line 21: Repairs and maintenance (of personal property used in the business)
- Line 22: Supplies
- Line 23: Taxes and licenses
- Line 24: Travel, meals, and entertainment
- Line 26: Wages
- Line 27: Other expenses (the total of all the items you've listed on the blank lines in Part V, such as food, toys, household items, cleaning supplies, and activity expenses)

Some of these major line items are covered in more detail in other parts of this book. For example, there's a section on vehicle expenses at the end of this chapter. The topic of depreciation is covered in chapter 3, and issues related to paying wages and hiring employees are covered in chapter 8. If you have any questions about how to calculate the deductions for any of these items, see the relevant part of this book.

If some of your business expenses don't seem to fit on any of the lines on **Schedule C**, bear in mind that it doesn't matter on which line you enter your expenses. The IRS won't penalize you for listing a business expense on one line rather than another. This means that you can make your own decision about what to categorize as supplies or office expenses or any other line on **Schedule C**; however, use the words *de minimis equipment* to describe toys, cribs, or other items that cost less than $2,500. (For suggestions on how to categorize your expenses, see the *Record-Keeping Guide*.)

To reduce your chance of an audit, don't lump large expense items together on one line. Instead, use the blank spaces under line 27, other expenses, to list items such as food, cleaning supplies, and activity expenses. If any line on your **Schedule C** is unusually high in comparison with your income, it may trigger an audit. For example, if your income on **Schedule C** is $15,000 and you list $8,000 for cleaning supplies, this will draw attention to your return. If your total expenses are reasonable, and you have just put all your food expenses, kitchen supplies, and children's supplies on line 22, then you don't need to worry. If you're audited, you will need to show the IRS all your records to demonstrate that your expenses are valid.

Calculating the Deductions for Your Business Expenses

You can deduct only the portion of an expense that relates to your business. To calculate how much you can deduct for each business expense, you need to follow the instructions given in chapters 1 through 3 for completing **Form 4562** and Part I of **Form 8829**. If you haven't completed those sections yet, you should do it now. (Calculating the deductions for your business expenses can be a complicated process. If you have any questions about this topic, refer to the *Record-Keeping Guide*, which lists over 1,000 potential business expenses and explains how to deduct them.)

As I described in the previous chapters of this book, you will need to divide all your expenses into three categories:

1. 100% personal use (such as jewelry and cigarettes)
2. 100% business use (such as child care food and the toys used only in your business)
3. Shared business and personal use (such as cleaning supplies and lightbulbs)

If an expense is 100% personal use, you can't deduct any of it as a business expense. If it is 100% business use, you can deduct all of it as a business expense. If it has both business and personal uses, you can deduct only part of it as a business expense.

There are two ways to determine the business portion of a shared expense; you can multiply the cost of the item either by your Time-Space percentage (covered in chapter 1) or by the item's actual business-use percentage. For most items, you will use your Time-Space percentage; for some items you may prefer to use an actual business-use percentage, especially if the expense was large and the business-use percentage is significantly higher than your Time-Space percentage.

Determining the Actual Business-Use Percentage

To determine the actual business-use percentage of an item, you need to track how much time you use the item for your business and how much time you use it for personal purposes. Divide the number of hours of business use by the total number of hours you used the item. For example, if you used an item three hours a week for business and nine hours a week for personal purposes, your business-use percentage would be 25% (3 ÷ [3 + 9]).

You must keep careful notes about how you calculated your business deductions and be able to support them if you are audited. Do your calculations on another sheet of paper, and enter only the business portion of your expenses on **Schedule C**. For example, let's say that you spent a total (business and personal) of $100 for paper towels last year. If your Time-Space percentage is 30%, you can enter $30 on **Schedule C** (probably on line 22). If you determine that 55% of the towels were used for your business, your business-use percentage is 55%, and you can enter $55 instead.

In addition, on line 18 for office expenses, you're claiming the following: books $50 (100% business); business birthday cards $20 (100% business); computer paper $15 (60% actual business use); internet access fees $250 (50% actual business use); office supplies $100 (40% Time-Space percentage); and magazines $50 (40% Time-Space percentage).

The best way to organize these expenses is to list them by category:

100% Business		Time-Space Percentage		Actual Business-Use Percentage		
books	$50	office supplies	$100	computer paper	$15 x 60% =	$9
birthday cards	$20	magazines	$50	internet fee	$250 x 50% =	$125
Subtotal:	$70	Subtotal:	$150	Subtotal:		$134
			x 40% = $60			

Total Office Expense: $264 ($70 + $60 + $134)

In this example, you would keep this calculation for your files and enter $264 on line 18.

If You Operate Two Home-Based Businesses

If you operate two businesses out of your home, you must file a separate **Schedule C** for each business and report your income and expenses for each business separately. If you earn money on child care–related activities (such as child care training or consulting), enter all your income and expenses for these activities on the same **Schedule C** as your child care business.

Allocate your expenses on a reasonable basis between the two **Schedule C**s. Transfer the net income from both of them to one **Form 1040 Schedule SE**. If you're entitled to claim the home office deduction for your other business, you must also file a separate **Form 8829** for each business. If your other business claims part of your home on **Form 8829**, you won't be able to claim a 100% Space percentage for your child care business.

How to Fill Out Schedule C

On the first few lines of **Schedule C**, enter your name and Social Security number (or employer identification number, if you have one) at the top of the page, and then proceed as follows:

Line A: Enter "Family Child Care."

Line B: Enter your principal business code: 624410 Child Day Care Services.

Line C: If your business has an official name, enter it here. If not, leave the line blank. See your state rules regarding any requirements for having a business name.

Line D: Enter your employer identification number, if you have one.

Line E: Enter your business address.

Line F: Select method (1) Cash. This doesn't mean that you're paid in cash; it means that you report your income when you receive it and your expenses when you incur them. For example, if a parent pays you in January of this year for services provided in December of last year, you will report the payment as income next tax season. If you received a check in December of last year that you don't deposit until January of this year, you count it as income for this tax season. If you buy something for your business with a credit card, you count it as an expense the month you sign the credit card receipt, not the month you pay your credit card bill. (Once you charge something on your credit card, you are legally obligated to pay the bill.)

Line G: Enter "yes." You are considered to have materially participated in your business if you meet any one of the following tests: (1) you worked more than 500 hours in the year, (2) you were the sole participant in your business (no employees), or (3) you worked more than 100 hours, and no other person worked more time than you.

Line H: If this is the first year you have filed **Schedule C**, check the box.

Line I: If you hired an independent contractor and paid any person $600 or more, you are required to file **Form 1099**. If this is true for you, check "yes." If not, check "no." See the form's instructions for details. If you paid a house cleaner, gardener, or someone to mow your lawn or plow your driveway, and you wrote a check to a company, rather than to an individual, you do not need to submit **Form 1099**. If you paid the individual directly, you do. Note: If you hire an assistant to help you care for children, this person is an employee, not an independent contractor; this is true no matter how little you pay the person. See chapter 8 for details.

Line J: If you are required to file **Form 1099**, check "yes." If you check "yes" on line I and fail to check it on line J, your chance of being audited will increase.

Part I: Income

Line 1: Enter all your income from parent fees here, including cash payments. Also enter any payments from social service agencies for care you provided to low-income parents.

Lines 2, 3, and 4: Leave these lines blank.

Line 5: Enter the amount from line 1.

Line 6: Enter any other business income you received, such as CACFP reimbursements, grants, gifts, and loans that have been forgiven.

Line 7: Add lines 5 and 6. This is your gross income.

Part II: Expenses

Line 8: **Advertising**. Enter any advertising expenses, which may include business cards, welcome mats, newspaper ads, keepsakes, and children's T-shirts (for more information, refer to the *Family Child Care Marketing Guide,* which lists over 100 advertising deductions).

Line 9: **Car and truck expenses**. Enter the vehicle expenses you have incurred for business purposes here. For information on how to calculate this amount, see the section on vehicle expenses at the end of this chapter.

Line 10: **Commissions and fees**. Leave blank.

Line 11: **Contract labor**. Enter the amount you paid to independent contractors (see pages 149–150).

Line 12: **Depletion**. Leave blank.

Line 13: **Depreciation**. Enter the amount from **Form 4562**, line 22 (see chapter 3). Make sure you have not included in this amount any depreciation expenses for your house or home improvements. Instead, claim these expenses on **Form 8829** (see chapter 2).

Line 14: **Employee benefit programs**. Enter the cost of any benefits you provide your employees such as health, life, or disability insurance.

Line 15: **Insurance**. Enter the total of any liability insurance you carry for your business and any workers' compensation insurance you purchase for yourself or your employees. Workers' compensation insurance protects a provider or employee who is injured while working. Insurance coverage can include medical benefits, disability income, rehabilitation expenses, and other costs. Liability and workers' compensation insurance is 100% deductible. Life insurance and disability income insurance for yourself are not deductible. Health insurance premiums for yourself aren't deductible on **Schedule C**, but they may be deductible on **Form 1040** (see chapter 6). Don't deduct your homeowners or renters insurance here; put these on **Form 8829** instead (see chapter 2). For a complete discussion of insurance, see the *Family Child Care Legal and Insurance Guide.*

Line 16: **Interest**. Enter the business portion of any interest you paid on items purchased for your business. For example, in January of last year, you bought some large play equipment on credit for $750. Your Time-Space percentage is 25%. By the end of last year, you paid $75 in interest on this purchase. In this case, you can deduct $18.75 ($75 x 25% = $18.75) as a business interest deduction on line 16.

You can put the business-use percentage of your vehicle loan interest on this line or include it in your vehicle expenses on line 9. Don't enter mortgage interest here; instead, enter it on **Form 8829** (see chapter 2). Report any interest you've earned on your business checking or saving accounts on **Schedule B**.

Loan Payments

You can't deduct the loan payments you make on an item purchased for your business. You can depreciate the item or take a Section 179 deduction, even if you're still making payments on it. You can also deduct the business portion of the interest you're paying on the loan.

Line 17: **Legal and professional services**. Enter the total of any legal and professional services you incurred for your business. This includes any costs you incur if you go to small-claims court over a business matter as well as the tax preparation fees to do your business tax forms (**Form 4562**, **Schedule C**, **Form 8829**, **Schedule SE**, **Form 1040-ES**, **Form 8826**, **Form 3115**, payroll tax forms, and others). Ask your tax preparer how much of the fee is for your business tax forms. (You can deduct the tax preparation fees for your personal tax forms as a miscellaneous itemized personal expense on **Schedule A**.)

Line 18: **Office expenses**. Enter the total of any office expenses you incurred (such as bank charges, books, magazines, desk supplies, receipt books), as well as any education or training expenses for yourself.

Line 19: **Pension and profit-sharing plans**. Enter the cost of any pension or profit-sharing plans you have set up for your employees.

Line 20: **Rent or lease**. Enter your total expenses for renting videotapes, carpet cleaning machines, and other business property. If you rent your home, don't enter that expense here; list it on line 19 of **Form 8829** (see chapter 2).

Line 21: **Repairs and maintenance**. Enter your total expenses for repair or maintenance of your personal property, such as appliance service contracts or repair of broken toys. Enter the costs of repair and maintenance of your home on **Form 8829**, line 20 (see chapter 2).

Line 22: **Supplies**. Enter your total expenses for supplies, such as children's supplies (craft items and games) and kitchen supplies (plastic wrap, garbage bags, and food containers).

Line 23: **Taxes and licenses**. Enter the total you've paid for taxes and licenses. Include any payroll taxes you've paid for the employer portion of Social Security, Medicare, and federal unemployment taxes. Also include any license fees you've paid. The sales taxes you've paid on items bought for your business can either be entered here or be included in the cost of each item. Enter your property taxes on **Form 8829**, line 11 (see chapter 2).

Line 24: **Travel, meals, and entertainment**. On line 24a, enter the total lodging and travel costs (such as airfare, bus fare, train fare, vehicle rental, or mileage) you incurred when traveling away from home overnight for a child care conference or other business activity.

On line 24b, enter your meal costs. You can keep receipts for all your meal expenses, or you can claim a per diem meal rate. For trips to many areas of the United States, that rate is $55 a day for 2020. (See the U.S. General Services Administration website for a list of the per diem rates across the country: www.gsa.gov/perdiem.) You don't need any receipts to claim the standard rate, but you must use only one of these methods for all your trips in the year.

You can deduct only 50% of your meal and entertainment expenses. Multiply the amount of your actual food costs or the per diem rate by 50% and enter the result on line 24b. Don't enter your food expenses for the children in your care on line 24b; enter them in Part V (see chapter 4).

If you go out and eat a meal with another child care provider, you can deduct 50% of the cost of your meal if the discussion during the meal is primarily business related. You should be fairly conservative in claiming such meals as business deductions. If you deduct a meal with another provider, keep a record of who attended the discussion and what topics were discussed. If you take the parent of a child in your care out for a meal, you can deduct 50% of the amount that you paid for your meal and the parent's meal on line 24b.

Line 25: **Utilities**. Don't enter your home utilities (gas, electricity, water, sewer, garbage, and cable television) here; put them on line 21 of **Form 8829**, where they'll be added to the home expenses you carry over to line 30 of **Schedule C** (see chapter 2).

The utilities expense that remains to be put on line 25 is usually telephone service. You can't claim a business deduction for basic monthly service for the first phone line into your home, even if you only installed the phone as a requirement to be licensed. If your phone bill is charged on a cost-per-minute basis, see line 21 on page 53.

If you install a second phone line and use it exclusively for your business, you can deduct 100% of this expense. If you use a second phone line partly for your business, you can deduct the Time-Space percentage of its cost.

Note: A cell phone is not deductible if it is the first line into your home. If you don't have a landline phone and have only one cell phone line, you cannot deduct any portion of your cell phone use.

You can deduct all other phone-related business expenses, such as long-distance calls, call waiting, an answering machine, and Yellow Pages advertising. If you wish, you can depreciate the cost of buying a phone (as other personal property; see chapter 3).

Schedule C versus Form 8829

Both **Schedule C** and **Form 8829** have lines for utilities, mortgage interest, repairs and maintenance, and insurance, which can give rise to some confusion about where to record certain expenses. The answer is that you should enter all the expenses related to your home on **Form 8829** and only the expenses related to your personal property on **Schedule C**. Here's a guide to which expenses to enter on each form:

Form 8829	Schedule C
Home utilities	Business repairs: toys, lawn mower, furniture, freestanding appliances, etc.
Real estate taxes	Payroll taxes
Mortgage interest	Liability insurance
Renters insurance	Insurance on personal property
Home repairs: furnace, plumbing, electrical, built-in appliances, etc.	Interest from home equity loan used to purchase nonhome items
Home maintenance	
Homeowners insurance	
Home depreciation	

If you run your business out of a building other than your home, don't follow this guide; instead, enter all your expenses for the building in which your business is located on **Schedule C**; you won't fill out **Form 8829** at all, since you don't have a home-based business.

Line 26: **Wages**. Enter any gross wages you paid to employees, including each employee's share of Social Security, Medicare, and any state taxes you have withheld. (For more information about paying employees, see chapter 8.)

Line 27: **Other expenses**. This is the total of the expenses listed on the blank lines in Part V of **Schedule C**. To get this total, go to Part V and list there all your remaining business expense categories, including food, toys, household items, cleaning supplies, and activity expenses (which are all major expenses for most family child care providers). Refer to the *Record-Keeping Guide* for many other kinds of expenses that you might include here. Because of the $2,500 rule (see pages 62–63), many more items may appear here rather than on **Form 4562**. These items could include furniture, appliances, playground equipment, fences, patios, and driveways. You can put them here on Line 27 and call them whatever you want: "$2,500 Property" or "Equipment" or "Household Items" or "Fence." It doesn't matter what you call these expenses. The following are special considerations for toys and gifts:

Toys. The IRS **Child Care Provider Audit Technique Guide** places special emphasis on toy expenses. If a provider is deducting a significant amount for toys, the guide suggests that the auditor investigate whether some of those expenses were really toys for her own children. You should keep receipts for the toys that you purchase for your own children to help prove that your business deduction is reasonable.

Gifts. You can deduct up to $25 per person each year for gifts to the parents of a child in your care. (You must spend the money on gifts to be able to take the deduction.) Any gifts you give to the children themselves may be a gift or it may be an activity expense. If it's an activity expense, there is no $25 per person limitation. A gift is an item that is used by only one child in your care, such as a gift card or clothing. A gift is also a wrapped present that the child opens at her own home and doesn't bring back to your home for the other children to play with it. An activity expense is a present you give to the child in your home who then allows the other children to play with it. It's still an activity even if the child then takes the present home and never returns with it. Don't list activity expenses as "gifts," or the IRS will assume that the $25 rule applies to them; instead, list them as activity expenses.

Line 28: Enter the subtotal of your direct business expenses by adding lines 8 through 27.

Line 29: Enter the total of line 28 minus line 7. This represents your tentative profit before subtracting the expenses for the business use of your home that you entered on **Form 8829**. You must complete **Form 8829** before you can continue with **Schedule C** (see chapter 2).

Line 30: A 2013 rule allows providers to choose between two methods when claiming house expenses. The first method is to claim these expenses from **Form 8829** (enter the amount from line 35). The second method (the Simplified Method) requires no receipts and involves using the following formula: $5 x your Time percentage x the number of square feet you use your home for your business (not to exceed 300 square feet). Almost all providers use at least 300 square feet of their home. Here's an example, if your Time percentage was 40%: $5 x 40% x 300 = $600. Thus, this provider would claim $600 on line 30 of **Schedule C**. She would also be entitled to claim 100% of her property tax and mortgage interest on **Schedule A**, if she itemized. Follow the instructions to **Schedule C** to use this method.

Warning: The vast majority of providers will be better off using their house expenses as shown on **Form 8829**, rather than using the Simplified Method. If you use the Simplified Method and later discover that you would have been better off using your **Form 8829** expenses, you cannot amend your tax return to fix this. Therefore, do not use the Simplified Method unless you have compared it to what you could have claimed using **Form 8829**.

Line 31: Subtract line 30 from line 29. This is your net profit or loss from your business. Enter this amount on **Form 1040 Schedule 1**, line 12, and **Schedule SE**, line 2.

Line 32: If you have a loss on line 31, check box 32a, "All investment is at risk."

Showing a Loss on Schedule C

If you don't show a profit at least three years out of every five, the IRS may look more closely at your tax returns to determine if you're really trying to make a profit. You must be able to show that you're acting in a businesslike manner in a serious effort to make a profit. Most providers won't need to worry about this, but if you only care for children infrequently, you should not try to claim a loss.

The IRS **Child Care Provider Audit Technique Guide** states that it is unusual for a family child care business to show a loss. Although this is an overstatement, if you have a legitimate loss, you should be prepared to defend it with good records.

If you claim regular losses, the IRS may take the position that you could have taken in more children or worked longer hours to make a profit. If it rules that you aren't in business to make a profit, it may reduce your business expenses.

Part III: Cost of Goods Sold

Lines 33–40: Skip this section; it doesn't apply to family child care businesses.

Part IV: Information on Your Vehicle

See the example under the section titled Standard Mileage Rate Method on the following pages for instructions on filling out this section.

Schedule C-EZ versus Schedule C

Small business owners can use the short form **Schedule C-EZ** instead of **Schedule C** if they meet all the following requirements:

- have business expenses of $5,000 or less
- have no employees
- don't have a net business loss
- don't claim automobile depreciation, personal property depreciation, land improvements, or home improvements
- don't claim any expenses for the business use of the home

It's to your advantage as a family child care provider to claim many of the deductions listed above, such as expenses for business use of your home. Therefore, almost every family child care provider will be better off using **Schedule C** instead of **Schedule C-EZ**.

Congratulations!

You have completed the second-most time-consuming tax form (according to the IRS). For most of you, the hard work is done. After calculating your Social Security tax on **Schedule SE**, you'll be ready to fill out **Form 1040** and file your return. If you need to fill out any other tax forms that address issues such as the Earned Income Credit, the sale of your home, or education credits, see the relevant chapters of this book. If you deliver child care out of a building that is not your home, enter all of your home expenses on **Schedule C** (mortgage interest, house depreciation, homeowners insurance, property tax, rent, house repairs, and utilities), not on **Form 8829**.

Vehicle Expenses (Line 9)

There are two ways to calculate the vehicle expenses that you deduct on line 9—the standard mileage rate method and the actual vehicle expenses method. Which method is better for you?

- The standard mileage rate method allows you simply to multiply your business miles by a set rate and claim the result as your deduction. In addition, you can claim the business portion of your vehicle loan interest and personal property tax, as well as your expenses for parking and tolls.
- The actual vehicle expenses method allows you to claim the business portion of all the expenses associated with your vehicle (gas, repairs, insurance, and so on). If you use this method, you must keep all your receipts for those expenses.

Traditionally, most providers have chosen the standard mileage rate over the actual vehicle expenses method, since the record keeping is simpler. Because of the increase in gas prices, however, more providers should consider using the actual vehicle expenses method. You can calculate your business deduction using both methods and use the one that offers the higher deduction.

If you are now considering using the actual vehicle expenses method, you should try hard to save all your receipts for vehicle expenses. You may be able to reconstruct some of these records; for example, if you bought gas with a credit card, save the copies of your credit card statements that show this. If you bought gas with cash, divide the miles you have driven by your car's average miles per gallon to calculate how many gallons of gas you have used. Then reconstruct what you spent by multiplying the number of gallons by the average price of gas over that period.

If you used the standard mileage rate method in 2019, you can switch to the actual vehicle expenses method in 2020. If you used the actual vehicle expenses method in the first year you used your vehicle for your business, you can't switch to the standard mileage rate method in later years. If you used the standard mileage rate in the first year you used your vehicle for your business, you can switch to the actual vehicle expenses method in later years. (After you change to the actual vehicle expenses method, you must use straight-line depreciation on your vehicle; see chapter 3. If you lease a vehicle, you cannot switch methods after the first year, no matter which method you use.)

Whichever method you use, you will need to track all your business miles, even if you use the vehicle 100% for business purposes. To track your business trips, refer to records such as receipts, canceled checks, credit card statements, field trip permission forms, training certificates, and calendar notations, or keep a mileage log. (The *Family Child Care Mileage-Keeper* makes it easy to record your mileage.)

If the Vehicle Isn't Registered in Your Name

If you are married, you can claim business expenses for both your vehicle and your spouse's vehicle, even if your name isn't on the vehicle registration.

If you aren't married and use a vehicle that isn't registered to you, you can't claim vehicle expenses for that vehicle. For example, if you use your boyfriend's vehicle, you can't claim any expenses for it, even if he drives it for your business trips.

If you pay your boyfriend for the use of his vehicle or to make a business trip for you, you can deduct these expenses as rent on **Schedule C**, line 20a, and your boyfriend will have to report this payment as income on line 21 of his **Form 1040**. The same is true if you pay anyone else for the use of a vehicle.

Is the Trip Business or Personal?

To determine the vehicle expenses you have incurred for your business, you need to decide which trips are deductible and which aren't. If you take a trip that involves both business and personal activities, you may still deduct the entire mileage as a business expense if the trip is primarily for business purposes.

What if you take a trip to the grocery store and buy both business and personal groceries? That can be the hardest kind of trip to judge, and there's no firm rule about whether you can deduct the mileage. The only rule is that if the trip was primarily to buy business groceries, you can deduct it as a business trip. Some factors that might make the trip a business expense include the following:

- You purchased more business than personal groceries.
- You spent more time shopping for business items than for personal items.
- You made other separate personal trips to the grocery store; this trip was for regular business shopping.

IRS Child Care Provider Audit Technique Guide on Car Expenses

The guide says that if there is a business destination and a personal destination in one trip that only the round trip miles to and from the business destination are deductible. For example, if a provider drove 5 miles to point A (business purpose) and then 3 miles to point B (personal purpose) and then 4 miles home she could count 10 miles as business miles (the round-trip miles to and from point A).

The Standard Mileage Rate Method

The standard mileage rate is $0.575 per business mile for 2020. In addition to your mileage, you may also deduct the following:

- parking fees and tolls
- bus, subway, and train fares for business trips
- any casualty or theft losses on your vehicle
- the business percentage of the interest payments on your vehicle loan
- the business percentage of the local personal property tax on your vehicle

Some tax preparers and IRS auditors are unaware that you are entitled to claim these last two deductions even when you're using the standard mileage rate. (See IRS **Publication 463** for a clear statement of this rule.)

When you use the standard mileage rate method, you need to keep adequate records of how many miles you have driven your vehicle for business. Here's how to calculate your deduction using the standard mileage rate method:

Step One

Go through your business records for last year and write down the destination of every trip you took for your business. Look through your checkbook receipts and calendar for evidence of business trips. If you took more than one trip to the same destination (grocery store, bank, and so on), count the number of trips to each destination.

Step Two

Determine the number of miles to each destination. Try to make a habit of recording your trip mileage as you make trips throughout the year. If you haven't done this, use an internet mapping service (such as MapQuest or Google Maps) to find the length of the trip (or drive to the destination again and record the mileage).

Step Three

Multiply the mileage to and from each destination by the number of trips you took to each destination last year. Add the miles together for all the destinations, and multiply the total by the standard mileage rate, which will give you your business-mileage deduction. Here's an example:

Al's Grocery Store	3 miles	x	48 trips	=	144 miles
First Bank	2 miles	x	60 trips	=	120 miles
Como Park	5 miles	x	12 trips	=	60 miles
Tots Toy Store	4 miles	x	10 trips	=	40 miles
Safeway Grocery Store	5 miles	x	40 trips	=	200 miles
Other trips (list)					266 miles
Total miles					830 miles

830 miles (Jan 1–Dec 31) x $0.575 = $477.25

Step Four

Add to the Step Three total any parking fees, tolls, or bus, subway, or train fares you paid while conducting business activities, and enter the total on **Schedule C**, line 9. Keep records showing how you calculated these amounts. If you drive more than one vehicle, you can claim the business mileage rate for both vehicles. Enter any expenses for renting or leasing a vehicle on **Schedule C**, line 20a.

The advantage of the standard mileage rate method is that you don't have to remember to record your mileage every time you take a business trip. Your check stubs, receipts, or notes on your calendar constitute evidence that a trip was taken. To make your record keeping easier, remember to record the odometer reading on your vehicle on January 1 of each year. Once you have measured the mileage to and from each destination, you can use that mileage number forever.

If you use the standard mileage rate method, you can't deduct the cost of vehicle insurance (even for a separate business policy) or vehicle repairs (even if the damage results from using the vehicle for business). To deduct these expenses, you must use the actual vehicle expenses method. When you use the standard mileage rate method, fill out **Schedule C**, Part IV, only if you don't have any depreciation expenses to show on **Form 4562**. Otherwise, fill out **Form 4562**, Part V, Section B, instead of **Schedule C**, Part IV.

Enter the date you first began using your vehicle for your business on line 43 of **Schedule C**. Enter the total business miles you drove last year on line 44a. (This may include mileage from more than one vehicle.) Don't enter anything under Commuting on line 44b. Put your personal vehicle miles on line 44c. Answer yes on line 45 if you use your car for personal purposes. Line 46 asks if your family had another vehicle available

Part IV **Information on Your Vehicle.** Complete this part **only** if you are claiming car or truck expenses on line 9 and are not required to file Form 4562 for this business. See the instructions for line 13 to find out if you must file Form 4562.

43 When did you place your vehicle in service for business purposes? (month/day/year) ▶ 1 / 1 / 2020

44 Of the total number of miles you drove your vehicle during 2020, enter the number of miles you used your vehicle for:

a Business 800 **b** Commuting (see instructions) ______ **c** Other 11,000

45 Was your vehicle available for personal use during off-duty hours? ☑ **Yes** ☐ **No**

46 Do you (or your spouse) have another vehicle available for personal use?. ☑ **Yes** ☐ **No**

47a Do you have evidence to support your deduction? ☑ **Yes** ☐ **No**

b If "Yes," is the evidence written? ☑ **Yes** ☐ **No**

for personal use. Answer yes to this question unless you don't have a second car. If you have kept records of the business use of your vehicle, answer yes to lines 47a and 47b.

You can use the standard mileage rate method even if you are operating more than one vehicle in your business. This is true whether or not you and your spouse are using each of your vehicles at the same time for business purposes. If you used more than one vehicle in your business during the year, report your business miles on **Form 4562** (lines 30–36), not on **Schedule C**.

Selling a Vehicle Used in Your Business

To report the sale of a vehicle used in your business, fill out **Form 4797 Sales of Business Property** (see chapter 11). If you sell a vehicle after using the standard mileage rate method for business expenses, you must reduce the business basis of the vehicle by a certain amount for every mile you drove for business purposes. This amount varies according to the year the vehicle was used. For 2020 it's $0.27 per mile. This means that if you drove your vehicle 10,000 business miles last year, your gain from selling it will be raised by $2,700 (10,000 miles x $0.27).

The Actual Vehicle Expenses Method

Under this method you can deduct the business portion of the following:

- gasoline, oil, antifreeze, and windshield wiper fluid
- tires, repairs, tune-ups, car washes, and waxes
- vehicle insurance, vehicle loan interest payments, and lease payments
- vehicle depreciation
- garage rent
- personal property tax on the vehicle and vehicle license fees
- membership in automobile clubs
- casualty or theft losses on the vehicle
- other actual vehicle expenses

In addition, you can still deduct your parking fees, tolls, and bus, subway, and train fares, as you can under the standard mileage rate method. Here's how to calculate your deduction using the actual vehicle expenses method:

STEP ONE

First, calculate the actual business-use percentage for each vehicle by dividing the number of business miles you drove the vehicle that year by the total miles you drove it that year. For example, if you drove your vehicle 12,875 miles, and 1,875 of those miles were for your business, your business use would be 15% (1,875 ÷ 12,875 = 15%).

STEP TWO

List all your actual expenses for all the vehicle expenses listed above (gasoline, oil, antifreeze, and so on). Make sure you have records for all the expenses you claim. Add up your vehicle expenses, and multiply the total by your business-use percentage. In the example below, the vehicle expenses total $1,550, and the vehicle deduction is $432.50.

Gasoline	$175.00	
Oil	$20.00	
Repairs	$205.00	
Insurance	$700.00	
Taxes and license	$100.00	
Vehicle loan interest	$350.00	
	$1,550.00 x 15% =	$232.50
Additional business vehicle insurance ($200 x 100%)		$200.00
Vehicle deduction		$432.50

STEP THREE

Add to the total from step two any parking fees, tolls, or bus, subway, or train fares you paid while conducting business activities, and enter the total on **Schedule C**, line 9. Keep the records showing how you calculated these amounts. Enter any expenses for renting or leasing a vehicle on **Schedule C**, line 20a (rent or lease of vehicle).

STEP FOUR

In addition to claiming your actual expenses, this method allows you to take a depreciation deduction for your vehicle. Claim this depreciation on **Form 4562**, Part V, Section B, not on **Schedule C**, Part IV. You will transfer the depreciation expense on **Form 4562** to **Schedule C**, line 13 (see chapter 3 for instructions on how to depreciate your vehicle).

Leasing versus Owning

For a leased vehicle, you can choose between the standard mileage rate method and the actual vehicle expenses method, even if you used the actual vehicle expenses method for the vehicle in earlier years. If your vehicle lease is actually a purchase contract and you want to claim the cost of the purchase contract by depreciating your vehicle, you must use the actual vehicle expenses method.

To use the standard mileage rate method for a leased vehicle, follow the rules described in this chapter. This method doesn't allow you to claim any portion of the cost of the lease. Once you start using the standard mileage rate method for a leased vehicle, you must continue to use it for the remainder of the lease term.

To use the actual vehicle expenses method for a leased vehicle, follow the rules described in this chapter. Calculate your business-use percentage, and apply it against your actual expenses (lease payments, gasoline, insurance, and any other expenses).

If the fair market value of a vehicle you leased in 2020 is more than $50,000 ($50,500 for a truck or van), you must include as income on **Schedule C**, line 6, a small amount for each year that you lease the vehicle (see IRS **Publication 463 Travel, Entertainment, Gift, and Car Expenses** for tables).

In general, you're better off purchasing a vehicle than leasing it. The benefits of leasing are that you get to drive a newer (and usually more expensive) vehicle than if you own one; however, leasing is usually more expensive than buying, and at the end of the lease period you must return the vehicle.

Should You and Your Spouse File Two Schedule Cs?

If you and your spouse work side by side caring for children, you have the option of each of you filing your own **Schedule C** and splitting the income and expenses.

Why would you do this? Because by doing so, your spouse could show a profit that could help him or her earn higher Social Security benefits. IRS rules allow a married couple in this situation to split the profit, pay Social Security taxes under both their names, and thus spread the future Social Security benefits between the two of them. This can be done without the couple filing as a partnership.

To do this, the two spouses should each file a separate **Schedule C**. They should split the income and expenses on these two forms and each pay Social Security taxes under their own names. This will not increase the total Social Security taxes they will pay. The two should split the income and expenses according to the amount of work they perform for the business. A spouse who works two hours a week doing the record keeping should not claim 50% of the income and expenses.

Warning

The reason to file two **Schedule C**s for one business is to allow the spouse to contribute more to his or her Social Security account and, later, earn higher benefits. However, before you take this action, I strongly recommend that you find out the long-term impact on the Social Security benefits for both you and your spouse.

Social Security rules are complex. You qualify to receive Social Security benefits by working for at least 10 years and earning enough income each of those years. If your spouse also works, you both can receive Social Security benefits. If your spouse dies, you can receive some of his or her benefits. Depending on how much you and your spouse have earned over the years, it may be more beneficial to have future earnings credited to your spouse.

To find out the impact of crediting the profit from your business to you alone or splitting it between you and your spouse, use the Social Security Retirement Estimator at www.socialsecurity.gov. Talk to someone at your local Social Security office if either of you are within five years of retiring. They can answer your questions to help you make the best decision.

Other Considerations

You can file two separate **Schedule C**s only if you are married under state law (including same-sex couples) and filing jointly. Unmarried couples cannot do this. You cannot do this if you are a Limited Liability Company (LLC) or a corporation.

If you do this, parents can still pay you, and, therefore, your husband does not need to obtain his own EIN. You don't have to put your husband's name on your child care license or contract. You don't have to change how you operate your program. You can stop filing two separate **Schedule C**s in future years if you want to.

For more information about the tax issues discussed in this chapter, refer to the related topics in the other chapters of this book and the Redleaf Press *Family Child Care Record-Keeping Guide*.

CHAPTER 6

Completing Your Tax Return

A significant change in IRS **Form 1040** affects all family child care providers. The form is shorter but not necessarily less complicated to fill out. This chapter explains how to fill out the remaining tax forms that most family child care providers are likely to need to complete their tax returns. It covers the following:

- **Schedule SE**, which you use to show how much self-employment tax you owe
- **Schedule EIC**, which you use to claim the Earned Income Credit
- **Form 8863**, which you use to claim education credits
- **Form 1040**, to which you transfer the amounts from your business tax forms to finish your individual tax return
- **Form 1040-ES**, which you use to estimate your quarterly taxes for the next tax year
- **Form 8995**, Qualified Business Income Deduction Simplified Computation

You may also need to fill out other tax forms, especially if you are affected by one of the special situations described in Part III; however, the forms covered in this chapter represent the remaining forms that most family child care providers will need to file for a normal tax year.

Note: A new rule allows providers to reduce their federal taxable income by 20% of either their profit or their family's taxable income, whichever is lower. See pages 129–130.

Filing an Extension

If you need more time to file your tax return, you can file for an extension. This may be helpful if you need more time to calculate your depreciation, sort your records, or deal with a family emergency; however, filing for an extension doesn't give you more time to pay your taxes. Your taxes are due on April 15. If at that time you aren't sure how much you'll owe, pay what you estimate you'll owe. If you underestimate this amount, you will owe interest on the taxes that you didn't pay on April 15.

You may file for an automatic extension of your tax return until October 15. The old rules allowed an automatic extension of four months and a second extension of two more months only after IRS approval. The new rules allow you to automatically extend the deadline for filing your tax return by six months. (There is no further extension after this.)

To get this extension, file **Form 4868 Application for Automatic Extension of Time to File U.S. Individual Income Tax Return**.

Self-Employment Tax: Schedule SE

This section explains how to fill out **Schedule SE Self-Employment Tax**. This form shows how much Social Security tax, if any, you owe for operating your business. Before you can complete it, you will have to fill out **Form 4562**, **Schedule C**, and **Form 8829**. A blank copy of **Schedule SE** is included in the tax forms in Part V of this book.

Self-employment tax is the tax that entitles you to Social Security benefits. If you have a net profit of $400 or more on **Schedule C**, line 31, you must pay this self-employment tax. If you're self-employed and have more than one business, you must pay this tax if you have a combined net profit of $400 or more for all your businesses.

If your spouse is self-employed, you owe self-employment tax only if the $400 threshold is met by each of your businesses. For example, if your net self-employment income is $300 and your spouse's net self-employment income is $20,000, then you don't have to pay self-employment tax and fill out **Schedule SE**, but your spouse does. (It doesn't matter if you're filing jointly or separately.)

Your Social Security benefits are based partly on the Social Security taxes you pay. To receive Social Security benefits, you or your spouse must pay into the Social Security fund. If you haven't worked much outside the home, you can make sure that you'll qualify for Social Security by paying self-employment tax.

Plan for Retirement

When you claim all your allowable deductions, you reduce your taxable income and Social Security taxes, which may result in lower Social Security benefits when you retire. To offset this, save money for retirement by investing in IRAs or other investment plans.

How to Fill Out Schedule SE

Since almost all child care providers can use the short version of the **Schedule SE** form, this chapter will describe only the short form. (See the note at the end of this section.)

Line 1: Leave blank.

Line 2: Enter your net profit from **Schedule C**, line 31.

Line 3: Enter the amount from line 2.

Line 4: Enter the total of line 3 multiplied by 92.35% (0.9235). If this amount is less than $400 or if you have a net loss from **Schedule C**, don't fill out the rest of **Schedule SE**.

Line 5: Enter the total of line 4 multiplied by 15.3% (0.153). This represents your self-employment tax. Enter this amount on **Schedule 4 Form 1040**, line 57. If line 4 is more than $137,700 see the instructions.

Line 6: Multiply line 5 by 50% and enter the result on **Schedule 4 Form 1040**, line 27.

You can deduct more than half of your self-employment tax from your income on **Schedule 1 Form 1040**, line 14, as an adjustment to your income. For example, if your self-employment tax is $1,000, put this amount on **Schedule 1 Form 1040**, line 14. This reduces your taxable income by $575.10. If you are in the 25% tax bracket, it would reduce your taxes by $144 ($575.10 x 25%).

SCHEDULE SE (Form 1040) — **Self-Employment Tax** — OMB No. 1545-0074 — **2020**

Department of the Treasury Internal Revenue Service (99)

▶ Go to *www.irs.gov/ScheduleSE* for instructions and the latest information.
▶ Attach to Form 1040, 1040-SR, or 1040-NR.

Attachment Sequence No. **17**

Name of person with self-employment income (as shown on Form 1040, 1040-SR, or 1040-NR): AMANDA WILSON

Social security number of person with **self-employment** income ▶ 123-56-6789

Part I Self-Employment Tax

Note: If your only income subject to self-employment tax is **church employee income,** see instructions for how to report your income and the definition of church employee income.

A If you are a minister, member of a religious order, or Christian Science practitioner **and** you filed Form 4361, but you had $400 or more of **other** net earnings from self-employment, check here and continue with Part I ▶ ☐

Skip lines 1a and 1b if you use the farm optional method in Part II. See instructions.

1a	Net farm profit or (loss) from Schedule F, line 34, and farm partnerships, Schedule K-1 (Form 1065), box 14, code A			1a	
b	If you received social security retirement or disability benefits, enter the amount of Conservation Reserve Program payments included on Schedule F, line 4b, or listed on Schedule K-1 (Form 1065), box 20, code AH			1b	( )
	Skip line 2 if you use the nonfarm optional method in Part II. See instructions.				
2	Net profit or (loss) from Schedule C, line 31; and Schedule K-1 (Form 1065), box 14, code A (other than farming). See instructions for other income to report or if you are a minister or member of a religious order			2	$1,000
3	Combine lines 1a, 1b, and 2			3	$1,000
4a	If line 3 is more than zero, multiply line 3 by 92.35% (0.9235). Otherwise, enter amount from line 3			4a	
	Note: If line 4a is less than $400 due to Conservation Reserve Program payments on line 1b, see instructions.				
b	If you elect one or both of the optional methods, enter the total of lines 15 and 17 here			4b	
c	Combine lines 4a and 4b. If less than $400, **stop;** you don't owe self-employment tax. **Exception:** If less than $400 and you had **church employee income,** enter -0- and continue ▶			4c	$923.50
5a	Enter your **church employee income** from Form W-2. See instructions for definition of church employee income	5a			
b	Multiply line 5a by 92.35% (0.9235). If less than $100, enter -0-			5b	
6	Add lines 4c and 5b			6	
7	Maximum amount of combined wages and self-employment earnings subject to social security tax or the 6.2% portion of the 7.65% railroad retirement (tier 1) tax for 2020			7	137,700
8a	Total social security wages and tips (total of boxes 3 and 7 on Form(s) W-2) and railroad retirement (tier 1) compensation. If $137,700 or more, skip lines 8b through 10, and go to line 11	8a			
b	Unreported tips subject to social security tax from Form 4137, line 10	8b			
c	Wages subject to social security tax from Form 8919, line 10	8c			
d	Add lines 8a, 8b, and 8c			8d	
9	Subtract line 8d from line 7. If zero or less, enter -0- here and on line 10 and go to line 11 ▶			9	
10	Multiply the **smaller** of line 6 or line 9 by 12.4% (0.124)			10	
11	Multiply line 6 by 2.9% (0.029)			11	
12	**Self-employment tax.** Add lines 10 and 11. Enter here and on **Schedule 2 (Form 1040), line 4**			12	$141.30
13	**Deduction for one-half of self-employment tax.** Multiply line 12 by 50% (0.50). Enter here and on **Schedule 1 (Form 1040), line 14**	13	$70.65		

Education Credits: Form 8863

If you or any members of your family attend a postsecondary school, even for just one class, you may be able to take advantage of the Lifetime Learning Credit or the American Opportunity Credit. Postsecondary schools include community colleges, vocational education schools, colleges, universities, and any U.S. institution eligible to participate in the Department of Education student aid program. You can't claim both of these credits for the same student in the same year.

The Lifetime Learning Credit

The Lifetime Learning Credit is for those who take a class at a postsecondary school, such as a class to obtain a Child Development Associate (CDA) credential. (The class does not have to be about family child care to be eligible for the credit.) The tax credit is 20% of up to $10,000 of tuition and related expenses incurred during the last year.

Unrelated expenses include books, meals, lodging, student activities, athletics, transportation, insurance, and personal living expenses.

To be eligible for this credit, your adjusted gross income must be less than $138,000 (if you're married and filing jointly) or $69,000 (if you're single). The credit is phased out when your adjusted gross income is between $118,000 and $138,000 (married filing jointly) or between $59,000 and $69,000 (single). There is a $2,000 maximum credit per family (you, your spouse, and your child). You don't need to be enrolled for any minimum amount of time or be trying to earn a degree.

American Opportunity Credit (Formerly the Hope Credit)

This credit covers the first four years of postsecondary education and is a refundable maximum tax credit of $2,500. To be eligible, your adjusted gross income must be less than $180,000 (married filing jointly) or $90,000 (all others). Education expenses that are eligible for this credit include tuition, fees, and course materials (books, supplies, and equipment). Students must be enrolled at least half-time.

To claim these credits, fill out **Form 8863 Education Credits**. Enter the amount of your credit from this form onto **Form 1040**, line 18c.

Caution about Education Credits

You should use these tax credits for courses that aren't related to family child care or for classes that are taken by other members of your family. If you're taking workshops or classes that are related to your business at a postsecondary school, it's better to claim your education costs as a direct business expense on **Schedule C** rather than using these tax credits.

For example, if you spend $100 on a child care workshop, claim it as a business deduction on **Schedule C**; if you are in the 12% bracket, you would save about $27 (12% income tax and 15% Social Security tax). If you are in the 24% bracket, you would save about $39 (24% income tax and 15% Social Security tax). On the other hand, if you used the Lifetime Learning Credit, your savings would be only $20 ($100 x 20% credit = $20).

You can't use the Lifetime Learning Credit for the $20 and claim the other $80 as a business deduction.

The Earned Income Credit: Schedule EIC

This section covers how to claim the Earned Income Credit using **Schedule EIC Earned Income Credit**. The Earned Income Credit is designed to help low-income families reduce their taxes. You don't have to spend any money on child care for your own children to be eligible for this credit. When you claim this credit, you will subtract the credit from the taxes you owe. Read the **Form 1040** instructions to determine if you are eligible for this credit. Here are the income eligibility limits and maximum benefits for 2020:

	Maximum Income		Maximum
Family Type	**Single or Head of Household**	**Married Filing Jointly**	**Benefit**
Families with 1 child	$41,756	$47,646	$3,584
Families with 2 children	$47,440	$53,330	$5,920
Families with 3 or more children	$50,954	$56,844	$6,660
Workers (25–64) without children	$15,820	$21,710	$538

Eligibility for the Earned Income Credit is based on your family's adjusted gross income, which is the amount on your **Form 1040**, line 8b. This amount includes your net income from **Schedule C**, line 31, any earned income from **Form 1040**, lines 1–7, and any money you received from a military housing allowance. You no longer need to add to this any nontaxable employee compensation, such as contributions to 401(k) retirement plans.

A child must meet all three of the following criteria to be eligible for this credit:

1. The child must be your son, daughter, adopted child, grandchild, stepchild, or eligible foster child. A brother, sister, stepbrother, or stepsister (or the child or grandchild of your brother, sister, stepbrother, or stepsister) may also be a qualifying child if you care for this individual as you would for your own child. A foster child is a child you care for as if she were your own child.
2. The child must be either under age 19 at the end of last year, under age 24 and a full-time student, or any age and permanently and totally disabled.
3. The child must have lived with you for more than six months last year (unless the child was born last year). If a foster child, he or she must have lived with you for more than half the year.

You can file under any filing status except married filing a separate return. You must provide a correct Social Security number for each child, as well as for yourself and your spouse. You can apply for a Social Security number by filing **Form SS-5** with your local Social Security Administration office. It takes about two weeks to receive a number. If you don't have the number by April 15, you can request an automatic extension (**Form 4868**) to October 15, but you must still pay your taxes by April 15. Or you can file your taxes without **Schedule EIC** and file an amended return (**Form 1040X**) after you receive the Social Security number.

How to Fill Out Schedule EIC

If you meet the above qualifications, you can either figure out the credit yourself or have the IRS do it for you. If you have a qualifying child and you want the IRS to figure out your credit, complete and attach **Schedule EIC** to your tax return. Proceed as follows:

- Instead of calculating the amount for line 18a on **Form 1040**, simply write "EIC" in that space.
- If you want to figure the credit yourself, use worksheet B in the instructions for **Form 1040** to determine your credit. Enter the credit amount on **Form 1040**, line 18a. Don't attach the worksheet to your return, but do keep it with your tax records. If you have a qualifying child, you must fill out **Schedule EIC** and file it with **Form 1040**.

Fraudulent Claims for the Earned Income Credit

Some taxpayers discover that if they lower some of their expenses on Form 8829 or **Schedule C**, they will be eligible for a higher EIC that would offset the taxes on their higher business profit. However, the IRS does not allow this. You may not adjust your expenses to claim a higher EIC.

If you make a fraudulent or reckless claim for the Earned Income Credit, you won't be entitled to receive it for either two years (if the IRS finds that you intentionally disregarded the rules) or ten years (if the IRS finds that you made a fraudulent claim).

IRS COMPLIANCE FORM TO PREVENT FRAUD

To reduce fraud, the IRS has begun a pilot program that uses **Form 8836 Qualifying Children Residency Statement** to certify that a child lived with a parent for more than half the year. This proof involves the signature of a child care provider, clergy, employer, health-care provider, landlord, school official, social service agency official, Indian tribal official, or community-based organization official who can certify where the child lived.

Although you can sign a parent's form, if you claim the EIC for your own child, you can't ask a parent of one of the children in your care to sign your form, since they aren't authorized to do so.

Other Tax Credits

Child Tax Credit

You may be eligible to claim the child tax credit for expenses associated with paying someone to care for your own child while you are working. This can be the case when you attend a training workshop or conference and have someone watch your child. It can also apply if you send your child to a preschool program while you are caring for child care children. To qualify for this tax credit, you must meet these tests:

- Your child must be age 12 or younger.
- The care must be provided while you are working. If you are married, your spouse must also be working during the time the care is provided.
- You cannot pay your spouse, the parent of the child, someone you can claim as a dependent, or your own child who is under age 19.
- Your child must have lived with you for more than half of the year.

The maximum amount of child care expenses you can claim for one child is $3,000 ($6,000 for two or more). The tax credit can be up to 35%, depending on your adjusted gross income.

For more information, see IRS **Publication 503 Child and Dependent Care Expenses**, and IRS **Form 2441 Child and Dependent Care Expenses**. Claim the credit on **Form 1040 Schedule 3**, line 2.

Saver's Credit

If you are a low-income taxpayer, you may be eligible to receive a tax credit for any contributions you have made to an IRA—a 401(k), traditional IRA, Roth IRA, Simplified Employee Pension (SEP), or SIMPLE IRA. This credit is in addition to the tax deductibility of the IRA contribution. If you are married filing jointly, your adjusted gross income must be less than $65,000 to qualify for this credit. If you are single, the income limit is $32,500. The tax credit ranges from 10% to 50% of an IRA contribution up to $2,000. To claim this credit, fill out **Form 8880 Credit for Qualified Retirement Savings Contribution**, and then put the credit amount on **Form 1040 Schedule 3**, line 4.

If you made a contribution to an IRA between 2017 and 2019 and did not claim this credit, you can still file an amended tax return (see chapter 9) this year and get a refund.

Completing Your Tax Return: Form 1040

This section explains how to enter the information from your child care tax forms onto your **Form 1040**. (There's a blank copy of **Form 1040** and the new schedules in Part V of this book.) You must fill out **Form 1040** rather than short **Form 1040A** or **1040EZ** because you are reporting income (or loss) from **Schedule C**. You must complete all your business tax forms before you can fill out **Form 1040**. The earlier chapters in this book have covered the business forms that you need to file along with **Form 1040**. Work carefully and make sure you transfer the numbers accurately from one form to another, as follows:

- Enter your depreciation expenses from **Form 4562** on **Schedule C**, line 13.
- Enter your home expenses from **Form 8829** on **Schedule C**, line 30.
- Enter your net profit (if any) from **Schedule C** on **Schedule SE**, line 2.

Once you have completed these business forms and your other personal tax forms (such as **Schedule A**, if you itemize), you're ready to begin filling out **Form 1040.**

The new Form 1040 looks different than it did before 2019! You must fill out a number of new schedules before completing the form.

Form 1040

Line 1: Enter any wages from your spouse or wages you earned outside of child care.

Line 7a: Enter amounts from **Schedule 1**, line 9 (see below).

Line 8a: Enter amounts from **Schedule 1**, line 22 (see below).

Line 9: Enter your standard deduction ($12,400 single or $24,800 married filing jointly).

Line 10: Enter your qualified business income deduction from **Form 8995** (see below).

Line 13a: Enter any eligible amounts for the child tax credit (see page 127).

Line 18a: Enter any eligible amounts for the Earned Income Credit (see pages 125–126).

Now let's look at the three new schedules for **Form 1040**.

Schedule 1 Additional Income and Adjustments to Income

Line 3: Report your profit from **Schedule C**, line 31 here.

Line 4: Report any capital gains or losses from **Form 4797** here (see chapter 11).

Line 14: Report one-half of your Social Security/Medicare tax form from **Schedule SE**, line 6 here.

Line 15: Report any contributions to a SEP or SIMPLE IRA plan here.

Line 16: If you aren't eligible to receive health insurance through an employer (usually your spouse's employer) and you buy health insurance for yourself, you can claim 100% of the insurance premium here. You may claim this deduction even if the health insurance isn't purchased in your name. You aren't eligible for this deduction if you qualify for insurance through your spouse's employer and choose not to purchase it. You also aren't eligible if you receive payments under COBRA. If you are eligible to claim this health insurance deduction, it can't exceed your net income on **Schedule C**, line 31.

Line 19: Report any contributions to a deductible IRA (not a SEP, SIMPLE, or Roth IRA) here. Enter the total from line 22 of this schedule onto **Form 1040**, line 6 (Total income). If you entered any amounts on lines 23–33 from this schedule, enter the amount from line 36 onto **Form 1040**, line 8a.

Schedule 2 Additional Taxes

Line 4: Enter your self-employment tax (Social Security/Medicare tax) from **Schedule SE**, line 5.

Schedule 3 Additional Credits and Payments

Line 2: Report any amounts eligible for the child and dependent credit. This is explained on page 132. Enter amounts from **Form 2441** if you are eligible.

Line 3: Enter any amounts for education credits from **Form 8863**. This is explained on pages 124–125.

Line 4: If you made a contribution to an IRA and were eligible for the Saver's Credit, enter your credit amount here. See page 127.

Line 5: If you are eligible for any residential energy credits, enter the amount from **Form 5695** here.

Line 7: Enter the totals from lines 1–6 on Form 1040, line 13b.

Line 8: Enter any 2020 estimated tax payments and amount applied from your 2019 return here.

Line 14: Enter the totals from lines 8–13 onto **Form 1040**, line 18d.

In summary, all providers must fill out **Schedule 1** and **Schedule 2**. Depending on your circumstances, you may have to fill out **Schedule 3**.

Standard Deduction vs. Itemized Deduction

All providers can reduce their federal taxable income by the higher of a standard deduction or itemized deductions on **Schedule A**. For 2020 the standard deduction has risen. If you are single, it rises from $12,200 (2019) to $12,400 (2020), and if you are married, from $24,400 to $24,800. This means that many more providers will find it beneficial to claim the standard deduction, rather than itemizing using **Schedule A**. **Schedule A** is where providers claimed the personal portion of their property tax and mortgage interest (as well as other personal expenses). **If you itemized in previous years and now claim the standard deduction, you will not lose the ability to claim the business portion of your property tax and mortgage interest on Form 8829 Expenses for Business Use of Your Home.**

Qualified Business Income Deduction

Perhaps the biggest change on **Form 1040** now allows providers to reduce their federal taxable income by 20% of the lower of their adjusted gross income or family's taxable income. Note: This rule does not affect your Social Security/Medicare tax or your state income tax (if any).

You are eligible to take advantage of this rule if your family's adjusted gross income is less than $163,300 (single) or $326,600 (married, filing jointly). If you make more than this, the deduction is subject to some limitations. You are not eligible for this rule if you are incorporated as a C corporation. Your adjusted gross income is on **Form 1040**, line 8b.

Your profit is found on **Schedule C**, line 31. If you have a loss on **Schedule C**, you aren't eligible for the Qualified Business Income Deduction. You would carry over any loss to your 2021 tax return to see if you would be eligible for this deduction in 2021. If your spouse is also self-employed or is incorporated (other than a C corporation) or in a partnership, you must net your business income. So if your spouse is self-employed and has a profit of $40,000 and your profit is $30,000, your joint profit is $70,000, which you would compare to your family's taxable income.

Here's how to calculate your qualified business income deduction. Note: I'm using a simple example and avoiding other tax issues, such as sale of property, retirement contributions, and health insurance deductions. Enter your profit from **Schedule C**, line 31, onto IRS **Form 1040 Schedule 1**, line 3. Then transfer this amount to IRS **Form 1040**, line 7a. If you are married, enter your spouse's income on **Form 1040**, line 1. Next, enter half of your Social Security/Medicare tax from **Form 1040 Schedule 1**, line 14, to **Form 1040**, line 8a. Subtract line 8a from line 7a. The result on line 8b is your family's adjusted gross income.

Enter your standard deduction of either $12,400 (single) or $24,800 (married filing jointly) on **Form 1040**, line 9.

Line 10 represents your qualified business income deduction. To calculate this number you will need to fill out the new IRS **Form 9885 Qualified Business Income Deduction Simplified Computation**. This new form for 2019 will tell you to compare two numbers and use the lower of the two. The first number is your business profit multiplied by 20%. The second number is your family's adjusted gross income (line 8b) minus your standard deduction and then multiplied by 20%. Put the lower of these two numbers on **Form 1040**, line 10. This is your qualified business income deduction.

Let's look at an example.

You are single and your business profit is $40,000. One-half of your Social Security/ Medicare tax is $2,826. Your standard deduction is $12,400.

First number: $40,000 x 20% = $8,000.

Second number: $40,000 – $2,826 – $12,400 = $24,774 x 20% = $4,955

The lower of these two numbers is $4,955, and that's your qualified business income deduction.

Here's how **Form 1040** and **Form 8995** would be filled out using this example:

Form 1040 Schedule 1

Line 3: $40,000 business profit

Line 9: $40,000 transfer to **Form 1040**, line 7a

Line 14: $2,826 half of your Social Security/Medicare tax

Line 22: $2,826 transfer to **Form 1040**, line 8a

Form 1040

Line 7a: $40,000

Line 7b: $40,000

Line 8a: $2,826

Line 8b: $40,000 – $2,826 = $37,174 adjusted gross income

Line 9: $12,400 standard deduction

Line 10: $4,995 based on filling out **Form 8995**

Form 8995

Lines 1, 2, and 4: $40,000 business profit

Line 5: $40,000 x 20% = $8,000

Lines 6–9: Zero

Line 10: $8,000

Line 11: $37,174 adjusted gross income – $12,400 standard deduction = $24,774

Line 13: $24,774

Line 14: $24,774 x 20% = $4,955

Compare line 5 ($8,000) with line 14 ($4,955) and transfer the lower number to **Form 1040**, line 10.

Form **1040** Department of the Treasury—Internal Revenue Service (99) **U.S. Individual Income Tax Return** **2020** OMB No. 1545-0074 IRS Use Only—Do not write or staple in this space.

Filing Status Check only one box. ☐ Single ☐ Married filing jointly ☐ Married filing separately (MFS) ☐ Head of household (HOH) ☐ Qualifying widow(er) (QW)
If you checked the MFS box, enter the name of your spouse. If you checked the HOH or QW box, enter the child's name if the qualifying person is a child but not your dependent ▶

Your first name and middle initial	Last name	**Your social security number**
If joint return, spouse's first name and middle initial	Last name	**Spouse's social security number**

Home address (number and street). If you have a P.O. box, see instructions.	Apt. no.	**Presidential Election Campaign** Check here if you, or your spouse if filing jointly, want $3 to go to this fund. Checking a box below will not change your tax or refund. ☐ You ☐ Spouse
City, town, or post office. If you have a foreign address, also complete spaces below.	State / ZIP code	
Foreign country name	Foreign province/state/county / Foreign postal code	

At any time during 2020, did you receive, sell, send, exchange, or otherwise acquire any financial interest in any virtual currency? ☐ Yes ☐ No

Standard Deduction **Someone can claim:** ☐ You as a dependent ☐ Your spouse as a dependent
☐ Spouse itemizes on a separate return or you were a dual-status alien

Age/Blindness **You:** ☐ Were born before January 2, 1956 ☐ Are blind **Spouse:** ☐ Was born before January 2, 1956 ☐ Is blind

Dependents (see instructions): If more than four dependents, see instructions and check here ▶ ☐

(1) First name Last name	(2) Social security number	(3) Relationship to you	(4) ✔ if qualifies for (see instructions): Child tax credit	Credit for other dependents
			☐	☐
			☐	☐
			☐	☐
			☐	☐

Attach Sch. B if required.

Standard Deduction for—
• Single or Married filing separately, $12,400
• Married filing jointly or Qualifying widow(er), $24,800
• Head of household, $18,650
• If you checked any box under *Standard Deduction,* see instructions.

1	Wages, salaries, tips, etc. Attach Form(s) W-2			1	
2a	Tax-exempt interest	2a	b Taxable interest	2b	
3a	Qualified dividends	3a	b Ordinary dividends	3b	
4a	IRA distributions	4a	b Taxable amount	4b	
5a	Pensions and annuities	5a	b Taxable amount	5b	
6a	Social security benefits	6a	b Taxable amount	6b	
7	Capital gain or (loss). Attach Schedule D if required. If not required, check here ▶ ☐			7	
8	Other income from Schedule 1, line 9			8	$40,000
9	Add lines 1, 2b, 3b, 4b, 5b, 6b, 7, and 8. This is your **total income** ▶			9	$40,000
10	Adjustments to income:				
a	From Schedule 1, line 22	10a	$2,826		
b	Charitable contributions if you take the standard deduction. See instructions	10b			
c	Add lines 10a and 10b. These are your **total adjustments to income** ▶			10c	$2,826
11	Subtract line 10c from line 9. This is your **adjusted gross income** ▶			11	$37,174
12	**Standard deduction or itemized deductions** (from Schedule A)			12	$12,400
13	Qualified business income deduction. Attach Form 8995 or Form 8995-A			13	$4,955
14	Add lines 12 and 13			14	$17,355
15	**Taxable income.** Subtract line 14 from line 11. If zero or less, enter -0-			15	$19,819

For Disclosure, Privacy Act, and Paperwork Reduction Act Notice, see separate instructions. Cat. No. 11320B Form **1040** (2020)

Form **8995** Department of the Treasury Internal Revenue Service	**Qualified Business Income Deduction Simplified Computation** ▶ Attach to your tax return. ▶ Go to *www.irs.gov/Form8995* for instructions and the latest information.	OMB No. 1545-0123 **2020** Attachment Sequence No. **55**

Name(s) shown on return	Your taxpayer identification number

Note. *You can claim the qualified business income deduction* **only** *if you have qualified business income from a qualified trade or business, real estate investment trust dividends, publicly traded partnership income, or a domestic production activities deduction passed through from an agricultural or horticultural cooperative. See instructions.*
Use this form if your taxable income, before your qualified business income deduction, is at or below $163,300 ($326,600 if married filing jointly), and you aren't a patron of an agricultural or horticultural cooperative.

1	(a) Trade, business, or aggregation name	(b) Taxpayer identification number	(c) Qualified business income or (loss)
i	FAMILY CHILD CARE		$40,000
ii			
iii			
iv			
v			

2	Total qualified business income or (loss). Combine lines 1i through 1v, column (c)	2	$40,000		
3	Qualified business net (loss) carryforward from the prior year	3	(---)		
4	Total qualified business income. Combine lines 2 and 3. If zero or less, enter -0-	4	$40,000		
5	Qualified business income component. Multiply line 4 by 20% (0.20)			5	$8,000
6	Qualified REIT dividends and publicly traded partnership (PTP) income or (loss) (see instructions)	6	---		
7	Qualified REIT dividends and qualified PTP (loss) carryforward from the prior year	7	(---)		
8	Total qualified REIT dividends and PTP income. Combine lines 6 and 7. If zero or less, enter -0-	8	$0		
9	REIT and PTP component. Multiply line 8 by 20% (0.20)			9	$0
10	Qualified business income deduction before the income limitation. Add lines 5 and 9			10	$8,000
11	Taxable income before qualified business income deduction	11	$24,774		
12	Net capital gain (see instructions)	12	---		
13	Subtract line 12 from line 11. If zero or less, enter -0-	13	$24,974		
14	Income limitation. Multiply line 13 by 20% (0.20)			14	$4,955
15	Qualified business income deduction. Enter the lesser of line 10 or line 14. Also enter this amount on the applicable line of your return ▶			15	$4,955
16	Total qualified business (loss) carryforward. Combine lines 2 and 3. If greater than zero, enter -0-			16	( )
17	Total qualified REIT dividends and PTP (loss) carryforward. Combine lines 6 and 7. If greater than zero, enter -0-			17	( )

For Privacy Act and Paperwork Reduction Act Notice, see instructions. Cat. No. 37806C Form **8995** (2020)

Personal Exemptions and the Child Tax Credit

Starting in 2019 you lost the ability to lower your federal taxable income by taking personal exemptions. In 2018 this was $4,150 per person for you, your spouse, and any eligible children. This used to appear on **Form 1040**, line 42. On the other hand, the Child Tax Credit has increased to $2,000 per eligible child, up from $1,000 in 2017.

Child Tax Credits

If you have dependents (including children, grandchildren, stepchildren, or foster children) who were under age 17 at the end of last year, you're entitled to up to a $2,000 tax credit (up from $1,000 in 2017) for each child if your adjusted gross income is less than

- $200,000 for married persons filing separately,
- $200,000 for single and head of household, or
- $400,000 for married filing jointly.

If you earn more than this, your credit will be reduced by $50 for each $1,000, or fraction thereof, above the limit. This credit is refundable (meaning it is payable to you even when you owe no taxes) up to $1,400.

This credit goes with the parent who claims the dependency exemption for the child. Be sure to check the box in column 4 on the Dependents section on page 1 of **Form 1040**. To get this credit, you must enter the name and Social Security number of each qualifying child on **Form 1040**. To claim the credit, fill out **Form 8862 Information to Claim Certain Credits After Disallowance** and then the Child Tax Credit worksheet in the instructions to **Form 1040** and enter the credit amount on line 13a.

If you have three or more children, you may be eligible for the Additional Child Tax Credit. This credit is for those who couldn't take full advantage of the Child Tax Credit. Use **Form 8812 Additional Child Tax Credit** to calculate this credit, and enter the credit amount on line 18b.

New Credit for Other Dependents

As of 2018 there is a new tax credit called the Credit for Other Dependents. You are eligible for this credit if you have a dependent who is under age 19 as of the end of the year, or under age 24 if they are a full-time student. This credit is worth $500. Complete **Form 8862** and the worksheet in the instructions to **Form 1040**. Enter the credit on line 13a on **Form 1040**.

Filing Quarterly Taxes: Form 1040-ES

As a family child care provider, you're self-employed and don't have any income taxes withheld from your earnings, unlike most wage-earning taxpayers. The IRS doesn't want to wait until the end of the year to get all the taxes you'll owe for 2020. If after subtracting all your withholding payments and estimated tax payments, you expect to owe $1,000 or more in federal taxes (federal income tax plus self-employment tax) this year, you may be subject to estimated quarterly tax payments. Many family child care providers aren't aware that they should be paying their taxes quarterly.

Estimated tax payments are due four times a year, on April 15, June 15, September 15, and January 15 of the next year. If you're reading this in early 2021, and you file your 2020 taxes by January 31, 2021, you won't have to file the fourth quarter estimated tax payment that is due on January 15. You may be able to avoid paying quarterly estimated taxes (see below), but if you can't avoid it, bear in mind that you can now pay these taxes with a credit card. (You may also have to pay quarterly estimated taxes to your state or locality; check your local laws.)

Avoiding the Quarterly Requirement

You don't have to pay any estimated taxes if you meet at least one of the following conditions:

- You estimate that you will receive a tax refund for the year on your individual, joint, or separate return.
- You estimate that you will owe less than $1,000 in taxes (after subtracting any withholding) by the end of the year.
- You estimate that the total tax payments that you or your spouse (if filing jointly) will make during the year will be at least 90% of your total tax bill for the year. Example: your husband has $6,400 in taxes withheld from his paycheck during 2020. You work only in your family child care business. You estimate that your total tax bill this year will be $7,000. Since $6,400 in withholding is 91% of your total tax bill, you won't have to pay estimated tax. If your husband had less than $6,300 in taxes withheld, you would have to pay some estimated tax.
- You had no income tax liability in the previous year.
- You estimate that the income tax that will be withheld from you and your spouse in 2021 will be equal to or greater than your total tax liability for 2020.

Another way to avoid worrying about estimated tax is to have your spouse file a new **Form W-4** to withhold more taxes to cover any taxes that are due because of your business earnings. For more information, see IRS **Publication 505**.

How to Fill Out Form 1040-ES

To find out if you will need to pay quarterly estimated tax this year, use the worksheet and payment vouchers on **Form 1040-ES**. The worksheet takes you through the calculations to determine how much tax you will owe by the end of 2021 after subtracting any withholding payments.

If you find that you need to make estimated tax payments, you will divide by four the total tax you will owe for the year after any withholding payments and pay this amount on April 15. For example, if you're single, have no other job besides your family child care business, and estimate that you will owe $4,000 in taxes by the end of this year, you will pay $1,000 ($4,000 ÷ 4) on April 15. In this case, you will have no withholding payments, because you do not earn a paycheck from an employer.

If your income or expenses rise or fall dramatically during the year, you can adjust your declared estimated tax and quarterly payments accordingly. There's a penalty for not paying enough estimated tax.

Form **1040-ES** Department of the Treasury Internal Revenue Service | **2020 Estimated Tax** | **Payment Voucher 4** | OMB No. 1545-0074

File only if you are making a payment of estimated tax by check or money order. Mail this voucher with your check or money order payable to **"United States Treasury."** Write your social security number and "2020 Form 1040-ES" on your check or money order. Do not send cash. Enclose, but do not staple or attach, your payment with this voucher.

Calendar year—Due Jan. 15, 2021

Amount of estimated tax you are paying by check or money order. Dollars $1,000 Cents 00

Print or type

Your first name and middle initial	Your last name	Your social security number
FRAN	ALLEN	183-62-4512
If joint payment, complete for spouse		
Spouse's first name and middle initial	Spouse's last name	Spouse's social security number
Address (number, street, and apt. no.) 28 PLAZA DRIVE		
City, state, and ZIP code. (If a foreign address, enter city, also complete spaces below.) BERKELEY, CA 94126		
Foreign country name	Foreign province/county	Foreign postal code

For Privacy Act and Paperwork Reduction Act Notice, see instructions. **Form 1040-ES (2020)**

-9-

The name you enter on this form must be shown exactly as it appears on your **Form 1040**. If your spouse's name is listed first on your **Form 1040**, list your spouse first on **Form 1040-ES**. If you separated from your spouse or were divorced last year, consult a tax professional before completing this form.

Example of Estimated Tax Calculations

Let's look at an example to determine whether you must make estimated tax payments. Assume it is January 2020. You care for four children and earn $600 a week.

Step One: Estimate Your Income

$600 week x 52 weeks = $31,200
Food Program reimbursement: $4,000
Total estimated income: $35,200

Step Two: Estimate Your Expenses

If you provided child care in 2020, revise your 2021 number to take into account any expected changes for 2021. If you have only been providing child care for a short time, calculate your average weekly expenses. Don't forget to include depreciation for your house and personal property. A rough rule of thumb might be to estimate that your expenses will be about 40% of your parent income.

Estimated expenses: $12,480

Step Three: Estimate Your Social Security Taxes

$22,720 net income x 92.35% x 13.3% = $2,790 (See **Form 1040-SE** for details.)

Step Four: Estimate Your Income Tax

Your federal income tax rate is determined by your family status and income. The tax brackets for 2020 are listed below. If your income is higher than the table below, there are higher tax brackets of 32%, 35%, and 37%.

	Tax Brackets			
Filing Status	**10%**	**12%**	**22%**	**24%**
Single/married filing sep.	$0–$9,875	$9,876–$40,125	$40,126–$85,525	$85,526–$163,300
Head of household	$0–$14,100	$14,101–$53,700	$53,701–$85,500	$85,501–$163,600
Married filing jointly	$0–$19,750	$19,751–$80,250	$80,251–$171,050	$171,051–$326,600

If you're single:

$22,720	Taxable income
$987	The first $9,875 is taxed at 10%
+$1,541	The remaining $12,845 is taxed at 12%
$2,528	Estimated income taxes due

Step Five: Total Your Estimated Taxes

$2,528	Estimated income taxes
+$2,790	Estimated Social Security tax
$5,318	Estimated total taxes due

If you're single and have no withholding payments to apply toward your taxes, you'll have to pay estimated taxes; however, your estimated tax payment will be less than shown above because you can subtract the standard deduction and personal exemptions from your income.

If you're married, you must make sure that your business income is offset by your spouse's withholding. If in our example none of your taxes are offset by the standard deduction or personal exemption, then by April 15 you should pay one-fourth of the taxes you will owe this year, which would be $5,318 x 0.25 = $1,329.50.

If your estimates change later in the year, you can adjust your estimated tax payments. If you pay too much, you'll get a refund at the end of the year. See the estimated tax worksheet in **Form 1040-ES**. If you're making estimated tax payments by filing **Form 1040-ES**, don't claim these payments as an expense on **Schedule C**. These payments represent your advanced tax deposits; you'll report them on **Form 1040 Schedule 3**, line 8.

Filing Your Tax Return Electronically or via the Internet

An increasing number of taxpayers are filing their tax returns electronically with the IRS e-file system. You can bring your completed tax return to an authorized IRS e-file provider or have a tax preparer prepare your tax return and have it electronically filed. To find an authorized IRS e-file provider, go to www.irs.gov. You can also purchase software and e-file your own tax return with your computer and an internet connection. For more information, go to www.irs.gov.

Paying Your Taxes Online

You can now pay all your federal taxes via a secure website, www.eftps.gov. Until now the Electronic Federal Tax Payment System (EFTPS) was only available via telephone or special software. Now you can pay directly via the internet, including your quarterly **Form 1040-ES** estimated tax payments. You must use the EFTPS system to pay any payroll taxes you may owe when you hire employees. See chapter 8 for details. On the EFTPS website, you can also review your tax payment history and print out a confirmation of your payment. To use this site to pay online, you need to enroll first, and the enrollments take two to four weeks to process. For enrollment information, go to www.eftps.gov or call 800-945-8400.

Save Your Records

You should save all the records you used to complete your tax return for at least three years after you file your return. (Your state laws may require you to save your federal tax records for longer than three years, so check with your state department of revenue.) If you file your federal tax return on March 1, you will need to save your tax records until March 1, 2024. Many family child care providers save their records for an extra year.

You must save records associated with items that you are depreciating for as long as you are depreciating the item plus three years. So if you bought a washer and dryer last year and filed your taxes on March 1, you would save the receipt until March 1, 2032 (eight years of depreciation, plus three years). But remember that in 2020 you probably won't be depreciating anything except your house, home improvements, and home additions.

When you go out of business, you need only to keep records of the items you are depreciating for three more years. We recommend that you keep copies of your tax returns for as long as you live.

For more information about the tax issues discussed in this chapter, refer to the related topics in the other chapters of this book and the Redleaf Press *Family Child Care Record-Keeping Guide.*

This concludes the Tax Workbook section of this book. The next chapter is a Tax Return Checklist that you can use to ensure that you haven't made any common errors or forgotten anything important while doing your taxes.

CHAPTER 7

Catching Your Errors: The Tax Return Checklist

The following checklist is designed to help you identify the most common mistakes before you send in your tax return. Review this list after you fill out all your tax forms.

Form 8829

Did you provide child care in a building that you didn't live in? You can't file **Form 8829**; instead, claim your house expenses directly on **Schedule C**.

Part I

- ❑ Did you enter the number of square feet of your home that you used on a regular basis for your business on line 1? *Regular use* means you used it at least two to three times per week on some business activity. You can count rooms that aren't used by the children in your care if *you* are using it for business purposes. This can include an office, laundry room, storage room, garage, and bedrooms used for storage.
- ❑ What should you include as the total number of square feet of your home on line 2? Make sure you also count your basement, garage (attached or unattached), and deck. Don't count a driveway, patio, or yard, since these areas aren't attached to your home. Count a shed if it is permanently attached to the ground.
- ❑ Does line 3 show 100%? Don't worry, it's not unusual.
- ❑ The instructions for this line—"Multiply days used for daycare during the year by hours used per day"—can be very misleading. So what should you enter? Put down the number of hours you worked in your home, including the number of hours children were present and the number of hours you used your home for business purposes when children were not present. Many providers fail to keep at least two months of careful records showing all the hours they spent on activities when children were not present: cleaning, record keeping, activity and meal preparation, time on the internet, and so on. If you didn't carefully track at least two months of hours for last year, plan ahead to do so for this year.
- ❑ Were you in business for the entire year? The default amount of 8,760 hours should appear on line 5. If you were not in business for the full year, enter the number of hours in the year for the weeks you were in business.
- ❑ Line 6 represents your Time percentage. If you cared for children 11 hours a day, 5 days a week, this would represent 33% of the year. After adding the number of hours

you worked on business activities when children were not present, this percentage would be close to 40% for most providers. If your percentage on this line is below 25%, this means that you either cared for children for fewer than 9 hours a day, 5 days a week—or you undercounted your hours.

- ❑ Is line 7 between 30% and 40%? This line represents your Time-Space percentage. But your Time-Space percentage can certainly be a lot higher if you work longer hours or have an exclusive-use room. If you used one or more rooms exclusively for your business, attach a statement to **Form 8829** showing how your Time-Space percentage was calculated. Lines 1–6 should be left blank. To have an exclusive-use room, you can never, ever use it for personal purposes.

Part II

- ❑ Line 8: Enter the amount from **Schedule C**, line 29 here. This number is called your tentative profit, since it is your profit before house expenses. Your deduction for house business expenses on **Form 8829** cannot exceed this amount. If it does, you will have to carry forward some of these expenses to the next year. See Part IV.
- ❑ Expenses entered under column (a): Direct expenses are those that are used 100% for your business. Expenses entered under column (b): Indirect expenses are those that are used for both business and personal purposes.
- ❑ Have you claimed expenses on **Schedule C**? Check to see that you are not claiming these same expenses on **Form 8829** on lines 9 through 22. This is most likely to happen with expenses for insurance, repairs, and utilities, since these categories appear on both forms. Check the following lines carefully. Utilities belong on **Form 8829**.
- ❑ Your full mortgage interest expense goes on line 10 in column (b) where it will be multiplied by your Time-Space percentage.
- ❑ Have real estate taxes? Enter the full amount on line 11 in column (b) where it will be multiplied by your Time-Space Percentage.
- ❑ Did you itemize your personal expenses on **Schedule A**? Check to see that you didn't claim 100% of your mortgage interest and real estate taxes there. These expenses should be split between **Schedule A** and **Form 8829**. If you didn't itemize using **Schedule A**, you are still entitled to your Time-Space percentage of these expenses on **Form 8829**.
- ❑ Enter your homeowners insurance in column (b) on line 18. Remember that your liability insurance goes on **Schedule C**, not here.
- ❑ Did you pay rent in 2020? Enter that amount on line 19 in column (b).
- ❑ List all your house repairs (for example, repairing a broken window, plumbing and electrical work, interior or exterior painting) on line 20. If you had repair expenses that were 100% business, enter them in column (a). Otherwise they should appear in column (b). Remember that repairs on your personal property used for your business (such as furniture, appliances, and equipment) go on **Schedule C**, not here.
- ❑ Enter your total utility expenses on line 21 in column (b). They can include gas, oil, electric, water, sewer, cable television, garbage, wood, and propane.
- ❑ Were you were not allowed to claim all of your house expenses from line 43 on your 2019 **Form 8829**? You should enter these amounts on line 25.

- ❑ Were you were not allowed to claim all of your house depreciation expenses from line 30 on your 2019 **Form 8829**? You should enter this amount on line 31.
- ❑ Line 36 represents the amount of house expenses from **Form 8829** that can be claimed on **Schedule C**, line 30.

Part III

- ❑ If you own your home, make sure you show an expense on line 37. You are always financially better off depreciating your home. Enter the lower of the purchase price of your home or its value at the time you first started using it for your business. For the most providers, this will be the original purchase price of your home, not its current value.
- ❑ If you used the purchase price of your home on line 37, enter the value of the land at the time you bought it on line 38. If you used the value of your home at the time you first started using it for your business, enter the value of the land at that time.
- ❑ If your expenses on **Form 8829** create or increase a loss on your **Schedule C**, you won't be able to claim all of your house depreciation this year and must carry it forward to the next year. See Part IV.
- ❑ Not your first year using your home for your business? Enter 2.564% on line 41 as you are depreciating your home over 39 years.
- ❑ The amount on line 42 represents your house depreciation deduction. It should also appear on line 30.

Part IV

- ❑ Subtract line 27 from line 26. You will enter this amount on line 43 and carry it over onto your 2021 **Form 8829**. This will happen when your house expenses exceed your tentative profit from **Schedule C**.
- ❑ Subtract line 33 from line 32. You will enter this amount on line 44 and carry it over onto your 2021 **Form 8829**. This will happen when your house depreciation expense exceeds your tentative profit from **Schedule C**.

Form 4562

Are you still depreciating items? Because of tax law changes in 2018, many family child care providers may no longer need to depreciate items used in their business. All items except a home, home improvement, and home addition can be deducted in one year, and it's usually better to deduct items in one year rather than depreciating them. If you use a tax preparer, and they are showing depreciation deductions on **Form 4562**, you should ask them to explain why. If you do need to depreciate items, ask for a copy of the worksheet they used to calculate the depreciation deduction. This worksheet will be helpful in preparing your 2021 tax return, especially if you do not use the same tax professional.

Part I

- ❑ Have you or your tax professional listed an item on line 6? Doing so means using the Section 179 rule to deduct the item in one year. Because of the restrictions to the Section 179 rule, in most cases it doesn't make sense to use this rule, but a home improvement that is used more than 50% for your business could be an exception. Items showing on this line should probably be moved to **Schedule C**.

Part II

- ❑ Did you have any items that individually cost more than $2,500 that you purchased in 2020? Enter them on line 14. Tax changes effective in 2018 allow providers to deduct in one year all items except a home, home improvement, and home addition. Items costing $2,500 or less belong on **Schedule C**.
- ❑ Enter items you purchased and began depreciating before 2020 on line 17. If you previously used a tax professional, get a copy of their worksheet showing how this number was calculated. If it's not clear to you where this number comes from, ask for clarification.
- ❑ Providers are entitled to claim deductions for items they owned before their business began. This includes furniture, appliances, and a host of household items. If you didn't claim these expenses under the Start-Up Rule, you may still be able to deduct them using **Form 3115 Application for Change in Accounting Method**. To claim previously unclaimed depreciation, you will need to conduct an inventory of these items and estimate their value at the time you first started using them in your business.
- ❑ Entering any expenses on lines 19(a–i) would be unusual. That's because most providers will no longer be depreciating items that can be deducted in one year. Again, it is almost always better to claim expenses in one year (on line 14 or on **Schedule C**) than to depreciate them here.
- ❑ Does a number appear on line 22? Make sure it also shows up on **Schedule C**, line 13.
- ❑ Are you depreciating your vehicle? Make sure "yes" is checked next to the two boxes on line 24.
- ❑ Items shown on lines 26 and 27 will probably be either a vehicle or a computer. If the computer costs $2,500 or less, it should be deducted in one year on **Schedule C** and not depreciated here. If the computer cost more than $2,500 and is used more than 50% of the time for your business, it should be deducted on line 14 in one year. If it is used less than 50% of the time for your business and costs more than $2,500, it should appear on line 26. The rules for depreciating a vehicle are complicated, and this deduction could appear on line 26 or 27. Recent changes in vehicle depreciation may allow you to deduct most or all the cost of the vehicle in the first year.
- ❑ Are you using the standard mileage rate for your vehicle expenses? You should still fill out lines 30–36.

Schedule C

Part I

- ❑ What goes on line 1? Enter all money received from parents, subsidy programs, and grants. This includes parent fees and copays. I recommend reporting your Food Program income on line 6, but you can put it here if you want. If you receive a **Form 1099** from your Food Program or a grant, enter these amounts on line 6.

- ❑ Have any amounts on lines 2–4? You shouldn't. You don't have any returns and allowances, and you aren't selling goods, so there is no need to fill out these lines or Part III.
- ❑ I recommend putting your Food Program income on line 6. Don't enter any reimbursements received for your own children, because they are not taxable.

Part II

- ❑ Did you know you are not required to list any of your deductions on any particular line on **Schedule C**? It doesn't matter if you put your calculator under Office Expenses (line 18) or under Supplies (line 22), but you need to know which deductions went on which line so you can produce receipts to support your return if you are ever audited.
- ❑ Do you do child care out of a home you do not live in? Do not fill out **Form 8829**—instead enter all your house-related expenses on **Schedule C**, including mortgage interest, property tax, rent, homeowners insurance, house repairs, utilities, and house depreciation. If you provide child care out of your home, do not enter these expenses on **Schedule C**.
- ❑ Want to reduce your chances of being audited? Make sure that the amount shown on any given line of 8–26 is not significantly larger than another. If you lump a lot of expenses under Supplies, this can attract the attention of the IRS. Instead, break out some of the expenses and put them in different categories.
- ❑ Did you claim the business portion of your car loan interest and any state personal property tax you pay each year on your car on line 9? You are always entitled to this deduction, even if you use the standard mileage rate method. If you used the actual vehicle expenses method for a vehicle, you can also claim depreciation for that vehicle. Check to see that your tax professional has entered that deduction on line 25 or 26 of **Form 4562**. You can't depreciate your vehicle if you use the standard mileage method.
- ❑ Do you have expenses from a house cleaner, gardener, music teacher, or other independent contractors? Those costs only belong here. If you hire someone to help you care for children, that person is likely an employee and you should be paying payroll taxes. Report these amounts on line 26.
- ❑ Did you claim any depreciation on **Form 4562**? The total from line 22 on that form should appear here on line 13.
- ❑ Enter the amount of your business liability insurance on line 15. Homeowners insurance belongs on **Form 8829**, line 18.
- ❑ Don't put your mortgage interest on line 16 (a)—that belongs on **Form 8829**.
- ❑ Enter the cost of tax preparation fees to file only your business tax forms on line 17.
- ❑ Not sure where to put your food expenses? You may enter them on line 24(b) or on line 27(a). If you enter them here, be sure you are deducting 100% of your business food expenses. If you take parents out to eat or you pay for a "business meal" with other providers, you can deduct only 50% of the cost of that food.
- ❑ Transfer the amount from **Form 8829**, line 36 to line 30. The vast majority of providers will not use the Simplified Method as described here. That's because your house

expenses from **Form 8829** are almost always going to be higher than what you could deduct using the Simplified Method.

Part III

- ❑ Lines 33–42: Since you do not sell any goods, you should not fill out this section.

Part IV

- ❑ Did you not file **Form 4562**? You should fill out this section. If you did file **Form 4562**, enter this same information on Part V of that form and leave this section blank.

Part V

- ❑ Not sure what to put here? You can create your own expense categories. I suggest using the following categories: Food, Household Items, Cleaning Supplies, Activity Expenses, and Toys. Do not use the category Gifts unless you are referring to items given to parents or children that are only used by them personally. You can deduct only up to $25 per year per person as a gift. If a child opens a present in your home before taking it to their home, this is an activity expense, not a gift.
- ❑ Compare your food expenses in Part V with the Food Program income you reported on line 6 of **Schedule C** (or line 1). If you received the higher Food Program reimbursement rate (Tier I) but served extra snacks that weren't reimbursed by the Food Program, your food deduction should be at least several hundred dollars higher than the amount on lines 1 or 6. If you received the lower Food Program reimbursement rate (Tier II), your deduction for food expenses should be at least twice as much as the amounts on line 1 or 6.

Schedule SE

- ❑ If you had a profit of more than $400 on **Schedule C**, line 31, you must fill out this form and pay Social Security taxes. Transfer this amount to **Form 1040 Schedule 4**, line 57.

Form 4797

- ❑ If you sold or traded in your vehicle last year and used the standard mileage rate method, did you check to see if you have a loss as a result of the sale or trade-in? Any business loss can be deducted on **Form 4797**. See chapter 11.

Form 1040

- ❑ Did you enter your profit from **Schedule C**, line 31, onto **Form 1040 Schedule 1**, line 3? Then transfer it to **Form 1040**, line 7a.
- ❑ Did you claim one-half of your self-employment tax on **Form 1040 Schedule 1**, line 14? Then transfer it to **Form 1040**, line 8a. Don't forget this deduction. See chapter 6.
- ❑ Your health insurance deduction on **Form 1040 Schedule 1**, line 16, may not exceed your net business income (**Schedule C**, line 31). If it does, reduce your health insurance deduction until it equals the amount on **Schedule C**, line 31.

- ❑ If you have children of your own who were under the age of 17 at the end of last year, did you claim the Child Tax Credit on **Form 1040**, line 13a? If so, did you also check the box on page 1 of **Form 1040**? See chapter 6.
- ❑ Did you enter the correct Social Security numbers for your spouse and your dependents on **Form 1040**?
- ❑ If you're married filing jointly, did both of you sign your **Form 1040**?
- ❑ Did you double-check the taxes you owe according to the tax tables in the IRS instruction book?
- ❑ Did you recheck the math on all your forms?

End-of-Year Record-Keeping Checklist

- ❑ Gather all your records together, and store them with your tax return.
- ❑ Record the odometer readings for all your vehicles on January 1, 2021.
- ❑ Collect receipts from all the parents indicating how much they paid you for the year. Have each parent sign your copy.
- ❑ Save all your canceled checks, from personal as well as business checking accounts.
- ❑ Ask your tax preparer for copies of all the backup worksheets or forms used to prepare your tax return.
- ❑ Organize your expense receipts by category (utilities, food, toys) rather than by month. If you're audited, this will make it easier to present your records to the IRS.
- ❑ Put all your tax records in a sealed plastic storage box (to protect them from water damage), and put the box in a safe place. Save the records for at least three years after the filing date.

PART III

Tax Instructions for Special Situations

CHAPTER 8

Hiring Employees and Paying Payroll Taxes

This chapter explains how to withhold and pay taxes for your employees. Although the rules are complicated, the consequences of not following them can be serious. This chapter covers only federal tax rules about employees; if you have employees, you'll need to find out if your state has other rules regarding state and local income taxes, state unemployment taxes, and/or workers' compensation insurance.

There are two types of workers—independent contractors and employees—and there are two types of employees—those who are family members and those who are not. First we will discuss the difference between an independent contractor and an employee, and then we will explain how to withhold and pay taxes for the two types of employees.

Domestic Workers versus Employees

Don't confuse the kinds of employees discussed in this chapter with household employees—domestic workers, such as nannies or house cleaners who work in the home. The people who work for your family child care business are not household employees.

Parents who hire a nanny to care for their children don't need to pay Social Security taxes if they pay $2,200 or less per year or hire someone under the age of 18. This rule does not apply to family child care employees, because they are considered to be hired by your business rather than as household employees.

Employee or Independent Contractor?

If you pay anyone else to work with the children in your care, you need to understand that in almost every case the IRS will consider those workers to be your employees rather than independent contractors—and this fact has major tax implications.

When you hire an independent contractor, you don't withhold any taxes; you simply deduct what you pay the person as a miscellaneous expense. When you hire an employee, you must withhold Social Security tax and income tax and pay federal unemployment and Social Security tax. You'll probably also have to withhold state taxes.

It doesn't matter if the person works for only a few hours. A person who works for you 20 hours every week is your employee, and so is a person whom you hire once as a substitute while you go to the doctor. The main reason why someone you hire to care for children is considered your employee is because you have the right to direct and control the work of this person.

Independent Contractors

There are two circumstances in which the IRS might consider a family child care worker to be an independent contractor. The following situations are the exceptions to the general rule that everyone you pay to help with the children in your care is your employee:

1. A person who comes into your home on special occasions to perform specific services is not usually considered an employee. Someone who cleans your home for your business, occasionally repairs your toys, or offers swimming lessons or other activities programs for the children in your care is not an employee. Since these people aren't working under your control and direction, they can be considered independent contractors.
2. A person who is in the business of providing backup child care or who serves as an employee to several other child care providers *may* be considered an independent contractor. To have a chance of being considered an independent contractor, a worker should meet the following conditions:
    - She should advertise to the public that she's available to provide substitute or part-time child care.
    - She should have her own federal (and state, if required) employer identification number and report her income on **Schedule C**.
    - She should work under a business name ("Sally's Substitute Service") that's registered with the state. She may also need a business license (check your state law).
    - She should provide a business contract for you to sign that states her rates and the fact that she's self-employed and in the business of providing substitute child care to the public.

Even if a worker meets all the above qualifications, there's no guarantee that the IRS will consider her to be an independent contractor. However, it's far more likely to occur if she meets these qualifications than if she doesn't.

For a full discussion of the issue of employees versus independent contractors, refer to the *Record-Keeping Guide.*

A Word to the Wise

Despite the above facts, many family child care providers don't consider their workers to be employees. If the IRS rules that you have employees, you'll be responsible for back Social Security taxes, interest, and penalties. You may also owe state and local taxes, interest, and penalties.

The most likely triggers for an IRS challenge are the following situations:

- One of your workers files an unemployment claim and lists you as a previous employer.
- One of your workers is injured on the job and files a workers' compensation claim. (Your state is likely to turn your name over to the IRS and penalize you for not having workers' compensation insurance.)

- You list a deduction for an employee on **Schedule C**, line 26.
- You file **Form 1099 Miscellaneous Income** for a worker (this form reports payments to an independent contractor). This often triggers an IRS investigation to determine if the payee is actually an independent contractor.

Although it may be tempting to avoid treating your workers as employees to avoid filing withholding forms and paying payroll taxes, you need to take your legal responsibilities seriously. I know how frustrated many family child care providers feel about trying to comply with the legal requirements; however, there are ways to satisfy them at a relatively low cost, such as the following (for more information, see the *Record-Keeping Guide*):

- You can hire a payroll service company to set up a payroll system, withhold the proper amount of taxes, and file the required forms at a relatively low cost. Payroll service companies include, but are not limited to, QuickBooks (https://quickbooks.intuit.com/payroll/online), Paychex (www.paychex.com/payroll/small-business-payroll), and ADP (www.adp.com/what-we-offer/payroll). See also the article "Best Payroll Services for 2020" (www.businessnewsdaily.com/7509-best-payroll-services.html). You can also look under Bookkeeping Services in the Yellow Pages. We do not recommend any particular company.
- You can use an employee leasing company instead of hiring your own employees. The advantage of this approach is that the leasing company will handle all the payroll and tax paperwork. Its disadvantage is that you won't be able to choose your own workers. Look under Employee Leasing Companies in the Yellow Pages. We do not recommend any particular company.

Note: If you have not treated your assistants as your employees in the past three years, there is some good news. The IRS will not audit you for your mistakes in past years if you apply for the Voluntary Classification Settlement Program. To be eligible, you must pay about 1% of the wages paid to your assistants for the past year; for $1,000 in wages paid, you'll owe $10.68. Apply for this program at least 60 days before the end of any tax quarter, and use IRS **Form 8952 Application for Voluntary Classification Settlement Program**. The IRS will not share this information with your state department of revenue. For more information, go to http://tinyurl.com/m9qm5rj.

Reporting Payments to Independent Contractors

If you pay any individual independent contractor $600 or more during the year, you must fill out **Form 1099 Miscellaneous Income** (box 7), give a copy to the independent contractor by January 31 of the following year, and file it with the IRS by January 31.

The purpose of **Form 1099** is to inform the IRS of payments that you make to independent contractors who are responsible for reporting that income to the IRS. If you don't file this form properly, you will be subject to a $50 penalty, but you won't be penalized if the independent contractor fails to report the income. If you didn't pay any independent contractors $600 or more during the year, you don't need to submit any records to the IRS.

9595 ☐ VOID ☐ CORRECTED

PAYER'S name, street address, city or town, state or province, country, ZIP or foreign postal code, and telephone no. SANDRA THOMPSON 628 WOODLEA COURT SAN JOSE, CA 95101		1 Rents $	OMB No. 1545-0115 2020	Miscellaneous Income
		2 Royalties $	Form 1099-MISC	
		3 Other income $	4 Federal income tax withheld $	Copy A For Internal Revenue Service Center
PAYER'S TIN	RECIPIENT'S TIN	5 Fishing boat proceeds $	6 Medical and health care payments $	File with Form 1096.
RECIPIENT'S name AMANDA FRANKLIN		7 Payer made direct sales of $5,000 or more of consumer products to a buyer (recipient) for resale ☐	8 Substitute payments in lieu of dividends or interest $	For Privacy Act and Paperwork Reduction Act Notice, see the 2020 General Instructions for Certain Information Returns.
Street address (including apt. no.) 1267 AMBER LANE, #6		9 Crop insurance proceeds $	10 Gross proceeds paid to an attorney $	
City or town, state or province, country, and ZIP or foreign postal code CUPERTINO, CA 95014		11	12 Section 409A deferrals $	
Account number (see instructions)	FATCA filing requirement ☐ 2nd TIN not. ☐	13 Excess golden parachute payments $	14 Nonqualified deferred compensation $ 750.00	
		15 State tax withheld $ $	16 State/Payer's state no.	17 State income $ $

Form 1099-MISC Cat. No. 14425J www.irs.gov/Form1099MISC Department of the Treasury - Internal Revenue Service

Do Not Cut or Separate Forms on This Page — Do Not Cut or Separate Forms on This Page

To report payments to independent contractors on your **Schedule C**, enter the total that you paid to independent contractors on line 11. *Don't enter anything on* ***Schedule C****, line 26, Wages* (unless you do have an employee). If you do, the IRS will assume that you have an employee and will check to see if you have withheld the proper amount of payroll taxes.

Employee Liability

Hiring an employee brings new risks and responsibilities. Before you start the hiring process, you need to check several things:

- Ask your licensor if there are any state regulations about the qualifications of your employees, if your state requires background checks of new employees, and if it requires you to buy workers' compensation insurance for employees.
- Find out if there are any deed restrictions, homeowners association covenants, or zoning laws that restrict your right to hire.
- Find out if your business liability insurance policy will cover you for any allegations of child abuse against your employees and for any medical expenses that are caused by the actions of your employees.

For a detailed discussion of the risks of having employees and how to reduce them, see the *Family Child Care Legal and Insurance Guide.*

Hiring Employees

When you hire someone, you must fill out the following forms and file them with the IRS: **Form SS-4**, **Form I-9**, and **Form W-4**. During the year you must file **Form 941**, and at the end of the year you must file **Form 940**, **Form W-2**, and **Form W-3**. You can avoid filing the quarterly **Form 941** (by filing a **Form 944**) if you pay less than $4,000 in total wages for the year. See this chapter for details.

All employers are also required to file a report with their state whenever they hire or rehire an employee (including their own children), usually within 15 to 30 days of hiring the employee. This usually involves filling out a simple form and usually doesn't cost anything. Submit this form to your state, not the IRS. Check with your state for further details.

When you hire someone, you must save all your employment records for four years after filing your tax return.

The Federal Minimum Wage

In 2020 the federal minimum wage was $7.25 per hour. The federal minimum wage applies only to a provider who hires more than one employee. It does not apply to a provider who hires her spouse or her own children.

Although you may not be required to pay a federal minimum wage to your employee, your state law may require you to pay a higher state minimum wage. If you are required to pay a federal minimum wage (because you have more than one employee) and your state minimum wage is higher than the federal rate, you must pay the higher state minimum wage. If the state or federal minimum wage law does apply to you and you pay someone to work more than 40 hours a week, you must pay that person overtime (one-and-a-half times the regular rate, or $10.88 per hour). You can pay a new employee who is younger than 20 years old $4.25 per hour for the first 90 days.

Even though you may not be required to pay a federal or state minimum wage, you can pay your employees these wage rates or higher. If you hire your own children, you may want to pay them the minimum wage to increase your business deductions.

Child Labor Laws

You may not hire anyone under age 14 who is not a family member. (Check with your state department of labor to see if your state laws restrict your ability to hire your own child under age 14.) If you hire someone under age 16 who is not a family member, there are restrictions on how many hours the person may work. Employees who are 14 and 15 years old may only work outside of school hours, no more than 3 hours on a school day and 8 hours on a nonschool day. They can only work 18 hours during a school week and 40 hours during a nonschool week.

Hiring Your Spouse or Children

Although the rules about hiring family members to work in your business are somewhat different from those for hiring nonfamily employees, you must still treat any family member you hire as an employee and fill out **Form SS-4**, **Form I-9**, **Form W-4**, **Form 941** (or possibly **Form 944**), and **Form 940**.

The IRS may also question the business expenses that you deduct for family employees. To protect yourself, you will need to keep good records that show specifically what work was done, how long it took, and how much you paid the employee for it.

Treat these financial transactions in a businesslike manner. For example, don't deposit the money that you pay to your spouse in a joint checking account; it will look as if you're simply paying yourself.

Your spouse or children must report the wages you pay them on their own **Form 1040**. For more information about the tax and financial benefits (and pitfalls) of hiring your spouse or children, see the *Record-Keeping Guide.*

Hiring Your Spouse

If you hire your spouse to work for your business, you must file the same tax forms as you would for any other employee, with one exception. The wages you pay to a spouse are not subject to federal unemployment taxes; however, you must still fill out **Form 940**. Your spouse's wages are subject to federal income tax withholding and Social Security and Medicare withholding. You must file **Form 941** (or possibly **Form 944**), **Form W-2**, and **Form W-3**. Your spouse must report all money earned by working in your business as wages and pay taxes on it.

Because your spouse will probably pay the same taxes that you would have paid if you had kept the money yourself, there's only a slight payroll tax advantage involved. The advantage is that you can deduct as a business expense the 7.65% you withhold as an employer for Social Security and Medicare taxes.

Hiring Your Own Children

Hiring your own children has two potential financial benefits. First, the wages you pay to a child under age 18 aren't subject to Social Security, Medicare, or federal unemployment taxes. Second, a child who earns less than $12,000 (up from $6,350 in 2017) doesn't have to file a tax return.

Between ages 18 and 21, children are subject to Social Security and Medicare withholding, but their wages are not subject to federal unemployment taxes. This means that there is little financial incentive to hire them rather than nonfamily employees. Wages paid to children over 21 are subject to federal unemployment taxes.

If you hire your own child, you will need to file all the usual federal tax forms: **Form W-4**, **Form 941**, **Form W-2**, and **Form W-3**. Your child can claim an exemption from income tax withholding if he or she doesn't anticipate owing any federal taxes. In this case, the child wouldn't need to file **Form 1040**, although if he or she also worked for another employer who did withhold taxes, the child could file **Form 1040** to get a refund.

Federal law allows parents to hire their own children under or over the age of 14. In some states, you can't hire your own children who are younger than age 14. Check your state and local laws for any other restrictions on hiring your own children. As with hiring your spouse, keeping good records and treating the work in a proper, businesslike fashion is important. This means that the child must be doing work for your business, and the wages you pay must be distinguished from the child's allowance. See the *Record-Keeping Guide* for more information. Here are some tips to follow:

- Prepare a job description that details the responsibilities of the job: play with the children, clean up before and after the children, prepare meals for the children, clean toys, keep records, and so on. Do not include personal activities such as shopping, mowing the lawn, and running family errands.
- Prepare a written agreement between you and your family member that describes the employment arrangement: days and hours of work, pay, and so on. Both parties should sign this agreement.
- Keep a daily record of when the work is done. If the work is done at the same time every day, simply record the days and hours worked: Monday 9:00 a.m.–10:00 a.m., Tuesday 9:00 a.m.–10:00 a.m., Wednesday 9:00 a.m.–10:00 a.m., and so on.
- Write out a receipt for each payment, get the family member to sign it, and keep a copy: "Payment of $25 cash for 5 hours of work January 3–7." It is not necessary to

pay by check; you can pay with cash. Make this payment out of a separate business account if you have one.

- Payments to family members must be reasonable. If you have a $15,000 business profit, it is unreasonable to pay your own children $6,000 in wages. Payment of $20 per hour to your 15-year-old is also unreasonable. The test of what is reasonable is probably how much you would be willing to pay someone who is not a family member.
- If you also give your child an allowance, keep a record of when you gave this allowance and how much it was.

Labor Law Posters

If you hire employees, you are required to post posters in your home explaining the rights of employees concerning minimum wage and workplace safety. You can put these posters in a back room, as long as it's accessible to employees. You can get these posters for free from the U.S. Department of Labor (www.dol.gov/general/topics/posters). This site also gives links to your state department of labor where there may be additional posters you must post. Scammers charge employers fees for these posters. Don't be fooled; you can get them for free.

Applying for an EIN

Before you can report your employment taxes, you must apply for an employer identification number (EIN). To get an EIN go to the IRS website at www.irs.gov. Enter "Online EIN" in the search box and answer the questions that appear on the screen. If you expect to pay less than $4,000 in total wages for the year, you may be eligible to file the annual **Form 944** rather than the quarterly **Form 941** (see this chapter for further information).

You can also get your EIN by filling out **Form SS-4** (available on the IRS website). Call the IRS Business and Specialty Tax Line (800-829-4933) for help in filling out this form.

If your employee doesn't have a Social Security number, she can apply for one by filling out **Form SS-5 Application for a Social Security Card**, which she can find at the nearest Social Security office.

Don't be fooled into paying anyone to receive your EIN. Some companies (EIN Filing Service, for one) charge a fee to help you get your EIN. Stay away from such "services."

Form I-9 Eligibility of the Employee

Every employer must verify that a new employee is a U.S. citizen or is eligible to work in the United States legally. To prove this, the employee must show evidence (such as a birth certificate, Social Security card, or passport) to the employer. Both parties must fill out and sign **Form I-9**.

The employer must keep **Form I-9** for three years after the date of hire or one year after the employment is terminated, whichever is later.

Form **SS-4** (Rev. December 2019) Department of the Treasury Internal Revenue Service

Application for Employer Identification Number

(For use by employers, corporations, partnerships, trusts, estates, churches, government agencies, Indian tribal entities, certain individuals, and others.)

► Go to *www.irs.gov/FormSS4* for instructions and the latest information.

► See separate instructions for each line. ► Keep a copy for your records.

OMB No. 1545-0003

EIN

Type or print clearly.

1 Legal name of entity (or individual) for whom the EIN is being requested
SONJA OLSON

2 Trade name of business (if different from name on line 1)
FAMILY CHILD CARE

3 Executor, administrator, trustee, "care of" name

4a Mailing address (room, apt., suite no. and street, or P.O. box)
421 PORTLAND AVENUE

5a Street address (if different) (Don't enter a P.O. box.)

4b City, state, and ZIP code (if foreign, see instructions)
BOISE, ID 83701

5b City, state, and ZIP code (if foreign, see instructions)

6 County and state where principal business is located
SMITH COUNTY, ID

7a Name of responsible party

7b SSN, ITIN, or EIN

8a Is this application for a limited liability company (LLC) (or a foreign equivalent)? ☐ Yes ☑ No

8b If 8a is "Yes," enter the number of LLC members ►

8c If 8a is "Yes," was the LLC organized in the United States? ☐ Yes ☐ No

9a **Type of entity** (check only one box). **Caution:** If 8a is "Yes," see the instructions for the correct box to check.

☑ Sole proprietor (SSN) 465-12-7748
☐ Partnership
☐ Corporation (enter form number to be filed) ►
☐ Personal service corporation
☐ Church or church-controlled organization
☐ Other nonprofit organization (specify) ►
☐ Other (specify) ►
☐ Estate (SSN of decedent)
☐ Plan administrator (TIN)
☐ Trust (TIN of grantor)
☐ Military/National Guard ☐ State/local government
☐ Farmers' cooperative ☐ Federal government
☐ REMIC ☐ Indian tribal governments/enterprises
Group Exemption Number (GEN) if any ►

9b If a corporation, name the state or foreign country (if applicable) where incorporated | State | Foreign country

10 **Reason for applying** (check only one box)

☐ Started new business (specify type) ►
☑ Hired employees (Check the box and see line 13.)
☐ Compliance with IRS withholding regulations
☐ Other (specify) ►
☐ Banking purpose (specify purpose) ►
☐ Changed type of organization (specify new type) ►
☐ Purchased going business
☐ Created a trust (specify type) ►
☐ Created a pension plan (specify type) ►

11 Date business started or acquired (month, day, year). See instructions.
1/1/2019

12 Closing month of accounting year

13 Highest number of employees expected in the next 12 months (enter -0- if none). If no employees expected, skip line 14.

Agricultural	Household	Other

14 If you expect your employment tax liability to be $1,000 or less in a full calendar year **and** want to file Form 944 annually instead of Forms 941 quarterly, check here. (Your employment tax liability generally will be $1,000 or less if you expect to pay $5,000 or less in total wages.) If you don't check this box, you must file Form 941 for every quarter. ☐

15 First date wages or annuities were paid (month, day, year). **Note:** If applicant is a withholding agent, enter date income will first be paid to nonresident alien (month, day, year) . . . ► 1/1/2020

16 Check **one** box that best describes the principal activity of your business.
☐ Health care & social assistance ☐ Wholesale-agent/broker
☐ Construction ☐ Rental & leasing ☐ Transportation & warehousing ☐ Accommodation & food service ☐ Wholesale-other ☐ Retail
☐ Real estate ☐ Manufacturing ☐ Finance & insurance ☑ Other (specify) ► FAMILY CHILD CARE

17 Indicate principal line of merchandise sold, specific construction work done, products produced, or services provided.

18 Has the applicant entity shown on line 1 ever applied for and received an EIN? ☐ Yes ☑ No
If "Yes," write previous EIN here ►

Third Party Designee

Complete this section **only** if you want to authorize the named individual to receive the entity's EIN and answer questions about the completion of this form.

Designee's name | Designee's telephone number (include area code)

Address and ZIP code | Designee's fax number (include area code)

Under penalties of perjury, I declare that I have examined this application, and to the best of my knowledge and belief, it is true, correct, and complete.

Name and title (type or print clearly) ► SONJA OLSON

Applicant's telephone number (include area code) (418) 222-7261

Applicant's fax number (include area code)

Signature ► Sonja Olson Date ► 1/5/2020

For Privacy Act and Paperwork Reduction Act Notice, see separate instructions. Cat. No. 16055N Form **SS-4** (Rev. 12-2019)

Employment Eligibility Verification
Department of Homeland Security
U.S. Citizenship and Immigration Services

USCIS
Form I-9
OMB No. 1615-0047
Expires 10/31/2022

►START HERE: Read instructions carefully before completing this form. The instructions must be available, either in paper or electronically, during completion of this form. Employers are liable for errors in the completion of this form.

ANTI-DISCRIMINATION NOTICE: It is illegal to discriminate against work-authorized individuals. Employers **CANNOT** specify which document(s) an employee may present to establish employment authorization and identity. The refusal to hire or continue to employ an individual because the documentation presented has a future expiration date may also constitute illegal discrimination.

Section 1. Employee Information and Attestation *(Employees must complete and sign Section 1 of Form I-9 no later than the **first day of employment**, but not before accepting a job offer.)*

Last Name *(Family Name)*	First Name *(Given Name)*	Middle Initial	Other Last Names Used *(if any)*
OLSON	SONJA		

Address *(Street Number and Name)*	Apt. Number	City or Town	State	ZIP Code
421 PORTLAND AVENUE			MN	55118

Date of Birth *(mm/dd/yyyy)*	U.S. Social Security Number	Employee's E-mail Address	Employee's Telephone Number
01/10/1990	123 - 45 - 6789		651-123-9876

I am aware that federal law provides for imprisonment and/or fines for false statements or use of false documents in connection with the completion of this form.

I attest, under penalty of perjury, that I am (check one of the following boxes):

- [√] 1. A citizen of the United States
- [ ] 2. A noncitizen national of the United States *(See instructions)*
- [ ] 3. A lawful permanent resident (Alien Registration Number/USCIS Number): ______
- [ ] 4. An alien authorized to work until (expiration date, if applicable, mm/dd/yyyy): ______
  Some aliens may write "N/A" in the expiration date field. *(See instructions)*

Aliens authorized to work must provide only one of the following document numbers to complete Form I-9: An Alien Registration Number/USCIS Number OR Form I-94 Admission Number OR Foreign Passport Number.

1. Alien Registration Number/USCIS Number: ______

OR

2. Form I-94 Admission Number: ______

OR

3. Foreign Passport Number: ______

Country of Issuance: ______

QR Code - Section 1
Do Not Write In This Space

Signature of Employee	Today's Date *(mm/dd/yyyy)*
Leland Mullen	01/01/2020

Preparer and/or Translator Certification (check one):

[ ] I did not use a preparer or translator. [ ] A preparer(s) and/or translator(s) assisted the employee in completing Section 1.

(Fields below must be completed and signed when preparers and/or translators assist an employee in completing Section 1.)

I attest, under penalty of perjury, that I have assisted in the completion of Section 1 of this form and that to the best of my knowledge the information is true and correct.

Signature of Preparer or Translator	Today's Date *(mm/dd/yyyy)*

Last Name *(Family Name)*	First Name *(Given Name)*

Address *(Street Number and Name)*	City or Town	State	ZIP Code

STOP *Employer Completes Next Page* STOP

Employment Eligibility Verification
Department of Homeland Security
U.S. Citizenship and Immigration Services

USCIS
Form I-9
OMB No. 1615-0047
Expires 10/31/2022

Section 2. Employer or Authorized Representative Review and Verification

(Employers or their authorized representative must complete and sign Section 2 within 3 business days of the employee's first day of employment. You must physically examine one document from List A OR a combination of one document from List B and one document from List C as listed on the "Lists of Acceptable Documents.")

Employee Info from Section 1	Last Name *(Family Name)*	First Name *(Given Name)*	M.I.	Citizenship/Immigration Status
	MULLEN	LELAND	P	1

List A Identity and Employment Authorization	OR	List B Identity	AND	List C Employment Authorization
Document Title: PASSPORT		Document Title:		Document Title:
Issuing Authority: US DEPARTMENT OF STATE		Issuing Authority:		Issuing Authority:
Document Number: 54321		Document Number:		Document Number:
Expiration Date *(if any) (mm/dd/yyyy)*: 09/04/2021		Expiration Date *(if any) (mm/dd/yyyy)*:		Expiration Date *(if any) (mm/dd/yyyy)*:
Document Title:				
Issuing Authority:				
Document Number:				
Expiration Date *(if any) (mm/dd/yyyy)*:				
Document Title:				
Issuing Authority:				
Document Number:				
Expiration Date *(if any) (mm/dd/yyyy)*:				

Additional Information

QR Code - Sections 2 & 3
Do Not Write In This Space

Certification: I attest, under penalty of perjury, that (1) I have examined the document(s) presented by the above-named employee, (2) the above-listed document(s) appear to be genuine and to relate to the employee named, and (3) to the best of my knowledge the employee is authorized to work in the United States.

The employee's first day of employment *(mm/dd/yyyy)*: 01/01/2020 ***(See instructions for exemptions)***

Signature of Employer or Authorized Representative	Today's Date *(mm/dd/yyyy)*	Title of Employer or Authorized Representative
Sonja Olson	01/01/2020	OWNER

Last Name of Employer or Authorized Representative	First Name of Employer or Authorized Representative	Employer's Business or Organization Name
OLSON	SONJA	CHILD CARE BUSINESS

Employer's Business or Organization Address (*Street Number and Name*)	City or Town	State	ZIP Code
421 PORTLAND AVE.	BOISE	ID	83701

Section 3. Reverification and Rehires *(To be completed and signed by employer or authorized representative.)*

A. New Name *(if applicable)*			**B.** Date of Rehire *(if applicable)*
Last Name *(Family Name)*	First Name *(Given Name)*	Middle Initial	Date *(mm/dd/yyyy)*

C. If the employee's previous grant of employment authorization has expired, provide the information for the document or receipt that establishes continuing employment authorization in the space provided below.

Document Title	Document Number	Expiration Date *(if any) (mm/dd/yyyy)*

I attest, under penalty of perjury, that to the best of my knowledge, this employee is authorized to work in the United States, and if the employee presented document(s), the document(s) I have examined appear to be genuine and to relate to the individual.

Signature of Employer or Authorized Representative	Today's Date *(mm/dd/yyyy)*	Name of Employer or Authorized Representative

The Rules of Tax Withholding

There are different requirements for withholding and paying payroll taxes for different types of employees. The federal payroll taxes that are subject to withholding include the following:

- federal income tax
- Social Security/Medicare taxes
- federal unemployment taxes

You need to fill out and file different forms for each of the above kinds of taxes, and you may also need to pay or withhold state and local taxes. Here's a chart that summarizes the employer's responsibilities for federal payroll taxes:

	Must withhold federal income taxes	**Must withhold and pay Social Security/ Medicare taxes**	**Must pay federal unemployment taxes*****
Nonfamily employee*	Yes**	Yes	Yes
Spouse	Yes	Yes	No
Provider's own child 18 or over	Yes**	Yes	No
Provider's own child under 18	Yes**	No	No
Independent contractor	No	No	No

For the purposes of payroll taxes, siblings, nieces or nephews, and other relatives with whom you don't have a parent-child relationship aren't considered to be family members, and you must withhold payroll taxes for them just as you would for a nonfamily employee. For example, if you hire your 16-year-old granddaughter, you must withhold Social Security and Medicare taxes from her wages.

If You Pay Small Amounts

If you pay a nonfamily member a small amount of money during the year, you still have to treat the person as an employee. If the total paid is small, you may not have to pay any unemployment taxes, but you'll still have to withhold Social Security and Medicare taxes and file the appropriate payroll forms. The minimum requirements for withholding are as follows:

- If you pay any amount, you must withhold Social Security and Medicare taxes.
- If you pay less than $1,500 in a calendar quarter, you don't have to pay any federal unemployment taxes.
- If the employee doesn't expect to owe any taxes, you don't have to withhold federal income taxes.

Federal Income Tax Withholding

To calculate how much federal income tax you must withhold, have the employee fill out **Form W-4**. Ask the employee to fill it out when she starts work. If your employee doesn't return a completed **Form W-4** to you, withhold taxes as if the employee were single with no withholding allowances. You won't generally file **Form W-4** with the IRS; instead, you'll keep it with your records to determine how much tax to withhold.

*A nonfamily employee is anyone except your spouse and your own children.

**Only if the employee requests that you do so.

***This assumes that the employer pays any employee $1,500 or more in any calendar quarter or that an employee worked for some part of a day in any 20 different weeks of the year. Unemployment tax is due for provider's own child age 21 or over.

Income tax withholding can be figured a number of ways; they're listed in **Circular E**. You must withhold income taxes for each payroll period. The payroll period is the period of service for which you usually pay wages (for example, once a week, once every two weeks). The amount you need to withhold will depend on the amount of wages, the number of withholding allowances, and if the employee is married or single.

Form **W-4**
Department of the Treasury Internal Revenue Service

Employee's Withholding Certificate
▶ Complete Form W-4 so that your employer can withhold the correct federal income tax from your pay.
▶ Give Form W-4 to your employer.
▶ Your withholding is subject to review by the IRS.

OMB No. 1545-0074
2020

Step 1: Enter Personal Information

(a) First name and middle initial: MANUEL
Last name: RUIZ
Address: 168 EAST CURTIS STREET
City or town, state, and ZIP code: ST. PETERSBURG, FL 81623
(b) Social security number: 416-22-5757
▶ **Does your name match the name on your social security card?** If not, to ensure you get credit for your earnings, contact SSA at 800-772-1213 or go to www.ssa.gov.

(c) ☑ **Single or Married filing separately**
☐ **Married filing jointly** (or Qualifying widow(er))
☐ **Head of household** (Check only if you're unmarried and pay more than half the costs of keeping up a home for yourself and a qualifying individual.)

Complete Steps 2–4 ONLY if they apply to you; otherwise, skip to Step 5. See page 2 for more information on each step, who can claim exemption from withholding, when to use the online estimator, and privacy.

Step 2: Multiple Jobs or Spouse Works

Complete this step if you (1) hold more than one job at a time, or (2) are married filing jointly and your spouse also works. The correct amount of withholding depends on income earned from all of these jobs.

Do **only one** of the following.

(a) Use the estimator at *www.irs.gov/W4App* for most accurate withholding for this step (and Steps 3–4); **or**

(b) Use the Multiple Jobs Worksheet on page 3 and enter the result in Step 4(c) below for roughly accurate withholding; **or**

(c) If there are only two jobs total, you may check this box. Do the same on Form W-4 for the other job. This option is accurate for jobs with similar pay; otherwise, more tax than necessary may be withheld . . . . . ▶ ☐

TIP: To be accurate, submit a 2020 Form W-4 for all other jobs. If you (or your spouse) have self-employment income, including as an independent contractor, use the estimator.

Complete Steps 3–4(b) on Form W-4 for only ONE of these jobs. Leave those steps blank for the other jobs. (Your withholding will be most accurate if you complete Steps 3–4(b) on the Form W-4 for the highest paying job.)

Step 3: Claim Dependents

If your income will be $200,000 or less ($400,000 or less if married filing jointly):

Multiply the number of qualifying children under age 17 by $2,000 ▶ $

Multiply the number of other dependents by $500 . . . . ▶ $

Add the amounts above and enter the total here . . . . **3** $

1

Step 4 (optional): Other Adjustments

(a) Other income (not from jobs). If you want tax withheld for other income you expect this year that won't have withholding, enter the amount of other income here. This may include interest, dividends, and retirement income . . . . **4(a)** $

(b) Deductions. If you expect to claim deductions other than the standard deduction and want to reduce your withholding, use the Deductions Worksheet on page 3 and enter the result here . . . . **4(b)** $

(c) Extra withholding. Enter any additional tax you want withheld each **pay period** . **4(c)** $

Step 5: Sign Here

Under penalties of perjury, I declare that this certificate, to the best of my knowledge and belief, is true, correct, and complete.

▶ *Manuel Ruiz*
Employee's signature (This form is not valid unless you sign it.)
▶ 3/4/2019
Date

Employers Only
Employer's name and address | First date of employment | Employer identification number (EIN)

For Privacy Act and Paperwork Reduction Act Notice, see page 3. Cat. No. 10220Q Form **W-4** (2020)

MAKING FEDERAL INCOME TAX DEPOSITS

The deadline for depositing the income taxes you've withheld depends on how much these taxes amount to. If you withhold $500 or more in income taxes, Social Security, and Medicare taxes in a three-month period, you should deposit the taxes monthly by the fifteenth day of the following month. If the total you withhold is less than $500 for a three-month period, you can deposit the taxes by the end of the month following that quarter. Your federal tax deposit must be made electronically using the Electronic Federal Tax Payment System (EFTPS). If you do not want to use the EFTPS, you can arrange for your tax professional, bank, or payroll service to make deposits on your behalf. The EFTPS is a free service. To enroll in the EFTPS, visit www.eftps.gov or call 800-555-4477. For more information, see IRS **Publication 966 Electronic Federal Tax Payment System: A Guide to Getting Started**.

Social Security and Medicare Withholding

You must also withhold and pay Social Security and Medicare taxes. For wages paid last year, the Social Security tax rate is 6.2% for you as an employer and 6.2% for the employee. The rate for Medicare is 1.45% for you as an employer and 1.45% for the employee. In other words, you must withhold a total of 7.65% of the gross wages you pay an employee. As the employer, you must pay 7.65% into the Social Security and Medicare fund. Refer to **Circular E** for the tables that show how much tax to withhold.

Making Social Security and Medicare Deposits

If you owe less than $2,500 in taxes for federal income tax, Social Security, and Medicare withholding (employer and employee share) in any calendar quarter, you must deposit the money by the end of the month following the calendar quarter (by April 30, July 31, October 31, and January 31). If you owe more than $2,500 in a quarter, you must file monthly. You must pay these taxes electronically using the EFTPS (www.eftps.gov).

Continue to file **Form 941** as long as you have an employee, even if you don't owe any payroll taxes, because it proves that you have an employee. Without this form, the IRS may assume that you don't have an employee and may not allow you to take employee expenses as a business deduction. If you temporarily stop hiring an employee, continue filing **Form 941** even if you have no taxes to report. When you stop paying wages, file a final return.

Form 944

You can avoid filing **Form 941** if you owe less than $1,000 in payroll taxes for the year. (The IRS created **Form 944 Employer's Annual Federal Tax Return** in response to my request to reduce the paperwork for taxpayers who pay small amounts to their employees.) Payroll taxes include Social Security and Medicare taxes (15.3%) and withheld federal income taxes (10% or 12% or 22% or 24% or more). You can use **Form 944** if you pay less than $4,000 in wages to all your employees during a year. This option is something to consider as you look forward to 2021. If you use **Form 944**, you must use the Electronic Federal Tax Payment System (EFTPS) to pay your payroll taxes.

You may have already been notified by the IRS to file **Form 944**. If not, and you wish to use **Form 944**, you must contact the IRS to request permission. Call the IRS at 800-829-4933 by April 1, 2021, or send a written request postmarked by March 15, 2021. See the instructions to **Form 944** for the mailing address.

If you are a new employer as of 2020, you can indicate that you want to file **Form 944** when you apply for an employer identification number (see page 153). For more information, visit www.irs.gov/form944.

Federal Unemployment Tax (FUTA)

If you paid an employee $1,500 or more in any calendar quarter or had any employee who worked for some part of a day in any 20 different weeks during the year, you must pay federal unemployment tax (FUTA). The unemployment tax is based on the first $7,000 of wages paid during the year to each employee. This rate assumes that you have paid state payroll or unemployment taxes on time. If not, you will owe unemployment taxes at a rate of .6%. You do not have to pay a FUTA tax on wages over $7,000 for each employee. (In some states, you may be entitled to a reduction in your federal unemployment tax because of your state unemployment tax rules.) The unemployment tax rate is 0.6% for 2020.

You must pay this tax in addition to the wages you pay your employee; you may not withhold or deduct these taxes from the employee's wages.

Making FUTA Deposits

If your total FUTA tax is less than $100 (or $12,500 in wages), pay it when you file your **Form 940**. You need to file this form by January 31 of the following year. If you owe more than $100 in FUTA taxes at the end of any quarter (you can accumulate the tax owed from one quarter to the next), you must make deposits by the end of the month following the quarter. You must pay your FUTA taxes electronically using the EFTPS. If you do not want to use the EFTPS, you can arrange for your tax professional, bank, or payroll service to make deposits on your behalf. The EFTPS is a free service. To enroll in the EFTPS, see www.eftps.gov or call 800-555-4477. For more information, see IRS **Publication 966**.

If You Haven't Filed Any Payroll Forms This Year

If you haven't yet filed the proper payroll forms and it's now early 2021, your best option is to file **Form 941** for the fourth quarter by January 31 and pay all the taxes you owe. You should file **Form 941** as soon as possible, even if you're filing late. The sooner you file, the less interest will accumulate on any taxes you owe. If you miss the January 31 deadline, you can file an amended tax return after April 15 and include the fourth-quarter filing of **Form 941** to cover the year.

Forms W-2 and W-3

In addition to the above forms, you must also file forms W-2 and W-3 at the end of the year for all types of employees:

- **Form W-2**
  You must file this form if you have withheld any income, Social Security, or Medicare taxes. It summarizes the wages you've paid and taxes you've withheld for each employee. You must give a copy to each employee as soon as possible after the end of the year, and no later than January 31. You must also send a copy of the W-2 to the IRS by January 31. An employee who stops working for you during the year may ask you to provide this form within 30 days.
- **Form W-3**
  Use this form to transmit a copy of **Form W-2** to the Social Security Administration. That agency will send the income tax data on **Form W-2** on to the IRS. You must submit **Form W-3** by January 31. Mail **Form W-2** and **Form W-3** to the address indicated on the instructions for **Form W-3**.

Note

If you withheld payroll taxes in 2020 that you did not send to the IRS until January 2021, you can still claim them as a business deduction in 2020. Payroll taxes that you pay (Social Security/Medicare tax, federal and state unemployment tax) are deductible in the year you pay them. So if you withheld $200 in Social Security/Medicare taxes for the last quarter of 2020 and sent them in to the IRS along with the employer share of these taxes ($200), you can deduct the withheld taxes in 2020, but you must wait until 2021 to deduct the employer share.

How to Fill Out Payroll Tax Forms

Filling out all the payroll tax forms for an employee can be a real pain in the neck, but the first year is usually the hardest. After that, it becomes easier because the forms are more familiar. And once you've completed all the proper forms, you'll be able to claim the wages and taxes (Social Security, Medicare, and federal and state unemployment taxes) that you paid as a business deduction on **Schedule C**, line 26. Let's look at three examples of filling out employee payroll tax forms—for a nonfamily employee, your own child under age 18, and your spouse. You'll find samples of some of the forms for the first two examples at the end of this chapter. (Check for other state or local rules in your area.)

Example 1: Hiring a Nonfamily Employee

You hire your first employee, Jill, on January 1 of last year. Jill works three days a week, eight hours a day, and you pay her $7.25 per hour. You write her a check at the end of every week. What obligations do you have to withhold and pay taxes to the IRS?

Step One: Employee Eligibility

When you hire Jill, ask her to fill out **Form I-9** to affirm that she isn't an undocumented worker.

Step Two: Employer Identification Number

As soon as you know that you will be hiring an employee, file **Form SS-4** to get an employer identification number. Use this number on all your employer forms.

Step Three: Federal Income Tax Withholding

Jill is single, has no dependents, and declares one withholding allowance on her **Form W-4**, which she filled out the day she started work. Her weekly wages amount to 8 hours x 5 days x $7.25/hour = $290. According to the the wage bracket tables, you need to withhold $22.30 in income tax. You therefore reduce Jill's weekly paycheck by $22.30 for income tax withholding.

In the first quarter of the year, Jill will earn $3,770 ($290 per week x 13 weeks). The income tax on this will be $289.90 ($22.30 x 13). Since this amount, plus Jill's quarterly Social Security and Medicare taxes, will be less than $2,500 per quarter, you don't have to deposit it with the IRS every month; you can wait and pay it when you file your quarterly **Form 941**.

Step Four: Social Security and Medicare Tax Withholding

To calculate Jill's Social Security and Medicare taxes, multiply her weekly wages by 7.65%: $290 x 7.65% = $22.19. This will further reduce her weekly paycheck by $22.19. Jill's actual take-home pay is now $290 – $22.30 – $22.19 = $245.51. Each week you must also pay $22.19 ($290 x 7.65%) of your own money into Social Security and Medicare.

Complete **Form 941** by April 30 to cover the first three months of the year. At this time you will owe the IRS $866.71 for Social Security and Medicare taxes:

$576.81	$290 x 13 x 15.3% (7.65% withheld plus 7.65% paid by you)
+$289.90	Income tax withheld ($22.30 x 13 weeks)
$866.71	Amount you owe the IRS

As long as Jill's hours and wages remain the same, you'll keep paying the IRS $866.71 every quarter. Pay this amount electronically using the EFTPS (www.eftps.gov).

STEP FIVE: FEDERAL UNEMPLOYMENT TAX

Jill earned $15,080 last year ($290 per week x 52 weeks). Since this is more than $1,500, you must pay federal unemployment tax (FUTA) on the first $7,000. At the end of the year, you will fill out **Form 940** and file it by January 31. You will owe $42 on **Form 940**:

$7,000	Jill's wages subject to FUTA tax
x 0.6%	FUTA tax
$42.00	Total FUTA tax

This amount is not withheld from Jill's paycheck; it's paid directly by you. Pay this amount electronically using the EFTPS (www.eftps.gov).

STEP SIX: END-OF-THE-YEAR REPORTING

At the end of the year, fill out **Form W-2** and **Form W-3**. These forms will show the following:

$15,080.00	Wages paid to Jill (**W-2** and **W-3**, lines 1, 3, and 5)
$1,159.60	Federal income tax withheld ($22.30 x 52 weeks) (**W-2** and **W-3**, line 2)
$934.96	Social Security tax withheld ($15,080 x 6.2%) (**W-2** and **W-3**, line 4)
$218.66	Medicare tax withheld ($15,080 x 1.45%) (**W-2** and **W-3**, line 6)

SUMMARY

$15,080.00	Jill's yearly wages
– $1,159.60	Federal income tax withheld
– $1,153.62	Social Security and Medicare tax withheld (7.65%)
$12,766.78	Jill's take-home pay

$1,153.62	Additional Social Security and Medicare taxes you paid (7.65%)
+ $42.00	Federal unemployment tax you paid
$1,195.62	Total taxes you paid for having Jill as an employee

Example 2: Hiring Your Own Child

You have hired your daughter Clarisse, age 16, to clean your home before children arrive in the morning. She works one hour a day, five days a week, and you pay her $5.00 per hour. You keep a record of the work she does and write her a check at the end of every week. You have an employment agreement stating her job description and pay. (See the *Record-Keeping Guide* for a sample.) Clarisse will earn $1,300 a year ($25 a week x 52 weeks). You keep records of your payments to her and make out a receipt each time you pay her. You must file the following IRS forms for this employee:

STEP ONE: EMPLOYEE ELIGIBILITY

Fill out **Form I-9**.

STEP TWO: EMPLOYER IDENTIFICATION NUMBER

File **Form SS-4**.

STEP THREE: FEDERAL INCOME TAX WITHHOLDING

Clarisse must fill out **Form W-4**. She declares no withholding allowance because she is a child and you don't have to withhold income tax on weekly wages of $25.

STEP FOUR: SOCIAL SECURITY AND MEDICARE TAX WITHHOLDING
Since Clarisse is under age 18, you don't have to withhold any Social Security or Medicare taxes for her. File **Form 941**, and check the box on line 4. Continue filing this form quarterly, even though you don't owe any taxes.

Note: Since you paid less than $4,000 in wages to Clarisse, you could use the annual **Form 944** instead of the quarterly **Form 941**. If you have not already been contacted by the IRS and told that you can use **Form 944**, fill out **Form 941**. To find out if you can use **Form 944**, call the IRS at 800-829-4933. See the end of this chapter for a sample of how to fill out **Form 944**.

Forms for Family Employees

If you have hired nonfamily employees or your own children, enter the total wages paid on line 2 of **Form 941**.

I've heard from some providers that the IRS told them it wasn't necessary to file **Forms 941**, **W-2**, and **W-3** when hiring their own children under age 18, since no taxes are due; however, I believe that it's important to file these forms as further evidence that the payments to your children were wages and not an allowance.

STEP FIVE: FEDERAL UNEMPLOYMENT TAX
Since Clarisse is under age 21, you don't owe any federal unemployment taxes. File **Form 940** and claim an exemption for wages on line 4.

STEP SIX: END-OF-THE-YEAR REPORTING
At the end of the year, fill out **Form W-2** and **Form W-3**.

SUMMARY

Wages paid to Clarisse	$1,300
Federal income tax withheld	$0
Social Security and Medicare taxes withheld	$0
Federal unemployment tax withheld	$0

Example 3: Hiring Your Spouse

You've hired your husband, John, to help with your business. He works five hours a week, and you pay him $10 per hour. You keep a record of the work he does and write him a check at the end of every week. John will earn $2,600 a year ($50 a week x 52 weeks).

STEP ONE: EMPLOYEE ELIGIBILITY
Fill out **Form I-9**.

STEP TWO: EMPLOYER IDENTIFICATION NUMBER
File **Form SS-4**.

STEP THREE: FEDERAL INCOME TAX WITHHOLDING
You can avoid withholding federal income tax if John is having enough withheld from the paycheck of another employer. If he does this, you don't have to fill out **Form W-4**.

STEP FOUR: SOCIAL SECURITY AND MEDICARE TAX WITHHOLDING

You must withhold Social Security and Medicare taxes on John's earnings. Multiply his weekly wages by 7.65%: $50 x 7.65% = $3.83. His weekly paycheck is now $46.17. You must pay $3.83 ($50 x 7.65%) of your own money into Social Security and Medicare. Complete **Form 941** by April to cover the first three months of the year. At the end of three months, John will have earned $650 ($50 x 13 weeks = $650). You will owe the IRS $99.45 for Social Security and Medicare taxes ($50 per week x 13 weeks x 15.3% [7.65% from John's paycheck and 7.65% from your pocket] = $99.45). Enter $99.45 on lines 5d, 6e, 10, and 13.

Note: Since you paid your husband less than $4,000 in wages, you can use the annual **Form 944** (see below) instead of the quarterly **Form 941** as long as you received permission to do so from the IRS. Call the IRS at 800-829-4933 to receive permission.

STEP FIVE: FEDERAL UNEMPLOYMENT TAX

You do not have to pay the federal unemployment tax.

STEP SIX: END-OF-THE-YEAR REPORTING

At the end of the year, fill out **Forms W-2** and **W-3**. You will show $322.40 in Social Security taxes withheld on line 4 ($2,600 x 12.4%) and $75.40 in Medicare taxes withheld on line 6 ($2,600 x 2.9%).

Example 4: Hiring a Part-Time Employee

You may be able to avoid filing the quarterly **Form 941** and instead use **Form 944** if you paid less than $4,000 in total wages last year. To be able to file **Form 944** for your taxes, you either must have been notified by the IRS or must call the IRS to receive permission. *Do not file **Form 944** unless you have IRS approval.*

Let's say you paid Ophelia Lopez $1,000 to provide substitute care for 50 hours last year. You should have withheld 7.65% of her pay ($76.50) when you paid her. Use **Form 944V** to make your payment. See pages 175–176 for how **Form 944** should be filled out. The deadline to file these forms is January 31. In this example, you would still file forms **I-9**, **W-2**, and **W-3**, but not **Form 941** or **Form 940** (because the amount paid was less than $1,500 in any calendar quarter).

Note: Most states still require you to file quarterly state payroll taxes (state unemployment) even when you file **Form 944**.

For more information about the tax issues discussed in this chapter, refer to the related topics in the other chapters of this book and the Redleaf Press *Family Child Care Record-Keeping Guide.*

For Employee Jill

Form **941 for 2020: Employer's QUARTERLY Federal Tax Return** 950120
(Rev. July 2020) Department of the Treasury — Internal Revenue Service OMB No. 1545-0029

Employer identification number (EIN) 9 2 – 1 2 3 4 5 6 7

Name *(not your trade name)* SONJA OLSON

Trade name *(if any)*

Address 421 PORTLAND AVENUE
Number Street Suite or room number

BOISE ID 83701
City State ZIP code

Foreign country name Foreign province/county Foreign postal code

Report for this Quarter of 2020
(Check one.)

- [√] **1:** January, February, March
- [ ] **2:** April, May, June
- [ ] **3:** July, August, September
- [ ] **4:** October, November, December

Go to *www.irs.gov/Form941* for instructions and the latest information.

Read the separate instructions before you complete Form 941. Type or print within the boxes.

Part 1: Answer these questions for this quarter.

1	**Number of employees who received wages, tips, or other compensation for the pay period including: *Sept. 12* (Quarter 3) or *Dec. 12* (Quarter 4)**	1	1
2	**Wages, tips, and other compensation**	2	$3,770 . 00
3	**Federal income tax withheld from wages, tips, and other compensation**	3	$67 . 56
4	**If no wages, tips, and other compensation are subject to social security or Medicare tax**		☐ **Check and go to line 6.**

		Column 1		Column 2
5a	**Taxable social security wages**	$3,770 . 00	× 0.124 =	$467 . 48
5a	(i) **Qualified sick leave wages**	.	× 0.062 =	.
5a	(ii) **Qualified family leave wages**	.	× 0.062 =	.
5b	**Taxable social security tips**	.	× 0.124 =	.
5c	**Taxable Medicare wages & tips**	.	× 0.029 =	.
5d	**Taxable wages & tips subject to Additional Medicare Tax withholding**	$3,770 . 00	× 0.009 =	$109 . 33

5e	**Total social security and Medicare taxes.** Add Column 2 from lines 5a, 5a(i), 5a(ii), 5b, 5c, and 5d	5e	$576 . 81
5f	**Section 3121(q) Notice and Demand—Tax due on unreported tips** (see instructions)	5f	.
6	**Total taxes before adjustments.** Add lines 3, 5e, and 5f	6	$644 . 37
7	**Current quarter's adjustment for fractions of cents**	7	.
8	**Current quarter's adjustment for sick pay**	8	.
9	**Current quarter's adjustments for tips and group-term life insurance**	9	.
10	**Total taxes after adjustments.** Combine lines 6 through 9	10	$644 . 37
11a	**Qualified small business payroll tax credit for increasing research activities.** Attach Form 8974	11a	.
11b	**Nonrefundable portion of credit for qualified sick and family leave wages from Worksheet 1**	11b	.
11c	**Nonrefundable portion of employee retention credit from Worksheet 1**	11c	.

▶ **You MUST complete all three pages of Form 941 and SIGN it.** Next ▶

For Privacy Act and Paperwork Reduction Act Notice, see the back of the Payment Voucher. Cat. No. 17001Z Form **941** (Rev. 7-2020)

950220

Name *(not your trade name)*	Employer identification number (EIN)
SONJA OLSON	92-1234567

Part 1: Answer these questions for this quarter. *(continued)*

11d	**Total nonrefundable credits.** Add lines 11a, 11b, and 11c	11d	.
12	**Total taxes after adjustments and nonrefundable credits.** Subtract line 11d from line 10	12	$644 . 37
13a	Total deposits for this quarter, including overpayment applied from a prior quarter and overpayments applied from Form 941-X, 941-X (PR), 944-X, or 944-X (SP) filed in the current quarter	13a	.
13b	**Deferred amount of social security tax**	13b	.
13c	**Refundable portion of credit for qualified sick and family leave wages from Worksheet 1**	13c	.
13d	**Refundable portion of employee retention credit from Worksheet 1**	13d	.
13e	**Total deposits, deferrals, and refundable credits.** Add lines 13a, 13b, 13c, and 13d	13e	.
13f	**Total advances received from filing Form(s) 7200 for the quarter**	13f	.
13g	**Total deposits, deferrals, and refundable credits less advances.** Subtract line 13f from line 13e	13g	.
14	**Balance due.** If line 12 is more than line 13g, enter the difference and see instructions	14	$644 . 37
15	**Overpayment.** If line 13g is more than line 12, enter the difference [.]	Check one:	☐ Apply to next return. ☐ Send a refund.

Part 2: Tell us about your deposit schedule and tax liability for this quarter.

If you're unsure about whether you're a monthly schedule depositor or a semiweekly schedule depositor, see section 11 of Pub. 15.

16 Check one:

☐ **Line 12 on this return is less than $2,500 or line 12 on the return for the prior quarter was less than $2,500, and you didn't incur a $100,000 next-day deposit obligation during the current quarter.** If line 12 for the prior quarter was less than $2,500 but line 12 on this return is $100,000 or more, you must provide a record of your federal tax liability. If you're a monthly schedule depositor, complete the deposit schedule below; if you're a semiweekly schedule depositor, attach Schedule B (Form 941). Go to Part 3.

☐ **You were a monthly schedule depositor for the entire quarter.** Enter your tax liability for each month and total liability for the quarter, then go to Part 3.

Tax liability:	**Month 1**	.
	Month 2	.
	Month 3	.
Total liability for quarter		. **Total must equal line 12.**

☐ **You were a semiweekly schedule depositor for any part of this quarter.** Complete Schedule B (Form 941), Report of Tax Liability for Semiweekly Schedule Depositors, and attach it to Form 941. Go to Part 3.

▶ **You MUST complete all three pages of Form 941 and SIGN it.** Next ▶

Page **2** Form **941** (Rev. 7-2020)

952920

Name *(not your trade name)* SONJA OLSON

Employer identification number (EIN) 92-1234567

Part 3: Tell us about your business. If a question does NOT apply to your business, leave it blank.

17 **If your business has closed or you stopped paying wages** . . . . ☐ Check here, and

enter the final date you paid wages [/ /]; also attach a statement to your return. See instructions.

18 **If you're a seasonal employer and you don't have to file a return for every quarter of the year** . . . ☐ Check here.

19	**Qualified health plan expenses allocable to qualified sick leave wages**	19	.
20	**Qualified health plan expenses allocable to qualified family leave wages**	20	.
21	**Qualified wages for the employee retention credit**	21	.
22	**Qualified health plan expenses allocable to wages reported on line 21**	22	.
23	**Credit from Form 5884-C, line 11, for this quarter**	23	.
24	**Deferred amount of the employee share of social security tax included on line 13b** . . .	24	.
25	**Reserved for future use**	25	.

Part 4: May we speak with your third-party designee?

Do you want to allow an employee, a paid tax preparer, or another person to discuss this return with the IRS? See the instructions for details.

☐ Yes. Designee's name and phone number

Select a 5-digit personal identification number (PIN) to use when talking to the IRS.

☐ No.

Part 5: Sign here. You MUST complete all three pages of Form 941 and SIGN it.

Under penalties of perjury, I declare that I have examined this return, including accompanying schedules and statements, and to the best of my knowledge and belief, it is true, correct, and complete. Declaration of preparer (other than taxpayer) is based on all information of which preparer has any knowledge.

X **Sign your name here** *Sonja Olson*

Print your name here: SONJA OLSON

Print your title here: OWNER

Date 4 / 11 / 2020

Best daytime phone 612-222-2222

Paid Preparer Use Only

Check if you're self-employed . . . ☐

Preparer's name		PTIN	
Preparer's signature		Date	/ /
Firm's name (or yours if self-employed)		EIN	
Address		Phone	
City	State	ZIP code	

Form **940 for 2020: Employer's Annual Federal Unemployment (FUTA) Tax Return** 850113

Department of the Treasury — Internal Revenue Service OMB No. 1545-0028

Employer identification number (EIN) 9 2 – 1 2 3 4 5 6 7

Name *(not your trade name)* SONJA OLSON

Trade name *(if any)*

Address 421 PORTLAND AVENUE

Number Street Suite or room number

BOISE ID 83701

City State ZIP code

Foreign country name Foreign province/county Foreign postal code

Type of Return
(Check all that apply.)

- ☐ **a.** Amended
- ☐ **b.** Successor employer
- ☐ **c.** No payments to employees in 2020
- ☐ **d.** Final: Business closed or stopped paying wages

Go to *www.irs.gov/Form940* for instructions and the latest information.

Read the separate instructions before you complete this form. Please type or print within the boxes.

Part 1: Tell us about your return. If any line does NOT apply, leave it blank. See instructions before completing Part 1.

1a	**If you had to pay state unemployment tax in one state only, enter the state abbreviation**	1a	
1b	**If you had to pay state unemployment tax in more than one state, you are a multi-state employer**	1b	☐ Check here. Complete Schedule A (Form 940).
2	**If you paid wages in a state that is subject to CREDIT REDUCTION**	2	☐ Check here. Complete Schedule A (Form 940).

Part 2: Determine your FUTA tax before adjustments. If any line does NOT apply, leave it blank.

3	**Total payments to all employees**	3	$15,080 .
4	**Payments exempt from FUTA tax**	4	.
	Check all that apply: 4a ☐ Fringe benefits; 4b ☐ Group-term life insurance; 4c ☐ Retirement/Pension; 4d ☐ Dependent care; 4e ☐ Other		
5	**Total of payments made to each employee in excess of $7,000**	5	$8,080 .
6	**Subtotal** (line 4 + line 5 = line 6)	6	$8,080 .
7	**Total taxable FUTA wages** (line 3 – line 6 = line 7). See instructions	7	$7,000 .
8	**FUTA tax before adjustments** (line 7 x 0.006 = line 8)	8	$42 .

Part 3: Determine your adjustments. If any line does NOT apply, leave it blank.

9	**If ALL of the taxable FUTA wages you paid were excluded from state unemployment tax, multiply line 7 by 0.054** (line 7 × 0.054 = line 9). Go to line 12	9	.
10	**If SOME of the taxable FUTA wages you paid were excluded from state unemployment tax, OR you paid ANY state unemployment tax late** (after the due date for filing Form 940), complete the worksheet in the instructions. Enter the amount from line 7 of the worksheet	10	.
11	**If credit reduction applies,** enter the total from Schedule A (Form 940)	11	.

Part 4: Determine your FUTA tax and balance due or overpayment. If any line does NOT apply, leave it blank.

12	**Total FUTA tax after adjustments** (lines 8 + 9 + 10 + 11 = line 12)	12	$42 .
13	**FUTA tax deposited for the year, including any overpayment applied from a prior year**	13	.
14	**Balance due.** If line 12 is more than line 13, enter the excess on line 14. • If line 14 is more than $500, you must deposit your tax. • If line 14 is $500 or less, you may pay with this return. See instructions	14	$42 .
15	**Overpayment.** If line 13 is more than line 12, enter the excess on line 15 and check a box below	15	.

► You **MUST** complete both pages of this form and **SIGN** it. Check one: ☐ Apply to next return. ☐ Send a refund.

Next ►

For Privacy Act and Paperwork Reduction Act Notice, see the back of the Payment Voucher. Cat. No. 11234O Form **940** (2020)

850212

Name *(not your trade name)* SONJA OLSON

Employer identification number (EIN) 92-1234567

Part 5: Report your FUTA tax liability by quarter only if line 12 is more than $500. If not, go to Part 6.

16 **Report the amount of your FUTA tax liability for each quarter; do NOT enter the amount you deposited. If you had no liability for a quarter, leave the line blank.**

16a **1st quarter** (January 1 – March 31)	16a	.
16b **2nd quarter** (April 1 – June 30)	16b	.
16c **3rd quarter** (July 1 – September 30)	16c	.
16d **4th quarter** (October 1 – December 31)	16d	.
17 **Total tax liability for the year** (lines 16a + 16b + 16c + 16d = line 17)	17	. **Total must equal line 12.**

Part 6: May we speak with your third-party designee?

Do you want to allow an employee, a paid tax preparer, or another person to discuss this return with the IRS? See the instructions for details.

☐ **Yes.** Designee's name and phone number

Select a 5-digit personal identification number (PIN) to use when talking to the IRS.

☐ **No.**

Part 7: Sign here. You MUST complete both pages of this form and SIGN it.

Under penalties of perjury, I declare that I have examined this return, including accompanying schedules and statements, and to the best of my knowledge and belief, it is true, correct, and complete, and that no part of any payment made to a state unemployment fund claimed as a credit was, or is to be, deducted from the payments made to employees. Declaration of preparer (other than taxpayer) is based on all information of which preparer has any knowledge.

X Sign your name here *Sonja Olson*

Print your name here: SONJA OLSON

Print your title here: OWNER

Date: 4 / 11 /2020

Best daytime phone: 612-222-2222

▼ **Detach Here and Mail With Your Payment and Form 940.** ▼

Form **940-V** — Department of the Treasury, Internal Revenue Service

Payment Voucher

▶ **Don't staple or attach this voucher to your payment.**

OMB No. 1545-0028

2020

1 Enter your employer identification number (EIN). 92-1234567

2 **Enter the amount of your payment.** ▶ Make your check or money order payable to **"United States Treasury"**

Dollars	Cents
$42	

3 Enter your business name (individual name if sole proprietor).
SONJA OLSON

Enter your address.
421 PORTLAND AVENUE

Enter your city, state, and ZIP code; or your city, foreign country name, foreign province/county, and foreign postal code.
BOISE, ID 83701

22222 | VOID ☐ | a Employee's social security number | For Official Use Only ▶ OMB No. 1545-0008

b Employer identification number (EIN) 92-1234567	1 Wages, tips, other compensation $15,080	2 Federal income tax withheld $292.76
c Employer's name, address, and ZIP code SONJA OLSON 421 PORTLAND AVENUE BOISE, ID 83701	3 Social security wages $15,080	4 Social security tax withheld $934.96
	5 Medicare wages and tips $15,080	6 Medicare tax withheld $218.66
	7 Social security tips	8 Allocated tips
d Control number	9	10 Dependent care benefits
e Employee's first name and initial JILL · Last name BROWN · Suff.	11 Nonqualified plans	12a See instructions for box 12
421 PORTLAND AVENUE BOISE, ID 83701	13 Statutory employee ☐ Retirement plan ☐ Third-party sick pay ☐	12b
	14 Other	12c
f Employee's address and ZIP code		12d

15 State	Employer's state ID number	16 State wages, tips, etc.	17 State income tax	18 Local wages, tips, etc.	19 Local income tax	20 Locality name

Form **W-2** **Wage and Tax Statement** **2020**

Department of the Treasury—Internal Revenue Service

For Privacy Act and Paperwork Reduction Act Notice, see the separate instructions.

Copy A—For Social Security Administration. Send this entire page with Form W-3 to the Social Security Administration; photocopies are **not** acceptable.

Cat. No. 10134D

Do Not Cut, Fold, or Staple Forms on This Page

DO NOT STAPLE

33333 | a Control number | **For Official Use Only ▶** **OMB No. 1545-0008**

b Kind of Payer (Check one): 941 ☑ Military ☐ 943 ☐ 944 ☐ CT-1 ☐ Hshld. emp. ☐ Medicare govt. emp. ☐

Kind of Employer (Check one): None apply ☑ 501c non-govt. ☐ State/local non-501c ☐ State/local 501c ☐ Federal govt. ☐

Third-party sick pay (Check if applicable) ☐

c Total number of Forms W-2 · d Establishment number	1 Wages, tips, other compensation $15,080.00	2 Federal income tax withheld $292.76
e Employer identification number (EIN) 92-1234567	3 Social security wages $15,080.00	4 Social security tax withheld $934.96
f Employer's name SONJA OLSON	5 Medicare wages and tips $15,080.00	6 Medicare tax withheld $218.66
421 PORTLAND AVENUE BOISE, ID 83701	7 Social security tips	8 Allocated tips
	9	10 Dependent care benefits
g Employer's address and ZIP code	11 Nonqualified plans	12a Deferred compensation
h Other EIN used this year	13 For third-party sick pay use only	12b
15 State · Employer's state ID number	14 Income tax withheld by payer of third-party sick pay	
16 State wages, tips, etc. · 17 State income tax	18 Local wages, tips, etc.	19 Local income tax
Employer's contact person	Employer's telephone number	For Official Use Only
Employer's fax number	Employer's email address	

Under penalties of perjury, I declare that I have examined this return and accompanying documents, and, to the best of my knowledge and belief, they are true, correct, and complete.

Signature ▶ *Sonja Olson* Title ▶ OWNER Date ▶ 01/01/2021

For Employee Clarisse

Form **941 for 2020: Employer's QUARTERLY Federal Tax Return** 950120
(Rev. July 2020) Department of the Treasury — Internal Revenue Service OMB No. 1545-0029

Employer identification number (EIN) 9 2 – 1 2 3 4 5 6 7

Name *(not your trade name)* SONJA OLSON

Trade name *(if any)*

Address 421 PORTLAND AVENUE
Number Street Suite or room number

BOISE ID 83701
City State ZIP code

Foreign country name Foreign province/county Foreign postal code

Report for this Quarter of 2020
(Check one.)

- [x] **1:** January, February, March
- [ ] **2:** April, May, June
- [ ] **3:** July, August, September
- [ ] **4:** October, November, December

Go to *www.irs.gov/Form941* for instructions and the latest information.

Read the separate instructions before you complete Form 941. Type or print within the boxes.

Part 1: Answer these questions for this quarter.

1	**Number of employees who received wages, tips, or other compensation for the pay period including:** ***Sept. 12*** **(Quarter 3) or** ***Dec. 12*** **(Quarter 4)**	1	1
2	**Wages, tips, and other compensation**	2	$325 . 00
3	**Federal income tax withheld from wages, tips, and other compensation**	3	.
4	**If no wages, tips, and other compensation are subject to social security or Medicare tax**		☐ **Check and go to line 6.**

		Column 1		Column 2
5a	**Taxable social security wages**	.	× 0.124 =	.
5a	**(i) Qualified sick leave wages**	.	× 0.062 =	.
5a	**(ii) Qualified family leave wages**	.	× 0.062 =	.
5b	**Taxable social security tips**	.	× 0.124 =	.
5c	**Taxable Medicare wages & tips**	.	× 0.029 =	.
5d	**Taxable wages & tips subject to Additional Medicare Tax withholding**	.	× 0.009 =	.

5e	**Total social security and Medicare taxes.** Add Column 2 from lines 5a, 5a(i), 5a(ii), 5b, 5c, and 5d	5e	$0 .
5f	**Section 3121(q) Notice and Demand—Tax due on unreported tips** (see instructions)	5f	.
6	**Total taxes before adjustments.** Add lines 3, 5e, and 5f	6	$0 .
7	**Current quarter's adjustment for fractions of cents**	7	.
8	**Current quarter's adjustment for sick pay**	8	.
9	**Current quarter's adjustments for tips and group-term life insurance**	9	.
10	**Total taxes after adjustments.** Combine lines 6 through 9	10	.
11a	**Qualified small business payroll tax credit for increasing research activities.** Attach Form 8974	11a	.
11b	**Nonrefundable portion of credit for qualified sick and family leave wages from Worksheet 1**	11b	.
11c	**Nonrefundable portion of employee retention credit from Worksheet 1**	11c	.

► **You MUST complete all three pages of Form 941 and SIGN it.** Next ►

For Privacy Act and Paperwork Reduction Act Notice, see the back of the Payment Voucher. Cat. No. 17001Z Form **941** (Rev. 7-2020)

950220

Name *(not your trade name)*	**Employer identification number (EIN)**
SONJA OLSON	92-1234567

Part 1: Answer these questions for this quarter. *(continued)*

11d	**Total nonrefundable credits.** Add lines 11a, 11b, and 11c	11d	.
12	**Total taxes after adjustments and nonrefundable credits.** Subtract line 11d from line 10	12	.
13a	**Total deposits for this quarter, including overpayment applied from a prior quarter and overpayments applied from Form 941-X, 941-X (PR), 944-X, or 944-X (SP) filed in the current quarter**	13a	.
13b	**Deferred amount of social security tax**	13b	.
13c	**Refundable portion of credit for qualified sick and family leave wages from Worksheet 1**	13c	.
13d	**Refundable portion of employee retention credit from Worksheet 1**	13d	.
13e	**Total deposits, deferrals, and refundable credits.** Add lines 13a, 13b, 13c, and 13d	13e	.
13f	**Total advances received from filing Form(s) 7200 for the quarter**	13f	.
13g	**Total deposits, deferrals, and refundable credits less advances.** Subtract line 13f from line 13e	13g	.
14	**Balance due.** If line 12 is more than line 13g, enter the difference and see instructions	14	$0 .

15 **Overpayment.** If line 13g is more than line 12, enter the difference [.] Check one: ☐ Apply to next return. ☐ Send a refund.

Part 2: Tell us about your deposit schedule and tax liability for this quarter.

If you're unsure about whether you're a monthly schedule depositor or a semiweekly schedule depositor, see section 11 of Pub. 15.

16 **Check one:**

☐ **Line 12 on this return is less than $2,500 or line 12 on the return for the prior quarter was less than $2,500, and you didn't incur a $100,000 next-day deposit obligation during the current quarter.** If line 12 for the prior quarter was less than $2,500 but line 12 on this return is $100,000 or more, you must provide a record of your federal tax liability. If you're a monthly schedule depositor, complete the deposit schedule below; if you're a semiweekly schedule depositor, attach Schedule B (Form 941). Go to Part 3.

☐ **You were a monthly schedule depositor for the entire quarter.** Enter your tax liability for each month and total liability for the quarter, then go to Part 3.

Tax liability:	**Month 1**	.
	Month 2	.
	Month 3	.
Total liability for quarter		. **Total must equal line 12.**

☐ **You were a semiweekly schedule depositor for any part of this quarter.** Complete Schedule B (Form 941), Report of Tax Liability for Semiweekly Schedule Depositors, and attach it to Form 941. Go to Part 3.

▶ **You MUST complete all three pages of Form 941 and SIGN it.** Next ▶

Page **2** Form **941** (Rev. 7-2020)

952920

Name *(not your trade name)*	**Employer identification number (EIN)**
SONJA OLSON	92-1234567

Part 3: Tell us about your business. If a question does NOT apply to your business, leave it blank.

17 **If your business has closed or you stopped paying wages** . . . ☐ Check here, and

enter the final date you paid wages [/ /] ; also attach a statement to your return. See instructions.

18 **If you're a seasonal employer and you don't have to file a return for every quarter of the year** . . . ☐ Check here.

19	**Qualified health plan expenses allocable to qualified sick leave wages**	19	.
20	**Qualified health plan expenses allocable to qualified family leave wages**	20	.
21	**Qualified wages for the employee retention credit**	21	.
22	**Qualified health plan expenses allocable to wages reported on line 21**	22	.
23	**Credit from Form 5884-C, line 11, for this quarter**	23	.
24	**Deferred amount of the employee share of social security tax included on line 13b**	24	.
25	**Reserved for future use**	25	.

Part 4: May we speak with your third-party designee?

Do you want to allow an employee, a paid tax preparer, or another person to discuss this return with the IRS? See the instructions for details.

☐ Yes. Designee's name and phone number

Select a 5-digit personal identification number (PIN) to use when talking to the IRS.

☐ No.

Part 5: Sign here. You MUST complete all three pages of Form 941 and SIGN it.

Under penalties of perjury, I declare that I have examined this return, including accompanying schedules and statements, and to the best of my knowledge and belief, it is true, correct, and complete. Declaration of preparer (other than taxpayer) is based on all information of which preparer has any knowledge.

X **Sign your name here** *Sonja Olson*

Print your name here: SONJA OLSON

Print your title here: OWNER

Date: 4 / 11 / 2020

Best daytime phone: 612-222-2222

Paid Preparer Use Only

Check if you're self-employed . . . ☐

Preparer's name		PTIN	
Preparer's signature		Date	/ /
Firm's name (or yours if self-employed)		EIN	
Address		Phone	
City	State	ZIP code	

 Form **941** (Rev. 7-2020)

22222 | VOID ☐ | a Employee's social security number | For Official Use Only ▶ OMB No. 1545-0008

b Employer identification number (EIN)
92-1234567

c Employer's name, address, and ZIP code
SONJA OLSON
421 PORTLAND AVENUE
BOISE, ID 83701

d Control number

e Employee's first name and initial: CLARISSE | Last name: OLSON | Suff.

421 PORTLAND AVENUE
BOISE, ID 83701

f Employee's address and ZIP code

1 Wages, tips, other compensation	$1,300	2 Federal income tax withheld	
3 Social security wages		4 Social security tax withheld	
5 Medicare wages and tips		6 Medicare tax withheld	
7 Social security tips		8 Allocated tips	
9		10 Dependent care benefits	
11 Nonqualified plans		12a See instructions for box 12	
13 Statutory employee ☐ Retirement plan ☐ Third-party sick pay ☐		12b	
14 Other		12c	
		12d	

15 State	Employer's state ID number	16 State wages, tips, etc.	17 State income tax	18 Local wages, tips, etc.	19 Local income tax	20 Locality name

Form **W-2** Wage and Tax Statement **2020**

Department of the Treasury—Internal Revenue Service
For Privacy Act and Paperwork Reduction Act Notice, see the separate instructions.
Cat. No. 10134D

Copy A—For Social Security Administration. Send this entire page with Form W-3 to the Social Security Administration; photocopies are **not** acceptable.

Do Not Cut, Fold, or Staple Forms on This Page

DO NOT STAPLE

33333 | a Control number | For Official Use Only ▶ OMB No. 1545-0008

b Kind of Payer (Check one): 941 ☑ | Military ☐ | 943 ☐ | 944 ☐ | CT-1 ☐ | Hshld. emp. ☐ | Medicare govt. emp. ☐

Kind of Employer (Check one): None apply ☑ | 501c non-govt. ☐ | State/local non-501c ☐ | State/local 501c ☐ | Federal govt. ☐

Third-party sick pay (Check if applicable) ☐

c Total number of Forms W-2		d Establishment number	
1 Wages, tips, other compensation	$1,300	2 Federal income tax withheld	
e Employer identification number (EIN)	92-1234567	3 Social security wages	
4 Social security tax withheld		f Employer's name	SONJA OLSON
5 Medicare wages and tips		6 Medicare tax withheld	
7 Social security tips		8 Allocated tips	
9		10 Dependent care benefits	
11 Nonqualified plans		12a Deferred compensation	
13 For third-party sick pay use only		12b	
14 Income tax withheld by payer of third-party sick pay			

421 PORTLAND AVENUE
BOISE, ID 83701

g Employer's address and ZIP code

h Other EIN used this year

15 State	Employer's state ID number	16 State wages, tips, etc.	17 State income tax	18 Local wages, tips, etc.	19 Local income tax

Employer's contact person | Employer's telephone number | For Official Use Only

Employer's fax number | Employer's email address

Under penalties of perjury, I declare that I have examined this return and accompanying documents, and, to the best of my knowledge and belief, they are true, correct, and complete.

Signature ▶ *Sonja Olson* Title ▶ OWNER Date ▶ 01/01/2021

For Employee Ophelia

Form **944 for 2020: Employer's ANNUAL Federal Tax Return**

Department of the Treasury — Internal Revenue Service

OMB No. 1545-2007

Employer identification number (EIN) 4 1 – 1 2 3 4 5 6 7

Name *(not your trade name)* SUSAN PROVIDER

Trade name *(if any)*

Address 1470 ASHLAND AVENUE

Number | Street | Suite or room number

ST. PAUL | MN | 55105

City | State | ZIP code

Foreign country name | Foreign province/county | Foreign postal code

Who Must File Form 944

You must file annual Form 944 instead of filing quarterly Forms 941 **only if the IRS notified you in writing.**

Go to *www.irs.gov/Form944* for instructions and the latest information.

Read the separate instructions before you complete Form 944. Type or print within the boxes.

Part 1: **Answer these questions for this year. Employers in American Samoa, Guam, the Commonwealth of the Northern Mariana Islands, the U.S. Virgin Islands, and Puerto Rico can skip lines 1 and 2, unless you have employees who are subject to U.S. income tax withholding.**

1	**Wages, tips, and other compensation**	1	$1,000 .
2	**Federal income tax withheld from wages, tips, and other compensation**	2	.
3	**If no wages, tips, and other compensation are subject to social security or Medicare tax**	3 ☐	**Check and go to line 5.**

4 Taxable social security and Medicare wages and tips:

	Column 1		Column 2
4a Taxable social security wages	$1,000 .	× 0.124 =	$124 .
4a (i) Qualified sick leave wages	.	× 0.062 =	.
4a (ii) Qualified family leave wages	.	× 0.062 =	.
4b Taxable social security tips	.	× 0.124 =	.
4c Taxable Medicare wages & tips	$1,000 .	× 0.029 =	$29 .
4d Taxable wages & tips subject to Additional Medicare Tax withholding	.	× 0.009 =	.

4e	**Total social security and Medicare taxes.** Add Column 2 from lines 4a, 4a(i), 4a(ii), 4b, 4c, and 4d	4e	$153 .
5	**Total taxes before adjustments.** Add lines 2 and 4e	5	$153 .
6	**Current year's adjustments** (see instructions)	6	.
7	**Total taxes after adjustments.** Combine lines 5 and 6	7	$153 .
8a	**Qualified small business payroll tax credit for increasing research activities.** Attach Form 8974	8a	.
8b	**Nonrefundable portion of credit for qualified sick and family leave wages from Worksheet 1**	8b	.
8c	**Nonrefundable portion of employee retention credit from Worksheet 1**	8c	.
8d	**Total nonrefundable credits.** Add lines 8a, 8b, and 8c	8d	.

► **You MUST complete all three pages of Form 944 and SIGN it.**

Next ►

Name (not your trade name): SUSAN PROVIDER | Employer identification number (EIN): 41-1234567

Part 1: Answer these questions for this year. *(continued)*

9	**Total taxes after adjustments and nonrefundable credits.** Subtract line 8d from line 7	9	$153.
10a	**Total deposits for this year, including overpayment applied from a prior year and overpayments applied from Form 944-X, 944-X (SP), 941-X, or 941-X (PR)**	10a	.
10b	**Deferred amount of the employer share of social security tax**	10b	.
10c	**Deferred amount of the employee share of social security tax**	10c	.
10d	**Refundable portion of credit for qualified sick and family leave wages from Worksheet 1**	10d	.
10e	**Refundable portion of employee retention credit from Worksheet 1**	10e	.
10f	**Total deposits, deferrals, and refundable credits.** Add lines 10a, 10b, 10c, 10d, and 10e	10f	.
10g	**Total advances received from filing Form(s) 7200 for the year**	10g	.
10h	**Total deposits, deferrals, and refundable credits less advances.** Subtract line 10g from line 10f	10h	.
11	**Balance due.** If line 9 is more than line 10h, enter the difference and see instructions	11	$153.
12	**Overpayment.** If line 10h is more than line 9, enter the difference ☐ . Check one: ☐ Apply to next return. ☐ Send a refund.		

Part 2: Tell us about your deposit schedule and tax liability for this year.

13 Check one: ☐ **Line 9 is less than $2,500. Go to Part 3.**

☐ **Line 9 is $2,500 or more. Enter your tax liability for each month. If you're a semiweekly schedule depositor or you became one because you accumulated $100,000 or more of liability on any day during a deposit period, you must complete Form 945-A instead of the boxes below.**

13a	Jan. .	13d	Apr. .	13g	July .	13j	Oct. .
13b	Feb. .	13e	May .	13h	Aug. .	13k	Nov. .
13c	Mar. .	13f	June .	13i	Sept. .	13l	Dec. .

Total liability for year. Add lines 13a through 13l. Total must equal line 9. 13m .

► **You MUST complete all three pages of Form 944 and SIGN it.**

Next ➡

Page 2 Form 944 (2020)

Name (not your trade name): SUSAN PROVIDER | Employer identification number (EIN): 41-1234567

Part 3: Tell us about your business. If any question does NOT apply to your business, leave it blank.

14 **If your business has closed or you stopped paying wages** ☐ Check here, and enter the final date you paid wages / / ; also attach a statement to your return. See instructions.

15	**Qualified health plan expenses allocable to qualified sick leave wages**	15	.
16	**Qualified health plan expenses allocable to qualified family leave wages**	16	.
17	**Qualified wages for the employee retention credit**	17	.
18	**Qualified health plan expenses allocable to wages reported on line 17**	18	.
19	**Credit from Form 5884-C, line 11, for the year**	19	.

Part 4: May we speak with your third-party designee?

Do you want to allow an employee, a paid tax preparer, or another person to discuss this return with the IRS? See the instructions for details.

☐ Yes. Designee's name and phone number

Select a 5-digit personal identification number (PIN) to use when talking to the IRS. ☐☐☐☐☐

☐ No.

Part 5: Sign here. You MUST complete all three pages of Form 944 and SIGN it.

Under penalties of perjury, I declare that I have examined this return, including accompanying schedules and statements, and to the best of my knowledge and belief, it is true, correct, and complete. Declaration of preparer (other than taxpayer) is based on all information of which preparer has any knowledge.

X Sign your name here: *Susan Provider*

Print your name here: SUSAN PROVIDER

Print your title here: OWNER

Date: 4/11/2021

Best daytime phone: 612-221-1111

Paid Preparer Use Only Check if you're self-employed ☐

Preparer's name		PTIN	
Preparer's signature		Date	
Firm's name (or yours if self-employed)		EIN	
Address		Phone	
City	State	ZIP code	

Page 3 Form 944 (2020)

CHAPTER 9

Amending Your Tax Return: Form 1040X

If you discover that you made a mistake on your tax returns in an earlier year, either by not claiming all your business income or by not deducting all your business expenses, you may be able to do something about it.

You can't e-file an amended return. Don't amend your return if you realize later you made a math error. The IRS will correct math errors when processing your original return. If you didn't include a required form or schedule, the IRS will send you a request for the missing item. If you are waiting for a refund from your original return, don't file your amended return until after you receive the refund. You may cash the refund check from your original return. Amended returns take up to 12 weeks to process.

You can amend your tax return by filing **Form 1040X** within three years of the date you filed the original return or two years from the time you paid the taxes on your original return, whichever is later. If you filed your return before April 15, it will be treated as if you had filed it on April 15. If you obtained an extension, you can count from the date you actually filed. This means that most people have until April 15, 2021 to file an amended return for the years 2019, 2018, and 2017. After April 15, it will be too late for most providers to file an amended return for 2017.

Don't be shy about filing an amended return. The IRS doesn't audit them any more often than original returns. If you think you may have missed some business deductions, check the list of more than 1,000 deductions in the *Record-Keeping Guide*. If you find that you were entitled to deductions that you didn't claim and you have adequate records to back this up, don't hesitate to file an amended return.

You must file a separate **Form 1040X** for each annual tax return that you are amending. If you're entitled to a refund and your original return also showed a refund, you'll get another refund check in addition to interest on the amount owed to you.

If you're claiming unclaimed depreciation on your amended tax return, you must use accelerated depreciation rules (see chapter 3). You can use straight-line rules only if you did so in the first year you began using the property in your business. The IRS allows you to elect to use the Section 179 rule when amending your 2017 or 2018 tax return. See chapter 3.

When you file **Form 1040X**, you must send with it copies of any tax forms for the year that is affected by the amended **Form 1040X**. (Don't send copies of your original tax forms, just amended versions of the forms that show changes.) A change on **Schedule C** will affect **Schedule SE** and **Form 1040**. A change in your Time-Space percentage will affect **Form 4562**, **Form 8829**, and **Schedule A**. For more information, see the instructions for **Form 1040X**, which also tell you where to mail your amended return. You can track the status of your amended return three weeks after you file by going online at www.irs.gov/Filing/Wheres-My-Amended-Return or by phone at 866-464-2050.

Amending your federal tax return will probably mean that you must also amend your state tax return. Check with your state for information on amending your state return.

How Much Will It Be Worth?

Here's how to estimate how much you might save by amending your federal tax return:

- If you're in the 12% federal tax bracket for 2020 (if married filing jointly, making less than $80,250):

  12% + 12% (net self-employment tax) = 24%.

  You'll get a refund of about $0.24 on every additional dollar of deductions you claim on your amended return.

- If you're in the 22% federal tax bracket for 2020 (if married filing jointly, making between $80,251 and $171,050):

  22% + 12% (net self-employment tax) = 34%.

  You'll get a refund of about $0.34 on every additional dollar of deductions you claim on your amended return.

Example of an Amended Return

Here is an example of how to amend your tax return, based on the sample tax return shown in appendix A. Note: The most recent IRS **Form 1040X** does not account for the new Qualified Business Income Deduction found on **Form 1040**, line 9. I expect a new **Form 1040X** to appear shortly to fix this. Therefore, for this chapter I have adjusted line 1 by reducing the adjusted gross income by the qualified business income deduction to make the numbers work.

Example

Sandy James filed her tax return (see appendix A) on April 15, 2021. In September 2021 she realizes that although she uses a 400-square-foot room exclusively for business, she didn't claim that on her last tax return. Here's her new Time-Space percentage:

Percentage for exclusive-use room: 400 ÷ 2,200 = 18%
Time-Space percentage for rest of home: 1,800 ÷ 2,200 = 81.8% x 39% Time percentage = 32%
Revised Time-Space percentage: 18% + 32% = 50%

Now Sandy must redo all the forms she filled out last tax season that are affected by this change:

- **Form 8829**

  Line 7 will now be 50%. Adjust the expenses on this form using this 50% Time-Space percentage. Line 36 will now be $7,641.

- **Form 4562**
  Recalculate the furniture and fence using the 50% Time-Space percentage. Line 22 will now be $9,206.
- **Schedule C**
  Line 13 will now be $9,206.
  Line 16b will now be $50.
  Line 21 will now be $65.
  Line 22 will now be $450.
  Line 27a will now be $11,351.
  Line 29 will now be $44,142.
  Line 30 from **Form 8829** will now be $7,641.
  Line 31 will now be $36,501, a reduction of net profit of $2,412.
- **Schedule SE**
  Line 5 will now be $5,158.
- **Schedule A**
  Since Sandy took the standard deduction, she won't file **Schedule A**.

See the sample **Form 1040X** to see how Sandy saved $583 in federal taxes by amending her return.

Because Sandy's business profit is lower, she is able to reduce her Social Security taxes as well as her federal income taxes. Do not fill out lines 23–31 unless you are changing the number of your exemptions.

For more information about the tax issues discussed in this chapter, refer to the related topics in the other chapters of this book and the Redleaf Press *Family Child Care Record-Keeping Guide.*

Form **1040-X** (Rev. January 2020)

Department of the Treasury—Internal Revenue Service

Amended U.S. Individual Income Tax Return

▶ Go to *www.irs.gov/Form1040X* for instructions and the latest information.

OMB No. 1545-0074

This return is for calendar year ☐ 2019 ☐ 2018 ☐ 2017 ☐ 2016

Other year. Enter one: calendar year 2018 **or** fiscal year (month and year ended):

Your first name and middle initial	Last name	Your social security number
SANDY	JAMES	123 45 6789
If joint return, spouse's first name and middle initial	Last name	Spouse's social security number
BILL	JAMES	987 65 4321

Current home address (number and street). If you have a P.O. box, see instructions.	Apt. no.	Your phone number
687 HOOVER STREET		212-541-7742

City, town or post office, state, and ZIP code. If you have a foreign address, also complete spaces below. See instructions.
HUDSON, OH 43287

Foreign country name	Foreign province/state/county	Foreign postal code

Amended return filing status. You **must** check one box even if you are not changing your filing status. **Caution:** In general, you can't change your filing status from a joint return to separate returns after the due date.

☐ **Full-year health care coverage (or, for amended 2018 returns only, exempt).** If amending a 2019 return, leave blank. See instructions.

☐ Single ☐ Married filing jointly ☐ Married filing separately (MFS) ☐ Qualifying widow(er) (QW) ☐ Head of household (HOH)

If you checked the MFS box, enter the name of spouse. If you checked the HOH or QW box, enter the child's name if the qualifying person is a child but not your dependent. ▶

Use Part III on the back to explain any changes		A. Original amount reported or as previously adjusted (see instructions)	B. Net change—amount of increase or (decrease)—explain in Part III	C. Correct amount
Income and Deductions				
1 Adjusted gross income. If a net operating loss (NOL) carryback is included, check here ▶ ☐	1	77,164	(2,242)	74,922
2 Itemized deductions or standard deduction	2	24,800	0	24,800
3 Subtract line 2 from line 1	3	52,364	(2,242)	50,122
4a Exemptions (amended 2017 or earlier returns only). **If changing,** complete Part I on page 2 and enter the amount from line 29	4a			
b Qualified business income deduction (amended 2018 or later returns only)	4b	7,783	(483)	7,300
5 Taxable income. Subtract line 4a or 4b from line 3. If the result is zero or less, enter -0-	5	44,581	(1,759)	42,822
Tax Liability				
6 Tax. Enter method(s) used to figure tax (see instructions):	6	4,987	(243)	4,744
7 Credits. If a general business credit carryback is included, check here ▶ ☐	7		---	
8 Subtract line 7 from line 6. If the result is zero or less, enter -0-	8	4,987	(243)	4,744
9 Health care: individual responsibility (amended 2018 or earlier returns only). See instructions	9			
10 Other taxes	10	5,498	(340)	5,158
11 Total tax. Add lines 8, 9, and 10	11	10,485	(583)	9,902
Payments				
12 Federal income tax withheld and excess social security and tier 1 RRTA tax withheld. (**If changing,** see instructions.)	12	9,000	---	9,000
13 Estimated tax payments, including amount applied from prior year's return	13			
14 Earned income credit (EIC)	14			
15 Refundable credits from: ☐ Schedule 8812 Form(s) ☐ 2439 ☐ 4136 ☐ 8863 ☐ 8885 ☐ 8962 or ☐ other (specify):	15			
16 Total amount paid with request for extension of time to file, tax paid with original return, and additional tax paid after return was filed			16	9,000
17 Total payments. Add lines 12 through 15, column C, and line 16			17	9,000
Refund or Amount You Owe				
18 Overpayment, if any, as shown on original return or as previously adjusted by the IRS			18	---
19 Subtract line 18 from line 17. (If less than zero, see instructions.)			19	9,000
20 **Amount you owe.** If line 11, column C, is more than line 19, enter the difference			20	902
21 If line 11, column C, is less than line 19, enter the difference. This is the amount **overpaid** on this return			21	
22 Amount of line 21 you want **refunded to you**			22	902
23 Amount of line 21 you want **applied to your (enter year):** estimated tax	23			

Complete and sign this form on page 2.

For Paperwork Reduction Act Notice, see instructions. Cat. No. 11360L Form **1040-X** (Rev. 1-2020)

Form 1040-X (Rev. 1-2020) Page **2**

Part I **Exemptions and Dependents**

Complete this part **only** if any information relating to exemptions (to dependents if amending your 2018 or later return) has changed from what you reported on the return you are amending. This would include a change in the number of exemptions (of dependents if amending your 2018 or later return).

CAUTION: *For amended 2018 or later returns only, leave lines 24, 28, and 29 blank. Fill in all other applicable lines.* **Note:** See the Forms 1040 and 1040-SR, or Form 1040A, instructions for the tax year being amended. See also the Form 1040-X instructions.		**A. Original number of exemptions or amount** reported or as previously adjusted	**B. Net change**	**C. Correct number or amount**
24 Yourself and spouse. **Caution:** If someone can claim you as a dependent, you can't claim an exemption for yourself. If amending your 2018 or later return, leave line blank	**24**			
25 Your dependent children who lived with you	**25**			
26 Your dependent children who didn't live with you due to divorce or separation	**26**			
27 Other dependents	**27**			
28 Total number of exemptions. Add lines 24 through 27. If amending your 2018 or later return, leave line blank	**28**			
29 Multiply the number of exemptions claimed on line 28 by the exemption amount shown in the instructions for line 29 for the year you are amending. Enter the result here and on line 4a on page 1 of this form. If amending your 2018 or later return, leave line blank	**29**			

30 List **ALL** dependents (children and others) claimed on this amended return. If more than 4 dependents, see inst. and ✓ here ▶ ☐

Dependents (see instructions): (a) First name	Last name	**(b)** Social security number	**(c)** Relationship to you	**(d)** ✓ if qualifies for (see instructions): Child tax credit	Credit for other dependents (amended 2018 or later returns only)
				☐	☐
				☐	☐
				☐	☐
				☐	☐

Part II **Presidential Election Campaign Fund**

Checking below won't increase your tax or reduce your refund.

☐ Check here if you didn't previously want $3 to go to the fund, but now do.

☐ Check here if this is a joint return and your spouse did not previously want $3 to go to the fund, but now does.

Part III **Explanation of Changes.** In the space provided below, tell us why you are filing Form 1040-X.

▶ Attach any supporting documents and new or changed forms and schedules.

The business use of home was miscalculated and is 50% rather than 39%.

Remember to keep a copy of this form for your records.

Under penalties of perjury, I declare that I have filed an original return and that I have examined this amended return, including accompanying schedules and statements, and to the best of my knowledge and belief, this amended return is true, correct, and complete. Declaration of preparer (other than taxpayer) is based on all information about which the preparer has any knowledge.

Sign Here

▶ Sandy James — 9/30/2021

Your signature | Date | Your occupation

▶ Bill James — 9/30/2021

Spouse's signature. If a joint return, **both** must sign. | Date | Spouse's occupation

Paid Preparer Use Only

▶

Preparer's signature | Date | Firm's name (or yours if self-employed)

Print/type preparer's name | Firm's address and ZIP code

☐ Check if self-employed

PTIN | Phone number | EIN

For forms and publications, visit *www.irs.gov.* Form **1040-X** (Rev. 1-2020)

CHAPTER 10

Recovering Your Unclaimed Depreciation: Form 3115

This chapter explains how to use **Form 3115 Application for Change in Accounting Method** to take advantage of any depreciation deductions you may have overlooked in previous years. Several IRS rulings (specifically, Revenue Procedure 2011-14) state that you can use **Form 3115** to deduct all the depreciation you haven't claimed for items that you've used in your business (with some restrictions; see below). Before these rulings, the only way you could deduct unclaimed depreciation without incurring a fee was to file an amended tax return—and you can only do that for the last three years.

If you have any unclaimed depreciation from earlier years, you can use **Form 3115** to deduct it on your tax return. (Note that you can't file **Form 3115** electronically.) Since family child care providers are entitled to depreciate a wide range of small and large household items, it's easy to overlook depreciation opportunities, yet by claiming them now, you could reap hundreds of dollars of deductions on this year's tax return.

For example, let's say that you started your business in 2011, and in 2012 you bought a sofa for $800; however, you've never claimed any depreciation for it. If your Time-Space percentage for 2012–2020 was 40%, you would have been entitled to depreciate $320 of the cost of the sofa ($800 x 40%), using seven-year accelerated depreciation (see chapter 3). Since you didn't claim any of this depreciation, you can use **Form 3115** to claim the entire $320 on your tax return. (You'll find a completed sample of **Form 3115** at the end of this chapter.)

Put items you owned before you went into business in one of two categories: items valued at $200 or less and items valued at $201 or more. You are entitled to deduct in one year under the Start-Up rule up to $5,000 worth of items you owned before you went into business valued at $200 or less. Amounts above this must be amortized over 180 months. For example, let's say you started your business in 2012 and at that time had 100 items each individually valued at less than $200 for a total of $7,000. Note: These numbers are after applying your Time-Space percentage. You can use **Form 3115** to deduct $5,000 of the $7,000 and amortize the other $2,000 over 180 months (15 years). Because it has been eight years (96 months), you can also deduct on **Form 3115** an additional $1,067 ($2,000 ÷ 180 months x 96 months = $1,067). On your 2020 tax return, you can also deduct $133 ($2,000 ÷ 180 months x 12 months = $133), representing the ninth year on **Form 4562**. Continue to deduct $133 on **Form 4562** for the remaining six years.

For items valued at more than $200, use the depreciation rules in effect in the year your business began to recapture previously unclaimed depreciation using **Form 3115**.

For example, if your business began in 2012, you would use the fifteen-year depreciation rule for a fence, patio, or driveway. If you purchased an $8,000 fence in 2012 and your Time-Space percentage was 40%, you were entitled to depreciate $3,200 over 15 years. You can use **Form 3115** to recapture about $1,700 for 2012–2019. You could claim an additional $213 for the tenth year of depreciation on **Form 4562**. Continue deducting $213 for the remaining 5 years. See my article "How to Recapture Previously Unclaimed Depreciation" (http://tomcopelandblog.com/?p=14623&preview=true) for more details.

For information about what kinds of property you can depreciate, see chapter 3 of this book (and refer to the *Record-Keeping Guide* for a comprehensive list). Here's a sampling of the items that family child care providers can typically depreciate:

- the home
- home appliances, such as a washer, dryer, freezer, stove, or refrigerator
- fences, outdoor play equipment, lawn mowers, snowblowers
- furniture, such as beds, chairs, or sofas
- televisions, DVD players, computers, home entertainment systems
- home improvements, such as remodeling or a new furnace

You can deduct unclaimed depreciation for property that you never previously depreciated and for property that you only partly depreciated. For example, let's say that you remodeled your basement in January 2014 but didn't start claiming depreciation until 2020 because you weren't aware that you could depreciate this expense. You would continue to claim the depreciation on your tax return (as year seven under the 39-year home improvement rules).

If you used the wrong depreciation method in earlier years, you can't use **Form 3115** to correct it. Let's say that you began depreciating a carpet over 39 years, and you realized several years later that you could have depreciated it over seven years. You can't use **Form 3115** to correct this error. You can only amend your tax return for the last three years and start claiming the proper depreciation amount in 2020.

Let's say that you started depreciating the carpet in 2016 over 39 years and discovered your error in 2020. It's too late to amend your 2016 tax return, but you can amend your 2017, 2018, and 2019 tax returns and claim the extra depreciation that you were entitled to, using the seven-year 200% declining balance method. In 2020 you would continue depreciating the carpet under the seven-year method by using the fifth-year percentage (8.93%) as shown on the depreciation tables in chapter 3.

Requirements for Using Form 3115

To be eligible to deduct your previously unclaimed depreciation by filing **Form 3115**, you must meet the following requirements:

1. You must still be in business.

If you go out of business for a year or two and then start up again, you can't use **Form 3115** to recapture any depreciation for the years before you closed your business. You also can't use **Form 3115** if you closed your child care business and used your home for some other business (such as renting out rooms).

2. You must own the property you are deducting.

You must own the property in question at the start of the year in which you deduct the unclaimed depreciation. For example, let's say that you began your business in 2013 and have never claimed any depreciation on your home. You decide to file **Form 3115** with your tax return to claim your home depreciation for the years 2015 to 2020. To be eligible to do this, you must still own the home and be in business on January 1, 2020.

If you sell the home before January 1, 2020, you can't claim any deductions on **Form 3115** for 2015–2019. If you sell the home during 2020, you can still deduct your home depreciation for the years 2015–2019 by filing **Form 3115** with your tax return. If you had sold the home in 2019, the only way you'd be able to claim the unclaimed depreciation would be to file an amended return for the years 2017–2019. (You can file an amended return only up to three years after filing the original return.)

3. You must be using the property you are deducting in your business.

You must have been using the item in your business on January 1, 2020. For example, if you used a sewing machine in your business from 2015 to 2019 but haven't used it since then, you can't use **Form 3115** to claim the unclaimed depreciation for it now.

You *can* use **Form 3115** for items you continue to use in your business after their depreciation life is over. For example, if you've been using a sofa in your business for more than seven years (its depreciation period), you can still use **Form 3115**, as long as you've used it for your business in the current year.

4. You must file Form 3115 by the tax deadline (including any extensions) for the year in which you are deducting your previously unclaimed depreciation.

To claim your past year's depreciation on your current tax return, you must file **Form 3115** no later than the due date of that tax return. In other words, to deduct previously unclaimed depreciation on your tax return, you must file **Form 3115** by April 15. If you file for an extension on your tax return, you could file **Form 3115** as late as October 15 and still claim the deductions on your tax return.

There is one way you could claim the deductions using **Form 3115** if you haven't filed it with your original tax return. You can amend your tax return up to October 15 using **Form 1040X**, attach **Form 3115** to your amended return, and file **Form 3115** before sending in your amended return. Write on the top of your amended return "Filed Pursuant to IRS Tax Code Section 301.9100-2."

There's no time limit for your right to claim your depreciation from previous years. You can do it anytime you discover that you haven't claimed earlier depreciation. If you file your tax return on April 15 and don't file **Form 3115** by that date, you can always claim the depreciation on your next tax return, as long as you're still in business, still own the property, and continue to use it in your business.

5. You can't claim an expense that you've already deducted.

You can't reclaim depreciation if you have already deducted the property under Section 179 (see chapter 3). For example, if you bought a computer in 2013 and deducted the entire business-use portion of its cost that year, you can't use **Form 3115** because you've already claimed all the expense you're entitled to deduct for that computer. You also can't use **Form 3115** to go back and use Section 179 on property you purchased in earlier years. You can use Section 179 only in the year you purchase the property.

6. You must not have depreciated the item for at least two years before using Form 3115.

To take advantage of filing **Form 3115**, you must not have claimed depreciation on the items you are recapturing for at least two years immediately preceding the year you use **Form 3115**. In other words, if you didn't claim depreciation on your furniture and appliances from 2014 to 2018, but you did claim depreciation on them in 2019, you can't use **Form 3115**. Also, if you amended your tax return for 2017 and 2018 to recapture depreciation, you can't use **Form 3115**.

7. You must use the proper depreciation method.

You can't use **Form 3115** to change the depreciation rules on an item that you've already started depreciating. For example, if you began depreciating a swing set in 2010 under straight-line rules, you can't use **Form 3115** to switch to accelerated depreciation and claim higher deductions for the earlier years.

Unless you've already started depreciating the item under straight-line rules, you must generally use accelerated depreciation rules on **Form 3115** to calculate your unclaimed depreciation for previous years. This is because you can't generally use straight-line depreciation for an item unless you chose this method in the first year you used the item in your business. If you didn't have the option of using straight-line depreciation in the first year you used the item, you must abide by the rules that were in effect at that time. Here are the rules you must use when claiming depreciation on **Form 3115**:

- Home (nonresidential real property): 39-year (or 31.5-year) straight-line
- Home improvements (nonresidential real property): 39-year (or 31.5-year) straight-line
- Land improvements (asset class 00.3): 15-year 150% declining balance
- Computers (asset class 00.12 information systems): if used 50% or less in business, 5-year straight-line; if used more than 50% in business, 5-year 200% declining balance
- Other personal property (asset class 00.11 office furniture, entertainment/recreation items, fixtures, and equipment): 7-year 200% declining balance
- Cars (asset class 00.22): 5-year 200% declining balance

Check Your State Rules

If you claim **Form 3115** depreciation deductions on your federal tax return, check to see if your state tax rules will permit you to include these deductions when calculating your state tax return. Some states don't allow you to transfer these deductions to your state tax return.

Unclaimed Depreciation and Losses on Schedule C

Although depreciation of personal property can always be used to claim a loss for your business, depreciation of a home or home improvement is not allowed to create a loss on **Schedule C**. You can carry forward those depreciation expenses to another year. (For a detailed explanation of how to depreciate property, see chapter 3.)

For example, let's say that you didn't claim any home depreciation for the years 2010–2015, and this year you're using **Form 3115** to claim that depreciation. You discover that the home depreciation deductions that you're claiming for 2010–2012 would have created a loss for your business if you had claimed them in those years; however, you would have been able to carry those deductions forward to 2013–2014 because your business made enough profit to cover the deductions in the later years. In a case like this, you would be able to claim all the home depreciation from 2010 to 2014 on this year's tax return.

If the deductions on your **Form 3115** create a loss for your business, you can't deduct the part of the depreciation for home or home improvements that creates a loss on your **Schedule C**. If you still have a loss after taking out all the depreciation for home and home improvements, that's fine; you can show that loss. You can also carry forward the unallowed portion of your home or home improvement depreciation from 2019 **Form 3115** to line 31 of 2020 **Form 8829**. (Enter "Section 481[a] Adjustment" on this line.)

You must also follow the usual instructions on **Form 8829** about deduction limitations. You may have to carry forward some of your deductions to your **Form 8829** for next tax season.

Claiming Depreciation on Vehicles

You can use **Form 3115** to claim depreciation on your vehicle only if you used the actual vehicle expenses method of claiming car expenses in earlier years or if you never claimed any car expenses. You can't claim past depreciation on your car if you used the standard mileage rate method. In calculating how much vehicle depreciation you can take, you must apply the yearly limitations on vehicle depreciation.

Will Filing Form 3115 Increase My Chances of Being Audited?

Your chances of being audited at all are very slim, and it's unlikely that you will be audited just because you file **Form 3115**—so don't base your decision about whether to claim depreciation on this. (If all your records are in order, you have nothing to worry about anyway.) If you don't claim all the depreciation you're entitled to, you're paying more taxes than you should.

What If You Don't Have the Receipts Anymore?

You need to calculate depreciation based on the lower of the cost of an item or its fair market value at the time you started using it for business (see chapter 3). But what if you don't know the cost of the item? Let's say that you've been using your freezer in your business since 2011, but you've never depreciated it and didn't save the receipt when you bought it because you didn't know it was deductible. What can you do?

Start by looking for other records you may have that show how much you paid for the item, such as a credit card statement, repair service contract, canceled check, or statement from the store where you purchased the item. If you can't find any of those kinds of records, estimate the value of the property when you began using it. Look up newspaper ads for used freezers from that year or visit a thrift store to get an idea of the fair market value of a used freezer.

See if you have any old family photos that show that you owned the item in 2011 or earlier. If your estimated fair market value of the item in 2011 is reasonable, you should be okay. Don't be aggressive by inflating the value of your item. The IRS should accept a reasonable estimate of its value, as long as you have some kind of evidence that you owned the item from 2011 to 2020.

Maximize Your Reclaimed Depreciation

Previously unclaimed depreciation could be one of your biggest deductions this year. Here are some ways to ensure that you'll be able to claim all the depreciation that you're entitled to:

- Recapture the biggest unclaimed depreciation first. This will probably be your home or home improvements. Don't worry that this will increase your taxes when you sell your home. The tax consequences of selling your home will be the same regardless of whether you've claimed all the depreciation you're entitled to (see chapter 12). The IRS rules state that all allowable depreciation must be treated as if it had been claimed, so any property that you haven't depreciated will be treated as if it had been depreciated. Therefore, you will have to pay the same amount later, and you should claim your depreciation today.
- Save all your receipts for home purchases, home improvements, furniture, appliances, and outdoor play equipment. To document items you bought in earlier years, dig out the receipts, canceled checks, or credit card statements. (It's easy to track these purchases and improvements if you use the *Inventory-Keeper*, which provides a room-by-room listing of depreciable items.)
- Don't throw away any household property you have used in earlier years for your business and are still using in your business. Remember, you can claim depreciation on an item this year only if you still own it as of January 1 of last year.

How important is it to deduct your unclaimed depreciation? Here's an example. Let's say that you've never depreciated the following property:

- Your home, which has a business basis of $30,000 ($100,000 adjusted basis x 30% Time-Space percentage)
- Your major appliances (washer, dryer, freezer, refrigerator, stove, microwave oven), which have a business basis of $1,000
- Your furniture (sofa, chairs, tables, bed, lawn mower), which has a business basis of $1,000

Applying 39-year straight-line rules to the house and 7-year 200% declining balance rules to the appliances and furniture, you would be entitled to a business deduction of about $1,019 for each year that you've used these items in your business. This would translate into a tax savings of $245 per year if you're in the 12% tax bracket (12% federal income tax and 12% net Social Security tax) and $346 if you're in the 22% tax bracket (22% federal income tax and 12% net Social Security tax). In addition, there may be state income tax savings. As you can see, your tax savings will rise quickly for every year that you haven't claimed the depreciation for this property.

Although **Form 3115** isn't the simplest tax form to fill out, you have a lot to gain by filing it. Even if you have to pay a tax preparer to do it for you, it may be well worth the extra cost. If you've been reluctant to claim all the depreciation you're entitled to, you should seriously consider filing this form; it can mean a substantial one-time business deduction.

How to Fill Out Form 3115

To start filling out **Form 3115**, write "Automatic method change under Rev. Proc. 2011-14" above the title. If you're filing jointly, enter the names and Social Security numbers of both spouses in the same order they appear on your **Form 1040**. If you have an employer identification number (see page 7), enter it here instead of your Social Security number. The principal business activity code number is 62441. Enter "1/1/19" as the date when the change begins. Enter "12/31/20" as the date when the change ends.

Check the box to indicate the applicant:
Check Individual (unless you are incorporated).

Check the appropriate box to indicate the type of accounting method change being requested:
Check Depreciation or Amortization.

Part I

Line 1: Enter "107" for the change number. Enter "recapture depreciation" under the description.

Line 2: Check the No column.

Line 3: Check the Yes column.

Part II

Line 4: Check the No column.

Line 5: Check the No column.

Line 6a: Check the No column, go to 7a.

Line 7a: Check the Yes column.

Line 7b: Check the "Not under exam" box.

Line 8a: Check the No column, go to line 9.

Line 9: Leave blank.

Line 10: Check the No column.

Line 11a: Check the No column, go to line 12.

Line 12: Check the No column.

Line 13: Check the No column.

Lines 14–16a: Attach a statement to the form to answer these questions. See the example shown later in this chapter.

Line 17: Check the Yes column.

Line 18: Check the No column.

Line 19: Leave blank.

Part III

Lines 20 and 23: Leave blank. Do not attach any documents.

Part IV

Line 25: Check the No column.

Line 26: Enter amount of recaptured depreciation you are claiming. See the example shown later in this chapter.

Line 27: Check the Yes column.

Line 28: Check the No column.

Schedule A: Change in Overall Method of Accounting

Leave the rest of pages 4–8 blank.

Transfer Your Unclaimed Depreciation to Schedule C

Enter the amount from **Form 3115**, Part IV, line 26, on one of the blank lines of **Schedule C**, Part V. Title that entry "Section 481(a) Adjustment." Include this amount in the total you enter on **Schedule C**, line 27 (other expenses).

Professional Help Is Recommended

The IRS rulings that allow you to claim previously unclaimed depreciation on **Form 3115** are relatively new, and they may require clarification. If you file **Form 3115**, you should consult a tax preparer to help you with it. If you aren't using a tax preparer, it would be worth it to hire one just to do (or review) your **Form 3115**.

Remember, there's no deadline for filing **Form 3115**. If you don't file it this year, you can do it next year, as long as you're still in business and still own the property you want to depreciate.

Two Examples of How to Fill Out Form 3115

The following examples show you how to fill out the remaining lines on **Form 3115**. In the first example, the depreciation period is over; in the second, it is still in progress.

EXAMPLE I

This example is shown on the forms and the attachment at the end of this chapter.

Karin Roth has been in business since 2012, and her Time-Space percentage each year has been 35%. In 2012 she bought a washer for $400 and a dryer for $300. She has never claimed any depreciation for these items. To claim it on her tax return, she'll have to file **Form 3115** by April 15 (unless she takes an extension). To answer questions 12, 13, and 25, Karin will write an attachment to **Form 3115** (see example at end of chapter). To calculate the proper amount of her depreciation, Karin will consult chapter 3. As her attachment shows, she was entitled to deduct $245 in depreciation over eight years. Because the eight-year recovery period has expired, she can claim all $245 as a deduction this year.

Karin will enter "–$245" on **Form 3115**, Part IV, line 26. Then she will enter $245 on one of the blank lines of her **Schedule C**, Part V, and write "Section 481(a) Adjustment" on that line.

EXAMPLE 2

In this case, Karin bought the washer and dryer in 2014, and her Time-Space percentages for the years 2016–2019 are as follows: 35%; 38%; 35%; 40%. Karin will fill out **Form 3115** in the same way, and her depreciation calculation will look like this:

2016: $700 x 35% = $245 x 14.29% = $35.01
2017: $700 x 38% = $266 x 24.49% = $65.14
2018: $700 x 35% = $245 x 17.49% = $42.85
2019: $700 x 40% = $280 x 12.49% = $34.97

Total depreciation allowed 2015–2018: $177.97

In this case, Karin will enter "–$178" on **Form 3115**, Part IV, line 26, and will claim this amount on her **Schedule C**, Part V. Karin is also entitled to claim $25 for the fifth year of depreciation on the washer and dryer for last year:

2020: $700 x 40% = $280 x 8.93% = $25

Karin will enter this $25.00 on line 1 of her **Form 4562**. Since there is still one more year of depreciation left, she will also be entitled to claim the sixth year of depreciation on the washer and dryer on her **Form 4562** next tax season:

2021: $700 x 40% = $280 x 8.92% = $24.98

Next year she will enter this $25 on line 17 of her **Form 4562**. (Although no attachment is shown for this example, Karin would complete **Form 3115** and the attachment in exactly the same way as example 1, except for her entry for question 26.)

How to File Form 3115

In the past, if you wanted to deduct previously unclaimed depreciation, you had to pay a hefty fee and get the consent of the commissioner of the IRS to change your accounting method. Now there is no fee for filing **Form 3115** and you can get automatic consent, if you proceed as follows:

1. Fill out **Form 3115**. Write "Automatic method change under Rev. Proc. 2015-13" above the title. Attach the original of **Form 3115** with your tax return.
2. Mail a copy of **Form 3115** by the filing deadline (April 15 or your extension deadline) to:

   Commissioner of Internal Revenue
   201 West Rivercenter Boulevard
   PIN Team Mail Stop 97
   Covington, KY 41011-1424

   Since you won't receive any acknowledgment that the IRS has received the form, send it by certified mail with a return receipt request in case you have to prove that it was delivered. If your **Form 3115** isn't postmarked by the deadline, the IRS will deny the deductions on your tax return. (You could file again next year and claim the deductions.) If for any reason the IRS does not consent to your **Form 3115**, it will notify you.

3. Attach a list of your previously unclaimed or underclaimed property to **Form 3115**, as shown at the end of this chapter. Be sure to include your name and Social Security number and indicate that this is an attachment to **Form 3115**.

A Note to Tax Professionals

The two types of unclaimed depreciation are **Schedule C** operating expenses depreciation (furniture, appliances, and other personal property) and **Form 8829** operating expenses depreciation (home and home improvements).

Calculate how much of each type of depreciation the provider was entitled to deduct for each unclaimed year. Check to see whether claiming this depreciation would have created a loss on **Form 8829** for each year in question. Higher **Schedule C** depreciation deductions may affect the provider's ability to claim some of the deductions on **Form 8829**.

After taking this into account, check to see if the provider is allowed to deduct all unclaimed depreciation on **Form 8829** each year. If so, the provider won't need to recalculate **Form 8829** each year. If not, she will need to recalculate the allowed deductions on **Form 8829** and carry forward any unallowed deductions to the next year's **Form 8829**. There may be a number of years of carry-forward deductions. The provider should keep copies of the recalculated **Form 8829**s as backup supporting statements.

Although **Form 8829** was introduced in 1991, the earlier rules were the same about the limitation on claiming home expenses that create a business loss. Consider the potential complexity of these calculations before agreeing to file **Form 3115**.

For more information about the tax issues discussed in this chapter, refer to the related topics in the other chapters of this book and the Redleaf Press *Family Child Care Record-Keeping Guide.*

Form **3115** (Rev. December 2018) Department of the Treasury Internal Revenue Service

Application for Change in Accounting Method

▶ Go to *www.irs.gov/Form3115* for instructions and the latest information.

OMB No. 1545-2070

Name of filer (name of parent corporation if a consolidated group) (see instructions)	**Identification number** (see instructions)
HANK AND KARIN ROTH	468-78-9123
	Principal business activity code number (see instructions) 62441
Number, street, and room or suite no. If a P.O. box, see the instructions. 466 WOBBLY LANE	Tax year of change begins (MM/DD/YYYY) 1/1/2019 Tax year of change ends (MM/DD/YYYY) 12/31/2019
City or town, state, and ZIP code DULUTH, MN 55671	Name of contact person (see instructions)
Name of applicant(s) (if different than filer) and identification number(s) (see instructions)	Contact person's telephone number

If the applicant is a member of a consolidated group, check this box . . . ▶ ☐

If **Form 2848,** Power of Attorney and Declaration of Representative, is attached (see instructions for when Form 2848 is required), check this box . . . ▶ ☐

Check the box to indicate the type of applicant.

☑ Individual
☐ Corporation
☐ Controlled foreign corporation (Sec. 957)
☐ 10/50 corporation (Sec. 904(d)(2)(E))
☐ Qualified personal service corporation (Sec. 448(d)(2))
☐ Exempt organization. Enter Code section ▶
☐ Cooperative (Sec. 1381)
☐ Partnership
☐ S corporation
☐ Insurance co. (Sec. 816(a))
☐ Insurance co. (Sec. 831)
☐ Other (specify) ▶

Check the appropriate box to indicate the type of accounting method change being requested. See instructions.

☑ Depreciation or Amortization
☐ Financial Products and/or Financial Activities of Financial Institutions
☐ Other (specify) ▶

Caution: To be eligible for approval of the requested change in method of accounting, the taxpayer must provide all information that is relevant to the taxpayer or to the taxpayer's requested change in method of accounting. This includes **(1)** all relevant information requested on this Form 3115 (including its instructions), and **(2)** any other relevant information, even if not specifically requested on Form 3115. **The taxpayer must attach all applicable statements requested throughout this form.**

Part I Information for Automatic Change Request

		Yes	No
1	Enter the applicable designated automatic accounting method change number ("DCN") for the requested automatic change. Enter only one DCN, except as provided for in guidance published by the IRS. If the requested change has no DCN, check "Other," and provide both a description of the change and a citation of the IRS guidance providing the automatic change. See instructions.		
a	(1) DCN: ____ (2) DCN: ____ (3) DCN: ____ (4) DCN: ____ (5) DCN: ____ (6) DCN: ____ (7) DCN: ____ (8) DCN: ____ (9) DCN: ____ (10) DCN: ____ (11) DCN: ____ (12) DCN: ____		
b	Other ☑ Description ▶ 107 RECAPTURE DEPRECIATION		
2	Do any of the eligibility rules restrict the applicant from filing the requested change using the automatic change procedures (see instructions)? If "Yes," attach an explanation.		✓
3	Has the filer provided all the information and statements required **(a)** on this form and **(b)** by the List of Automatic Changes under which the applicant is requesting a change? See instructions.	✓	
	Note: Complete Part II and Part IV of this form, and, Schedules A through E, if applicable.		

Part II Information for All Requests

		Yes	No
4	During the tax year of change, did or will the applicant **(a)** cease to engage in the trade or business to which the requested change relates, or **(b)** terminate its existence? See instructions.		✓
5	Is the applicant requesting to change to the principal method in the tax year of change under Regulations section 1.381(c)(4)-1(d)(1) or 1.381(c)(5)-1(d)(1)?		✓
	If "No," go to line 6a. If "Yes," the applicant cannot file a Form 3115 for this change. See instructions.		

Sign Here

Under penalties of perjury, I declare that I have examined this application, including accompanying schedules and statements, and to the best of my knowledge and belief, the application contains all the relevant facts relating to the application, and it is true, correct, and complete. Declaration of preparer (other than applicant) is based on all information of which preparer has any knowledge.

Signature of filer (and spouse, if joint return)	Date	Name and title (print or type)
Hank Roth Karin Roth	1/10/2020	HANK ROTH, KARIN ROTH

Preparer (other than filer/applicant)

Print/Type preparer's name	Preparer's signature	Date

Firm's name ▶

For Privacy Act and Paperwork Reduction Act Notice, see the instructions. Cat. No. 19280E Form **3115** (Rev. 12-2018)

Form 3115 (Rev. 12-2018) Page 2

Part II Information for All Requests *(continued)*

		Yes	No
6a	Does the applicant (or any present or former consolidated group in which the applicant was a member during the applicable tax year(s)) have any federal income tax return(s) under examination (see instructions)? If "No," go to line 7a.		✓
b	Is the method of accounting the applicant is requesting to change an issue under consideration (with respect to either the applicant or any present or former consolidated group in which the applicant was a member during the applicable tax year(s))? See instructions.		
c	Enter the name and telephone number of the examining agent and the tax year(s) under examination. Name ▶ ______ Telephone number ▶ ______ Tax year(s) ▶ ______		
d	Has a copy of this Form 3115 been provided to the examining agent identified on line 6c?		
7a	Does audit protection apply to the applicant's requested change in method of accounting? See instructions. If "No," attach an explanation.	✓	
b	If "Yes," check the applicable box and attach the required statement. ☑ Not under exam ☐ 3-month window ☐ 120 day: Date examination ended ▶ ______ ☐ Method not before director ☐ Negative adjustment ☐ CAP: Date member joined group ▶ ______ ☐ Audit protection at end of exam ☐ Other		
8a	Does the applicant (or any present or former consolidated group in which the applicant was a member during the applicable tax year(s)) have any federal income tax return(s) before Appeals and/or a federal court? If "No," go to line 9.		✓
b	Is the method of accounting the applicant is requesting to change an issue under consideration by Appeals and/or a federal court (for either the applicant or any present or former consolidated group in which the applicant was a member for the tax year(s) the applicant was a member)? See instructions. If "Yes," attach an explanation.		
c	If "Yes," enter the name of the (check the box) ☐ Appeals officer and/or ☐ counsel for the government, telephone number, and the tax year(s) before Appeals and/or a federal court. Name ▶ ______ Telephone number ▶ ______ Tax year(s) ▶ ______		
d	Has a copy of this Form 3115 been provided to the Appeals officer and/or counsel for the government identified on line 8c?		
9	If the applicant answered "Yes" to line 6a and/or 8a with respect to any present or former consolidated group, attach a statement that provides each parent corporation's **(a)** name, **(b)** identification number, **(c)** address, and **(d)** tax year(s) during which the applicant was a member that is under examination, before an Appeals office, and/or before a federal court.		
10	If for federal income tax purposes, the applicant is either an entity (including a limited liability company) treated as a partnership or an S corporation, is it requesting a change from a method of accounting that is an issue under consideration in an examination, before Appeals, or before a federal court, with respect to a federal income tax return of a partner, member, or shareholder of that entity?		✓
11a	Has the applicant, its predecessor, or a related party requested or made (under either an automatic or non-automatic change procedure) a change in method of accounting within any of the five tax years ending with the tax year of change? If "No," go to line 12.		✓
b	If "Yes," for each trade or business, attach a description of each requested change in method of accounting (including the tax year of change) and state whether the applicant received consent.		
c	If any application was withdrawn, not perfected, or denied, or if a Consent Agreement granting a change was not signed and returned to the IRS, or the change was not made or not made in the requested year of change, attach an explanation.		
12	Does the applicant, its predecessor, or a related party currently have pending any request (including any concurrently filed request) for a private letter ruling, change in method of accounting, or technical advice?		✓
	If "Yes," for each request attach a statement providing **(a)** the name(s) of the taxpayer, **(b)** identification number(s), **(c)** the type of request (private letter ruling, change in method of accounting, or technical advice), and **(d)** the specific issue(s) in the request(s).		
13	Is the applicant requesting to change its **overall** method of accounting? If "Yes," complete Schedule A on page 4 of the form.		✓

Form **3115** (Rev. 12-2018)

Form 3115 (Rev. 12-2018) Page **3**

Part II **Information for All Requests** *(continued)* | Yes | No

14 If the applicant is either **(i) not** changing its overall method of accounting, or **(ii)** changing its overall method of accounting **and** changing to a special method of accounting for one or more items, attach a detailed and complete description for each of the following (see instructions):

a The item(s) being changed.

b The applicant's present method for the item(s) being changed.

c The applicant's proposed method for the item(s) being changed.

d The applicant's present overall method of accounting (cash, accrual, or hybrid).

15a Attach a detailed and complete description of the applicant's trade(s) or business(es). See section 446(d).

b If the applicant has more than one trade or business, as defined in Regulations section 1.446-1(d), describe **(i)** whether each trade or business is accounted for separately; **(ii)** the goods and services provided by each trade or business and any other types of activities engaged in that generate gross income; **(iii)** the overall method of accounting for each trade or business; and **(iv)** which trade or business is requesting to change its accounting method as part of this application or a separate application.

Note: If you are requesting an automatic method change, see the instructions to see if you are required to complete lines 16a–16c.

16a Attach a full explanation of the legal basis supporting the proposed method for the item being changed. Include a detailed and complete description of the facts that explains how the law specifically applies to the applicant's situation and that demonstrates that the applicant is authorized to use the proposed method.

b Include all authority (statutes, regulations, published rulings, court cases, etc.) supporting the proposed method.

c Include either a discussion of the contrary authorities or a statement that no contrary authority exists.

17 Will the proposed method of accounting be used for the applicant's books and records and financial statements? For insurance companies, see the instructions. . . . . | Yes: ✓ | No:

If "No," attach an explanation.

18 Does the applicant request a conference with the IRS National Office if the IRS National Office proposes an adverse response? | Yes: | No: ✓

19a If the applicant is changing to either the overall cash method, an overall accrual method, or is changing its method of accounting for any property subject to section 263A, any long-term contract subject to section 460 (see 19b), or inventories subject to section 474, enter the applicant's gross receipts for the 3 tax years preceding the tax year of change.

1st preceding year ended: mo. yr.	2nd preceding year ended: mo. yr.	3rd preceding year ended: mo. yr.
$	$	$

b If the applicant is changing its method of accounting for any long-term contract subject to section 460, in addition to completing 19a, enter the applicant's gross receipts for the 4th tax year preceding the tax year of change:

4th preceding year ended: mo. ________ yr. ____ $ ______________________

Part III **Information for Non-Automatic Change Request** | Yes | No

20 Is the applicant's requested change described in any revenue procedure, revenue ruling, notice, regulation, or other published guidance as an automatic change request? . . . .

If "Yes," attach an explanation describing why the applicant is submitting its request under the non-automatic change procedures.

21 Attach a copy of all documents related to the proposed change (see instructions).

22 Attach a statement of the applicant's reasons for the proposed change.

23 If the applicant is a member of a consolidated group for the year of change, do all other members of the consolidated group use the proposed method of accounting for the item being changed? . . . .

If "No," attach an explanation.

24a Enter the amount of **user fee** attached to this application (see instructions). ▶ $ ______________

b If the applicant qualifies for a reduced user fee, attach the required information or certification (see instructions).

Form 3115 (Rev. 12-2018) Page 4

Part IV Section 481(a) Adjustment

		Yes	No
25	Does published guidance require the applicant (or permit the applicant and the applicant is electing) to implement the requested change in method of accounting on a cut-off basis? If "Yes," attach an explanation and do not complete lines 26, 27, and 28 below.		✓
26	Enter the section 481(a) adjustment. Indicate whether the adjustment is an increase (+) or a decrease (-) in income. ▶ $ ______ Attach a summary of the computation and an explanation of the methodology used to determine the section 481(a) adjustment. If it is based on more than one component, show the computation for each component. If more than one applicant is applying for the method change on the application, attach a list of the **(a)** name, **(b)** identification number, and **(c)** the amount of the section 481(a) adjustment attributable to each applicant.		
27	Is the applicant making an election to take the entire amount of the adjustment into account in the tax year of change? If "Yes," check the box for the applicable elective provision used to make the election (see instructions). ☐ $50,000 de minimis election ☐ Eligible acquisition transaction election	✓	
28	Is any part of the section 481(a) adjustment attributable to transactions between members of an affiliated group, a consolidated group, a controlled group, or other related parties? If "Yes," attach an explanation.		✓

Schedule A—Change in Overall Method of Accounting (If Schedule A applies, Part I below must be completed.)

Part I Change in Overall Method (see instructions)

1 Check the appropriate boxes below to indicate the applicant's present and proposed methods of accounting.

Present method: ☐ Cash ☐ Accrual ☐ Hybrid (attach description)

Proposed method: ☐ Cash ☐ Accrual ☐ Hybrid (attach description)

2 Enter the following amounts as of the close of the tax year preceding the year of change. If none, state "None." Also, attach a statement providing a breakdown of the amounts entered on lines 2a through 2g.

		Amount
a	Income accrued but not received (such as accounts receivable)	$
b	Income received or reported before it was earned (such as advanced payments). Attach a description of the income and the legal basis for the proposed method.	
c	Expenses accrued but not paid (such as accounts payable).	
d	Prepaid expenses previously deducted	
e	Supplies on hand previously deducted and/or not previously reported	
f	Inventory on hand previously deducted and/or not previously reported. Complete Schedule D, Part II.	
g	Other amounts (specify). Attach a description of the item and the legal basis for its inclusion in the calculation of the section 481(a) adjustment. ▶	
h	**Net section 481(a) adjustment** (Combine lines 2a–2g.) Indicate whether the adjustment is an increase (+) or decrease (-) in income. Also enter the net amount of this section 481(a) adjustment amount on Part IV, line 26.	$

3 Is the applicant also requesting the recurring item exception under section 461(h)(3)? ☐ **Yes** ☐ **No**

4 Attach copies of the profit and loss statement (Schedule F (Form 1040) for farmers) and the balance sheet, if applicable, as of the close of the tax year preceding the year of change. Also attach a statement specifying the accounting method used when preparing the balance sheet. If books of account are not kept, attach a copy of the business schedules submitted with the federal income tax return or other return (such as, tax-exempt organization returns) for that period. If the amounts in Part I, lines 2a through 2g, do not agree with the amounts shown on both the profit and loss statement and the balance sheet, attach a statement explaining the differences.

5 Is the applicant making a change to the overall cash method as a small business taxpayer (see instructions)? ☐ **Yes** ☐ **No**

Part II Change to the Cash Method for Non-Automatic Change Request (see instructions)

Applicants requesting a change to the cash method must attach the following information:

1 A description of inventory items (items whose production, purchase, or sale is an income-producing factor) and materials and supplies used in carrying out the business.

2 An explanation as to whether the applicant is required to use the accrual method under any section of the Code or regulations.

Form **3115** (Rev. 12-2018)

Attachment to Form 3115 for Tax Year 2020
Hank and Karin Roth
SS #123-45-6789, 987-65-4321

Answers to Questions:

14a) Applicant is deducting unclaimed depreciation for a washer bought for $400 in 2012 and a dryer bought for $300 in the same year.

14b) Present method: Applicant has previously not depreciated this property.

14c) Proposed method: Applicant is depreciating this property under the 7-year MACRS 200% declining balance method under Section 168.

14d) Overall method of accounting: Cash basis.

15a) The applicant is a family child care provider. She takes care of children in her home. The business activity code is 62441.

26) Depreciation Calculation

Washer (asset class 00.11):	$400
Dryer (asset class 00.11):	$300
Total:	$700

The Time-Space percentage was 35% for all the years of depreciation.

2012: $700 x 35% = $245 x 14.29%	=	$35.01
2013: $700 x 35% = $245 x 24.49%	=	$60.00
2014: $700 x 35% = $245 x 17.49%	=	$42.85
2015: $700 x 35% = $245 x 12.49%	=	$30.60
2016: $700 x 35% = $245 x 8.93%	=	$21.88
2017: $700 x 35% = $245 x 8.92%	=	$21.85
2018: $700 x 35% = $245 x 8.93%	=	$21.88
2019: $700 x 35% = $245 x 4.46%	=	$10.93
Total depreciation allowed 2012–2019	=	$245.00

CHAPTER 11

Selling Your Business Property: Form 4797

If you sold items you used for your business this year, you may be able to claim some additional tax deductions by filing **Form 4797** Sales of Business Property with your income tax forms. You should fill out **Form 4797** if you experienced any of the following situations last year:

- An item you're depreciating wears out before the end of its depreciation period.
- You sell your car.
- You sell your home or land.
- You sell property that was used in your business while you were still in business.
- Your business use drops to 50% or less for an item you depreciated under Section 179 or accelerated rules, and you must recapture (pay back) some of the depreciation you've claimed.

To illustrate these situations, we'll look at ten examples. Examples 1 and 2 show how to handle an item that wears out before the end of its depreciation period. Examples 3 through 6 deal with selling items you're using in your business. Examples 7 through 9 show how to handle the sale of a vehicle, and example 10 explains how to recapture depreciation. Report the net gain or loss for all the sales (except for the car) you show on **Form 4797** and on **Form 8829**, line 8.

Selling Your Home

The IRS rules issued in December 2002 have greatly simplified the tax consequences of selling your home. Most family child care providers will now be able to avoid paying any taxes on the profit made by selling a home but will still have to pay taxes on the home depreciation that has been claimed since May 6, 1997. For more information, see chapter 12.

An Item Wears Out during the Depreciation Period

Example 1

You've been providing child care since 2014. In January 2015 you install a new deck for $2,000. In March 2020 the deck is rotted out, and you demolish it. Later that year you build a new deck and start depreciating it (see chapter 3 for instructions). You were depreciating the first deck over 39 years as a home improvement. Your Time-Space percentages have been as follows: 2015: 30%; 2016: 28%; 2017: 27%; 2018: 31%; 2019: 32%; 2020: 33%. Your depreciation deductions for 2014–2018 were as follows:

2015: $2,000 x 30% = $600 x 2.461% = $14.77
2016: $2,000 x 28% = $560 x 2.564% = $14.36
2017: $2,000 x 27% = $540 x 2.564% = $13.85
2018: $2,000 x 31% = $620 x 2.564% = $15.90
2019: $2,000 x 32% = $640 x 2.564% = $16.41

Total claimed so far: $75.29

For 2020 you must first calculate the amount of depreciation you're entitled to for the last year you used the old deck in your business (2020):

$2,000 x 33% = $660 x 2.564% = $16.92

Under the Half-Year Convention rules (see chapter 3), you can claim only half the normal depreciation for 2020 (you last used the deck in March 2020). Therefore, enter $8.46 ($16.92 x 50% = $8.46) on **Form 4562**, line 17, as your depreciation for 2020.

So far you've claimed a total of $83.75 for the old deck ($75.29 for 2015–2019 and $8.46 for 2020). Since the deck has now worn out, you're also entitled to claim the rest of the depreciation for the deck this year. The remaining depreciation you haven't yet claimed amounts to $576.25 ($2,000 x 33% Time-Space percentage for 2020 = $660 – $83.75).

You'll claim this $576.25 as a loss on Part I of **Form 4797** because the deck was used in business for more than one year. (See example form at the end of chapter 11.) It is a loss because you weren't able to claim all the depreciation before the deck wore out. You'll carry over the total of this amount and any other amounts you enter here to **Form 1040**, line 14, where it will reduce your taxable income and thus your taxes.

If you are no longer in business when the deck wears out, you won't be able to claim this remaining depreciation; you can only claim a business loss if you're still in business.

Example 2

In 2017 you bought a microwave oven for $300 and started using it in your business. In 2020 the oven breaks down; you discard it and buy a new one. Your Time-Space percentages have been as follows: 2017: 35%; 2018: 38%; 2019: 37%; 2020: 36%. You've been depreciating the oven under seven-year 200% declining balance rules. Your depreciation deductions for 2017–2019 were as follows:

2017: $300 x 35% = $105 x 14.29% = $15.00
2018: $300 x 38% = $114 x 24.49% = $27.92
2019: $300 x 37% = $111 x 17.49% = $19.41

Total claimed so far: $62.33

In 2020 the business basis of the microwave oven is $108 ($300 x 36% Time-Space percentage), so you can claim $6.74 in depreciation ($108 x 12.49% x 50%) on **Form 4562**, line 17. You can claim the remaining depreciation, $38.93 ($108 – $62.33 – $6.74), as a loss on Part I of **Form 4797**. You'll carry over this loss (and any other amounts in this section) to **Form 1040**, line 14. (This example is not shown on the forms at the end of this chapter.)

You Sell an Item You've Used for Business

You must follow special rules when you sell items you've used in your business, and the reporting procedures differ depending on whether you have a gain or a loss on the sale. To determine that, follow these steps:

1. If you bought the item while you were in business, start with its original cost. If you bought it before you went into business, use the lesser of its original cost or its fair market value when you began using it for business. (This will usually be the item's fair market value.) This is the basis of the item.
2. Determine the total depreciation you were entitled to claim on the item while using it for your business, using straight-line depreciation rules. Determine the total depreciation you actually claimed for the item. Use the larger of these two amounts for the next step.
3. Subtract the item's total depreciation (step 2) from the item's basis (step 1). You must subtract all the depreciation you could have claimed, even if you didn't claim it all. The result is the item's adjusted basis.
4. Subtract the adjusted basis (step 3) from the price you got for the item when you sold it. The result is your gain or loss on the sale.

If You're No Longer in Business

If you sell an item after you're no longer in business (or no longer using the item in your business), use the above calculations to determine if you have a gain or a loss, adjusting the basis of the item by any depreciation you were entitled to claim. If you have a gain, enter it on **Schedule D** and **Form 1040** but not on **Form 4797**. If you have a loss, you have no further forms to fill out. Since you're no longer using the item in your business, you can't claim a deduction for a business loss.

If the Item Was Originally a Gift

If someone gave you the item as a gift or as payment for child care services, use the donor's basis to determine your gain or loss for the item. The donor's basis is the lesser of the donor's adjusted basis (usually the original cost) of the item or its fair market value when it was given to you.

- If someone bought a $1,000 swing set in 2017 and gave it to you in that same year, you would use $1,000 as its basis and follow the calculations above.
- If someone bought a $1,000 swing set in 2013 and gave it to you in 2017, its 2017 fair market value would be less than $1,000. If you estimate it to be worth $600 in 2017, you would use $600 as your basis instead of the $1,000 purchase price.

Example 3: Item Used 100% for Business and Sold at a Gain

You started your business in 2015. In 2018 you buy a swing set to use 100% for your business. You're still in business on May 1, 2020, when you sell the swing set for $900.

$1,000	purchase price of swing set (2018)
– $475	depreciation claimed 2018–2020 (7-year 200% declining balance)
	2018: $1,000 x 14.29% = $142.90
	2019: $1,000 x 24.49% =$244.90
	2020: $1,000 x 17.49% x 50% =$87.45
	Total: $475.25
$525	adjusted basis of swing set
$900	sale price of swing set in 2020
– $525	adjusted basis
$375	gain

Report this gain on **Form 4797**, Part I, and carry it over to **Schedule D**, line 10 (see end-of-chapter example), along with any other amounts you've reported in this section. The amounts on line 8 will be totaled on line 17 and carried over to **Form 1040**, line 13, where they will increase your taxable income. Since this is not a business gain, you won't owe any additional Social Security tax on it.

Charitable Contributions

If you give an item to a charitable organization, either while you're in business or after you've closed your business, your deduction for it would be the lower of the fair market value of the item at the time you donated it or the adjusted basis of the item. Since a self-employed person can't claim a business deduction for a charitable contribution, report the donation on **Schedule A**, line 16.

For example, if you had given the swing set in example 3 to a charity on May 1, 2020, you could claim a charitable deduction of $525 ($1,000 – $475 depreciation = $525 adjusted basis) if its fair market value at that time was more than $525. If it was worth $500 at that time, you would deduct $500.

If you give an item away but *not* to a charitable organization before it's fully depreciated, you can't take any more depreciation deductions for that item.

Example 4: Item Used 40% for Business and Sold at a Gain

How would example 3 change if your own children also used the swing set and your Time-Space percentage was 40% each year?

$400	business basis of swing set ($1,000 purchase price x 40% Time-Space percentage)
– $190	depreciation claimed 2018–2020 (7-year 200% declining balance)
	2018: $400 x 14.29% = $57.16
	2019: $400 x 24.49% = $97.96
	2020: $400 x 17.49% x 50% = $34.98 (only a half year of depreciation because it was sold during the year)
	Total: $190.10
$210	adjusted business basis of swing set
$360	business basis of swing set sale ($900 x 40%)
– $210	adjusted business basis
$150	gain

You'll report this gain on **Form 4797**, Part I, and **Form 8949**, Part II, and then transfer the gain to **Schedule D** (see example at end of chapter) and **Form 1040**. Since you've also used the swing set for personal use, there may also be personal tax consequences:

$600	personal basis of swing set ($1,000 purchase price x 60% personal use)
$540	personal basis of swing set sale ($900 x 60%)
$540	personal basis of sale
– $600	personal basis of purchase
($60)	personal loss

Since you can't deduct a personal loss, in this case you won't fill out any other forms; however, if you had a personal gain on the sale, you'd report it as income on **Schedule D**.

Example 5: Item Used 100% for Business and Sold at a Loss

How would Example 3 change if you sold the swing set in 2020 for $500?

$500	sale price of swing set in 2020
– $525	adjusted basis
($25)	loss

In this case, you would deduct the $25 loss as a business expense on **Form 4797**, Part I. (This example is not shown on the forms at the end of this chapter.)

Example 6: Item Used 40% for Business and Sold at a Loss

How would Example 3 change if you sold the swing set for $400, your own children used the swing set, and your Time-Space percentage was 40% each year?

$160	business basis of sale price ($400 x 40%)
– $190	adjusted business basis
($30)	business loss

Enter this $30 as a loss on **Form 4797**, Part I (see example at end of chapter). If your total gains and losses on **Form 4797** result in a loss, enter that amount onto **Form 1040**, line 14.

What If You Sell an Item at a Garage Sale?

The tax impact of selling an item at a garage sale is the same as in examples 3 through 6. You must take depreciation into account and calculate an adjusted basis for the item:

- If you never used the item sold in your business, report any gain you made on the sale on **Schedule D** and **Form 1040**. If you have a loss on the sale, don't report it on any tax form.
- If you're in business and you sell an item used in your business, report the business gain or loss on **Form 4797** and any personal gain on **Schedule D**.
- If you're no longer in business and you sell an item used in your business for a profit, report it as a gain on **Schedule D**. If you have a loss on the sale, don't report it on any tax form.

Because of the low prices at garage sales, it's unlikely you'll have any gains to report on **Form 4797**, **Schedule D**, and **Form 1040**. You may, however, have business losses you can claim on **Form 4797** and **Form 1040**. Although you're entitled to claim these losses, many child care providers probably wouldn't do so, and there's no penalty for not claiming them.

You Sell a Vehicle You've Used for Business

Calculating a gain or loss on the sale of a vehicle is a little more complicated than it is for other items; however, it's good to follow the special rules about selling a vehicle because often they'll allow you to claim a business loss and save taxes. The procedure you'll follow will depend on which method you've used to deduct your vehicle expenses.

Actual Vehicle Expenses Method

If you used the actual vehicle expenses method to claim your vehicle expenses, you have claimed a depreciation deduction. When the vehicle is sold, you will take your depreciation deductions into account as shown in the previous examples.

Standard Mileage Rate Method

If you used the standard mileage rate method to claim your vehicle expenses, you must do a special calculation to determine how much depreciation to apply to the sale. Each year you use the standard mileage rate method, part of the deduction is considered to be depreciation. Here are the depreciation amounts for the last several years:

2020	$0.27 per mile
2019	$0.26 per mile
2018	$0.25 per mile
2017	$0.25 per mile
2015–16	$0.24 per mile
2014	$0.22 per mile
2012–13	$0.23 per mile
2011	$0.22 per mile
2010	$0.23 per mile
2008–2009	$0.21 per mile
2007	$0.19 per mile
2004–2006	$0.17 per mile
2003	$0.16 per mile
2001–2002	$0.15 per mile

Multiply your business miles for each year you used your vehicle in business by the appropriate depreciation amount. Add these results together to get the total depreciation you will use to determine the adjusted basis of your vehicle.

Example 7: Sale of a Vehicle without a Trade-In (Standard Mileage Rate)

In 2015 you buy a $15,000 vehicle and use it for business. You drive it 1,500 business miles in 2015, 1,400 miles in 2016, 1,700 miles in 2017, 1,452 miles in 2018, 1,130 miles in 2019, and 800 miles in 2020. You sell the vehicle in September 2020 for $4,000.

You use the standard mileage rate method every year, and your average business-use percentage this tax season is 20%. Here's how you would calculate your gain or loss on the sale:

Depreciation per year	
1,500 miles in 2015 x $0.24 =	$360
1,400 miles in 2016 x $0.24 =	$336
1,700 miles in 2017 x $0.25 =	$425
1,452 miles in 2018 x $0.25 =	$363
1,130 miles in 2019 x $0.26 =	$293.80
800 miles in 2020 x $0.27 =	$216
Total:	$1,993.80

$3,000	business basis of vehicle ($15,000 purchase price x 20% business use)
– $1,994	depreciation claimed as part of standard mileage rate method
$1,006	adjusted business basis
$800	business basis of vehicle sold ($4,000 x 20% business use)
– $1,006	adjusted business basis
($206)	business loss

You can deduct this loss as a business expense on **Form 4797**, Part I. Enter –$206 on lines 11, 18a, and 18b and transfer –$206 to **Form 1040**, line 14.

Example 8: Sale of a Vehicle without a Trade-In (Actual Vehicle Expenses)

If you had used the actual vehicle expenses method instead, you'd use the depreciation that you could have claimed over the years (even if you didn't actually claim it). This example is otherwise like example 7 except that you're depreciating the vehicle based on 20% business use. After six years of use, you would have claimed the full amount of depreciation ($15,000 purchase price x 20% = $3,000).

$3,000	business basis of vehicle
– $3,000	depreciation claimed under actual vehicle expenses method
0	adjusted basis
$800	business basis of vehicle sold
– 0	adjusted basis
$800	business gain

You would report this gain as shown in example 3.

Selling a Vehicle with a Trade-In

If you trade your vehicle for another vehicle, you won't have a taxable gain or loss because this transaction is considered to be a like-kind exchange. If you used the standard mileage rate method on your traded-in vehicle and the same method on your new vehicle, there is no tax consequence at the time of the trade-in. If you eventually sell your new vehicle without trading it in, you should follow the procedure in example 7.

If you used the standard mileage rate method on your traded-in vehicle and the actual vehicle expenses method (or Section 179) on your new vehicle, then you would base the depreciation for the new vehicle on the actual cash you paid for it, without reference to the amount you received for the trade-in. In other words, if your new vehicle cost $30,000 and you paid $22,000 in cash in addition to the $8,000 you received for the trade-in value of the old vehicle, you would base your depreciation deduction on $22,000.

If you use the actual vehicle expenses method on both your traded-in vehicle and your new vehicle, follow this procedure to determine the depreciation amount on the new car: Take the original price of the old car and subtract it from the depreciation amount you claimed for the years you used it in your business. Then add the amount you paid for the new car. For example, if you paid $28,000 for the old car, claimed $3,449 in depreciation for the old car, and paid $10,000 (plus the traded-in old car) for the new car, the adjusted basis for depreciating the new car is $34,551 ($28,000 – $3,449 + $10,000).

Example 9: Sale of a Vehicle with a Trade-In

You originally purchased a car in 2017 for $28,000, and for the last three years you have been using the actual vehicle expenses method to deduct your expenses for that vehicle. Your business-use percentage for all three years was 20%. In 2020 you bought a new car for $10,000 ($10,000 cash plus the trade-in value for your old car). Here's how you would claim your depreciation deduction for 2020:

Traded-in car: $28,000 x 20% business use = $5,600
x 20% (4th year straight-line depreciation) = $1,120

Since the depreciation deduction limitation is $395 ($1,975 x 20% = $395), you can only claim $375. The depreciation basis for the new car is $34,551 (see above). See also page 91.

New car: $34,551 x 20% business use = $6,910
x 10% (1st year straight-line depreciation) = $691

Since the depreciation deduction limitation is $2,000 ($10,000 x 20% = $2,000), you can claim $691 this year.

Total depreciation claimed: $1,007 ($395 + $691)
Enter $1,086 on **Form 4562**, line 27.

IRS **Notice 2002-4** doesn't clarify how to calculate the depreciation on the traded-in vehicle if your business-use percentage fluctuated during the years you used it in your business. I assume that you should use an average business-use percentage for the years you used it in your business and continue using this average percentage for the remaining depreciation period.

You Have to Recapture Some Depreciation

For a description of the many circumstances under which you might have to recapture depreciation, see chapter 3. This example is one of the most common scenarios: you used Section 179 to deduct the entire business portion of an item in the year you bought it, and then your business-use percentage dropped to 50% or below before the end of the item's depreciation period. In this case, you'll have to recapture some of the depreciation you've claimed by filling out Part IV of **Form 4797**.

Example 10: Business Use Drops below 50% after Using Section 179

In 2018 you used Section 179 to deduct a $1,000 set of children's furniture. Since you expected to use it 100% for business purposes, you deducted the entire $1,000 in 2018. In 2020 your own children began using the furniture 40% of the time. Since your business-use percentage dropped below 50% in 2020, you must recapture some of the Section 179 deduction you claimed by filling out lines 33–35 of **Form 4797** as follows:

Line 33: Enter "$1,000."

Line 34: Enter the amount of depreciation you would have been entitled to claim each year through 2020, under straight-line rules, if you had not used Section 179.

2018: $1,000 x 100% business use = $1,000 x 7.14%	= $71.40
2019: $1,000 x 100% business use = $1,000 x 14.29%	= $142.90
2020: $1,000 x 40% business use = $400 x 14.29%	= $57.16
Total:	$271.46

Line 35: Subtract line 34 from line 33:

$1,000 – $271.46 = $728.54

Part IV **Recapture Amounts Under Sections 179 and 280F(b)(2) When Business Use Drops to 50% or Less** (see instructions)

			(a) Section 179	(b) Section 280F(b)(2)
33	Section 179 expense deduction or depreciation allowable in prior years.	33	$1,000	
34	Recomputed depreciation. See instructions	34	$271	
35	Recapture amount. Subtract line 34 from line 33. See the instructions for where to report	35	$729	

Form **4797** (2020)

Also enter $729 on **Schedule C**, line 6 (other income). You'll have to pay Social Security tax and income tax on this amount. You could still claim $57.16 as a depreciation deduction for 2020 on **Form 4562**.

If you went out of business by the end of 2020, you'd report the $729 as income on **Schedule C** and wouldn't be able to take any further depreciation deductions on the furniture.

If you remain in business, you'd report the $729 as income but would now be able to claim depreciation on the furniture in 2021 and beyond. (2021 would be the fourth year of depreciation; you'd be able to deduct $57.12 [$1,000 x 40% Time-Space percentage = $400 x 14.28% = $57.12]. You'd enter this amount on **Form 4562**, line 17.)

For more information about the tax issues discussed in this chapter, refer to the related topics in the other chapters of this book and the Redleaf Press *Family Child Care Record-Keeping Guide.*

Form **4797**

Department of the Treasury
Internal Revenue Service

Sales of Business Property

(Also Involuntary Conversions and Recapture Amounts Under Sections 179 and 280F(b)(2))

▶ Attach to your tax return.

▶ Go to *www.irs.gov/Form4797* for instructions and the latest information.

OMB No. 1545-0184
2020
Attachment Sequence No. **27**

Name(s) shown on return: LUPE SERANNO | **Identifying number**: 621-33-7454

1 Enter the gross proceeds from sales or exchanges reported to you for 2020 on Form(s) 1099-B or 1099-S (or substitute statement) that you are including on line 2, 10, or 20. See instructions 1

Part I **Sales or Exchanges of Property Used in a Trade or Business and Involuntary Conversions From Other Than Casualty or Theft—Most Property Held More Than 1 Year** (see instructions)

2 (a) Description of property	(b) Date acquired (mo., day, yr.)	(c) Date sold (mo., day, yr.)	(d) Gross sales price	(e) Depreciation allowed or allowable since acquisition	(f) Cost or other basis, plus improvements and expense of sale	(g) Gain or (loss) Subtract (f) from the sum of (d) and (e)
#1 DECK	1/8/2014	3/1/2020	$0	$84	$660	($576)
#3 SWING SET	1/1/2017	5/1/2020	$900	$475	$1,000	$375
#4 SWING SET	1/1/2017	5/1/2020	$360	$190	$400	$150
#6 SWING SET	1/1/2017	5/1/2020	$160	$190	$400	($30)
#7 VEHICLE	1/1/2014	9/1/2020	$800	$1,174	$3,000	($374)

3 Gain, if any, from Form 4684, line 39 3

4 Section 1231 gain from installment sales from Form 6252, line 26 or 37 4

5 Section 1231 gain or (loss) from like-kind exchanges from Form 8824 5

6 Gain, if any, from line 32, from other than casualty or theft 6

7 Combine lines 2 through 6. Enter the gain or (loss) here and on the appropriate line as follows 7

Form **8949**

Department of the Treasury
Internal Revenue Service

Sales and Other Dispositions of Capital Assets

▶ Go to *www.irs.gov/Form8949* for instructions and the latest information.

▶ File with your Schedule D to list your transactions for lines 1b, 2, 3, 8b, 9, and 10 of Schedule D.

OMB No. 1545-0074
2020
Attachment Sequence No. **12A**

Name(s) shown on return: LUPE SERANNO | **Social security number or taxpayer identification number**: 621-33-7454

Part II **Long-Term.** Transactions involving capital assets you held more than 1 year are generally long-term (see instructions). For short-term transactions, see page 1.

Note: You may aggregate all long-term transactions reported on Form(s) 1099-B showing basis was reported to the IRS and for which no adjustments or codes are required. Enter the totals directly on Schedule D, line 8a; you aren't required to report these transactions on Form 8949 (see instructions).

You *must* check Box D, E, *or* F below. Check only one box. If more than one box applies for your long-term transactions, complete a separate Form 8949, page 2, for each applicable box. If you have more long-term transactions than will fit on this page for one or more of the boxes, complete as many forms with the same box checked as you need.

☐ **(D)** Long-term transactions reported on Form(s) 1099-B showing basis was reported to the IRS (see **Note** above)

☐ **(E)** Long-term transactions reported on Form(s) 1099-B showing basis **wasn't** reported to the IRS

☑ **(F)** Long-term transactions not reported to you on Form 1099-B

1 (a) Description of property (Example: 100 sh. XYZ Co.)	(b) Date acquired (Mo., day, yr.)	(c) Date sold or disposed of (Mo., day, yr.)	(d) Proceeds (sales price) (see instructions)	(e) Cost or other basis. See the **Note** below and see *Column (e)* in the separate instructions	Adjustment, if any, to gain or loss. If you enter an amount in column (g), enter a code in column (f). **See the separate instructions.** (f) Code(s) from instructions	(g) Amount of adjustment	(h) **Gain or (loss).** Subtract column (e) from column (d) and combine the result with column (g)
#3 SWING SET	1/1/2017	5/1/2020	$900	$1,000		($475)	$375
#4 SWING SET	1/1/2017	5/1/2020	$360	$400		($190)	$150

SCHEDULE D
(Form 1040)

Department of the Treasury
Internal Revenue Service (99)

Capital Gains and Losses

► Attach to Form 1040, 1040-SR, or 1040-NR.
► Go to *www.irs.gov/ScheduleD* for instructions and the latest information.
► Use Form 8949 to list your transactions for lines 1b, 2, 3, 8b, 9, and 10.

OMB No. 1545-0074
2020
Attachment Sequence No. **12**

Name(s) shown on return: LUPE SERRANO | **Your social security number** 621-33-7454

Did you dispose of any investment(s) in a qualified opportunity fund during the tax year? ☐ **Yes** ☐ **No**
If "Yes," attach Form 8949 and see its instructions for additional requirements for reporting your gain or loss.

Part I **Short-Term Capital Gains and Losses—Generally Assets Held One Year or Less** (see instructions)

See instructions for how to figure the amounts to enter on the lines below. This form may be easier to complete if you round off cents to whole dollars.	**(d)** Proceeds (sales price)	**(e)** Cost (or other basis)	**(g)** Adjustments to gain or loss from Form(s) 8949, Part I, line 2, column (g)	**(h) Gain or (loss)** Subtract column (e) from column (d) and combine the result with column (g)
1a Totals for all short-term transactions reported on Form 1099-B for which basis was reported to the IRS and for which you have no adjustments (see instructions). However, if you choose to report all these transactions on Form 8949, leave this line blank and go to line 1b .				
1b Totals for all transactions reported on Form(s) 8949 with **Box A** checked				
2 Totals for all transactions reported on Form(s) 8949 with **Box B** checked				
3 Totals for all transactions reported on Form(s) 8949 with **Box C** checked				

4 Short-term gain from Form 6252 and short-term gain or (loss) from Forms 4684, 6781, and 8824	**4**	
5 Net short-term gain or (loss) from partnerships, S corporations, estates, and trusts from Schedule(s) K-1	**5**	
6 Short-term capital loss carryover. Enter the amount, if any, from line 8 of your **Capital Loss Carryover Worksheet** in the instructions	**6**	( )
7 **Net short-term capital gain or (loss).** Combine lines 1a through 6 in column (h). If you have any long-term capital gains or losses, go to Part II below. Otherwise, go to Part III on the back	**7**	

Part II **Long-Term Capital Gains and Losses—Generally Assets Held More Than One Year** (see instructions)

See instructions for how to figure the amounts to enter on the lines below. This form may be easier to complete if you round off cents to whole dollars.	**(d)** Proceeds (sales price)	**(e)** Cost (or other basis)	**(g)** Adjustments to gain or loss from Form(s) 8949, Part II, line 2, column (g)	**(h) Gain or (loss)** Subtract column (e) from column (d) and combine the result with column (g)
8a Totals for all long-term transactions reported on Form 1099-B for which basis was reported to the IRS and for which you have no adjustments (see instructions). However, if you choose to report all these transactions on Form 8949, leave this line blank and go to line 8b .				
8b Totals for all transactions reported on Form(s) 8949 with **Box D** checked				
9 Totals for all transactions reported on Form(s) 8949 with **Box E** checked				
10 Totals for all transactions reported on Form(s) 8949 with **Box F** checked.	**#3 SWING $900** **#4 SWING $360**	**$1,000** **$400**	**($475)** **($190)**	**$375** **$150**

11 Gain from Form 4797, Part I; long-term gain from Forms 2439 and 6252; and long-term gain or (loss) from Forms 4684, 6781, and 8824	**11**	
12 Net long-term gain or (loss) from partnerships, S corporations, estates, and trusts from Schedule(s) K-1	**12**	
13 Capital gain distributions. See the instructions	**13**	
14 Long-term capital loss carryover. Enter the amount, if any, from line 13 of your **Capital Loss Carryover Worksheet** in the instructions	**14**	( )
15 **Net long-term capital gain or (loss).** Combine lines 8a through 14 in column (h). Then, go to Part III on the back	**15**	

For Paperwork Reduction Act Notice, see your tax return instructions. Cat. No. 11338H **Schedule D (Form 1040) 2020**

CHAPTER 12

Selling Your Home: Form 4797 and Schedule D

When you sell your home, you potentially face two taxes. The first tax is on the depreciation you claimed (or were entitled to claim) for all the years you used your home for your business. The second tax is on the profit of the sale of your home. Almost every provider must pay the first tax, and some may have to pay the second tax.

The Tax on the Depreciation of Your Home

When you use your home for business, you are entitled to depreciate its value. You always want to depreciate your home because doing so will usually generate a substantial deduction each year.

Here's a very simple example. You purchase your home for $200,000. Each year, your Time-Space percentage is 35%. You run your family child care business for seven years and then stop offering child care. Years later you sell your home:

$200,000 x 35% = $70,000
Homes are depreciated over 39 years: $70,000 ÷ 39 = $1,795
You used your home for your business for 7 years: $1,795 x 7 years = $12,565

Over the seven years, you were entitled to claim $12,565 of business deductions. (See chapter 3 for a discussion of how to depreciate your home.) As a result, when you sell your home, you will owe taxes on $12,565.

The tax rate you will pay on this amount depends on your tax bracket in the year you sell your home. The current tax rates are as follows:

- 10% if you are in the 10% tax bracket
- 12% if you are in the 12% tax bracket
- 22% if you are in the 22% or higher tax bracket (see page 135 for a description of the 2020 tax brackets)

If you sold your home in 2020 and you were in the 12% tax bracket, you would owe $1,508 in taxes ($12,565 x 12% = $1,508).

Important Note: Always Depreciate Your Home!

In the above example, you would owe $1,508 in taxes even if you didn't claim house depreciation for the seven years you were in business; this tax is due if you were entitled to claim house depreciation—even if you didn't! The IRS rules clearly state that if you were entitled to claim house depreciation in any tax year, you will be treated as if you did when you sell your home. You will owe this tax even if you do not offer child care services for many years before you sell your home. The only situation in which you would not be entitled to claim house depreciation (and therefore not have to pay taxes on it when you sell your home) is if you showed a loss in your business in any year. For example, if you showed a business loss for the last two tax years, you wouldn't owe any tax on depreciation for those years.

When you consider the above information, you should realize that you always want to depreciate your home, no matter what! You will owe the same amount in taxes on your home later, even if you didn't depreciate it. Depreciating your home can mean a significant tax deduction each year, so don't let anyone tell you it's not a good idea. If you did not depreciate your home in earlier years, you can amend your tax return (going back up to three years) or use **Form 3115** (see chapter 10) to recapture the depreciation (going back many years). The amount of depreciation subject to tax is the lower of the amount of depreciation claimed or the gain from the sale of the home.

Note: The tax on house depreciation is only due for depreciation claimed—or entitled to be claimed—after May 6, 1997.

The Tax on the Profit on the Sale of Your Home

Normally, when you sell something for a profit, you will owe a tax on this profit. So, if you bought your home for $200,000 and sold it for $275,000, you earned a profit of $75,000 that would be subject to taxes.

However, there is a rule that may allow you to avoid paying taxes on the first $250,000 ($500,000 if you are married) of the profit on the sale of your home. To take advantage of this rule, you must meet two tests. First, you must be able to show that you owned your home for two of the last five years before you sold it. Second, you must show that you lived in your home (as your main home) for two of the last five years before you sold it.

Because most providers will not make a profit of $250,000 (or $500,000) on the sale of their homes, it may appear that they will not have to pay tax on the profit. Unfortunately, it's not that simple. The tax rules regarding the sale of your home are extremely complicated when you have used your home for your child care business. Essentially, you must treat your home sale as two sales: a sale of the personal portion of your home and a sale of the business portion of your home. Because of this, you may owe some taxes on the profit on the sale of your home in addition to tax on the depreciation you claimed (or were entitled to claim). The longer you have used your home for your business, the more likely you may owe some tax on the profit on the sale of the home.

In previous editions of this book, I used an example of how to fill out tax forms to report taxes on home depreciation (**Form 8949** and **Schedule D**). After speaking with several tax professionals this past year, I've come to understand how complicated the sale of a home is and realized that my past explanation was incomplete because I did not address the issue of possibly paying some taxes on the profit on the sale of the home. Therefore, I am no longer attempting to explain how to fill out the proper forms.

Get Professional Help

I strongly recommend that providers get help from a tax professional if they sell their home. I would not rely on any tax software (TurboTax, H&R Block, and so on) to correctly calculate your taxes. IRS **Publication 523 Selling Your Home** (www.irs.gov/pub523) does cover this topic, but you will find it extremely difficult to fill out the proper forms correctly even if you try to follow these directions. I wish the sale of home rules were simpler! I apologize for not alerting readers to the possibility of owing taxes on the profit on the sale of the home in earlier editions of this book.

Other Points to Consider

The longer you use your home for business after May 6, 1997, the more tax you'll have to pay on depreciation when you sell your home. For example, let's say that the basis of your home is $100,000, you use 39-year depreciation rules, and your Time-Space percentage is 35%. If you sell your home five years after May 6, 1997, you'll owe tax on $4,485. If you sell it ten years after May 6, 1997, you'll owe tax on $8,970. If you sell it fifteen years after May 6, 1997, you'll owe tax on $13,455. (This assumes that your gain on the sale is at least equal to these amounts.)

Home Improvements

If you've made home improvements while living in your home, you can reduce the profit on the sale of your home. You can increase the basis of the home by the cost of the improvement and then decrease the basis by the amount of depreciation you claimed (or were entitled to claim) on the improvement. The more home improvements you make on your home, the lower your gain will be when you sell your home.

Land Improvements

If you've been depreciating land improvements using the 150% declining balance method (see chapter 3), you may need to recapture some of that depreciation when you sell your home. The amount you will have to recapture and pay income tax on is the difference between the depreciation you claimed using the 150% declining balance method and the depreciation you would have claimed with the straight-line method. Report this amount on **Form 4797**, Part IV, and then transfer it to **Schedule C**, line 6.

Like-Kind Exchanges

One way to avoid paying the tax on the sale of a home is to conduct a like-kind exchange. If you expect to make a profit on the sale of your home over the limits of $250,000 or $500,000, you may want to consider a like-kind exchange. The Tax Code states that "no gain or loss shall be recognized if property held for productive use in trade or business . . . is exchanged solely for property of a like-kind to be held for productive use in trade or business." This means that you can exchange your old home for a new one and avoid most of the taxes you would otherwise owe, even if you don't meet the two-year test. (Doing a like-kind exchange does allow you to defer paying taxes on depreciation claimed after May 6, 1997, but eventually you will have to pay tax on this depreciation.) To take advantage of the like-kind exchange rules, you have to intend to continue providing child care in your new home.

The best way to do a like-kind exchange is to hire an intermediary to handle the transactions and ensure that all the proper rules are followed. You are allowed 180 days after closing on your old home, but before you've received the money from the sale, to conduct a like-kind exchange. Once you've accepted the money from the sale of your home, you can no longer do a like-kind exchange.

Conducting a like-kind exchange is far more complicated than described here. You should hire a qualified intermediary to handle this complicated transaction. I strongly urge you to talk to a tax professional before you sell your home and use a tax preparer, lawyer, or real estate professional to help you follow the requirements of the law.

Changes in Marital Status

Changes in your marital status can complicate the tax impact of selling your home. If you're planning to marry or divorce, you should consult a tax professional to find out how the home sale rules will apply in your situation.

In June 2013 the U.S. Supreme Court struck down the Defense of Marriage Act (DOMA) and ended federal discrimination against same-sex couples who are legally married under state law. This means a family child care provider who is legally married to a same-sex partner can take advantage of the ability to depreciate her home, even if the home is in her spouse's name. It also means that the same provider will be taxed on this depreciation when the home is sold.

For more information about the tax issues discussed in this chapter, refer to the related topics in the other chapters of this book and the Redleaf Press *Family Child Care Record-Keeping Guide.*

CHAPTER 13

Closing Your Child Care Business

From a tax point of view, it's almost as easy to close your child care business as it is to start it. You don't need to notify the IRS of your decision to quit. (Check your state revenue department to see if your state has any special requirements.) If you ended your business in 2020, however, there are some tax issues that you should review carefully, especially in regard to depreciation.

Depreciation Issues

General Depreciation Rule

In general, if you go out of business before you have fully depreciated your property, you stop claiming depreciation and forfeit the ability to claim the remainder of the depreciation. In addition, you don't have to report any of the depreciation you have already claimed as income. This includes any depreciation you claimed using the 50% or 100% bonus depreciation rules. There are two exceptions to this general depreciation rule: Section 179 depreciation and accelerated depreciation on a vehicle (see next page).

The Half-Year Convention

For items you've been depreciating under the Half-Year Convention rules (see chapter 3), you can claim only a half-year's worth of the normal depreciation in the year you end your business. The items covered by this convention include personal property, land improvements, and vehicles.

For example, you bought a washer in 2018 for $500 and used it in your business until you closed your business in 2020. Your Time-Space percentage in 2020 is 35%, and you've been using straight-line depreciation. Your depreciation deduction for the washer in 2020 would normally be $25 ($500 x 35% x 14.29% [Year 3 depreciation rate] = $25); however, if you went out of business last year, you can only claim half of this amount, or $12.50.

If you bought these items in 2020 and went out of business in 2019, you would deduct the business portion in 2020 without having to depreciate them.

The Mid-Month Convention

For items you've been depreciating under the Mid-Month Convention rules (see chapter 3), you can claim only a prorated part of the normal depreciation in the year you end your business, based on the month you quit. The items covered by this convention include your home and home improvements.

For example, you bought a new roof in 2019 for $6,000 and went out of business in July 2020. Your Time-Space percentage in 2020 is 30%. Your normal depreciation for all of 2020 would be $46.15 ($6,000 x 30% x 2.564%). You are considered to be in business for 6.5 months in 2020, because the month you go out of business counts for half of a month. Thus, multiply $46.15 by 6.5 months and divide by 12 months. The result, $25.00, is your depreciation deduction for 2020.

Section 179

If you used Section 179 rules (see chapter 3) on any personal property items while you were in business, check to see whether the recovery period has run out for each item. This period is five years for computers and vehicles, and seven years for furniture, appliances, TVs, VCRs, DVD players, and large play equipment. If the recovery period is still in effect, you'll have to pay additional taxes to recapture the unused depreciation (see chapter 11).

Recapturing Accelerated Depreciation on a Vehicle

If you use accelerated depreciation (the 200% declining balance method) to depreciate a vehicle you use more than 50% for business, and your business use of the vehicle falls below 50% during the five-year recovery period, you will have to recapture some of the depreciation you claimed and report it as income. Use the rules for recapturing depreciation described in chapter 11. You would also need to recapture some depreciation if you had used the 50% or 100% bonus depreciation rules on the vehicle. You do not have to recapture depreciation if you used the 50% or 100% bonus depreciation rules on any other property.

Going Out of Business Checklist

If you closed your business in 2020, here's a checklist of some other business reminders and tax issues that could affect your tax return:

- ❑ Make sure you've taken all the depreciation you're entitled to on your home and other property used in your business. If you haven't, use **Form 3115** to take these deductions in 2020 (see chapter 10). They can add up to a large amount, and if you went out of business in 2020, this will be your last chance to claim them.
- ❑ If you paid employees in 2020 (including your spouse and children), be sure to file **Form 941** or **Form 944** to report wages for Social Security and Medicare taxes for the quarter you quit. Check the box at the top of the form to indicate that you won't be filing any more of these forms. File **Form 940** at the end of the year, as usual. You must file **Form W-2** by the date the next **Form 941** is due and file **Form W-3** one month later (see chapter 8).
- ❑ If you weren't in business until December 31, adjust the number of hours on **Form 8829**, line 5. For example, if you ended your business on August 31, write in 5,856 hours (the number of hours from January 1 to August 31). Enter on **Form 8829** only expenses that you incurred during this time period. In this case, you would enter only 66% (5,832 hours ÷ 8,760 total hours in the year) of your mortgage interest, real estate taxes, and homeowners insurance, and you would enter your actual expenses for utilities, home repairs, and maintenance for these months.

- ❑ It's a good idea to send a letter to the parents of the children in your care officially informing them of your decision to end your business. Keep a copy of the letter for your files. Take photographs that show you have converted your play areas back to personal use.
- ❑ If you're planning to sell your home in the next few years, consult a tax professional about how to reduce your tax liability when selling your home.
- ❑ Since you'll file your final business forms this tax season, you won't need to file **Schedule C**, **Form 4562**, **Form 8829**, or **Schedule SE** for 2021.
- ❑ If you have any carryover expenses from **Form 8829** in your last year of business, you won't be able to claim them after your business ends.
- ❑ Notify your state regulatory department, local child care resource and referral agency, Food Program sponsor, and local family child care association that you are going out of business so they can update their records.
- ❑ If you sell any items you've used in your business *before* you go out of business, you may be entitled to a business deduction or (more rarely) need to report some additional business income. See chapter 11 for details.
- ❑ Contact your insurance agent to review your policies (homeowners, business liability, and car) to see if you are entitled to a refund.

The IRS does not consider you to have gone out of business if you simply move from one home to another and continue your child care business in your new home. Your business has continued, even if you're operating at a new location. You'll still file one **Schedule C**, **Form 4562**, and **Schedule SE**. You will need to file two **Form 8829**s, showing your Time-Space percentage and expenses for each home separately.

If you go out of business and later decide to start up again, just start claiming your income and expenses as if you were beginning your business for the first time. To claim depreciation for items that you used before, use the lower of the item's fair market value or its adjusted basis at the time you start using it again for your business (see chapter 3).

For more information about the tax issues discussed in this chapter, refer to the related topics in the other chapters of this book and the Redleaf Press *Family Child Care Record-Keeping Guide.*

CHAPTER 14

Dealing with an Audit

Although your chances of being audited are less than 1%, if you are audited, your best defense is to have good records for your business. You should keep documents such as receipts, bills, record books, and menus for at least three years after the date you file your tax return. Keep the records for items you are depreciating (such as your home, personal property, and business equipment) for the depreciation period plus three years. In other words, if you began depreciating your stove in 2015, you should keep the receipt for eight years (the depreciation period) plus three years, or until the year 2026.

You may wish to bring another person with you to the audit, such as your spouse, a friend, your tax preparer, a certified public accountant, an enrolled agent, an enrolled federal tax accountant, or an attorney. Sometimes it can help to have another person in the room, especially someone who is more objective or familiar with the audit process.

When auditing a family child care business, IRS auditors often target the following five areas of the tax return:

- unreported income
- Time-Space percentage
- food expenses
- shared business and personal expenses
- business mileage

Unreported Income

The first thing the auditor is likely to do is ask you to identify the source of all the deposits to your personal and business bank accounts. You should mark the source of every deposit on the deposit slip, your check register, or your computer software program, even if they are simply transfers from one account to another. Label each business deposit by the parent's name. If you can't account for a deposit, the IRS is likely to assume that it is business income and will tax it.

Time-Space Percentage

The auditor may challenge your Time-Space percentage. You need to have records showing the hours you worked and that the space you are claiming was used on a regular basis for your business. The higher your Time-Space percentage is, the more closely the IRS will examine your records. Don't let the auditor challenge your right to count the hours you spent cooking, cleaning, and planning activities for your business (see chapter 1).

Food Expenses

With the passage of the standard meal allowance rule (see chapter 4), the IRS may be less likely to challenge your food expenses in an audit. The only question is likely to be whether you can prove that you served the number of meals and snacks you are claiming. The meals reimbursed by the Food Program will appear on your monthly claim forms, but you must keep very careful daily records of all the meals and snacks you serve that aren't reimbursed by the Food Program. If you are claiming food expenses based on the actual cost of food, be sure to keep all your business and personal food receipts.

Shared Business and Personal Expenses

The auditor may try to claim that some of your business expenses are personal, especially items such as household supplies and repairs. To support your case, you can take pictures that show children using the item or get letters from parents.

Business Mileage

Auditors have sometimes held that a provider can't deduct any miles for a trip in which some personal items were purchased; however, this is not what the law says. It says that you may deduct all the miles for a trip if it is *primarily* for business purposes.

Avoiding an Audit

No one wants to be audited by the IRS. It's a scary prospect that most of us would do just about anything to avoid. Instead of worrying about whether you'll be audited, focus on keeping the proper records for your business. If your records are complete and organized, you have nothing to fear from an audit.

For example, I often hear people say, "I don't claim all my allowable expenses because I'm afraid I'll be audited" or "I used a lower Time-Space percentage than I really had because I didn't want to trigger an audit." It isn't a good idea to think like this. You have little control over *if* you'll be audited; your real concern should be "If I'm audited, do I have the records to back up my deductions?" If the answer is yes, you have little to worry about.

People also ask, "If I claim many deductions that I haven't claimed before, my expenses will be a lot higher than usual. Will the IRS notice and audit my return?" Again, don't worry about this. Just claim the deductions you're entitled to and keep the records to back them up.

In an audit you can submit records and receipts for expenses that you didn't originally claim on your tax return to offset any deductions the auditor disallows (or even to give you a refund). For example, you could claim a higher Time-Space percentage or a larger business food expense. (If you discover additional deductions after the audit is completed, ask the IRS to reopen your case. If the IRS won't do this, you can file an amended return up to three years after you filed the original return, even after being audited.)

Errors by Your Tax Preparer

You're always responsible for paying the proper taxes, even if your tax preparer has made a mistake on your return. That's why it's important to make sure you understand what your tax preparer has done. If the mistake was the tax preparer's error, a good tax preparer will pay some, if not all, of the interest that is because of the mistake. (Tax preparers aren't required to pay this, however.) If you knew that what your tax preparer did was wrong, you should pay the penalty. If you didn't know that it was wrong, ask your tax preparer to pay the penalty. (It's best to find out your tax preparer's policy on this issue when you hire the preparer.)

You Have the Right to Appeal

Remember that some auditors aren't familiar with the unique way the tax rules apply to family child care businesses, so an auditor may not be aware of all the deductions you're entitled to. When this happens, some providers have told the auditor, "Tom Copeland said I could do it in his *Tax Workbook*!" Although I've tried to interpret the tax laws and show you how to apply them in a reasonable manner, in any specific situation they may be subject to various interpretations. If there's a dispute, ask your auditor to justify his or her interpretation with a written reference. (If you need more help, refer to the resources listed below.)

If you don't agree with your auditor's findings, you have a right to ask that the auditor's supervisor review the problem. If you aren't satisfied with the supervisor's decision, you have the right to appeal. Do your best to settle the matter with the auditor and the supervisor first.

Appealing the decision is a relatively simple matter. Tell your auditor that you want to appeal. Better yet, put your request for an appeal in writing. When you appeal, your auditor will write up the facts of your case and pass them on to an appeals officer; however, your auditor (or your auditor's supervisor) may offer to settle your case before sending it to appeal.

Appearing before the appeals officer is an informal affair. Bring your tax preparer (or even better, have your tax preparer appear without you). If you can't resolve the case here, you can appeal to the U.S. Tax Court. There is a $60 filing fee to appeal to the Tax Court (there's no fee for the appeals up to this point). You can choose to go before the "S-Court," which handles disputes that involve only a few thousand dollars. Although you don't need a lawyer to appear before the Tax Court, it's common to hire professional assistance at this level. (For more information on this process, refer to **Publication 556**.)

Get the Help You Need

If you're audited, you don't have to do it alone; get the help you need. We recommend that you hire a tax professional to assist you. To be qualified to represent you before the IRS, this person must be an enrolled agent, a certified public accountant, or an attorney.

- Check my website, www.tomcopelandblog.com, for a wealth of resource materials and a special section on audits. This site has copies of all the IRS rulings and Tax Court cases that involve family child care businesses.

- Get the text of the IRS **Child Care Provider Audit Technique Guide** at my website (www.tomcopelandblog.com) or the IRS website (www.irs.gov/pub/irs-utl/child_care_provider.pdf). Although this guide doesn't have the force of law, it can help you understand what your auditor may be looking for. You can challenge its interpretations, but if you do you should be prepared to cite some other authority for your position. (The statements in the **Child Care Provider Audit Technique Guide** may need to be modified based on new laws, Tax Court cases, IRS Revenue Rulings, and IRS Revenue Procedures that have been released since its publication.)

IRS Taxpayer Advocate Service

If you have one of the following problems or an ongoing issue with the IRS that hasn't been resolved through normal processes, you can call the IRS Taxpayer Advocate Service (877-777-4778, 24 hours a day) for help:

- You're suffering, or are about to suffer, a significant hardship.
- You're facing an immediate threat of adverse action.
- You're about to incur significant costs (including fees for professional representation).
- You haven't received a response or resolution by the date promised.
- You've experienced a delay of more than 30 days to resolve an issue.

For more information about the tax issues discussed in this chapter, refer to the related topics in the other chapters of this book and the Redleaf Press *Family Child Care Record-Keeping Guide.*

PART IV

Appendixes

Sample Tax Return

Sandy James began her child care business on January 1, 2017. She has one child of her own, Vanessa, age three, and she cares for six children, ages two through eight. Sandy's husband, Bill, earned $41,000 in 2020 as a construction worker. His **Form W-2** shows that he had $9,000 withheld in federal taxes and $1,200 withheld in state taxes. He paid $4,104 in medical bills in 2020. Sandy's Time-Space percentage is 39%. In 2020 Sandy and Bill received a federal stimulus check for $2,900. Of this, $1,200 was for Bill, $1,200 was for Sandy, and $500 was for their child. None of this is taxable income and will not appear on their tax return. Let's see how Sandy should fill out her tax forms.

Sandy's first task will be to organize her records by income and expense categories, using the worksheets in the Tax Organizer. Next, she'll place the worksheets next to the proper tax form. A step-by-step process of how she'll fill out her tax forms follows. You can also refer to the copies of her completed forms at the end of this appendix.

In this example, the numbers on the tax forms will be rounded to the nearest dollar, as you should also do on your tax forms. (The deductions in this sample tax return aren't intended to be used as a guideline. Your deductions may be significantly more or less than shown here.)

Form 8829 Expenses for Business Use of Your Home

Lines 1–7: Sandy has a Time-Space percentage of 39%.

Line 8: Sandy carries forward her tentative profit from **Schedule C**, line 29, to this line on **Form 8829**.

Lines 16–17: Because Sandy is claiming the standard deduction, she will enter her mortgage interest and real estate taxes on lines 16 and 17. If she chose to itemize her personal expenses on **Schedule A**, she would enter these expenses on lines 10 and 11. Sandy enters her deductible mortgage interest ($5,000) and real estate taxes ($3,000) in column (b) because they also have a personal component.

Lines 18–25: Homeowners insurance ($1,500) and utilities (gas, electricity, water, sewer, cable TV, and trash hauling = $2,000) go in column (b) because they have a personal component. A $15 replacement of a window broken by a child in her care is a 100% business expense and goes on line 20, column (a). A screen door that cost $85 to repair was damaged by normal wear and tear and goes on line 20, column (b). Sandy multiplies the total of the items in column (b) ($11,585) by her Time-Space percentage (39%) from line 7. She adds to the result ($4,518) the $15 from column (a) and enters the total ($4,533) on line 26.

Lines 30, and 37–42: Sandy purchased her home in 2009 for $150,000 ($15,000 of this was the value of the land). In 2011 she remodeled her kitchen for $8,000. In 2012 she hired a contractor to paint her living room and bedrooms for $750. Here's how she'll calculate her depreciation for her home:

$150,000	Purchase price of home
+ $8,000	Kitchen improvement done before business began
$158,000	
– $15,000	Land
$143,000	Basis of home
x 39%	Time-Space percentage
$55,770	Business basis of home
x 2.564%	(Because Sandy began depreciating her home after May 13, 1993, she uses 39-year depreciation rules. This is the percentage she uses after the first year.)
$1,430	Home depreciation

Since the painting was a repair, it isn't added to this calculation. Sandy can't claim a business expense for it because it was done before she began her business.

Enter the $1,430 on **Form 8829**, line 42.

Sandy skips to Part III to enter her home depreciation. Sandy enters "2.564%" on line 41 because that's the percentage for a full year of depreciation for a home that was first used for business in 2017. She enters "$1,430" on line 42 and line 30.

Line 36: When she finishes this form, Sandy will transfer the amount on line 36 ($5,963) to **Schedule C**, line 30. Then she'll be able to calculate her net profit on **Schedule C**.

Sandy could choose to use the IRS Simplified Method or claim her expenses from **Form 8829** on her **Schedule C**. If she used the Simplified Method, her maximum deduction for house expenses would be $585 (300 square feet x $5 x 39%). Since her actual house expenses ($5,963 – **Form 8829**, line 36) are more than this, she will use her **Form 8829** expenses.

Form 4562 Depreciation and Amortization

Sandy added a new deck in March 2020 that cost $9,000. This is a home improvement that would normally be depreciated over 39 years. However, because Sandy cares for six children and one of her own, she determines she uses her deck more than half the time in her business. She tracked the actual use of her deck for two months and calculated that she used it 80% of the time for her business. She is therefore eligible for the Section 179 exception that allows her to deduct the business portion on the deck in one year (See pages 74–75).

$9,000 deck x 80% business use = $7,200.

Enter this on **Form 4562**, line 6. The amount to enter on line 11 is Sandy's profit from **Schedule C** ($38,913 minus this Section 179 deduction = $31,713).

Other Personal Property

In 2017 Sandy began depreciating some appliances and furniture worth $3,300. She owned these items before she went into business and began using them in her business in 2017. Here's how she'll calculate her depreciation for these expenses:

Furniture/appliances: $3,300 purchased before 2017

$3,300 x 39% (T/S%) = $1,254

$1,254 x 12.49% (7-year 200% DB method, year 4) = $157

Sandy will enter "$157" on line 17.

LAND IMPROVEMENTS

In June 2020 Sandy bought a $3,600 fence for her backyard. She will use the 100% bonus depreciation rule.

$3,600 x 39% (T/S%) = $1,404
Enter on **Form 4562**, line 14.

Part V: Sandy will record her vehicle mileage in Part V, Section B.

Schedule C Profit or Loss from Business

PART I INCOME

Sandy earned $68,080 in parent fees last year. Of this amount, she received $80 in January 2020 for care she provided in December 2020. Another $140 is a bounced check that a parent never honored. Sandy also received $2,300 in reimbursements from the Food Program. Here's how she'll report this income:

Line 1b:

$68,080	
– $80	Received
$68,000	
– $140	Bounced check
$67,860	

Line 6: $2,300

PART II EXPENSES

Line 8: **Advertising**: Sandy paid $150 for business cards, newspaper ads, and so on.

Line 9: **Automobile expenses**: The value of Sandy's vehicle on January 1, 2017 (when she first used it for business), was $4,000. She drove the vehicle 14,241 miles in 2020, and 3,480 of those miles were for business trips. Sandy's actual vehicle expenses were

Gas, oil, repairs	$600
Vehicle insurance	$800
Extra vehicle insurance for her business	$200
Vehicle loan interest	$237
Parking for business trips	$15
Vehicle property tax	$150

Here's how Sandy will calculate her deduction for vehicle expenses—first, to decide whether to use the standard mileage rate method or the actual vehicle expenses method, she calculates her vehicle expenses using both methods:

STANDARD MILEAGE RATE METHOD		
3,480 business miles (Jan–Dec) x $0.575	=	$2,001.40
Vehicle loan interest:		
$237 x 24.9% (3,546 ÷ 14,241)	=	$59
Parking		$15
Vehicle property tax:		
$150 x 24.9%	=	$37
Total		$2,112.40

ACTUAL VEHICLE EXPENSES METHOD

3,546 miles ÷ 14,241 miles = 24.9% business use

Gas, oil, repairs	$600	
Vehicle insurance	$800	
Vehicle loan interest	$237	
Vehicle property tax	$150	
Total	$1,787 x 24.99% =	$447
Extra vehicle insurance		$200
Parking		$15
Total		$662

Vehicle depreciation (5-year straight-line, year 3):

	$4,000	
	x 24.99%	
	$1,000 x 20.0% =	$200
Total		$862

Sandy will use the standard mileage rate method because it gives her a larger deduction ($2,112 vs. $862). She enters "$2,112" on **Schedule C**, line 9. Sandy will not fill out Part IV because she must fill out **Form 4562**.

If Sandy were to use the actual vehicle expenses method, she would report her $59 loan interest on line 16b and her $37 property tax on line 23.

Line 13: **Depreciation**: Sandy enters "$8,761" from **Form 4562**, line 22.

Line 15: **Insurance**: Sandy paid $427 for business liability insurance premiums. This is 100% deductible.

Line 16b: **Interest**: Sandy paid $100 in interest on her credit card for her dining room furniture.

$100 x 39% Time-Space percentage = $39

Line 17: **Legal and professional services**: Last year Sandy paid a tax preparer to file her tax return. The tax preparer charged her $500 to file her business tax forms and $250 to file her personal tax forms. Sandy will enter "$500" here.

Line 18: **Office expenses**: Sandy purchased the following items last year:

Notebooks, calculator, copies, postage	$84.00
Subscriptions to child care magazines	$40.00
Child care books/calendar (*Tax Workbook, Record-Keeping Guide,* and *KidKare Software*)	$133.90
Membership fee in local child care association	$15.00
Training workshops	$37.00
Long-distance calls to parents of children in her care	$25.39
Total:	$335.29

Since these expenses were used 100% for her business, she will enter "$335" on line 18. Sandy also spent $300 on her monthly phone bill, but none of this is deductible.

Line 20b: **Rent of business property**: Sandy purchased Netflix and showed movies for the children in her care. $95.88 x 39% Time-Space percentage = $37.39. Enter "$38" on line 20b.

Line 21: **Repairs and maintenance**: Sandy spent $130 on a service contract for her refrigerator and microwave oven.

$130 x 39% Time-Space percentage = $51.00

Line 22: **Supplies**: Sandy purchased the following supplies last year:

Kitchen supplies (soap, scrubbers, napkins)	$50
Can opener	$20
Children's games and toys	$440
Total:	$510

Since these items were also used for personal purposes, she can claim only her Time-Space percentage:

$510 x 39% = $211

This year Sandy also purchased the following:

Arts and crafts supplies	$240
Household supplies (paper towels, toilet paper, etc.)	$150
Total:	$390

Sandy calculated that these items were used 50% in her business ($390 x .50 = $195). This gives her a new total of $406 ($211 + $195), which she enters on line 22.

Line 24: **Travel**: Sandy traveled to a three-day family child care conference in Orlando in July and incurred these expenses:

Plane ticket	$675	
Hotel	$520	
Taxis	$40	
Total:	$1,235	Enter on line 24a.

IRS **Publication 1542 Per Diem Rates** lists the amount of meal expenses you can claim for a business trip without having to keep food receipts. The general meal rate is $55 per day, but some cities have a higher rate. Orlando, Florida, has a higher rate of $66 per day, so Sandy can claim $198 ($66 x 3 days) with this method. But she can deduct only 50% of meal expenses, so she enters "$99" on line 24b.

Line 27: **Other Expenses**: In April 2020 Sandy purchased a $2,000 swing set used by her business and her own children. Under the $2,500 rule she can deduct the business portion of $780 ($2,000 x 39% = $780) here. No need to depreciate it. To elect this rule she must attach a statement to her tax return (see page 237).

In February 2020 Sandy purchased a computer for $3,000 used 100% in her business. Because of the $2,500 rule, Sandy can deduct her computer in full and doesn't have to depreciate it.

On the blank lines of Part V, Sandy has entered the following line items:

Food for children in her care	$5,802
Swing set	$780
Computer	$3,000
Fire extinguisher (required by licensing)	$45
Security locks	$102
Cleaning supplies	$422
Activity expenses	$380
Toys	$600
Total:	$11,131

Sandy will enter "$11,131" on line 27a.

Schedule SE Self-Employment Tax

This form is easy to complete. Sandy transfers her net profit from **Schedule C**, line 31, onto line 2 of this form and follows the directions to calculate her self-employment tax of $5,498. Then she transfers this total to **Form 1040 Schedule 2**, line 4.

Schedule A Itemized Deductions

Because the 2020 standard deduction for married couples filing jointly is $24,800 (up from $24,400 in 2019), Sandy and Bill will not itemize their taxes on **Schedule A** and will use the new, higher standard deduction.

Schedule EIC Earned Income Credit

Sandy and Bill earned more than the limit of $47,646 in adjusted gross income (**Form 1040**, line 17a), so they aren't eligible for this credit.

Form 1040 U.S. Individual Income Tax Return

Sandy and Bill can now transfer the amounts from their other tax forms to **Form 1040**. She will also fill out **Schedule 1** and **Schedule 2**.

Form 8995 Qualified Income Deduction Simplified Computation

All providers who show a profit on **Schedule C** should fill out this form.

Line 1: Enter profit from **Schedule C**, line 31 = $38,913

Line 5: Multiply line 4 by 20%: $38,913 x 20% = $7,783

Line 11: The formula for this line is: Total income ($77,164 from **Form 1040**, line 11) minus the standard deduction ($24,800 from **Form 1040**, line 12) = $52,364

Line 13: Enter the same amount on line 13.

Line 14: Multiply line 13 by 20% = $10,473

Line 15: Enter the lesser of line 10 or line 14: $7,783

Form **8829**

Department of the Treasury
Internal Revenue Service (99)

Expenses for Business Use of Your Home

▶ File only with Schedule C (Form 1040). Use a separate Form 8829 for each home you used for business during the year.

▶ Go to *www.irs.gov/Form8829* for instructions and the latest information.

OMB No. 1545-0074

2020

Attachment Sequence No. **176**

Name(s) of proprietor(s)	Your social security number
SANDY JAMES	123-45-6789

Part I Part of Your Home Used for Business

1	Area used regularly and exclusively for business, regularly for daycare, or for storage of inventory or product samples (see instructions)		1	2,200
2	Total area of home		2	2,200
3	Divide line 1 by line 2. Enter the result as a percentage		3	100 %
	For daycare facilities not used exclusively for business, go to line 4. All others, go to line 7.			
4	Multiply days used for daycare during year by hours used per day	4 — 3,399 hr.		
5	If you started or stopped using your home for daycare during the year, see instructions; otherwise, enter 8,784	5 — 8,760 hr.		
6	Divide line 4 by line 5. Enter the result as a decimal amount	6 — .39		
7	Business percentage. For daycare facilities not used exclusively for business, multiply line 6 by line 3 (enter the result as a percentage). All others, enter the amount from line 3 ▶		7	39 %

Part II Figure Your Allowable Deduction

8	Enter the amount from Schedule C, line 29, **plus** any gain derived from the business use of your home, **minus** any loss from the trade or business not derived from the business use of your home. See instructions.				8	$38,913
	See instructions for columns (a) and (b) before completing lines 9–22.		**(a)** Direct expenses	**(b)** Indirect expenses		
9	Casualty losses (see instructions)	9				
10	Deductible mortgage interest (see instructions)	10				
11	Real estate taxes (see instructions)	11				
12	Add lines 9, 10, and 11	12				
13	Multiply line 12, column (b), by line 7		13			
14	Add line 12, column (a), and line 13				14	
15	Subtract line 14 from line 8. If zero or less, enter -0-				15	$38,913
16	Excess mortgage interest (see instructions)	16		$5,000		
17	Excess real estate taxes (see instructions)	17		$3,000		
18	Insurance	18		$1,500		
19	Rent	19				
20	Repairs and maintenance	20	$15	$85		
21	Utilities	21		$2,000		
22	Other expenses (see instructions)	22				
23	Add lines 16 through 22	23	$15	$11,585		
24	Multiply line 23, column (b), by line 7		24	$4,518		
25	Carryover of prior year operating expenses (see instructions)		25	$0		
26	Add line 23, column (a), line 24, and line 25				26	$4,533
27	Allowable operating expenses. Enter the **smaller** of line 15 or line 26				27	$4,533
28	Limit on excess casualty losses and depreciation. Subtract line 27 from line 15				28	$34,380
29	Excess casualty losses (see instructions)		29			
30	Depreciation of your home from line 42 below		30	$1,430		
31	Carryover of prior year excess casualty losses and depreciation (see instructions)		31			
32	Add lines 29 through 31				32	$1,430
33	Allowable excess casualty losses and depreciation. Enter the **smaller** of line 28 or line 32				33	$1,430
34	Add lines 14, 27, and 33				34	$5,963
35	Casualty loss portion, if any, from lines 14 and 33. Carry amount to **Form 4684.** See instructions				35	
36	**Allowable expenses for business use of your home.** Subtract line 35 from line 34. Enter here and on Schedule C, line 30. If your home was used for more than one business, see instructions. ▶				36	$5,963

Part III Depreciation of Your Home

37	Enter the **smaller** of your home's adjusted basis or its fair market value. See instructions	37	$158,000
38	Value of land included on line 37	38	$15,000
39	Basis of building. Subtract line 38 from line 37	39	$143,000
40	Business basis of building. Multiply line 39 by line 7	40	$55,770
41	Depreciation percentage (see instructions)	41	2.564 %
42	Depreciation allowable (see instructions). Multiply line 40 by line 41. Enter here and on line 30 above	42	$1,430

Part IV Carryover of Unallowed Expenses to 2021

43	Operating expenses. Subtract line 27 from line 26. If less than zero, enter -0-	43	
44	Excess casualty losses and depreciation. Subtract line 33 from line 32. If less than zero, enter -0-	44	

For Paperwork Reduction Act Notice, see your tax return instructions. Cat. No. 13232M Form **8829** (2020)

Form **4562**

Department of the Treasury
Internal Revenue Service (99)

Depreciation and Amortization

(Including Information on Listed Property)

▶ Attach to your tax return.

▶ Go to *www.irs.gov/Form4562* for instructions and the latest information.

OMB No. 1545-0172

2020

Attachment Sequence No. **179**

Name(s) shown on return	Business or activity to which this form relates	Identifying number
SANDY JAMES	FAMILY CHILD CARE	123-45-6789

Part I Election To Expense Certain Property Under Section 179

Note: If you have any listed property, complete Part V before you complete Part I.

1	Maximum amount (see instructions)	1	$1,000,000
2	Total cost of section 179 property placed in service (see instructions)	2	
3	Threshold cost of section 179 property before reduction in limitation (see instructions)	3	$500,000
4	Reduction in limitation. Subtract line 3 from line 2. If zero or less, enter -0-	4	0
5	Dollar limitation for tax year. Subtract line 4 from line 1. If zero or less, enter -0-. If married filing separately, see instructions	5	$500,000

6	(a) Description of property	(b) Cost (business use only)	(c) Elected cost
	Deck	$7,200	$7,200

7	Listed property. Enter the amount from line 29	7	
8	Total elected cost of section 179 property. Add amounts in column (c), lines 6 and 7	8	$7,200
9	Tentative deduction. Enter the **smaller** of line 5 or line 8	9	$7,200
10	Carryover of disallowed deduction from line 13 of your 2019 Form 4562	10	
11	Business income limitation. Enter the smaller of business income (not less than zero) or line 5. See instructions	11	$31,713
12	Section 179 expense deduction. Add lines 9 and 10, but don't enter more than line 11	12	$7,200
13	Carryover of disallowed deduction to 2021. Add lines 9 and 10, less line 12 ▶	13	

Note: Don't use Part II or Part III below for listed property. Instead, use Part V.

Part II Special Depreciation Allowance and Other Depreciation (Don't include listed property. See instructions.**)**

14	Special depreciation allowance for qualified property (other than listed property) placed in service during the tax year. See instructions	14	$1,404
15	Property subject to section 168(f)(1) election	15	
16	Other depreciation (including ACRS)	16	

Part III MACRS Depreciation (Don't include listed property. See instructions.**)**

Section A

17	MACRS deductions for assets placed in service in tax years beginning before 2020	17	$157
18	If you are electing to group any assets placed in service during the tax year into one or more general asset accounts, check here ▶ ☐		

Section B—Assets Placed in Service During 2020 Tax Year Using the General Depreciation System

(a) Classification of property	(b) Month and year placed in service	(c) Basis for depreciation (business/investment use only—see instructions)	(d) Recovery period	(e) Convention	(f) Method	(g) Depreciation deduction
19a 3-year property						
b 5-year property						
c 7-year property						
d 10-year property						
e 15-year property						
f 20-year property						
g 25-year property			25 yrs.		S/L	
h Residential rental			27.5 yrs.	MM	S/L	
property			27.5 yrs.	MM	S/L	
i Nonresidential real			39 yrs.	MM	S/L	
property				MM	S/L	

Section C—Assets Placed in Service During 2020 Tax Year Using the Alternative Depreciation System

(a) Classification of property	(b) Month and year placed in service	(c) Basis for depreciation	(d) Recovery period	(e) Convention	(f) Method	(g) Depreciation deduction
20a Class life					S/L	
b 12-year			12 yrs.		S/L	
c 30-year			30 yrs.	MM	S/L	
d 40-year			40 yrs.	MM	S/L	

Part IV Summary (See instructions.)

21	Listed property. Enter amount from line 28	21	
22	**Total.** Add amounts from line 12, lines 14 through 17, lines 19 and 20 in column (g), and line 21. Enter here and on the appropriate lines of your return. Partnerships and S corporations—see instructions	22	$8,761
23	For assets shown above and placed in service during the current year, enter the portion of the basis attributable to section 263A costs	23	

For Paperwork Reduction Act Notice, see separate instructions. Cat. No. 12906N Form **4562** (2020)

Form 4562 (2020) Page **2**

Part V **Listed Property** (Include automobiles, certain other vehicles, certain aircraft, and property used for entertainment, recreation, or amusement.)

Note: For any vehicle for which you are using the standard mileage rate or deducting lease expense, complete **only** 24a, 24b, columns (a) through (c) of Section A, all of Section B, and Section C if applicable.

Section A—Depreciation and Other Information (Caution: See the instructions for limits for passenger automobiles.**)**

24a Do you have evidence to support the business/investment use claimed? ☐ **Yes** ☐ **No** **24b** If "Yes," is the evidence written? ☐ **Yes** ☐ **No**

(a) Type of property (list vehicles first)	(b) Date placed in service	(c) Business/investment use percentage	(d) Cost or other basis	(e) Basis for depreciation (business/investment use only)	(f) Recovery period	(g) Method/Convention	(h) Depreciation deduction	(i) Elected section 179 cost
25 Special depreciation allowance for qualified listed property placed in service during the tax year and used more than 50% in a qualified business use. See instructions .						25		
26 Property used more than 50% in a qualified business use:								
		%						
		%						
		%						
27 Property used 50% or less in a qualified business use:								
		%				S/L –		
		%				S/L –		
		%				S/L –		
28 Add amounts in column (h), lines 25 through 27. Enter here and on line 21, page 1 .						28		
29 Add amounts in column (i), line 26. Enter here and on line 7, page 1							29	

Section B—Information on Use of Vehicles

Complete this section for vehicles used by a sole proprietor, partner, or other "more than 5% owner," or related person. If you provided vehicles to your employees, first answer the questions in Section C to see if you meet an exception to completing this section for those vehicles.

	(a) Vehicle 1		(b) Vehicle 2		(c) Vehicle 3		(d) Vehicle 4		(e) Vehicle 5		(f) Vehicle 6	
30 Total business/investment miles driven during the year (**don't** include commuting miles) .												
31 Total commuting miles driven during the year												
32 Total other personal (noncommuting) miles driven												
33 Total miles driven during the year. Add lines 30 through 32												
	Yes	**No**	**Yes**	**No**	**Yes**	**No**	**Yes**	**No**	**Yes**	**No**	**Yes**	**No**
34 Was the vehicle available for personal use during off-duty hours?												
35 Was the vehicle used primarily by a more than 5% owner or related person? . .												
36 Is another vehicle available for personal use?												

Section C—Questions for Employers Who Provide Vehicles for Use by Their Employees

Answer these questions to determine if you meet an exception to completing Section B for vehicles used by employees who **aren't** more than 5% owners or related persons. See instructions.

	Yes	**No**
37 Do you maintain a written policy statement that prohibits all personal use of vehicles, including commuting, by your employees?		
38 Do you maintain a written policy statement that prohibits personal use of vehicles, except commuting, by your employees? See the instructions for vehicles used by corporate officers, directors, or 1% or more owners . .		
39 Do you treat all use of vehicles by employees as personal use?		
40 Do you provide more than five vehicles to your employees, obtain information from your employees about the use of the vehicles, and retain the information received?		
41 Do you meet the requirements concerning qualified automobile demonstration use? See instructions.		
Note: If your answer to 37, 38, 39, 40, or 41 is "Yes," don't complete Section B for the covered vehicles.		

Part VI **Amortization**

(a) Description of costs	(b) Date amortization begins	(c) Amortizable amount	(d) Code section	(e) Amortization period or percentage	(f) Amortization for this year
42 Amortization of costs that begins during your 2020 tax year (see instructions):					
43 Amortization of costs that began before your 2020 tax year				43	
44 **Total.** Add amounts in column (f). See the instructions for where to report				44	

Form **4562** (2020)

SCHEDULE C (Form 1040)

Department of the Treasury Internal Revenue Service (99)

Profit or Loss From Business

(Sole Proprietorship)

▶ Go to *www.irs.gov/ScheduleC* for instructions and the latest information.

▶ Attach to Form 1040, 1040-SR, 1040-NR, or 1041; partnerships generally must file Form 1065.

OMB No. 1545-0074

2020

Attachment Sequence No. **09**

Name of proprietor	Social security number (SSN)
SANDY JAMES	123-45-6789
A Principal business or profession, including product or service (see instructions)	**B** Enter code from instructions
FAMILY CHILD CARE	▶ 6 2 4 4 1 0
C Business name. If no separate business name, leave blank.	**D** Employer ID number (EIN) (see instr.)

E Business address (including suite or room no.) ▶ 687 HOOVER ROAD

City, town or post office, state, and ZIP code HUDSON, OH 42383

F Accounting method: (1) ☑ Cash (2) ☐ Accrual (3) ☐ Other (specify) ▶

G Did you "materially participate" in the operation of this business during 2020? If "No," see instructions for limit on losses . ☑ Yes ☐ No

H If you started or acquired this business during 2020, check here . . . ▶ ☐

I Did you make any payments in 2020 that would require you to file Form(s) 1099? See instructions . . . ☐ Yes ☑ No

J If "Yes," did you or will you file required Form(s) 1099? . . . ☐ Yes ☐ No

Part I Income

1	Gross receipts or sales. See instructions for line 1 and check the box if this income was reported to you on Form W-2 and the "Statutory employee" box on that form was checked . . . ▶ ☐	1	$67,860
2	Returns and allowances . . .	2	$67,860
3	Subtract line 2 from line 1 . . .	3	
4	Cost of goods sold (from line 42) . . .	4	$67,860
5	**Gross profit.** Subtract line 4 from line 3 . . .	5	
6	Other income, including federal and state gasoline or fuel tax credit or refund (see instructions) . . .	6	$2,300
7	**Gross income.** Add lines 5 and 6 . . . ▶	7	$70,160

Part II Expenses. Enter expenses for business use of your home **only** on line 30.

8	Advertising . . .	8	$150	18	Office expense (see instructions)	18	$335
9	Car and truck expenses (see instructions) . . .	9	$2,129	19	Pension and profit-sharing plans .	19	
				20	Rent or lease (see instructions):		
10	Commissions and fees .	10		a	Vehicles, machinery, and equipment	20a	
11	Contract labor (see instructions)	11		b	Other business property . . .	20b	$38
12	Depletion . . .	12		21	Repairs and maintenance . . .	21	$51
13	Depreciation and section 179 expense deduction (not included in Part III) (see instructions) . . .	13	$8,761	22	Supplies (not included in Part III) .	22	$406
				23	Taxes and licenses . . .	23	
				24	Travel and meals:		
14	Employee benefit programs (other than on line 19) . .	14		a	Travel . . .	24a	$1,235
				b	Deductible meals (see instructions) . . .	24b	$99
15	Insurance (other than health)	15	$410				
16	Interest (see instructions):			25	Utilities . . .	25	
a	Mortgage (paid to banks, etc.)	16a		26	Wages (less employment credits) .	26	
b	Other . . .	16b	$39	27a	Other expenses (from line 48) . .	27a	$11,131
17	Legal and professional services	17	$500	b	**Reserved for future use** . . .	27b	

28	**Total expenses** before expenses for business use of home. Add lines 8 through 27a . . . ▶	28	$25,284
29	Tentative profit or (loss). Subtract line 28 from line 7 . . .	29	$44,876
30	Expenses for business use of your home. Do not report these expenses elsewhere. Attach Form 8829 unless using the simplified method. See instructions. **Simplified method filers only:** Enter the total square footage of (a) your home: ______ and (b) the part of your home used for business: ______ . Use the Simplified Method Worksheet in the instructions to figure the amount to enter on line 30 . . .	30	$5,963
31	**Net profit or (loss).** Subtract line 30 from line 29. • If a profit, enter on both **Schedule 1 (Form 1040), line 3,** and on **Schedule SE, line 2.** (If you checked the box on line 1, see instructions). Estates and trusts, enter on **Form 1041, line 3.** • If a loss, you **must** go to line 32.	31	$38,913

32 If you have a loss, check the box that describes your investment in this activity. See instructions.

- If you checked 32a, enter the loss on both **Schedule 1 (Form 1040), line 3**, and on **Schedule SE, line 2.** (If you checked the box on line 1, see the line 31 instructions). Estates and trusts, enter on **Form 1041, line 3.**
- If you checked 32b, you **must** attach **Form 6198.** Your loss may be limited.

32a ☐ All investment is at risk.
32b ☐ Some investment is not at risk.

For Paperwork Reduction Act Notice, see the separate instructions. Cat. No. 11334P **Schedule C (Form 1040) 2020**

Schedule C (Form 1040) 2020 Page **2**

Part III **Cost of Goods Sold** (see instructions)

33 Method(s) used to value closing inventory: **a** ☐ Cost **b** ☐ Lower of cost or market **c** ☐ Other (attach explanation)

34 Was there any change in determining quantities, costs, or valuations between opening and closing inventory? If "Yes," attach explanation . . . ☐ **Yes** ☐ **No**

35	Inventory at beginning of year. If different from last year's closing inventory, attach explanation	**35**	
36	Purchases less cost of items withdrawn for personal use	**36**	
37	Cost of labor. Do not include any amounts paid to yourself	**37**	
38	Materials and supplies	**38**	
39	Other costs	**39**	
40	Add lines 35 through 39	**40**	
41	Inventory at end of year	**41**	
42	**Cost of goods sold.** Subtract line 41 from line 40. Enter the result here and on line 4	**42**	

Part IV **Information on Your Vehicle.** Complete this part **only** if you are claiming car or truck expenses on line 9 and are not required to file Form 4562 for this business. See the instructions for line 13 to find out if you must file Form 4562.

43 When did you place your vehicle in service for business purposes? (month/day/year) ▶ / /

44 Of the total number of miles you drove your vehicle during 2020, enter the number of miles you used your vehicle for:

a Business ______ **b** Commuting (see instructions) ______ **c** Other ______

45 Was your vehicle available for personal use during off-duty hours? . . . ☐ **Yes** ☐ **No**

46 Do you (or your spouse) have another vehicle available for personal use?. . . ☐ **Yes** ☐ **No**

47a Do you have evidence to support your deduction? . . . ☐ **Yes** ☐ **No**

b If "Yes," is the evidence written? . . . ☐ **Yes** ☐ **No**

Part V **Other Expenses.** List below business expenses not included on lines 8–26 or line 30.

SWING SET		$780
COMPUTER		$3,000
TIER II PROVIDER FOOD		$5,802
HOUSEHOLD ITEMS		$147
CLEANING SUPPLIES		$422
ACTIVITY SUPPLIES		$380
TOYS		$600
		$11,131
48 **Total other expenses.** Enter here and on line 27a	**48**	

Schedule C (Form 1040) 2020

SCHEDULE SE (Form 1040)

Department of the Treasury
Internal Revenue Service (99)

Self-Employment Tax

▶ Go to *www.irs.gov/ScheduleSE* for instructions and the latest information.
▶ Attach to Form 1040, 1040-SR, or 1040-NR.

OMB No. 1545-0074
2020
Attachment Sequence No. **17**

Name of person with self-employment income (as shown on Form 1040, 1040-SR, or 1040-NR): SANDY JAMES

Social security number of person with **self-employment** income ▶ 123-45-6789

Part I Self-Employment Tax

Note: If your only income subject to self-employment tax is **church employee income,** see instructions for how to report your income and the definition of church employee income.

A If you are a minister, member of a religious order, or Christian Science practitioner **and** you filed Form 4361, but you had $400 or more of **other** net earnings from self-employment, check here and continue with Part I . . . . ▶ ☐

Skip lines 1a and 1b if you use the farm optional method in Part II. See instructions.

Line	Description		Amount
1a	Net farm profit or (loss) from Schedule F, line 34, and farm partnerships, Schedule K-1 (Form 1065), box 14, code A	1a	
b	If you received social security retirement or disability benefits, enter the amount of Conservation Reserve Program payments included on Schedule F, line 4b, or listed on Schedule K-1 (Form 1065), box 20, code AH	1b	( )

Skip line 2 if you use the nonfarm optional method in Part II. See instructions.

Line	Description		Amount
2	Net profit or (loss) from Schedule C, line 31; and Schedule K-1 (Form 1065), box 14, code A (other than farming). See instructions for other income to report or if you are a minister or member of a religious order	2	$38,913
3	Combine lines 1a, 1b, and 2	3	$38,913
4a	If line 3 is more than zero, multiply line 3 by 92.35% (0.9235). Otherwise, enter amount from line 3. **Note:** If line 4a is less than $400 due to Conservation Reserve Program payments on line 1b, see instructions.	4a	$35,936
b	If you elect one or both of the optional methods, enter the total of lines 15 and 17 here	4b	
c	Combine lines 4a and 4b. If less than $400, **stop;** you don't owe self-employment tax. **Exception:** If less than $400 and you had **church employee income,** enter -0- and continue ▶	4c	
5a	Enter your **church employee income** from Form W-2. See instructions for definition of church employee income — 5a		
b	Multiply line 5a by 92.35% (0.9235). If less than $100, enter -0-	5b	
6	Add lines 4c and 5b	6	
7	Maximum amount of combined wages and self-employment earnings subject to social security tax or the 6.2% portion of the 7.65% railroad retirement (tier 1) tax for 2020	7	137,700
8a	Total social security wages and tips (total of boxes 3 and 7 on Form(s) W-2) and railroad retirement (tier 1) compensation. If $137,700 or more, skip lines 8b through 10, and go to line 11 — 8a		
b	Unreported tips subject to social security tax from Form 4137, line 10 — 8b		
c	Wages subject to social security tax from Form 8919, line 10 — 8c		
d	Add lines 8a, 8b, and 8c	8d	
9	Subtract line 8d from line 7. If zero or less, enter -0- here and on line 10 and go to line 11 ▶	9	
10	Multiply the **smaller** of line 6 or line 9 by 12.4% (0.124)	10	
11	Multiply line 6 by 2.9% (0.029)	11	
12	**Self-employment tax.** Add lines 10 and 11. Enter here and on **Schedule 2 (Form 1040), line 4**	12	$5,498
13	**Deduction for one-half of self-employment tax.** Multiply line 12 by 50% (0.50). Enter here and on **Schedule 1 (Form 1040), line 14** — 13: 2,749		

Part II Optional Methods To Figure Net Earnings (see instructions)

Farm Optional Method. You may use this method **only** if **(a)** your gross farm income[1] wasn't more than $8,460, **or (b)** your net farm profits[2] were less than $6,107.

Line	Description		Amount
14	Maximum income for optional methods	14	5,640
15	Enter the **smaller** of: two-thirds (2/3) of gross farm income[1] (not less than zero) **or** $5,640. Also, include this amount on line 4b above	15	

Nonfarm Optional Method. You may use this method **only** if **(a)** your net nonfarm profits[3] were less than $6,107 and also less than 72.189% of your gross nonfarm income,[4] **and (b)** you had net earnings from self-employment of at least $400 in 2 of the prior 3 years. **Caution:** You may use this method no more than five times.

Line	Description		Amount
16	Subtract line 15 from line 14	16	
17	Enter the **smaller** of: two-thirds (2/3) of gross nonfarm income[4] (not less than zero) **or** the amount on line 16. Also, include this amount on line 4b above	17	

[1] From Sch. F, line 9; and Sch. K-1 (Form 1065), box 14, code B.
[2] From Sch. F, line 34; and Sch. K-1 (Form 1065), box 14, code A—minus the amount you would have entered on line 1b had you not used the optional method.
[3] From Sch. C, line 31; and Sch. K-1 (Form 1065), box 14, code A.
[4] From Sch. C, line 7; and Sch. K-1 (Form 1065), box 14, code C.

For Paperwork Reduction Act Notice, see your tax return instructions. Cat. No. 11358Z **Schedule SE (Form 1040) 2020**

Form **1040** Department of the Treasury—Internal Revenue Service (99) **U.S. Individual Income Tax Return** **2020** OMB No. 1545-0074 IRS Use Only—Do not write or staple in this space.

Filing Status Check only one box. ☐ Single ☐ Married filing jointly ☐ Married filing separately (MFS) ☐ Head of household (HOH) ☐ Qualifying widow(er) (QW)

If you checked the MFS box, enter the name of your spouse. If you checked the HOH or QW box, enter the child's name if the qualifying person is a child but not your dependent ▶

Your first name and middle initial	Last name	Your social security number
SANDY	JAMES	123 45 6789
If joint return, spouse's first name and middle initial	**Last name**	**Spouse's social security number**
BILL	JAMES	987 65 4321

Home address (number and street). If you have a P.O. box, see instructions. 687 Hoover Street Apt. no.

City, town, or post office. If you have a foreign address, also complete spaces below. Hudson, Ohio 42387 State ZIP code

Foreign country name Foreign province/state/county Foreign postal code

Presidential Election Campaign Check here if you, or your spouse if filing jointly, want $3 to go to this fund. Checking a box below will not change your tax or refund. ☐ You ☐ Spouse

At any time during 2020, did you receive, sell, send, exchange, or otherwise acquire any financial interest in any virtual currency? ☐ Yes ☐ No

Standard Deduction **Someone can claim:** ☐ You as a dependent ☐ Your spouse as a dependent ☐ Spouse itemizes on a separate return or you were a dual-status alien

Age/Blindness You: ☐ Were born before January 2, 1956 ☐ Are blind **Spouse:** ☐ Was born before January 2, 1956 ☐ Is blind

Dependents (see instructions): If more than four dependents, see instructions and check here ▶ ☐

(1) First name	Last name	(2) Social security number	(3) Relationship to you	(4) ✔ if qualifies for (see instructions): Child tax credit	Credit for other dependents
Vanessa	James	124 56 4411	Daughter	☑	☐
				☐	☐
				☐	☐
				☐	☐

Attach Sch. B if required.

Standard Deduction for— • Single or Married filing separately, $12,400 • Married filing jointly or Qualifying widow(er), $24,800 • Head of household, $18,650 • If you checked any box under *Standard Deduction*, see instructions.

1	Wages, salaries, tips, etc. Attach Form(s) W-2	1	$41,000
2a	Tax-exempt interest 2a / b Taxable interest	2b	
3a	Qualified dividends 3a / b Ordinary dividends	3b	
4a	IRA distributions 4a / b Taxable amount	4b	
5a	Pensions and annuities 5a / b Taxable amount	5b	
6a	Social security benefits 6a / b Taxable amount	6b	
7	Capital gain or (loss). Attach Schedule D if required. If not required, check here ▶ ☐	7	
8	Other income from Schedule 1, line 9	8	$38,913
9	Add lines 1, 2b, 3b, 4b, 5b, 6b, 7, and 8. This is your **total income** ▶	9	$79,913
10	Adjustments to income:		
a	From Schedule 1, line 22 — 10a $2,749		
b	Charitable contributions if you take the standard deduction. See instructions — 10b		
c	Add lines 10a and 10b. These are your **total adjustments to income** ▶	10c	$2,749
11	Subtract line 10c from line 9. This is your **adjusted gross income** ▶	11	$77,164
12	**Standard deduction or itemized deductions** (from Schedule A)	12	$24,800
13	Qualified business income deduction. Attach Form 8995 or Form 8995-A	13	$7,783
14	Add lines 12 and 13	14	$32,583
15	**Taxable income.** Subtract line 14 from line 11. If zero or less, enter -0-	15	$44,581

For Disclosure, Privacy Act, and Paperwork Reduction Act Notice, see separate instructions. Cat. No. 11320B Form **1040** (2020)

Form 1040 (2020) Page **2**

16	**Tax** (see instructions). Check if any from Form(s): 1 ☐ 8814 2 ☐ 4972 3 ☐ $4,987	16	$4,987
17	Amount from Schedule 2, line 3	17	
18	Add lines 16 and 17	18	$4,987
19	Child tax credit or credit for other dependents	19	
20	Amount from Schedule 3, line 7	20	
21	Add lines 19 and 20	21	0
22	Subtract line 21 from line 18. If zero or less, enter -0-	22	$4,987
23	Other taxes, including self-employment tax, from Schedule 2, line 10	23	$5,498
24	Add lines 22 and 23. This is your **total tax** ▶	24	$10,485
25	Federal income tax withheld from:		
a	Form(s) W-2 — 25a $9,000		
b	Form(s) 1099 — 25b		
c	Other forms (see instructions) — 25c		
d	Add lines 25a through 25c	25d	$9,000
26	2020 estimated tax payments and amount applied from 2019 return	26	
27	Earned income credit (EIC) — 27		
28	Additional child tax credit. Attach Schedule 8812 — 28		
29	American opportunity credit from Form 8863, line 8 — 29		
30	Recovery rebate credit. See instructions — 30		
31	Amount from Schedule 3, line 13 — 31		
32	Add lines 27 through 31. These are your **total other payments and refundable credits** ▶	32	---
33	Add lines 25d, 26, and 32. These are your **total payments** ▶	33	$9,000

• If you have a qualifying child, attach Sch. EIC. • If you have nontaxable combat pay, see instructions.

Refund

34	If line 33 is more than line 24, subtract line 24 from line 33. This is the amount you **overpaid**	34	
35a	Amount of line 34 you want **refunded to you.** If Form 8888 is attached, check here ▶ ☐	35a	
▶ b	Routing number ▶ c Type: ☐ Checking ☐ Savings		
▶ d	Account number		
36	Amount of line 34 you want **applied to your 2021 estimated tax** ▶ 36		

Direct deposit? See instructions.

Amount You Owe For details on how to pay, see instructions.

37	Subtract line 33 from line 24. This is the **amount you owe now** ▶	37	$1,485
	Note: Schedule H and Schedule SE filers, line 37 may not represent all of the taxes you owe for 2020. See Schedule 3, line 12e, and its instructions for details.		
38	Estimated tax penalty (see instructions) ▶ 38		

Third Party Designee Do you want to allow another person to discuss this return with the IRS? See instructions ▶ ☐ **Yes.** Complete below. ☐ **No**

Designee's name ▶ Phone no. ▶ Personal identification number (PIN) ▶

Sign Here Under penalties of perjury, I declare that I have examined this return and accompanying schedules and statements, and to the best of my knowledge and belief, they are true, correct, and complete. Declaration of preparer (other than taxpayer) is based on all information of which preparer has any knowledge.

Joint return? See instructions. Keep a copy for your records.

Your signature	Date	Your occupation	If the IRS sent you an Identity Protection PIN, enter it here (see inst.) ▶
Sandy James	4/3/2021	child care provider	
Spouse's signature. If a joint return, both must sign.	**Date**	**Spouse's occupation**	**If the IRS sent your spouse an Identity Protection PIN, enter it here (see inst.) ▶**
Bill James	4/3/2021	Construction	

Phone no. Email address

Paid Preparer Use Only

Preparer's name	Preparer's signature	Date	PTIN	Check if: ☐ Self-employed

Firm's name ▶ Phone no.

Firm's address ▶ Firm's EIN ▶

Go to *www.irs.gov/Form1040* for instructions and the latest information. Form **1040** (2020)

SCHEDULE 1 (Form 1040) — Department of the Treasury, Internal Revenue Service

Additional Income and Adjustments to Income

▶ Attach to Form 1040, 1040-SR, or 1040-NR.
▶ Go to *www.irs.gov/Form1040* for instructions and the latest information.

OMB No. 1545-0074 — **2020** — Attachment Sequence No. **01**

Name(s) shown on Form 1040, 1040-SR, or 1040-NR: SANDY and BILL JAMES — **Your social security number**: 123-45-6789

Part I Additional Income

1	Taxable refunds, credits, or offsets of state and local income taxes	1	
2a	Alimony received	2a	
b	Date of original divorce or separation agreement (see instructions) ▶		
3	Business income or (loss). Attach Schedule C	3	$38,913
4	Other gains or (losses). Attach Form 4797	4	
5	Rental real estate, royalties, partnerships, S corporations, trusts, etc. Attach Schedule E	5	
6	Farm income or (loss). Attach Schedule F	6	
7	Unemployment compensation	7	
8	Other income. List type and amount ▶	8	
9	Combine lines 1 through 8. Enter here and on Form 1040, 1040-SR, or 1040-NR, line 8	9	$38,913

Part II Adjustments to Income

10	Educator expenses	10	
11	Certain business expenses of reservists, performing artists, and fee-basis government officials. Attach Form 2106	11	
12	Health savings account deduction. Attach Form 8889	12	
13	Moving expenses for members of the Armed Forces. Attach Form 3903	13	
14	Deductible part of self-employment tax. Attach Schedule SE	14	$2,749
15	Self-employed SEP, SIMPLE, and qualified plans	15	
16	Self-employed health insurance deduction	16	
17	Penalty on early withdrawal of savings	17	
18a	Alimony paid	18a	
b	Recipient's SSN ▶		
c	Date of original divorce or separation agreement (see instructions) ▶		
19	IRA deduction	19	
20	Student loan interest deduction	20	
21	Tuition and fees deduction. Attach Form 8917	21	
22	Add lines 10 through 21. These are your **adjustments to income.** Enter here and on Form 1040, 1040-SR, or 1040-NR, line 10a	22	$2,749

For Paperwork Reduction Act Notice, see your tax return instructions. Cat. No. 71479F **Schedule 1 (Form 1040) 2020**

SCHEDULE 2 (Form 1040) — Department of the Treasury, Internal Revenue Service

Additional Taxes

▶ Attach to Form 1040, 1040-SR, or 1040-NR.
▶ Go to *www.irs.gov/Form1040* for instructions and the latest information.

OMB No. 1545-0074 — **2020** — Attachment Sequence No. **02**

Name(s) shown on Form 1040, 1040-SR, or 1040-NR: Sandy and Bill James — **Your social security number**: 123-45-6789

Part I Tax

1	Alternative minimum tax. Attach Form 6251	1	
2	Excess advance premium tax credit repayment. Attach Form 8962	2	
3	Add lines 1 and 2. Enter here and on Form 1040, 1040-SR, or 1040-NR, line 17	3	

Part II Other Taxes

4	Self-employment tax. Attach Schedule SE	4	$5,498
5	Unreported social security and Medicare tax from Form: **a** ☐ 4137 **b** ☐ 8919	5	
6	Additional tax on IRAs, other qualified retirement plans, and other tax-favored accounts. Attach Form 5329 if required	6	
7a	Household employment taxes. Attach Schedule H	7a	
b	Repayment of first-time homebuyer credit from Form 5405. Attach Form 5405 if required	7b	
8	Taxes from: **a** ☐ Form 8959 **b** ☐ Form 8960 **c** ☐ Instructions; enter code(s)	8	
9	Section 965 net tax liability installment from Form 965-A — 9		
10	Add lines 4 through 8. These are your **total other taxes.** Enter here and on Form 1040 or 1040-SR, line 23, or Form 1040-NR, line 23b	10	$5,498

For Paperwork Reduction Act Notice, see your tax return instructions. Cat. No. 71478U **Schedule 2 (Form 1040) 2020**

Form **8995**

Department of the Treasury
Internal Revenue Service

Qualified Business Income Deduction Simplified Computation

▶ Attach to your tax return.

▶ Go to *www.irs.gov/Form8995* for instructions and the latest information.

OMB No. 1545-0123

2020

Attachment Sequence No. **55**

Name(s) shown on return | **Your taxpayer identification number**

Note. *You can claim the qualified business income deduction* **only** *if you have qualified business income from a qualified trade or business, real estate investment trust dividends, publicly traded partnership income, or a domestic production activities deduction passed through from an agricultural or horticultural cooperative. See instructions.*
Use this form if your taxable income, before your qualified business income deduction, is at or below $163,300 ($326,600 if married filing jointly), and you aren't a patron of an agricultural or horticultural cooperative.

1	(a) Trade, business, or aggregation name	(b) Taxpayer identification number	(c) Qualified business income or (loss)
i	Family Child Care		$38,913
ii			
iii			
iv			
v			

2	Total qualified business income or (loss). Combine lines 1i through 1v, column (c)	2	$38,913		
3	Qualified business net (loss) carryforward from the prior year	3	( )		
4	Total qualified business income. Combine lines 2 and 3. If zero or less, enter -0-	4	$38,913		
5	Qualified business income component. Multiply line 4 by 20% (0.20)			5	$7,783
6	Qualified REIT dividends and publicly traded partnership (PTP) income or (loss) (see instructions)	6	---		
7	Qualified REIT dividends and qualified PTP (loss) carryforward from the prior year	7	(---)		
8	Total qualified REIT dividends and PTP income. Combine lines 6 and 7. If zero or less, enter -0-	8	---		
9	REIT and PTP component. Multiply line 8 by 20% (0.20)			9	$0
10	Qualified business income deduction before the income limitation. Add lines 5 and 9			10	$7,783
11	Taxable income before qualified business income deduction	11	$52,364		
12	Net capital gain (see instructions)	12	---		
13	Subtract line 12 from line 11. If zero or less, enter -0-	13	$52,364		
14	Income limitation. Multiply line 13 by 20% (0.20)			14	$10,473
15	Qualified business income deduction. Enter the lesser of line 10 or line 14. Also enter this amount on the applicable line of your return ▶			15	$7,783
16	Total qualified business (loss) carryforward. Combine lines 2 and 3. If greater than zero, enter -0-			16	( )
17	Total qualified REIT dividends and PTP (loss) carryforward. Combine lines 6 and 7. If greater than zero, enter -0-			17	( )

For Privacy Act and Paperwork Reduction Act Notice, see instructions. Cat. No. 37806C Form **8995** (2020)

$2,500 Election

For the year ending December 31, 2021 I am electing the de minimus safe harbor rule under Treas. Reg. Section 1.263(a)-1(f) for my business expenses of less than $2,500.

Sandy James (signature) 4/3/2021

Sandy James Date

Taxpayer identification number: 26-389187
Address: 687 Hoover Street, Hudson, Ohio 42387

APPENDIX B

How and When to Depreciate an Item

Step 1: Does It Cost More Than $2,500?

If the answer is yes, go to step 2. If no, deduct it in one year. If it's part of a home improvement, see step 4.

Step 2: Is It a Repair?

The definition of a repair was greatly expanded in 2014. If the answer is yes, deduct it in one year, regardless of the cost. If not, go to step 3.

Step 3: Choose a Depreciation Category

Office equipment (computer, printer, copy machine)
Personal property (furniture, appliances, play equipment)
Land improvement (fence, patio, driveway)
Home improvement (house, deck, new addition, major remodeling)
Home

Step 4: Follow the Directions for Each Depreciation Category

Office equipment:

- Costing less than $2,500: deduct in one year and attach statement to your tax return.
- Costing more than $2,500:
    - If you use less than 50% for your business, depreciate over five years.
    - If you use 50% or more for your business:
        - use the Section 179 rule, or
        - use the 100% bonus depreciation rule and deduct in one year, or
        - depreciate over five years.

Personal property:

- Costing less than $2,500: deduct in one year and attach statement to your tax return.
- Costing more than $2,500:
    - use 100% bonus depreciation rule and deduct in one year, or
    - depreciate over seven years.

- If you use 50% or more for your business:
    - can use the Section 179 rule.

Land improvement:

- Costing less than $2,500: deduct in one year and attach statement to your tax return.
- Costing more than $2,500:
    - Does the Safe Harbor for Small Taxpayers rule apply (effective 2014 and after)?
        - If yes, deduct in one year.
        - If no, use the 100% bonus depreciation rule and deduct in one year, or depreciate over 15 years.

Home improvement:

- Costing less than $2,500: deduct in one year and attach statement to your tax return.
- Costing more than $2,500:
    - Does the Safe Harbor for Small Taxpayers rule apply (effective 2014 and after)?
        - If yes, deduct in one year.
        - If no, depreciate over 39 years, or if used more than 50% for business, use the Section 179 rule.

Home:

- Depreciate over 39 years.

APPENDIX C

IRS Resources

You can call the IRS Business and Specialty Tax Line at 800-829-4933 with any tax question. This toll-free number for business questions should make it easier for you to get through to an IRS employee who can answer your questions. If you aren't sure if the answer you are given is correct, ask the IRS employee to tell you which IRS publication or part of the Tax Code the answer is based on. If you have a hearing impairment and TDD equipment, you can call 800-829-4059. If you live outside the United States and have a tax question, call your U.S. Embassy. In Puerto Rico call 787-622-8929.

You can find IRS forms and publications at local IRS offices, banks, libraries, and post offices. You can also call 800-829-3676 to have any IRS form mailed to you. The IRS has its own website (www.irs.gov) from which you can download any IRS form, publication, or instruction book. The site also has other information that may help you with your taxes.

You can also get IRS tax forms by fax. Dial 703-368-9694 from the voice unit of your fax machine and follow the voice prompts. Tax forms must be on plain paper, not thermal paper, to be acceptable for filing. (You can copy the form if necessary.) For help with transmission problems, call the Fed World Help Desk at 703-487-4608.

If you want to report that another taxpayer (an illegal child care provider, for example) is cheating, call the IRS criminal investigation informant hotline at 800-829-0433. Your name will be kept confidential, and you are eligible for a reward if the IRS collects taxes due.

Below is a list of the IRS publications and Tax Court cases that address family child care tax issues. You can find copies at www.tomcopelandblog.com.

Child Care Provider Audit Technique Guide

This guide from the IRS is a must if you are audited. It contains guidance on the many unique tax issues facing child care providers. You can find the guide at www.tomcopelandblog.com.

Publication 587 Business Use of Your Home

Under the section Day-Care Facility, this publication clarifies that providers who have applied for, have been granted, or are exempt from a license, certification, or registration under applicable state law can claim home expenses as shown on **Form 8829**. This publication also discusses how to calculate the Time-Space percentage in filling out **Form 8829**. It includes a discussion of how to claim food expenses and report Food Program income.

Instructions for Form 8829 Expenses for Business Use of Your Home

Under the section Special Computation for Certain Day-Care Facilities, the instructions spell out how to calculate the Time-Space percentage of the home when at least one of the rooms in the home is used exclusively for the business.

IRS Revenue Ruling 92-3

This Revenue Ruling, based on an audit of a family child care provider, clarifies how to calculate the Time-Space percentage. It also defines what "regular use" means.

Tax Court Cases

***Robert Neilson and Dorothy Neilson v. Commissioner,* 94-1, 1990**

In this case, the court ruled that a provider could claim 75 hours a week (including preparation and cleanup time) in determining her Time-Space percentage. The court also allowed the provider to deduct a portion of her lawn care expenses.

Uphus and Walker v. Commissioner

Tax Court Memo 1994-71, February 23, 1994

In these two cases, the court ruled that providers could claim rooms (laundry room, basement storage area, garage, and furnace area) as regularly used for the business even if the children in care never entered the rooms. The use of these rooms by the provider for business purposes was enough to meet the regular-use test.

Hewett v. Commissioner

Tax Court Memo 1996-110

In this case, the court allowed a taxpayer to claim an exclusive-use area for a grand piano that occupied a small recessed section of the living room and had no partition separating it from the rest of the home. The court ruled that it wasn't necessary to have a physical barrier to prove that an area was used exclusively for business.

Scott C. and Patricia A. Simpson v. Commissioner

Tax Court Memo 1997-223, May 12, 1997

In this case, a new provider was not allowed to claim most of her first two years of expenses because they were not related to her business. These expenses included cross-country ski machine, personal food expenses, payments to wineries, and much more. Despite the loss of many deductions, the court did allow her to show a loss of \$2,000–\$3,000 for these two years. The court also acknowledged that cable TV and water were proper business deductions.

Peter and Maureen Speltz v. Commissioner

Tax Court Summary Opinion 2006-25

A provider hired her husband and set up a medical reimbursement plan without paying him a salary. The court ruled that the plan was valid, the husband was a bona fide employee, and the provider was allowed to deduct thousands of dollars in medical expenses.

Jonelle Broady v. Commissioner
Tax Court Summary Opinion 2008-63
An illegal provider was entitled to claim business expenses such as advertising, car expenses, office supplies, repairs and maintenance, and supplies and food. Illegal providers are not entitled to claim expenses associated with the home.

Tax Help on the internet
Commercial internet services have special sites on which you can get tax assistance; however, be careful about accepting advice from these sources, because none of the information is guaranteed.

State Tax Information and Forms
If you need state tax information and forms, contact your state tax office.

List of IRS Forms and Publications

Here's a list of the IRS forms and publications that are mentioned in this book:

Form W-5 Earned Income Credit Advance Payment Certificate
Form W-10 Dependent Care Provider's Identification and Certification
Form 1040 U.S. Individual Income Tax Return
Form 1040-ES Estimated Tax for Individuals
Form 1040-SE Self-Employment Tax
Form 1040X Amended U.S. Individual Income Tax Return
Form 3115 Application for Change in Accounting Method
Form 4562 Depreciation and Amortization
Form 4684 Casualties and Thefts
Form 4797 Sales of Business Property
Form 4868 Application for Automatic Extension of Time to File U.S. Individual Income Tax Return
Form 5305-SEP Simplified Employee Pension
Form 5695 Residential Energy Credits
Form 8109 Federal Tax Deposit Coupon
Form 8812 Additional Child Tax Credit
Form 8824 Like-Kind Exchange
Form 8829 Expenses for Business Use of Your Home
Form 8863 Education Credits
Form 8880 Credit for Qualified Retirement Savings Contributions
Form 8949 Sales and Other Dispositions of Capital Assets
Publication 463 Travel, Entertainment, Gift, and Car Expenses
Publication 505 Tax Withholding and Estimated Tax
Publication 523 Selling Your Home
Publication 534 Depreciating Property Placed in Service Before 1987
Publication 544 Sales and Other Dispositions of Assets
Publication 556 Examination of Returns, Appeal Rights, and Claims for Refund
Publication 583 Starting a Business and Keeping Records
Publication 587 Business Use of Your Home

Publication 590 Individual Retirement Arrangements
Publication 596 Earned Income Credit
Publication 946 How to Depreciate Property
Publication 1542 Per Diem Rates
Schedule A Itemized Deductions
Schedule B Interest and Dividend Income
Schedule C Profit or Loss from Business
Schedule D Capital Gains and Losses
Schedule EIC Earned Income Credit
Schedule SE Self-Employment Tax

Employee and Payroll Tax Forms

Circular E Employer's Tax Guide
Form I-9 Employment Eligibility Verification
Form SS-4 Application for Employer Identification Number
Form SS-5 Application for a Social Security Card
Form W-2 Wages and Tax Statement
Form W-3 Transmittal of Income and Tax Statements
Form W-4 Employee's Withholding Allowance Certificate
Form 940 Employer's Annual Federal Unemployment Tax Return (FUTA)
Form 941 Employer's Quarterly Federal Tax Return
Form 944 Employer's Annual Federal Tax Return
Form 1099 Miscellaneous Income

APPENDIX D

Finding and Working with a Tax Professional

Tax Professional Directory

The National Association for Family Child Care (NAFCC) maintains a list of tax professionals around the country who have experience filing tax returns for family child care providers. This list is posted at www.nafcc.org. It is available for members only.

Working with a Tax Professional

When hiring or working with a tax professional, follow these guidelines:

- Get referrals from other providers who have a good tax professional.
- Ask the professionals you are considering about their training, experience, and knowledge of the unique tax laws that affect family child care providers (see pages xx–xxi).
- Always review your tax return before signing it, and ask questions if you don't understand something on your return.
- Never sign a blank tax form or one that has been filled out in pencil.
- Keep a copy of your return for your records.
- Remember that you are ultimately responsible for your tax return even if your tax professional makes an error.
- Watch out for the following warning signs of an unscrupulous tax professional:
  Someone who says that he or she can obtain larger refunds than other preparers.
  Someone who bases his or her fee on a percentage of the amount of the refund.
  Someone who refuses to sign your return or give you a copy for your records.

PART V

Tax Forms

Form **W-10**
(Rev. October 2020)
Department of the Treasury
Internal Revenue Service

Dependent Care Provider's Identification and Certification

▶ **Do NOT file Form W-10 with your tax return. Instead, keep it for your records.**
▶ **Go to *www.irs.gov/FormW10* for the latest information.**

Part I Dependent Care Provider's Identification (see instructions)

Please Print or Type	Name of dependent care provider	**Provider's taxpayer identification number**
	Address (number, street, and apt. no.)	If the above number is a social security number, check here ▶ . . . . ☐
	City, state, and ZIP code	

Certification and Signature of Dependent Care Provider. Under penalties of perjury, I, as the dependent care provider, certify that my name, address, and taxpayer identification number shown above are correct.

Please Sign Here	**Dependent care provider's signature**	**Date**

Part II Name and Address of Person Requesting Part I Information (see instructions)

Name, street address, apt. no., city, state, and ZIP code of person requesting information

____

For calendar year 2020, I paid $ ______________ (amount paid) to
______________________ (name of provider) for the care of
______________________ (name of child(ren)).

______________________ ______________
Signature of Parent Date

______________________ ______________
Signature of Provider Date

Form **W-10**
(Rev. October 2020)
Department of the Treasury
Internal Revenue Service

Dependent Care Provider's Identification and Certification

▶ **Do NOT file Form W-10 with your tax return. Instead, keep it for your records.**
▶ **Go to *www.irs.gov/FormW10* for the latest information.**

Part I Dependent Care Provider's Identification (see instructions)

Please Print or Type	Name of dependent care provider	**Provider's taxpayer identification number**
	Address (number, street, and apt. no.)	If the above number is a social security number, check here ▶ . . . . ☐
	City, state, and ZIP code	

Certification and Signature of Dependent Care Provider. Under penalties of perjury, I, as the dependent care provider, certify that my name, address, and taxpayer identification number shown above are correct.

Please Sign Here	**Dependent care provider's signature**	**Date**

Part II Name and Address of Person Requesting Part I Information (see instructions)

Name, street address, apt. no., city, state, and ZIP code of person requesting information

____

For calendar year 2020, I paid $ ______________ (amount paid) to
______________________ (name of provider) for the care of
______________________ (name of child(ren)).

______________________ ______________
Signature of Parent Date

______________________ ______________
Signature of Provider Date

Electing the $2,500 Safe Harbor Rule

If you bought items costing $2,500 or less that you want to deduct in 2020, rather than depreciating, attach this statement to your 2020 tax return.

For the year ending December 31, 2020, I am electing the de minimis safe harbor under Treas. Reg. Section 1.263(a)-1(f) for my business expenses of less than $2,500.

____________________________ ________________

Signature Date

Taxpayer identification number:

Address:

Electing the Small Taxpayer Safe Harbor Rule

If you bought home improvements or a fence, a patio, or a driveway that cost the lesser of $10,000 or 2% of the unadjusted basis of your home, you can deduct them in one year if you attach this statement to your 2020 tax return.

For the year ending December 31, 2020, I am electing the safe harbor election for small taxpayers under Treas. Reg. Section 1.263(a)-3(g) for the following: [list your improvements].

____________________________ ________________

Signature Date

Taxpayer identification number:

Address:

Form **1040** Department of the Treasury—Internal Revenue Service (99)
U.S. Individual Income Tax Return **2020** OMB No. 1545-0074 IRS Use Only—Do not write or staple in this space.

Filing Status Check only one box.
☐ Single ☐ Married filing jointly ☐ Married filing separately (MFS) ☐ Head of household (HOH) ☐ Qualifying widow(er) (QW)
If you checked the MFS box, enter the name of your spouse. If you checked the HOH or QW box, enter the child's name if the qualifying person is a child but not your dependent ▶

Your first name and middle initial	Last name	**Your social security number**
If joint return, spouse's first name and middle initial	Last name	**Spouse's social security number**

Home address (number and street). If you have a P.O. box, see instructions. | Apt. no.
City, town, or post office. If you have a foreign address, also complete spaces below. | State | ZIP code
Foreign country name | Foreign province/state/county | Foreign postal code

Presidential Election Campaign Check here if you, or your spouse if filing jointly, want $3 to go to this fund. Checking a box below will not change your tax or refund. ☐ **You** ☐ **Spouse**

At any time during 2020, did you receive, sell, send, exchange, or otherwise acquire any financial interest in any virtual currency? ☐ **Yes** ☐ **No**

Standard Deduction **Someone can claim:** ☐ You as a dependent ☐ Your spouse as a dependent
☐ Spouse itemizes on a separate return or you were a dual-status alien

Age/Blindness **You:** ☐ Were born before January 2, 1956 ☐ Are blind **Spouse:** ☐ Was born before January 2, 1956 ☐ Is blind

Dependents (see instructions):
If more than four dependents, see instructions and check here ▶ ☐

(1) First name / Last name	**(2)** Social security number	**(3)** Relationship to you	**(4)** ✔ if qualifies for (see instructions): Child tax credit	Credit for other dependents
			☐	☐
			☐	☐
			☐	☐
			☐	☐

Attach Sch. B if required.

1	Wages, salaries, tips, etc. Attach Form(s) W-2			1	
2a	Tax-exempt interest	2a	**b** Taxable interest	2b	
3a	Qualified dividends	3a	**b** Ordinary dividends	3b	
4a	IRA distributions	4a	**b** Taxable amount	4b	
5a	Pensions and annuities	5a	**b** Taxable amount	5b	
6a	Social security benefits	6a	**b** Taxable amount	6b	
7	Capital gain or (loss). Attach Schedule D if required. If not required, check here ▶ ☐			7	
8	Other income from Schedule 1, line 9			8	
9	Add lines 1, 2b, 3b, 4b, 5b, 6b, 7, and 8. This is your **total income** ▶			9	
10	Adjustments to income:				
a	From Schedule 1, line 22		10a		
b	Charitable contributions if you take the standard deduction. See instructions		10b		
c	Add lines 10a and 10b. These are your **total adjustments to income** ▶			10c	
11	Subtract line 10c from line 9. This is your **adjusted gross income** ▶			11	
12	**Standard deduction or itemized deductions** (from Schedule A)			12	
13	Qualified business income deduction. Attach Form 8995 or Form 8995-A			13	
14	Add lines 12 and 13			14	
15	**Taxable income.** Subtract line 14 from line 11. If zero or less, enter -0-			15	

Standard Deduction for—
- Single or Married filing separately, $12,400
- Married filing jointly or Qualifying widow(er), $24,800
- Head of household, $18,650
- If you checked any box under *Standard Deduction,* see instructions.

For Disclosure, Privacy Act, and Paperwork Reduction Act Notice, see separate instructions. Cat. No. 11320B Form **1040** (2020)

Form 1040 (2020) Page **2**

16	**Tax** (see instructions). Check if any from Form(s): 1 ☐ 8814 2 ☐ 4972 3 ☐ ______		16	
17	Amount from Schedule 2, line 3		17	
18	Add lines 16 and 17		18	
19	Child tax credit or credit for other dependents		19	
20	Amount from Schedule 3, line 7		20	
21	Add lines 19 and 20		21	
22	Subtract line 21 from line 18. If zero or less, enter -0-		22	
23	Other taxes, including self-employment tax, from Schedule 2, line 10		23	
24	Add lines 22 and 23. This is your **total tax** ▶		24	
25	Federal income tax withheld from:			
a	Form(s) W-2	25a		
b	Form(s) 1099	25b		
c	Other forms (see instructions)	25c		
d	Add lines 25a through 25c		25d	
26	2020 estimated tax payments and amount applied from 2019 return		26	
27	Earned income credit (EIC)	27		
28	Additional child tax credit. Attach Schedule 8812	28		
29	American opportunity credit from Form 8863, line 8	29		
30	Recovery rebate credit. See instructions	30		
31	Amount from Schedule 3, line 13	31		
32	Add lines 27 through 31. These are your **total other payments and refundable credits** ▶		32	
33	Add lines 25d, 26, and 32. These are your **total payments** ▶		33	

- If you have a qualifying child, attach Sch. EIC.
- If you have nontaxable combat pay, see instructions.

Refund

Direct deposit? See instructions.

34	If line 33 is more than line 24, subtract line 24 from line 33. This is the amount you **overpaid**		34	
35a	Amount of line 34 you want **refunded to you.** If Form 8888 is attached, check here ▶ ☐		35a	
▶ b	Routing number ▶ c Type: ☐ Checking ☐ Savings			
▶ d	Account number			
36	Amount of line 34 you want **applied to your 2021 estimated tax** ▶	36		

Amount You Owe

For details on how to pay, see instructions.

37	Subtract line 33 from line 24. This is the **amount you owe now** ▶		37	
	Note: Schedule H and Schedule SE filers, line 37 may not represent all of the taxes you owe for 2020. See Schedule 3, line 12e, and its instructions for details.			
38	Estimated tax penalty (see instructions) ▶	38		

Third Party Designee

Do you want to allow another person to discuss this return with the IRS? See instructions ▶ ☐ **Yes.** Complete below. ☐ **No**

Designee's name ▶ Phone no. ▶ Personal identification number (PIN) ▶

Sign Here

Under penalties of perjury, I declare that I have examined this return and accompanying schedules and statements, and to the best of my knowledge and belief, they are true, correct, and complete. Declaration of preparer (other than taxpayer) is based on all information of which preparer has any knowledge.

Joint return? See instructions. Keep a copy for your records.

Your signature	Date	Your occupation	If the IRS sent you an Identity Protection PIN, enter it here (see inst.) ▶
Spouse's signature. If a joint return, **both** must sign.	Date	Spouse's occupation	If the IRS sent your spouse an Identity Protection PIN, enter it here (see inst.) ▶
Phone no.	Email address		

Paid Preparer Use Only

Preparer's name	Preparer's signature	Date	PTIN	Check if: ☐ Self-employed
Firm's name ▶			Phone no.	
Firm's address ▶			Firm's EIN ▶	

Go to *www.irs.gov/Form1040* for instructions and the latest information. Form **1040** (2020)

SCHEDULE 1 (Form 1040)
Department of the Treasury Internal Revenue Service

Additional Income and Adjustments to Income

▶ Attach to Form 1040, 1040-SR, or 1040-NR.
▶ Go to *www.irs.gov/Form1040* for instructions and the latest information.

OMB No. 1545-0074
2020
Attachment Sequence No. 01

Name(s) shown on Form 1040, 1040-SR, or 1040-NR | **Your social security number**

Part I Additional Income

1	Taxable refunds, credits, or offsets of state and local income taxes	1	
2a	Alimony received	2a	
b	Date of original divorce or separation agreement (see instructions) ▶		
3	Business income or (loss). Attach Schedule C	3	
4	Other gains or (losses). Attach Form 4797	4	
5	Rental real estate, royalties, partnerships, S corporations, trusts, etc. Attach Schedule E	5	
6	Farm income or (loss). Attach Schedule F	6	
7	Unemployment compensation	7	
8	Other income. List type and amount ▶	8	
9	Combine lines 1 through 8. Enter here and on Form 1040, 1040-SR, or 1040-NR, line 8	9	

Part II Adjustments to Income

10	Educator expenses	10	
11	Certain business expenses of reservists, performing artists, and fee-basis government officials. Attach Form 2106	11	
12	Health savings account deduction. Attach Form 8889	12	
13	Moving expenses for members of the Armed Forces. Attach Form 3903	13	
14	Deductible part of self-employment tax. Attach Schedule SE	14	
15	Self-employed SEP, SIMPLE, and qualified plans	15	
16	Self-employed health insurance deduction	16	
17	Penalty on early withdrawal of savings	17	
18a	Alimony paid	18a	
b	Recipient's SSN ▶		
c	Date of original divorce or separation agreement (see instructions) ▶		
19	IRA deduction	19	
20	Student loan interest deduction	20	
21	Tuition and fees deduction. Attach Form 8917	21	
22	Add lines 10 through 21. These are your **adjustments to income.** Enter here and on Form 1040, 1040-SR, or 1040-NR, line 10a	22	

SCHEDULE 2 (Form 1040)

Department of the Treasury Internal Revenue Service

Additional Taxes

▶ Attach to Form 1040, 1040-SR, or 1040-NR.
▶ Go to *www.irs.gov/Form1040* for instructions and the latest information.

OMB No. 1545-0074
2020
Attachment Sequence No. **02**

Name(s) shown on Form 1040, 1040-SR, or 1040-NR | **Your social security number**

Part I Tax

1	Alternative minimum tax. Attach Form 6251	1	
2	Excess advance premium tax credit repayment. Attach Form 8962	2	
3	Add lines 1 and 2. Enter here and on Form 1040, 1040-SR, or 1040-NR, line 17	3	

Part II Other Taxes

4	Self-employment tax. Attach Schedule SE	4	
5	Unreported social security and Medicare tax from Form: **a** ☐ 4137 **b** ☐ 8919	5	
6	Additional tax on IRAs, other qualified retirement plans, and other tax-favored accounts. Attach Form 5329 if required	6	
7a	Household employment taxes. Attach Schedule H	7a	
b	Repayment of first-time homebuyer credit from Form 5405. Attach Form 5405 if required	7b	
8	Taxes from: **a** ☐ Form 8959 **b** ☐ Form 8960 **c** ☐ Instructions; enter code(s)	8	
9	Section 965 net tax liability installment from Form 965-A — 9		
10	Add lines 4 through 8. These are your **total other taxes.** Enter here and on Form 1040 or 1040-SR, line 23, or Form 1040-NR, line 23b	10	

For Paperwork Reduction Act Notice, see your tax return instructions. Cat. No. 71478U **Schedule 2 (Form 1040) 2020**

SCHEDULE 3 (Form 1040)

Department of the Treasury Internal Revenue Service

Additional Credits and Payments

▶ Attach to Form 1040, 1040-SR, or 1040-NR.
▶ Go to *www.irs.gov/Form1040* for instructions and the latest information.

OMB No. 1545-0074
2020
Attachment Sequence No. **03**

Name(s) shown on Form 1040, 1040-SR, or 1040-NR | **Your social security number**

Part I Nonrefundable Credits

1	Foreign tax credit. Attach Form 1116 if required	1	
2	Credit for child and dependent care expenses. Attach Form 2441	2	
3	Education credits from Form 8863, line 19	3	
4	Retirement savings contributions credit. Attach Form 8880	4	
5	Residential energy credits. Attach Form 5695	5	
6	Other credits from Form: **a** ☐ 3800 **b** ☐ 8801 **c** ☐	6	
7	Add lines 1 through 6. Enter here and on Form 1040, 1040-SR, or 1040-NR, line 20	7	

Part II Other Payments and Refundable Credits

8	Net premium tax credit. Attach Form 8962	8	
9	Amount paid with request for extension to file (see instructions)	9	
10	Excess social security and tier 1 RRTA tax withheld	10	
11	Credit for federal tax on fuels. Attach Form 4136	11	
12	Other payments or refundable credits:		
a	Form 2439 — 12a		
b	Qualified sick and family leave credits from Schedule(s) H and Form(s) 7202 — 12b		
c	Health coverage tax credit from Form 8885 — 12c		
d	Other: — 12d		
e	Deferral for certain Schedule H or SE filers (see instructions) — 12e		
f	Add lines 12a through 12e	12f	
13	Add lines 8 through 12f. Enter here and on Form 1040, 1040-SR, or 1040-NR, line 31	13	

For Paperwork Reduction Act Notice, see your tax return instructions. Cat. No. 71480G **Schedule 3 (Form 1040) 2020**

SCHEDULE C (Form 1040)

Department of the Treasury Internal Revenue Service (99)

Profit or Loss From Business

(Sole Proprietorship)

▶ Go to *www.irs.gov/ScheduleC* for instructions and the latest information.

▶ Attach to Form 1040, 1040-SR, 1040-NR, or 1041; partnerships generally must file Form 1065.

OMB No. 1545-0074

2020

Attachment Sequence No. **09**

Name of proprietor | **Social security number (SSN)**

A Principal business or profession, including product or service (see instructions) | **B Enter code from instructions** ▶

C Business name. If no separate business name, leave blank. | **D Employer ID number (EIN)** (see instr.)

E Business address (including suite or room no.) ▶

City, town or post office, state, and ZIP code

F Accounting method: **(1)** ☐ Cash **(2)** ☐ Accrual **(3)** ☐ Other (specify) ▶

G Did you "materially participate" in the operation of this business during 2020? If "No," see instructions for limit on losses . ☐ **Yes** ☐ **No**

H If you started or acquired this business during 2020, check here . . . ▶ ☐

I Did you make any payments in 2020 that would require you to file Form(s) 1099? See instructions . . . ☐ **Yes** ☐ **No**

J If "Yes," did you or will you file required Form(s) 1099? . . . ☐ **Yes** ☐ **No**

Part I Income

1	Gross receipts or sales. See instructions for line 1 and check the box if this income was reported to you on Form W-2 and the "Statutory employee" box on that form was checked . . . ▶ ☐	1	
2	Returns and allowances . . .	2	
3	Subtract line 2 from line 1 . . .	3	
4	Cost of goods sold (from line 42) . . .	4	
5	**Gross profit.** Subtract line 4 from line 3 . . .	5	
6	Other income, including federal and state gasoline or fuel tax credit or refund (see instructions) . . .	6	
7	**Gross income.** Add lines 5 and 6 . . . ▶	7	

Part II Expenses. Enter expenses for business use of your home **only** on line 30.

8	Advertising . . .	8		18	Office expense (see instructions)	18	
9	Car and truck expenses (see instructions) . . .	9		19	Pension and profit-sharing plans .	19	
10	Commissions and fees .	10		20	Rent or lease (see instructions):		
11	Contract labor (see instructions)	11		a	Vehicles, machinery, and equipment	20a	
12	Depletion . . .	12		b	Other business property . . .	20b	
13	Depreciation and section 179 expense deduction (not included in Part III) (see instructions) . . .	13		21	Repairs and maintenance . . .	21	
				22	Supplies (not included in Part III) .	22	
				23	Taxes and licenses . . .	23	
				24	Travel and meals:		
14	Employee benefit programs (other than on line 19) . .	14		a	Travel . . .	24a	
15	Insurance (other than health)	15		b	Deductible meals (see instructions) . . .	24b	
16	Interest (see instructions):			25	Utilities . . .	25	
a	Mortgage (paid to banks, etc.)	16a		26	Wages (less employment credits) .	26	
b	Other . . .	16b		27a	Other expenses (from line 48) . .	27a	
17	Legal and professional services	17		b	**Reserved for future use** . . .	27b	

28	**Total expenses** before expenses for business use of home. Add lines 8 through 27a . . . ▶	28	
29	Tentative profit or (loss). Subtract line 28 from line 7 . . .	29	
30	Expenses for business use of your home. Do not report these expenses elsewhere. Attach Form 8829 unless using the simplified method. See instructions. **Simplified method filers only:** Enter the total square footage of (a) your home: ________ and (b) the part of your home used for business: ________ . Use the Simplified Method Worksheet in the instructions to figure the amount to enter on line 30 . . .	30	
31	**Net profit or (loss).** Subtract line 30 from line 29. • If a profit, enter on both **Schedule 1 (Form 1040), line 3,** and on **Schedule SE, line 2.** (If you checked the box on line 1, see instructions). Estates and trusts, enter on **Form 1041, line 3.** • If a loss, you **must** go to line 32.	31	

32 If you have a loss, check the box that describes your investment in this activity. See instructions.

- If you checked 32a, enter the loss on both **Schedule 1 (Form 1040), line 3,** and on **Schedule SE, line 2.** (If you checked the box on line 1, see the line 31 instructions). Estates and trusts, enter on **Form 1041, line 3.**
- If you checked 32b, you **must** attach **Form 6198.** Your loss may be limited.

32a ☐ All investment is at risk.
32b ☐ Some investment is not at risk.

For Paperwork Reduction Act Notice, see the separate instructions. Cat. No. 11334P **Schedule C (Form 1040) 2020**

Schedule C (Form 1040) 2020 Page **2**

Part III Cost of Goods Sold (see instructions)

33 Method(s) used to value closing inventory: a ☐ Cost b ☐ Lower of cost or market c ☐ Other (attach explanation)

34 Was there any change in determining quantities, costs, or valuations between opening and closing inventory? If "Yes," attach explanation . . . ☐ Yes ☐ No

35	Inventory at beginning of year. If different from last year's closing inventory, attach explanation	35	
36	Purchases less cost of items withdrawn for personal use	36	
37	Cost of labor. Do not include any amounts paid to yourself	37	
38	Materials and supplies	38	
39	Other costs	39	
40	Add lines 35 through 39	40	
41	Inventory at end of year	41	
42	**Cost of goods sold.** Subtract line 41 from line 40. Enter the result here and on line 4	42	

Part IV Information on Your Vehicle.

Complete this part **only** if you are claiming car or truck expenses on line 9 and are not required to file Form 4562 for this business. See the instructions for line 13 to find out if you must file Form 4562.

43 When did you place your vehicle in service for business purposes? (month/day/year) ▶ ____ / ____ / ____

44 Of the total number of miles you drove your vehicle during 2020, enter the number of miles you used your vehicle for:

a Business ____________ b Commuting (see instructions) ____________ c Other ____________

45 Was your vehicle available for personal use during off-duty hours? . . . ☐ Yes ☐ No

46 Do you (or your spouse) have another vehicle available for personal use? . . . ☐ Yes ☐ No

47a Do you have evidence to support your deduction? . . . ☐ Yes ☐ No

b If "Yes," is the evidence written? . . . ☐ Yes ☐ No

Part V Other Expenses.

List below business expenses not included on lines 8–26 or line 30.

48 Total other expenses. Enter here and on line 27a	48

SCHEDULE SE (Form 1040)

Department of the Treasury Internal Revenue Service (99)

Self-Employment Tax

► Go to *www.irs.gov/ScheduleSE* for instructions and the latest information.
► Attach to Form 1040, 1040-SR, or 1040-NR.

OMB No. 1545-0074
2020
Attachment Sequence No. **17**

Name of person with self-employment income (as shown on Form 1040, 1040-SR, or 1040-NR) | Social security number of person with **self-employment** income ►

Part I Self-Employment Tax

Note: If your only income subject to self-employment tax is **church employee income,** see instructions for how to report your income and the definition of church employee income.

A If you are a minister, member of a religious order, or Christian Science practitioner **and** you filed Form 4361, but you had $400 or more of **other** net earnings from self-employment, check here and continue with Part I . . . . ► ☐

Skip lines 1a and 1b if you use the farm optional method in Part II. See instructions.

Line	Description			Line	Amount
1a	Net farm profit or (loss) from Schedule F, line 34, and farm partnerships, Schedule K-1 (Form 1065), box 14, code A			1a	
b	If you received social security retirement or disability benefits, enter the amount of Conservation Reserve Program payments included on Schedule F, line 4b, or listed on Schedule K-1 (Form 1065), box 20, code AH			1b	( )
	Skip line 2 if you use the nonfarm optional method in Part II. See instructions.				
2	Net profit or (loss) from Schedule C, line 31; and Schedule K-1 (Form 1065), box 14, code A (other than farming). See instructions for other income to report or if you are a minister or member of a religious order			2	
3	Combine lines 1a, 1b, and 2			3	
4a	If line 3 is more than zero, multiply line 3 by 92.35% (0.9235). Otherwise, enter amount from line 3			4a	
	Note: If line 4a is less than $400 due to Conservation Reserve Program payments on line 1b, see instructions.				
b	If you elect one or both of the optional methods, enter the total of lines 15 and 17 here			4b	
c	Combine lines 4a and 4b. If less than $400, **stop;** you don't owe self-employment tax. **Exception:** If less than $400 and you had **church employee income,** enter -0- and continue ►			4c	
5a	Enter your **church employee income** from Form W-2. See instructions for definition of church employee income	5a			
b	Multiply line 5a by 92.35% (0.9235). If less than $100, enter -0-			5b	
6	Add lines 4c and 5b			6	
7	Maximum amount of combined wages and self-employment earnings subject to social security tax or the 6.2% portion of the 7.65% railroad retirement (tier 1) tax for 2020			7	137,700
8a	Total social security wages and tips (total of boxes 3 and 7 on Form(s) W-2) and railroad retirement (tier 1) compensation. If $137,700 or more, skip lines 8b through 10, and go to line 11	8a			
b	Unreported tips subject to social security tax from Form 4137, line 10	8b			
c	Wages subject to social security tax from Form 8919, line 10	8c			
d	Add lines 8a, 8b, and 8c			8d	
9	Subtract line 8d from line 7. If zero or less, enter -0- here and on line 10 and go to line 11 ►			9	
10	Multiply the **smaller** of line 6 or line 9 by 12.4% (0.124)			10	
11	Multiply line 6 by 2.9% (0.029)			11	
12	**Self-employment tax.** Add lines 10 and 11. Enter here and on **Schedule 2 (Form 1040), line 4**			12	
13	**Deduction for one-half of self-employment tax.** Multiply line 12 by 50% (0.50). Enter here and on **Schedule 1 (Form 1040), line 14**	13			

Part II Optional Methods To Figure Net Earnings (see instructions)

Farm Optional Method. You may use this method **only** if **(a)** your gross farm income[1] wasn't more than $8,460, **or (b)** your net farm profits[2] were less than $6,107.

14	Maximum income for optional methods	14	5,640
15	Enter the **smaller** of: two-thirds (2/3) of gross farm income[1] (not less than zero) **or** $5,640. Also, include this amount on line 4b above	15	

Nonfarm Optional Method. You may use this method **only** if **(a)** your net nonfarm profits[3] were less than $6,107 and also less than 72.189% of your gross nonfarm income,[4] **and (b)** you had net earnings from self-employment of at least $400 in 2 of the prior 3 years. **Caution:** You may use this method no more than five times.

16	Subtract line 15 from line 14	16	
17	Enter the **smaller** of: two-thirds (2/3) of gross nonfarm income[4] (not less than zero) **or** the amount on line 16. Also, include this amount on line 4b above	17	

[1] From Sch. F, line 9; and Sch. K-1 (Form 1065), box 14, code B.
[2] From Sch. F, line 34; and Sch. K-1 (Form 1065), box 14, code A—minus the amount you would have entered on line 1b had you not used the optional method.
[3] From Sch. C, line 31; and Sch. K-1 (Form 1065), box 14, code A.
[4] From Sch. C, line 7; and Sch. K-1 (Form 1065), box 14, code C.

For Paperwork Reduction Act Notice, see your tax return instructions. Cat. No. 11358Z **Schedule SE (Form 1040) 2020**

Schedule SE (Form 1040) 2020 | Attachment Sequence No. **17** | Page **2**

Part III Maximum Deferral of Self-Employment Tax Payments

If line 4c is zero, skip lines 18 through 20, and enter -0- on line 21.

18	Enter the portion of line 3 that can be attributed to March 27, 2020, through December 31, 2020	**18**	
19	If line 18 is more than zero, multiply line 18 by 92.35% (0.9235); otherwise, enter the amount from line 18	**19**	
20	Enter the portion of lines 15 and 17 that can be attributed to March 27, 2020, through December 31, 2020	**20**	
21	Combine lines 19 and 20	**21**	

If line 5b is zero, skip line 22 and enter -0- on line 23.

22	Enter the portion of line 5a that can be attributed to March 27, 2020, through December 31, 2020	**22**	
23	Multiply line 22 by 92.35% (0.9235)	**23**	
24	Add lines 21 and 23	**24**	
25	Enter the smaller of line 9 or line 24	**25**	
26	Multiply line 25 by 6.2% (0.062). Enter here and see the instructions for line 12e of Schedule 3 (Form 1040)	**26**	

Schedule SE (Form 1040) 2020

Form **4562**

Department of the Treasury
Internal Revenue Service (99)

Depreciation and Amortization

(Including Information on Listed Property)

▶ Attach to your tax return.

▶ Go to *www.irs.gov/Form4562* for instructions and the latest information.

OMB No. 1545-0172

2020

Attachment Sequence No. **179**

Name(s) shown on return	Business or activity to which this form relates	**Identifying number**

Part I Election To Expense Certain Property Under Section 179

Note: If you have any listed property, complete Part V before you complete Part I.

1	Maximum amount (see instructions)	1	
2	Total cost of section 179 property placed in service (see instructions)	2	
3	Threshold cost of section 179 property before reduction in limitation (see instructions)	3	
4	Reduction in limitation. Subtract line 3 from line 2. If zero or less, enter -0-	4	
5	Dollar limitation for tax year. Subtract line 4 from line 1. If zero or less, enter -0-. If married filing separately, see instructions	5	

6	**(a)** Description of property	**(b)** Cost (business use only)	**(c)** Elected cost

7	Listed property. Enter the amount from line 29	7	
8	Total elected cost of section 179 property. Add amounts in column (c), lines 6 and 7	8	
9	Tentative deduction. Enter the **smaller** of line 5 or line 8	9	
10	Carryover of disallowed deduction from line 13 of your 2019 Form 4562	10	
11	Business income limitation. Enter the smaller of business income (not less than zero) or line 5. See instructions	11	
12	Section 179 expense deduction. Add lines 9 and 10, but don't enter more than line 11	12	
13	Carryover of disallowed deduction to 2021. Add lines 9 and 10, less line 12 ▶	13	

Note: Don't use Part II or Part III below for listed property. Instead, use Part V.

Part II Special Depreciation Allowance and Other Depreciation (Don't include listed property. See instructions.**)**

14	Special depreciation allowance for qualified property (other than listed property) placed in service during the tax year. See instructions	14	
15	Property subject to section 168(f)(1) election	15	
16	Other depreciation (including ACRS)	16	

Part III MACRS Depreciation (Don't include listed property. See instructions.**)**

Section A

17	MACRS deductions for assets placed in service in tax years beginning before 2020	17	
18	If you are electing to group any assets placed in service during the tax year into one or more general asset accounts, check here ▶ ☐		

Section B—Assets Placed in Service During 2020 Tax Year Using the General Depreciation System

(a) Classification of property	**(b)** Month and year placed in service	**(c)** Basis for depreciation (business/investment use only—see instructions)	**(d)** Recovery period	**(e)** Convention	**(f)** Method	**(g)** Depreciation deduction
19a 3-year property						
b 5-year property						
c 7-year property						
d 10-year property						
e 15-year property						
f 20-year property						
g 25-year property			25 yrs.		S/L	
h Residential rental property			27.5 yrs.	MM	S/L	
			27.5 yrs.	MM	S/L	
i Nonresidential real property			39 yrs.	MM	S/L	
				MM	S/L	

Section C—Assets Placed in Service During 2020 Tax Year Using the Alternative Depreciation System

20a Class life					S/L	
b 12-year			12 yrs.		S/L	
c 30-year			30 yrs.	MM	S/L	
d 40-year			40 yrs.	MM	S/L	

Part IV Summary (See instructions.)

21	Listed property. Enter amount from line 28	21	
22	**Total.** Add amounts from line 12, lines 14 through 17, lines 19 and 20 in column (g), and line 21. Enter here and on the appropriate lines of your return. Partnerships and S corporations—see instructions	22	
23	For assets shown above and placed in service during the current year, enter the portion of the basis attributable to section 263A costs	23	

For Paperwork Reduction Act Notice, see separate instructions. Cat. No. 12906N Form **4562** (2020)

Form 4562 (2020) Page **2**

Part V **Listed Property** (Include automobiles, certain other vehicles, certain aircraft, and property used for entertainment, recreation, or amusement.)

Note: For any vehicle for which you are using the standard mileage rate or deducting lease expense, complete **only** 24a, 24b, columns (a) through (c) of Section A, all of Section B, and Section C if applicable.

Section A—Depreciation and Other Information (Caution: See the instructions for limits for passenger automobiles.**)**

24a Do you have evidence to support the business/investment use claimed? ☐ **Yes** ☐ **No** | **24b** If "Yes," is the evidence written? ☐ **Yes** ☐ **No**

(a) Type of property (list vehicles first)	(b) Date placed in service	(c) Business/ investment use percentage	(d) Cost or other basis	(e) Basis for depreciation (business/investment use only)	(f) Recovery period	(g) Method/ Convention	(h) Depreciation deduction	(i) Elected section 179 cost
25 Special depreciation allowance for qualified listed property placed in service during the tax year and used more than 50% in a qualified business use. See instructions .						**25**		
26 Property used more than 50% in a qualified business use:								
		%						
		%						
		%						
27 Property used 50% or less in a qualified business use:								
		%				S/L –		
		%				S/L –		
		%				S/L –		
28 Add amounts in column (h), lines 25 through 27. Enter here and on line 21, page 1 .						**28**		
29 Add amounts in column (i), line 26. Enter here and on line 7, page 1							**29**	

Section B—Information on Use of Vehicles

Complete this section for vehicles used by a sole proprietor, partner, or other "more than 5% owner," or related person. If you provided vehicles to your employees, first answer the questions in Section C to see if you meet an exception to completing this section for those vehicles.

	(a) Vehicle 1		(b) Vehicle 2		(c) Vehicle 3		(d) Vehicle 4		(e) Vehicle 5		(f) Vehicle 6	
30 Total business/investment miles driven during the year (**don't** include commuting miles) .												
31 Total commuting miles driven during the year												
32 Total other personal (noncommuting) miles driven												
33 Total miles driven during the year. Add lines 30 through 32												
	Yes	**No**	**Yes**	**No**	**Yes**	**No**	**Yes**	**No**	**Yes**	**No**	**Yes**	**No**
34 Was the vehicle available for personal use during off-duty hours?												
35 Was the vehicle used primarily by a more than 5% owner or related person? . .												
36 Is another vehicle available for personal use?												

Section C—Questions for Employers Who Provide Vehicles for Use by Their Employees

Answer these questions to determine if you meet an exception to completing Section B for vehicles used by employees who **aren't** more than 5% owners or related persons. See instructions.

	Yes	**No**
37 Do you maintain a written policy statement that prohibits all personal use of vehicles, including commuting, by your employees?		
38 Do you maintain a written policy statement that prohibits personal use of vehicles, except commuting, by your employees? See the instructions for vehicles used by corporate officers, directors, or 1% or more owners . .		
39 Do you treat all use of vehicles by employees as personal use?		
40 Do you provide more than five vehicles to your employees, obtain information from your employees about the use of the vehicles, and retain the information received?		
41 Do you meet the requirements concerning qualified automobile demonstration use? See instructions.		
Note: If your answer to 37, 38, 39, 40, or 41 is "Yes," don't complete Section B for the covered vehicles.		

Part VI **Amortization**

(a) Description of costs	(b) Date amortization begins	(c) Amortizable amount	(d) Code section	(e) Amortization period or percentage	(f) Amortization for this year
42 Amortization of costs that begins during your 2020 tax year (see instructions):					
43 Amortization of costs that began before your 2020 tax year				**43**	
44 **Total.** Add amounts in column (f). See the instructions for where to report				**44**	

Form **4562** (2020)

Form **8829** Department of the Treasury Internal Revenue Service (99)	**Expenses for Business Use of Your Home** ▶ **File only with Schedule C (Form 1040). Use a separate Form 8829 for each home you used for business during the year.** ▶ **Go to *www.irs.gov/Form8829* for instructions and the latest information.**	OMB No. 1545-0074 **2020** Attachment Sequence No. **176**

Name(s) of proprietor(s)	**Your social security number**

Part I Part of Your Home Used for Business

1	Area used regularly and exclusively for business, regularly for daycare, or for storage of inventory or product samples (see instructions)			1	
2	Total area of home			2	
3	Divide line 1 by line 2. Enter the result as a percentage			3	%
	For daycare facilities not used exclusively for business, go to line 4. All others, go to line 7.				
4	Multiply days used for daycare during year by hours used per day	4	hr.		
5	If you started or stopped using your home for daycare during the year, see instructions; otherwise, enter 8,784	5	hr.		
6	Divide line 4 by line 5. Enter the result as a decimal amount	6	.		
7	Business percentage. For daycare facilities not used exclusively for business, multiply line 6 by line 3 (enter the result as a percentage). All others, enter the amount from line 3 ▶			7	%

Part II Figure Your Allowable Deduction

			(a) Direct expenses	(b) Indirect expenses		
8	Enter the amount from Schedule C, line 29, **plus** any gain derived from the business use of your home, **minus** any loss from the trade or business not derived from the business use of your home. See instructions.				8	
	See instructions for columns (a) and (b) before completing lines 9–22.		**(a)** Direct expenses	**(b)** Indirect expenses		
9	Casualty losses (see instructions)	9				
10	Deductible mortgage interest (see instructions)	10				
11	Real estate taxes (see instructions)	11				
12	Add lines 9, 10, and 11	12				
13	Multiply line 12, column (b), by line 7		13			
14	Add line 12, column (a), and line 13				14	
15	Subtract line 14 from line 8. If zero or less, enter -0-				15	
16	Excess mortgage interest (see instructions)	16				
17	Excess real estate taxes (see instructions)	17				
18	Insurance	18				
19	Rent	19				
20	Repairs and maintenance	20				
21	Utilities	21				
22	Other expenses (see instructions)	22				
23	Add lines 16 through 22	23				
24	Multiply line 23, column (b), by line 7		24			
25	Carryover of prior year operating expenses (see instructions)		25			
26	Add line 23, column (a), line 24, and line 25				26	
27	Allowable operating expenses. Enter the **smaller** of line 15 or line 26				27	
28	Limit on excess casualty losses and depreciation. Subtract line 27 from line 15				28	
29	Excess casualty losses (see instructions)		29			
30	Depreciation of your home from line 42 below		30			
31	Carryover of prior year excess casualty losses and depreciation (see instructions)		31			
32	Add lines 29 through 31				32	
33	Allowable excess casualty losses and depreciation. Enter the **smaller** of line 28 or line 32				33	
34	Add lines 14, 27, and 33				34	
35	Casualty loss portion, if any, from lines 14 and 33. Carry amount to **Form 4684.** See instructions				35	
36	**Allowable expenses for business use of your home.** Subtract line 35 from line 34. Enter here and on Schedule C, line 30. If your home was used for more than one business, see instructions. ▶				36	

Part III Depreciation of Your Home

37	Enter the **smaller** of your home's adjusted basis or its fair market value. See instructions	37	
38	Value of land included on line 37	38	
39	Basis of building. Subtract line 38 from line 37	39	
40	Business basis of building. Multiply line 39 by line 7	40	
41	Depreciation percentage (see instructions)	41	%
42	Depreciation allowable (see instructions). Multiply line 40 by line 41. Enter here and on line 30 above	42	

Part IV Carryover of Unallowed Expenses to 2021

43	Operating expenses. Subtract line 27 from line 26. If less than zero, enter -0-	43	
44	Excess casualty losses and depreciation. Subtract line 33 from line 32. If less than zero, enter -0-	44	

For Paperwork Reduction Act Notice, see your tax return instructions. Cat. No. 13232M Form **8829** (2020)

Form **8995**

Department of the Treasury
Internal Revenue Service

Qualified Business Income Deduction Simplified Computation

▶ Attach to your tax return.

▶ Go to *www.irs.gov/Form8995* for instructions and the latest information.

OMB No. 1545-0123

2020

Attachment Sequence No. 55

Name(s) shown on return	Your taxpayer identification number

Note. *You can claim the qualified business income deduction* ***only*** *if you have qualified business income from a qualified trade or business, real estate investment trust dividends, publicly traded partnership income, or a domestic production activities deduction passed through from an agricultural or horticultural cooperative. See instructions.*
Use this form if your taxable income, before your qualified business income deduction, is at or below $163,300 ($326,600 if married filing jointly), and you aren't a patron of an agricultural or horticultural cooperative.

1	**(a)** Trade, business, or aggregation name	**(b)** Taxpayer identification number	**(c)** Qualified business income or (loss)
i			
ii			
iii			
iv			
v			

2	Total qualified business income or (loss). Combine lines 1i through 1v, column (c)	2			
3	Qualified business net (loss) carryforward from the prior year	3	( )		
4	Total qualified business income. Combine lines 2 and 3. If zero or less, enter -0-	4			
5	Qualified business income component. Multiply line 4 by 20% (0.20)			5	
6	Qualified REIT dividends and publicly traded partnership (PTP) income or (loss) (see instructions)	6			
7	Qualified REIT dividends and qualified PTP (loss) carryforward from the prior year	7	( )		
8	Total qualified REIT dividends and PTP income. Combine lines 6 and 7. If zero or less, enter -0-	8			
9	REIT and PTP component. Multiply line 8 by 20% (0.20)			9	
10	Qualified business income deduction before the income limitation. Add lines 5 and 9			10	
11	Taxable income before qualified business income deduction	11			
12	Net capital gain (see instructions)	12			
13	Subtract line 12 from line 11. If zero or less, enter -0-	13			
14	Income limitation. Multiply line 13 by 20% (0.20)			14	
15	Qualified business income deduction. Enter the lesser of line 10 or line 14. Also enter this amount on the applicable line of your return ▶			15	
16	Total qualified business (loss) carryforward. Combine lines 2 and 3. If greater than zero, enter -0-			16	( )
17	Total qualified REIT dividends and PTP (loss) carryforward. Combine lines 6 and 7. If greater than zero, enter -0-			17	( )

For Privacy Act and Paperwork Reduction Act Notice, see instructions. Cat. No. 37806C Form **8995** (2020)

Using Redleaf Record-Keeping Tools

This chart shows how the books in the Redleaf business series work together to help you prepare and pay your taxes and communicate with the IRS. If you use these resources throughout the tax year, it will be much easier to complete your tax forms at the end of the year.

Learn how to keep records → *Record-Keeping Guide*, 9th Edition: identifies tax laws and allowable deductions; explains how to keep accurate records

↓

Track income and expenses → and

- *Redleaf Calendar-Keeper:* tracks monthly income and expenses; updated annually
- *Mileage-Keeper:* tracks vehicle expenses
- *Business Receipt Book:* tracks payments from parents
- *Inventory-Keeper:* tracks property to help with depreciation

↓

File tax returns

- **By yourself**: Use the *Family Child Care Tax Workbook and Organizer*, which explains how to fill out IRS forms related to family child care, with examples; includes tax forms and a tax organizer; updated annually
- **With a tax preparer**: Use the *Family Child Care Tax Companion*, which contains worksheets to help your tax preparer avoid mistakes; updated annually